KINGS, QUEENS
& COURTIERS

KINGS, QUEENS & COURTIERS

Intimate Portraits of the Royal House of Windsor
from its foundation to the present day

KENNETH ROSE

WEIDENFELD AND NICOLSON
LONDON

First published in Great Britain in 1985 by

George Weidenfeld and Nicolson Limited
91 Clapham High Street, London sw4 7ta

Designed by Helen Lewis
assisted by Sheila Sherwen

isbn 0 297 78733 0

Filmset by Keyspools Limited, Golborne, Lancashire
Printed and bound in Italy

Note: entries relating to families, such as the Kents or
the Gloucesters, appear in chronological order.

Facing title page:
Detail of a souvenir postcard celebrating
the Coronation of King George v.

Jacket illustrations:

Front (left to right):
George v by Lance Calkin (National Portrait Gallery),
Queen Elizabeth ii by Annigoni (Camera Press, London),
Lord Mountbatten (Bern Schwartz), Lady Diana Cooper by Ambrose McEvoy
(e.t. Archive, private collection),
Lord Stamfordham (BBC Hulton Picture Library)
Back (Left to right):
Kenneth Clark (Camera Press, London),
Queen Elizabeth the Queen Mother (Tim Graham),
Lord Snowdon (Camera Press, London, photo by Dmitri Kasterini),
Anthony Blunt (Camera Press, London),
Queen Mary (By kind permission of the House of Lords),
Noel Coward (Camera Press, London)

Also by Kenneth Rose

SUPERIOR PERSON:
A Portrait of Curzon and his Circle in late
Victorian England

THE LATER CECILS

KING GEORGE V

For Marie-Sygne

Four Sovereigns: Queen Victoria holding the future Edward VIII in her arms; the Prince of Wales and Prince George

CONTENTS

BY THE KING.

A PROCLAMATION

Declaring that the Name of Windsor is to be borne by His Royal House and Family and relinquishing the use of all German Titles and Dignities.

GEORGE R.I.

WHEREAS WE, having taken into consideration the Name and Title of Our Royal House and Family, have determined that hencefor Our House and Family shall be styled and known as the House and Family of Windsor:

AND WHEREAS We have further determined for Ourselves and for and on behalf of Our descendants and all other the descendants Our Grandmother Queen Victoria of blessed and glorious memory to relinquish and discontinue the use of all German Titles and Dignitie

AND WHEREAS We have declared these Our determinations in Our Privy Council:

NOW, THEREFORE, We, out of Our Royal Will and Authority, do hereby declare and announce that as from the date of this O Royal Proclamation Our House and Family shall be styled and known as the House and Family of Windsor, and that all the descendants the male line of Our said Grandmother Queen Victoria who are subjects of these Realms, other than female descendants who may marry may have married, shall bear the said Name of Windsor:

And do hereby further declare and announce that We for Ourselves and for and on behalf of Our descendants and all other t descendants of Our said Grandmother Queen Victoria who are subjects of these Realms, relinquish and enjoin the discontinuance of the u of the Degrees, Styles, Dignities, Titles and Honours of Dukes and Duchesses of Saxony and Princes and Princesses of Saxe-Coburg a Gotha, and all other German Degrees, Styles, Dignities, Titles, Honours and Appellations to Us or to them heretofore belonging appertaining.

Given at Our Court at Buckingham Palace, this Seventeenth day of Jul in the year of our Lord One thousand nine hundred and seventeen, an in the Eighth year of Our Reign.

GOD SAVE THE KING.

LONDON: Printed by EYRE AND SPOTTISWOODE, LIMITED, Printers to the King's most Excellent Majesty

INTRODUCTION

With an inspired flamboyance worthy of any medieval monarch, King George v renounced his German ancestry and proclaimed the House of Windsor on 17 July 1917. Born in the turmoil of the First World War as a gesture of appeasement to anti-German hysteria, the House of Windsor has since rooted itself in the history of the nation and the hearts of her people.

In *King George V*, published in 1983, I told the story of the founder of the dynasty: a man of shrewd sense and salty humour who without seeking popularity became the best-loved of British Sovereigns. Now I have broadened the canvas to depict not only King George, his immediate family and his descendants down to the third and fourth generation; but also a selection of those courtiers, advisers and friends who even in an age of democracy are required to support the structure of monarchy.

There are Lord Chamberlains and Ladies of the Bedchamber, doctors and lawyers, secretaries and chaplains; Poets Laureate and librarians, portrait painters and photographers, cooks and couturiers; tutors and gamekeepers and racehorse trainers; a Master of the Horse, a Lord Lyon King of Arms and a Clerk of the Privy Council. Nor have the black sheep been forgotten: a blackmailer and a gambler, an embezzler and a spy.

These brief lives jostle each other in alphabetical order. Some of them run to no more than a few lines, others to several thousand words. Their treatment, like their choice, has been capricious. Many are drawn from personal knowledge, buttressed by almost half a century of desultory reading and correspondence and talk. But I have not knowingly broken private confidences or the intimacies of friendship. Although a bibliography would be both ponderous and pretentious, I am grateful to those fellow writers whose labours I have pillaged: works of reference and newspapers, memoirs and biographies.

This is a self-indulgent book which I hope may be of interest to others and perhaps add a footnote or two to history.

KENNETH ROSE

The Proclamation of the House of Windsor, 17 July 1917

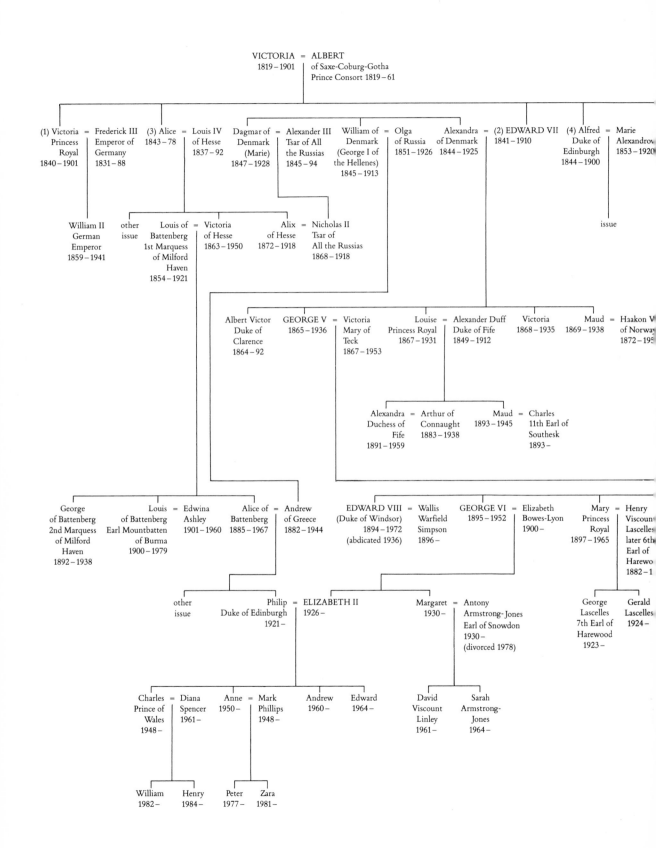

Family tree of those referred to in the book

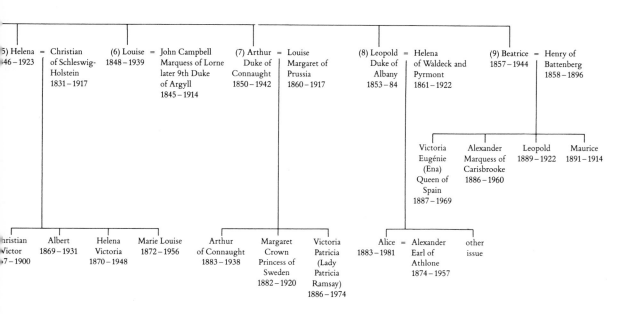

(5) Helena
846–1923 = Christian
of Schleswig-
Holstein
1831–1917

(6) Louise
1848–1939 = John Campbell
Marquess of Lorne
later 9th Duke
of Argyll
1845–1914

(7) Arthur
Duke of
Connaught
1850–1942 = Louise
Margaret of
Prussia
1860–1917

(8) Leopold
Duke of
Albany
1853–84 = Helena
of Waldeck and
Pyrmont
1861–1922

(9) Beatrice
1857–1944 = Henry of
Battenberg
1858–1896

Victoria
Eugénie
(Ena)
Queen of
Spain
1887–1969

Alexander
Marquess of
Carisbrooke
1886–1960

Leopold
1889–1922

Maurice
1891–1914

hristian
Victor
7–1900

Albert
1869–1931

Helena
Victoria
1870–1948

Marie Louise
1872–1956

Arthur
of Connaught
1883–1938

Margaret
Crown
Princess of
Sweden
1882–1920

Victoria
Patricia
(Lady
Patricia
Ramsay)
1886–1974

Alice
1883–1981 = Alexander
Earl of
Athlone
1874–1957

other
issue

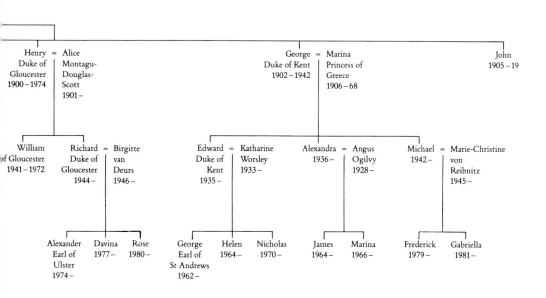

Henry
Duke of
Gloucester
1900–1974 = Alice
Montagu-
Douglas-
Scott
1901–

George
Duke of Kent
1902–1942 = Marina
Princess of
Greece
1906–68

John
1905–19

William
of Gloucester
1941–1972

Richard
Duke of
Gloucester
1944– = Birgitte
van
Deurs
1946–

Edward
Duke of
Kent
1935– = Katharine
Worsley
1933–

Alexandra
1936– = Angus
Ogilvy
1928–

Michael
1942– = Marie-Christine
von
Reibnitz
1945–

Alexander
Earl of
Ulster
1974–

Davina
1977–

Rose
1980–

George
Earl of
St Andrews
1962–

Helen
1964–

Nicholas
1970–

James
1964–

Marina
1966–

Frederick
1979–

Gabriella
1981–

For the family tree of Queen Mary, see p.13

THE FAMILY OF QUEEN MARY

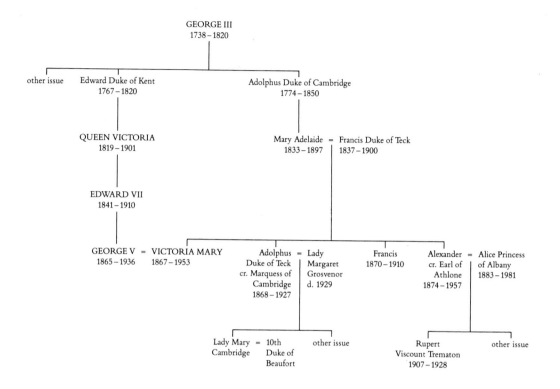

See also the family tree on pp. 10-11

Adeane, Sir Michael, 1st Baron (1910–1984).

Private Secretary to the Queen, 1953–72. He was the son of Captain Henry Adeane, Coldstream Guards, killed in action in 1914, and Victoria Eugenie Bigge, elder daughter of Lord Stamfordham (q.v.). Educated at Eton and Magdalene College, Cambridge, where he took a First Class in History, he was commissioned in 1931 into his father's old regiment. After serving as aide-de-camp to Lord Tweedsmuir, Governor-General of Canada, he was appointed in 1937 an Assistant Private Secretary to King George VI. On the outbreak of war he returned to active service with the Coldstream Guards, was wounded and mentioned in despatches. In 1945 he resumed his appointment at Buckingham Palace until 1953, when he succeeded Sir Alan Lascelles (q.v.) as Private Secretary to the Queen.

Like his grandfather, small, slim and resilient, he also inherited Stamfordham's habits of industry and self-effacement. 'Because you happen to be in Whitehall terms the equivalent of a Permanent Under-Secretary,' he would say, 'it is no use thinking you are a mandarin. You must also be a nanny. One moment you may be writing to the Prime Minister. The next you are carrying a small boy's mac.' His dedication to a life of sevice left him in no doubt as to the duty of others. When Richard Crossman, Lord President of the Council in a Labour Government, tried to excuse himself from taking part in the ceremonial Opening of Parliament, Michael Adeane told him: 'Of course, the Queen has as strong a feeling of dislike of public ceremonies as you do. I don't disguise from you the fact that it will certainly occur to her to ask herself why you should be excused when she has to go, since you are both officials.'

From a mournful little office cheered only by a painting of a fat white dog and an old-fashioned grate adorned with pleated white paper, Adeane bore a vast burden: the Queen's business, not only as Sovereign of the United Kingdom but also as Head of the Commonwealth. By his own wish, for he disliked delegation, his staff was tiny. When in 1971 he described to the House of Commons Select Committee on the Civil List the treadmill to which hereditary monarchs are chained, the following exchange took place:

Mr Houghton: You have spoken of the Queen's heavy day. What about your own?
Sir Michael Adeane: Well, it is not killing me.
Mr Houghton: Are you over worked too?
Sir Michael Adeane: No, but I am adequately worked. We have our holidays like everybody else and at the moment I should be sorry to see our office increased because I think it would become less efficient.

He disliked committees, and indeed any discussion which postponed an obvious decision. Yet even when hard pressed he rarely displayed temper or impatience. There is a classic story of how, leaving Buckingham Palace one day, he was accosted by a royal biographer with a problem. Adeane listened sympathetically, although the visitor did detect just the faintest impression that Adeane would like to be moving on. It was another minute or two before he said: 'I do hope you'll forgive me, but I've just heard that my house is on fire. I wouldn't mind, but as it's part of St James's Palace . . . .'

No man who remained Private Secretary for almost twenty years could have escaped all criticism. There were some who said that he was too cautious, others that he remained too long. During the Suez crisis of 1956 the Palace was a house divided: Adeane in favour of armed intervention, the two Assistant Private Secretaries, Martin Charteris and Edward Ford (qq.v.) against.

The part he played in the selection of Lord Home as Prime Minister in 1963 has also been questioned. Adeane's critics maintained that he should, on behalf of the Queen, have made his own extensive soundings of Conservative opinion instead of leaving the task to the outgoing – and ailing – Prime Minister, Harold

Sir Michael Adeane

for an honour chose the lavatory of a club, of all unlikely places, to plead his cause as they stood side by side. And when a friend congratulated Adeane on receiving the GCVO, he replied with Lord Curzon's immortal reference to 'the series of Grand Crosses with which the Sovereign has recognized my distinguished services.'

On his retirement in 1972 Adeane was rewarded with a peerage and the Royal Victorian Chain. He became chairman of the Royal Commission on Historical Monuments, a member of the British Library Board and a director of several important companies.

In 1939 he married Helen Chetwynd-Stapylton. They had two children, a daughter who died in childhood and a son, Edward, who, after some years at the Bar specializing in libel, followed in the family tradition as Private Secretary to Charles, Prince of Wales from 1979 to 1985.

Agnew, Sir Godfrey
(1913–   )

Macmillan. Home, it is said, might not then have emerged as 'the preponderant first choice.' There is at least one simple answer to this: that the constitutional duty of the Queen was to find a Prime Minister who could command a majority in the House of Commons. It was not her responsibility to choose necessarily the best of several well-qualified candidates. The supposed views of the Conservative Party which Macmillan garnered from his sick-bed, read to the Queen, and then presented to Adeane, did at least ensure that.

Throughout his long years at the Palace, Adeane never lost that humour and sense of the ridiculous which courtiers need more than most. He once took the present writer to his London gunsmiths to look at a printed card showing all the monograms and coronets that could be engraved on the stock of a shotgun. With glee, he pointed to a tiny mitre for the use of sporting bishops. He also loved to relate how a supplicant

Clerk of the Privy Council, 1953–74. From his father-in-law, Captain Charles Moore (q.v.), the Queen's racing manager, he acquired a knowledge of horses. Over the years he was able to combine his two interests by summoning meetings of the Privy Council at country houses where the Queen happened to be staying for the races. There were three at Goodwood, home of the Duke of Richmond (q.v.); three at nearby Arundel, home of the Duke of Norfolk (q.v.); and one at Sandbeck Park, in Yorkshire, home of the Earl of Scarbrough, her host for the St Leger meeting at Doncaster.

Agnew was once asked by a Labour Minister, whether the Queen preferred Conservative Ministers to Labour since, as he put it, 'they are our social superiors.' Agnew's reply was illuminating. 'I don't think so,' he said. 'The Queen doesn't make fine distinctions between politicians of different parties. They all roughly belong to the same social category in her view.'

Ainslie, James

Butler to King George VI. He was a man of imposing presence and engaging phrase. After being lightly admonished by the Master of the Household, Sir Piers Legh, he replied: 'Let me assure you, Sir Piers, that my sole object is to obey the orders of the Master of the Household and give pleasure to the ladies-in-waiting.'

He did, however, unbutton on the birth of Prince Charles in 1948, when he was heard to shout to some lesser member of the staff: 'Get your flipping skates on and bring the champagne.'

Airlie, David Ogilvy, 13th Earl of (1926–)

Lord Chamberlain of the Household since 1984. The eldest son of the 12th Earl of Airlie and his wife, a daughter of the 3rd Earl of Leicester (q.v.), he was brought up, as it were, on the steps of the throne. His father was for almost thirty years Lord Chamberlain to Queen Elizabeth, later the Queen Mother; his grandmother, Mabell Countess of Airlie (q.v.), was for more than fifty years lady-in-waiting and confidante to Queen Mary; his younger brother, the Hon. Angus Ogilvy is married to Princess Alexandra (qq.v); and his own wife Virginia, a granddaughter of the American financier Otto Kahn, is a lady-in-waiting to the Queen.

Educated at Eton, Airlie joined the Scots Guards and saw service in Germany and Malaya, looked after the family estates, then went into the City as a merchant banker. In 1984 he retired from Schroder's as chairman of its holding company, thus relinquishing an annual salary of £168,000. But he remains on the boards of other companies, including the Royal Bank of Scotland, Scottish and Newcastle Breweries and

General Accident Fire and Life Assurance.

As Lord Chamberlain, Airlie attends the Queen on ceremonial occasions at court, where he is required to walk backwards carrying his white stave of office. He organizes State visits and garden parties and investitures. He is the arbiter of such teasing problems as protocol and precedence and the minutiae of stars and ribbons. Although the Lord Chamberlain is no longer required to censor plays – that burden was detached from the office in 1968 – he remains the intermediary between the Sovereign and both the House of Lords and the Diplomatic Corps.

Airlie is well qualified for all these duties. On the verge of sixty, he is a handsome man: tall, thin, with an ascetic face and all his hair.

Airlie, Mabell, Countess of (1866–1956)

Lifelong friend and lady-in-waiting to Queen Mary. The eldest daughter of the 5th Earl of Arran, Lady Mabell Gore was married in 1886 to the 11th Earl of Airlie, who was killed in 1900 leading a cavalry charge against the Boers. The Princess of Wales, later Queen Mary, her friend from childhood, invited the thirty-four-year-old widow to join her household as a lady-in-waiting: an appointment which Lady Airlie accepted with reluctance but continued to hold until the old Queen's death more than half a century later.

So free was their relationship from the usual constraints of court life that they could have been mistaken for devoted twin sisters. Both were stately in appearance, lively of mind and methodical in business. Lady Airlie resented the inferior education to which aristocratic custom had condemned her. 'I remember teaching myself the Greek alphabet in secret,' she recalled, 'but when this illicit study was discovered, the book was confiscated and I was ordered to do some needlework instead.'

In spite of this early handicap, she managed the family estates in Scotland, 69,000 far from remunerative acres, until her eldest son came of age. She also edited several attractive volumes of family letters and wrote some illuminating memoirs which no chronicler of the House of Windsor should ignore. The title, *Thatched with Gold*, is taken from one of her own letters: 'When you are young you always expect your house to be thatched with gold; when you grow older you are thankful that it is thatched at all.'

Although never exactly roofless, Lady Airlie's last years were shadowed by domestic difficulties. Living in two rooms of her little Scottish castle, she did the housework, looked after the garden and even chopped the firewood. When at length her strength could no longer match her self-discipline, she moved to London. But rather

Mabell, Countess of Airlie

than be a burden on her children, who asked her to share their homes, she took rooms in a succession of modest hotels.

Mabell Airlie died in 1956 at the age of ninety. Seven years later, her grandson Angus Ogilvy married Princess Alexandra (qq.v.), granddaughter of her mistress and friend, Queen Mary.

Alexandra, Queen
(1844–1925)

Consort of King Edward VII and mother of King George V. She was born in Copenhagen, the second child of the future King Christian IX of Denmark. Hans Andersen, a friend of her parents, was a familiar figure of her childhood. In 1862 she was betrothed to the Prince of Wales (later King Edward VII) after some discreet marriage-broking on the part of his eldest sister, the Crown Princess of Prussia. Their wedding, which took place in St George's Chapel, Windsor, on 10 March 1863, was heralded by the celebrated lines of Tennyson:

> Sea King's daughter from over the sea,
> > Alexandra!
> Saxon and Norman and Dane are we,
> But all of us Danes in our welcome of thee,
> > Alexandra!

There were two sons and three daughters of the marriage. The eldest child, Prince Albert Victor, born in 1864 and created Duke of Clarence in 1890, died in 1892 of pneumonia. His younger brother, Prince George, was born in 1865 and reigned as King George V from 1910 to his death in 1936. The three daughters were Princess Louise, Duchess of Fife; Princess Victoria; and Princess Maud, afterwards Queen of Norway (qq.v.).

The Princess of Wales's third confinement, that of Princess Louise in 1867, was complicated by rheumatic fever that left her with a slight limp. Some considered it a becoming attribute in so beautiful a woman. It was the prelude, however, to a more tragic consequence: a progressive and ultimately total deafness. The Princess bore her affliction bravely. She refused to curtail her charitable and other public duties, yet was increasingly obliged to withdraw from the social world of which she and her husband were acknowledged leaders. Although she was skilful in disguising how little she heard, the time came when only a few familiar voices could penetrate her prison of silence. She found consolation in home and family, in flowers and animals and the tranquillity of country life. Yet one sure refuge of the deaf was denied her. She

Queen Alexandra

had never acquired the habit of reading. Nor in truth had her husband. 'The melancholy thing', Lady Frederick Cavendish confided to her diary, 'is that neither he nor the darling Princess ever care to open a book.' But whereas the Prince could learn the ways of the world in conversation – and thus in time acquire a shrewdness of judgment from those about him – his wife could not. She radiated every generous instinct, she bubbled with humour and fantasy, she won every heart; her mind, however, remained that of an adolescent.

Long after her children had embarked upon lives of their own, she clung to the endearments of the cradle. She would write to Prince George: 'With a great big kiss for your lovely little face.' Her son was then a bearded naval officer of twenty-five in command of a gunboat. It caused him no embarrassment. Well into manhood he would begin his own letters to her, 'My own darling sweet little beloved Motherdear', and end them, 'Your loving little Georgie.'

The Princess's mawkish style did not exclude common sense. Even Queen Victoria recognized her insistence upon 'great simplicity and an absence of all pride' in the upbringing of her children. They also acquired from her an uncomplicated Christianity and habits of devotion that sustained them throughout life. The Princess was less well equipped to expand their minds, to rouse their curiosity, to unveil the joys of literature and the arts. Their intellectual progress was slow and reluctant.

Both as Princess of Wales and as Queen, she suffered from her husband's neglect and barely concealed infidelities. In turn she caused that punctilious master of ceremonies acute annoyance by her dilatory ways. Rarely was she on time for a meal or even for a royal engagement. In Buckingham Palace on the morning of their Coronation in 1902, the King burst into her room, watch in hand. 'My dear Alix', he remonstrated, 'if you don't come immediately you won't be crowned Queen.' It was on that occasion, too, that she displayed another sort of wilfulness. 'I know better than all the milliners and antiquaries,' she declared, 'I shall wear exactly what I like, and so shall my ladies.' Always she carried herself gracefully, choosing both clothes and jewels with stylish confidence. When the driver of the royal train applied the brakes too suddenly during dinner, a footman upset a dish of quails over her, leaving one bird suspended in her hair. With peals of laughter, she described how she would arrive *coiffée de cailles*.

Neither that beauty nor the popular affection it inspired grew less with the years. 'Your Majesty is sixty-two today,' Admiral Fisher telegraphed in 1906, 'may you live till you look it.' They shared an intense dislike of Germany and the Kaiser, for she could never forgive Prussia's aggression against her native Denmark; and when in 1890 the future King George v had been obliged to accept honorary command of a Prussian regiment, she wrote: 'And so my Georgie boy has become a real live filthy bluecoated *Pickelhaube* German soldier !!!' She even mocked his efforts to learn German, 'that old *Sauerkraut* language,' as she called it.

Whatever the tribulations of Queen Alexandra's marriage, the death of King Edward VII in 1910 left her miserable and bewildered. Her strong-willed sister, Marie Feodorovna, the Dowager Russian Empress, prompted her to claim precedence over the wife of the reigning Sovereign: a custom followed in St Petersburg but unknown to the Court of St James's. With characteristic restraint, neither King George nor Queen Mary was willing to challenge the widow's pretensions. At the funeral, therefore, Queen Alexandra stood at the foot of her husband's coffin, accompanied only by her sister, while Queen Mary was relegated to an inferior place.

There were smouldering discussions about the ownership of certain jewels, including King Edward's insignia of the Garter and the diamond circlet or crown worn by the Queen at the opening of Parliament. Another dispute concerned the standard to be flown by Queen Alexandra. The Royal Standard, bearing the arms of the United Kingdom, may be flown only by the Sovereign; a widowed Queen

Consort who flies a standard must impale the royal arms with those she has borne before marriage. Queen Alexandra nevertheless continued to fly the Royal Standard itself over Buckingham Palace. So trivial an infringement of precedent, it may be thought, was scarcely worthy of notice. Yet the mystique of monarchy has long rested on symbolism, and Queen Alexandra's flouting of tradition evoked dismay. When writing to her son, she similarly refused to address the envelopes in the expected style, 'The King'. Regarding him as hardly more than the surrogate of her late husband, she would instead write, 'King George.'

That dutiful son did not attempt to hasten his mother's departure from either Buckingham Palace or Windsor, where with determined indecision she lingered on, immobilized in a sargasso sea of possessions. At last, in her own time, she returned to Marlborough House, where as Princess of Wales she had lived for forty years. She also retained Sandringham, bequeathed to her by King Edward for her lifetime, together with a legacy of £200,000. As the widow of a Sovereign she received a Civil List of £70,000 a year. Since the new King paid for much of the upkeep of Sandringham, even two such large establishments would have been within her means had she agreed to curb her extravagance and her generosity. As it was, she insisted on a profusion of cut flowers and left no charitable appeal unanswered. When urged to economize, she took refuge in deafness. The King had no option but to make her a private allowance of £10,000 a year. In 1920, however, he was relieved of this burden when the Treasury, displaying rare indulgence, remitted five-sevenths of the tax it had previously levied on Queen Alexandra's income.

So she lived on in those two huge houses peopled by ghosts of the Edwardian Age, stone deaf and almost blind. 'But she retains her old grace and charm and her wonderful smile,' a friend wrote in the last year of her life. 'She never complains and keeps her slim pretty figure.' Three devoted companions sustained Queen Alexandra to the end: Princess Victoria, her only unmarried daughter, and two ageing courtiers, Sir Dighton Probyn and Miss Charlotte Knollys (qq.v.). She died at Sandringham in her eighty-first year, and is commemorated by an annual Alexandra Rose Day that raises money for hospitals.

Alexandra, Princess
Wife of Prince Arthur of Connaught and, in her own right, 2nd Duchess of Fife
(1891–1959)

The elder daughter of the 1st Duke of Fife and his wife Princess Louise, the Princess Royal (qq.v.) she was married in 1913 to Prince Arthur of Connaught, only son of the Duke of Connaught (qq.v.). Prince Arthur died in 1938. They had one son, who died in 1943.

Princess Arthur, as she was known, devoted much of her life to nursing and served throughout both world wars in London hospitals. She boasted of once having amputated someone's thumb under general anaesthetic but perhaps exaggerated her surgical skill. She did, however, write a paper on eclampsia, the convulsions or fits which may occur as a complication of pregnancy. For ten years Princess Arthur ran her own nursing home, selling it only when acute rheumatoid arthritis obliged her to take permanently to her bed. Both as matron and patient, she proved exacting, even formidable.

Until her health deteriorated she was a notable shot with a rifle. In 1939 she stalked and killed seventy-five stags in five weeks on her Scottish estate of Mar, in Aberdeenshire. At her death she left Mar to Captain Alexander Ramsay, only son of her sister-in-law Lady Patricia Ramsay (q.v.). The contents of Mar Lodge went to another nephew, James, Lord Carnegie, only son of her late sister Princess Maud (q.v.). Princess Arthur had on the death of her father in 1912 inherited the dukedom of Fife by special remainder through the female line. This too now passed to Lord Carnegie, who thereupon became the 3rd Duke of Fife.

Alexandra, Princess
(1936–)

The only daughter of Prince George, Duke of Kent, and Princess Marina, Duchess of Kent (qq.v.). She was born on Christmas Day: a happy augury, even if it reduced the twice-yearly bounty of presents enjoyed by other children to a single bonanza. She was educated at Heathfield, a girls' boarding school near Ascot, then studied French while living with the family of the Comte de Paris, claimant to the throne of France. In 1957 she did a short nursing course at the Great Ormond Street Hospital for Children. Princess Alexandra further broadened her experience when, as she listened to the cases in a London juvenile court, a resentful offender threw a chair at the bench.

After touring South America with her mother in 1959, the Princess undertook her first official tour alone, to Queensland, Australia. In 1960 she represented the Queen at the independence celebrations in Nigeria, winning many hearts by her insistence that the hood of her Rolls-Royce should remain down even while she drove in procession through tropical rain. On her return she was made a Dame Grand Cross of the Royal Victorian Order.

In Westminster Abbey on 24 April 1963 she was married to Angus Ogilvy (q.v.), second son of the 12th Earl of Airlie and one of her oldest friends. They share a common ancestor in Mary Queen of Scots. Princess Alexandra and her husband live in Thatched House Lodge, Richmond Park. There are two children of the marriage: James, born in 1964, and Marina, born in 1966. The Princess has over the years carried out a full programme of public engagements, only occasionally accompanied by her husband, who leads his own life as a company director and active worker for many charities. With the exception of the Queen Mother, no member of the royal family radiates such intense and unfeigned enjoyment, whether as Colonel-in-

Chief of a regiment, Chancellor of Lancaster University or among children the world over. With a beauty less classic but more English than that of her Danish great-grandmother, she is also well cast as president of Alexandra Rose Day. Her cheerful simplicity, however, does not exclude a touch of Marie-Antoinette. After travelling on a bus she declared: 'I like to try anything once.'

Alice, Princess, Countess of Athlone
(1883–1981)

The only daughter of Prince Leopold, Duke of Albany, Queen Victoria's youngest son, and Princess Helen of Waldeck-Pyrmont, she was born at Windsor Castle. The Home Secretary, who by tradition attended all royal births, wrote to her father: 'I trust that the infant princess may remain all her life as lively and cheerful as I can testify to her having been in the first minutes of her experience of this troubled world.' The prophecy was to be well-fulfilled. Her sparkling personality enchanted all who knew her for the next ninety-eight years.

Princess Alice's introduction to royal duty came even while she was a child. Staying with her grandmother at Windsor, she would build walls with ministerial despatch boxes while the old Queen laboured over her papers. The Duke of Albany died of haemophilia little more than a year after her birth, and she was brought up by her widowed mother at Claremont House, near Esher. Lewis Carroll, who met this other Alice with the Cecil family at Hatfield when she was six, described her as 'a sweet little girl, though with unruly spirits.' She too had reservations about their supposed friendship: 'He was always making grown-up jokes to us, and we thought him awfully silly.'

In 1904, the Princess was married to her kinsman Prince Alexander of Teck, a brother of Queen Mary and a serving officer in the British Army; in 1917 he abandoned his German title and was created Earl of Athlone (q.v.).

The Great War of 1914–18 brought them the sorrow and anxiety of a family divided. A generation earlier, the right of succession to the Duchy of Coburg had passed through the Prince Consort to the sons whom Queen Victoria had borne him. When the future King Edward VII relinquished his claim, the Duchy was inherited by the next brother, Prince Alfred, Duke of Edinburgh, who reigned from 1893 until his death in 1900. On the death of his only son and heir in 1899, the succession was offered to Prince Alfred's younger brother, the Duke of Connaught (q.v.); and when he waived his claim, as well as that of his son Prince Arthur of Connaught (q.v.), it passed to Prince Charles Edward, only son of the late Duke of Albany and thus Princess Alice's brother. At the age of fifteen the boy was taken away from Eton to be brought up as a German princeling. In 1900 the young Duke of Albany, known in the family as Charlie, succeeded his Uncle Alfred as Duke of Coburg, became a general in the German Army and fought for his adopted country on the

Princess Alice, Countess of Athlone, 1950

Queen Alexandra by Lafayette

Russian Front. At the end of the war he lost his German duchy and was stripped of his British dukedom of Albany. Later he became a fervent supporter of the Nazi regime and turned up at the funeral of King George V wearing a steel helmet and swastika armband. These events naturally distressed Princess Alice, whose heart was torn between patriotism and affection for an only brother.

As wife of the Governor-General of South Africa in 1923–31 and of Canada in 1940–6, Princess Alice proved a memorable proconsul in her own right: graceful, sympathetic and perpetually amused. But tragedy struck again in 1928. Her only son, Rupert, Viscount Trematon, had inherited the haemophilia or bleeding disease of his grandfather, Prince Leopold. He died of injuries in a motoring accident from which others might have recovered. There were also two daughters of the marriage; one died in infancy, the other married a soldier, Colonel Sir Henry Abel Smith.

With the death of Lord Athlone in 1957, Princess Alice embarked on a widowhood that was both vigorous and convivial. She wrote, with professional help, an entertaining volume of memoirs called *For My Grandchildren*. She maintained a prodigious correspondence in her own clear sloping hand. She loved seeing her friends in their houses, often arriving by bus and always doing justice to the good things they laid before her; and in turn she welcomed them to the sunlit warmth of Kensington Palace and the marble scrutiny of her grandparents, Queen Victoria and the Prince Consort. Year after year, too, she would combine a winter holiday with her duties as Chancellor of the University of the West Indies; she preferred travelling by banana boat with an armful of the latest biographies and her favourite Trollope novels.

Deafness led her to shun large gatherings, but *tête à tête* she was an entrancing talker. With the vivacious gestures of her generation, she would describe how at the Coronation of Edward VII she had driven in the same carriage as the Duke of Cambridge, born in the reign of George III; how George V would mock the frivolity of her hats; how Queen Mary had ferreted out of a box of Queen Victoria's abandoned bric-a-brac a huge engraved ruby presented by an Indian prince, then forgotten. Nor did Princess Alice ever forgive Mr Gladstone for having cheated her family of a whole year's Civil List when her father died a few days before the start of the fiscal year; or Winston Churchill sixty years later for filling her drawing-room with pungent cigar smoke.

Even as she reminisced, Princess Alice would be bent over her needlework. That was the essentially Victorian quality of her life: not a moment must ever be wasted. An awed lady-in-waiting used to say: 'Princess Alice is the only woman I have ever known who continues to knit while walking up a Balmoral mountain.'

Princess Alexandra and Angus Ogilvy, 1982

Amies, Hardy
(1909–)

Couturier to the Queen. He was born at Maida Vale into a modest, middle-class family. His father worked in the land valuation department of the London County Council, his mother as a saleswoman at a court dressmaker's, where little Hardy was sometimes allowed to play with pieces of material. On leaving Brentwood School he studied languages in France and Germany. In 1934, without specialist training, he became the designer for the House of Lachasse. Amies served throughout the war in the Intelligence Corps, becoming head of the Special Forces Mission to Belgium, with the rank of lieutenant-colonel.

In 1946 he founded his own dressmaking business in Savile Row and first made clothes for the Queen when, as Princess Elizabeth, she toured Canada in 1951. His designs are both striking and practical: a royal frock must sometimes be worn throughout a whole day yet never show a crease. He has built up a prosperous empire by branching out into men's clothes and making licensing agreements in nearly fifty countries.

His eye is sharp and severe. When Princess Elizabeth and Princess Margaret first came to Savile Row, Princess Margaret dropped a glove and Amies picked it up. There was a hole in it. 'Hmm,' he thought, but did not say, 'she hasn't got a very good maid.' As the Queen's couturier, he is allowed to use the Privy Purse entrance to Buckingham Palace; his staff must use the side entrance. Among the many qualities of the Queen he most admires is her ability to put on a tiara while going downstairs. In 1977 this court-ly couturier became a CVO.

The 'Royal Team' of Hardy Amies (*third from left*) leaves Savile Row for Clarence House.

Andrew, Prince

(1960–   )

Second son of Queen Elizabeth II and Prince Philip, Duke of Edinburgh. He was born at Buckingham Palace on 19 February 1960, and from Heatherdown, his preparatory school, followed his father and elder brother to Gordonstoun. His fondest memory of Kurt Hahn's (q.v.) spartan foundation is that it had gone co-educational in the year before he arrived. 'They were a great bunch of girls,' he recalled. 'They were the frontier ladies of Gordonstoun, much the same as they were in the gold rush, and they came up and had a go.' He spent some months at Lakefield College School, Ontario; passed through the Royal Naval College, Dartmouth; was commissioned as a midshipman and learned to fly.

Prince Andrew served throughout the Falklands campaign of 1982 in the aircraft carrier *Invincible*. As a sub-lieutenant in 820 Squadron, he flew innumerable patrols in Sea King helicopters, sometimes acting as a decoy to lure the enemy's Exocet missiles away from HMS *Invincible*. He returned victorious, a rose between his teeth, and was welcomed home by the Queen and Prince Philip. On being asked what he had most missed, he replied: 'Quietness, the smell of grass and fresh milk.' His pleasures, as it soon turned out, were not exclusively pastoral. The handsome young Prince's holiday in the West Indies with a pretty actress called Koo Stark evoked a whole spectrum of emotions, from admiration and amusement to envy and outrage.

In common with his two brothers, he enjoys acting. 'I become bored with myself,' he once explained, 'and like taking on other roles and characters.' During a visit to a housing renovation project in Los Angeles, he did a Marx Brothers act by spraying a group of photographers with paint. In a country where there is an exaggerated respect for the Press, his conduct was harshly condemned. He is himself, as it

Prince Andrew, 1984

happens, an accomplished photographer, with a flair for producing commercial calendars. But Prince Andrew's career continues to lie in the Royal Navy. He was promoted lieutenant in 1984 and appointed a personal Aide-de-Camp to the Queen.

Anne, Princess
(1950–   )

Only daughter of Queen Elizabeth II and Prince Philip, Duke of Edinburgh. She was born at Clarence House on 15 August 1950. At the age of five she makes a spirited appearance in the memoirs of her great-aunt, Princess Alice, Duchess of Gloucester, plunging a dirk through

Princess Anne in The Gambia, 1984

the eiderdown, sheets, blankets and mattress of a guest's bed at Balmoral, saying: 'I've always wanted to do this.' A similar story is told of the Queen Mother as a child, shredding a pair of new sheets with scissors. Perhaps there is something about Scottish beds which frays the temper.

At thirteen she was sent to Benenden, a girls' boarding school in Kent. She emerged five years later with six O levels, two A levels and a robust self-confidence that has been the mark of her character ever since. Already an accomplished equestrian, she won the European Three-Day Event Championship in 1971, and in 1976 was selected for the British team at the Olympic Games in Montreal. 'When I appear in public,' she said, 'people expect me to neigh, grind my teeth, paw the ground and swish my tail.' They were not far wrong. At a dinner party, the story went, she talked to one of her neighbours about horses throughout the entire meal, utterly ignoring the other. At last she turned: 'Could I have the sugar please?' The slighted young man placed two lumps on his palm and held them out

to the hippomane. There were constant brushes with the Press, too, whom she accused of frightening her horses and wanting to see her fall off. Even her good-natured hosts in the United States found her irritable and uncooperative.

In 1973 she was married to Captain Mark Phillips (q.v.), an equally dedicated and dashing equestrian. 'I'd prefer a quiet wedding,' the bride was reported to have said, 'but Mummy wants Westminster Abbey.' There are two children of the marriage. In 1974 she suffered a nightmare experience when, returning to Buckingham Palace with her husband after a charity film show, she was stopped in the Mall by a car swerving in front of her own. Its driver, who was later found to be mentally deranged, then tried to kidnap her. In the struggle, her police officer, Chief Inspector Beaton, shielded her with his body, was shot and later awarded the George Cross for his gallantry. She scarcely turned a hair. 'That man didn't know what he was taking on,' the Queen Mother said.

Princess Anne has grown no less forthright with the years or determined to guard her private life. Increasingly she resembles one of those resonant-voiced ladies in leopard-skin coat and regimental brooch who used to haunt first-class railway carriages. But any exasperation she may have provoked by her lack of royal affability is nowadays far outweighed by public admiration. No severity of climate or terrain deters the president of the Save the Children Fund from worldwide tours of inspection wherever there is disaster or need. Like Florence Nightingale, however, she can still bare her teeth. When asked why she thought the Press were troubling her less at her home in Gloucestershire, she replied: 'It's far enough from London for most reporters . . . and the pubs are fairly widely scattered in that area.'

Athlone, Alexander Cambridge, 1st Earl of
formerly Prince Alexander of Teck
(1874–1957)

Born at Kensington Palace, London, he was the youngest son of the 1st Duke of Teck and Princess Mary of Cambridge; he was thus a brother of Queen Mary and a great-uncle of Queen Elizabeth II.

Prince Alexander of Teck, as he was known until 1917, went to Eton, the first member of the Victorian royal family to be sent to a public school. When his mother was asked what advantage Eton could offer over private tutors, she replied: 'He will learn to cook his own tea. Every good soldier should be able to do that.' At the Royal Military College, Sandhurst, he was a few months senior to Winston Churchill, to whom he took a lifelong dislike. Commissioned into the 7th Hussars, Prince Alexander fought in the Matabele campaign and in the South African War; he marched to the relief of Mafeking and was awarded the DSO. Later he transferred to the 2nd Life Guards. In 1904 he married Princess Alice (q.v.), only daughter of Prince Leopold, Duke of Albany, Queen Victoria's fourth son.

In the summer of 1914, Prince Alexander agreed to a flattering request that he should

succeed his wife's uncle, the Duke of Connaught, as Governor-General of Canada. His inexperience attracted criticism, and the outbreak of war a few weeks later gave him a convenient excuse to withdraw. So the Duke remained at his post and Prince Alexander served on the Western Front, mostly on the staff. In 1917, on the instructions of King George v, he reluctantly relinquished his princely German title, exchanged his family name of Teck for that of Cambridge, and emerged as the 1st Earl of Athlone.

His appointment as Governor-General of South Africa in 1923 was more successful than any could have forecast. He was undismayed by occasional friction with the Nationalist Government of General Hertzog; and by his tact, Lord Athlone persuaded the Prime Minister to retain the Union Jack in the central panel of the new South African flag. At the request of the same Government, his term of office was extended until 1931. In 1935 Athlone was for the second time invited by the Canadian Government to become Governor-General. But King George v demurred. Not having long to live, he asked the Athlones to remain in England so that when the

The Earl of Athlone and Princess Alice await their guests at the Governor General's Garden Party in Capetown,

time came – as it did in January 1936 – they could comfort his widow in her loneliness. The offer was renewed in 1940, and although by now approaching his sixty-sixth birthday he agreed to accept it for two years. In the event he remained as Governor General for the full term of five years.

Lord Athlone enjoyed his busy Canadian life encouraging the war effort, travelling the length and breadth of every province, entertaining allied statesmen, including President Roosevelt, at Government House. His relations with the Prime Minister, Mackenzie King, demanded exceptional courtesy and care. King, sensitive and insecure, resented that the Governor-General should take even ceremonial precedence over the Prime Minister, and he would imagine a royal snub where none was intended. He wrote sullenly of the Athlones' failure to congratulate him on an election victory. 'I am beginning more and more,' the Prime Minister continued, 'to see that the upholding of the monarchy is a form of idolatry.' The Governor-General seemed serenely unaware of Mackenzie King's resentment. But later he said to a Canadian historian: 'Your man King, knew him quite well, actually. Bit of a puzzle. Great man and all that. And you know, he just missed being quite a decent fellow.'

Even at eighty, Athlone remained strikingly handsome and carried himself with the same majestic bearing as his sister, Queen Mary. Unlike her, however, he never mastered his Teck temper, which sometimes erupted over trivialities. Morbidly tidy, for ever fiddling with pictures and ornaments until they were arranged to his satisfaction, he would bellow with rage at a brush left by his valet an inch or two out of alignment. And although a genial host, with a royal memory for persons and places, Athlone marred the gift by an unwillingness to attach names to either. When he inquired of a guest, 'How are they?' he might have been referring to the visitor's family, but equally to the new false teeth he had noticed when last they met. It was a habit which bemused but kept everyone on their toes.

Austin, Alfred
(1835–1913)

Lord Salisbury appointed him Poet Laureate to Queen Victoria in 1896, and he survived into the reign of King George v. The Prime Minister, asked why he had chosen so unremarkable a poet, replied: 'Because he wanted it.' It was in fact Austin's reward for having supported the Conservative Party as a political journalist. Gladstone wrote some illuminating words to the old Queen about the difficulty of filling the office:

'Could there always be at hand a great poet, such as Wordsworth or Tennyson, beyond competition, and almost beyond criticism, the path would lie open and easy. But the case appears to have been this: that, in the absence of these conspicuous and unassailable claims, the person appointed becomes the object of envy, sarcasm, and ridicule; and further that what is intended perhaps only to strike the holder of the office disparages the office itself.'

The most memorable lines attributed to Austin were on the illness of the Prince of Wales, later Edward vii, in 1872, although his authorship has been disputed:

Across the wires the electric message came:
'He is no better, he is much the same.'

Alfred Austin,
Poet Laureate

King George V so little esteemed this unmelodious versifier that on Austin's death in 1913 he wanted the appointment of Poet Laureate to lapse. Then Asquith pressed the name of Robert Bridges, and the King relented.

Battenberg, Admiral Prince Louis of
see *Milford Haven, Marquess of*

Beaton, Sir Cecil
(1904–1980)

Photographer, stage designer and diarist. The son of a London timber merchant, he was educated at Harrow and St John's College, Cambridge. Only after a battle of wills with his father did he escape from a clerk's stool in the City into a small and primitive dark-room. There he practised photography with increasing success. His likenesses of fashionable women were imaginative, even inspired, yet not always free from syrup.

He took many photographs of Mrs Ernest Simpson – what he called the Wallis Collection – during her entanglement with King Edward VIII; and on the eve of their wedding in 1937 they asked him to the Château de Candé, near Tours, to record the nuptials twenty-four hours before they took place. The first professional photographer with social pretensions, he was disappointed not to be invited to stay on for the true ceremony – he had brought a bag with him just in case. On the death of the Duke of Windsor a generation later, Beaton was still aggrieved. He wrote in his diary: 'I felt callously indifferent, no pang of nostalgia ... throughout the years, the Duke had never shown any affection for or interest in me.'

Beaton achieved the triumph of his career in the summer of 1939 when summoned to photograph the Queen, later Queen Elizabeth the Queen Mother, in the gilded rooms and garden of Buckingham Palace. During the sittings he stole one of her handkerchiefs, scented with

tuberoses and gardenias. He wrote about his affection for the actress Greta Garbo with the same romantic abandon. By contrast, Beaton served as an official photographer for the RAF, throughout the war, flying many thousands of miles in unaccustomed austerity.

Although pleased to take the first photographs of the infant Prince Charles in 1948 and to be chosen as official photographer at the Coronation five years later, Beaton hankered after stage design and was much applauded for the costumes of *My Fair Lady*.

Cecil Beaton, who never married, was held in high regard by his intimates, a close-knit and sophisticated circle. Successive volumes of his diaries, however, exposed the faults of friends scarcely less savagely than those of enemies; nor did he hesitate to publish these observant but spiteful pages in his victims' lifetime. For his services to photography and other arts he was made CBE in 1957 and knighted in 1972.

Cecil Beaton with a costume for *My Fair Lady*

Princess Beatrice at Queen Victoria's Jubilee Drawing-Room, May 1887. On the Queen's left are the Princess of Wales, Princess Beatrice, Princess Louise of Wales, the Duke of Cambridge and the Duke of Teck.

Beatrice, Princess
later Princess Henry of Battenberg
(1857–1944)

The youngest child of Queen Victoria and the Prince Consort, she was only four years old when her father's death consigned her to a role of filial servitude. 'The Queen can only pray,' the bereaved Sovereign wrote, 'that this flower of the flock … may never leave her, but be the prop, comfort and companion of her widowed mother to old age.' The intelligent young princess acquired a love of music and a talent for drafting those imperious telegrams with which the Queen liked to ginger up her Ministers. But as the guardian of State secrets, she was discreet to the point of dullness; and those who dined next to her could expect only talk of the weather or a shy silence.

At the age of twenty-eight, Princess Beatrice

fell in love with Prince Henry of Battenberg. But the Queen, fearing to lose her only unmarried daughter, declared that the match 'would never do.' She gave way only on the understanding that the couple should make their home with her, sharing her annual migrations between Windsor, Osborne and Balmoral. The wedding took place in Whippingham Church, near Osborne, in July 1885. There were four children of the marriage. (See *Victoria Eugénie, Queen of Spain*; and *Carisbrooke, Marquess of*)

Princess Beatrice continued to act as her mother's confidential secretary. Prince Henry was given the less demanding duties of Governor of the Isle of Wight and Honorary Colonel of the Isle of Wight Rifles. Bored by inactivity, he once slipped away for a few days to Corsica with his brother Louis (see *Milford Haven, 1st Marquess of*), but was retrieved by a man-of-war sent at the Queen's express command. In 1896, however, he insisted on volunteering as military secretary to the commander of the British

Menu for the wedding breakfast at Osborne after the marriage of Princess Beatrice to Prince Henry of Battenberg, July 1885

expedition to Ashanti, in West Africa. There he contracted fever, dying on his way home to England.

Princess Beatrice, not yet forty, lived on for almost half a century. The Queen, whose sight had begun to fail, increasingly depended on her daughter both to read aloud the contents of her official boxes and to act as a link with her official household. This her private secretaries had cause to resent. One of them, Frederick Ponsonby (q.v.) confided to his mother in 1898: 'The most absurd mistakes occur and the Queen is not even *au courant* with the ordinary topics of the present day. Imagine Beatrice trying to explain the vaccination question or our policy on the East. Bigge or I may write out long précis of these things but they are often not read to H.M. as Beatrice is in a hurry to develop a photograph or wants to paint a flower for a bazaar.'

Posterity also has reason to regret Princess Beatrice's industry after her mother's death. The Queen bequeathed to her all her private manuscript journals, with the injunction that she should modify or destroy any passages she thought unsuitable for preservation. For more than forty years the Princess worked away at this task of literary emasculation. Page by page, she copied out only what was anodyne into a series of notebooks, then burned the original manuscript. Historians have since been able to collate the expurgated text, now in the Royal Archives, with certain passages from the original journal: these were copied during the Queen's lifetime and with her permission, for use by Sir Theodore Martin in his official biography of the Prince Consort. From this comparison it is possible to estimate the incalculable loss of the Queen's journal: more than sixty years of insight and illumination.

Stout of person and kindly of heart, Princess Beatrice survived to mourn two of her sons and to perform many works of charity. She died in the reign of King George VI, the last of those five sisters who, as their niece Princess Alice puts it, 'were authoritarian, part of a conscious royal caste, telling people what to do and getting on each other's nerves.'

Beaufort, Henry Somerset, 10th Duke of
(1900–1984)

The Queen with the Duke of Beaufort, the Queen Mother, and Princess Margaret at the International Horse Trials at Badminton, 1956

Master of the Horse 1936–78. The only son of the 9th Duke, he was educated at Eton and the Royal Military College, Sandhurst, and commissioned into the Royal Horse Guards. In 1923, the year before he succeeded to the family honours, he married (as Earl of Worcester) Lady Mary Cambridge, elder daughter of the 1st Marquess of Cambridge (see *Beaufort, Mary, Duchess of*).

A considerable landowner in Gloucestershire and elsewhere, the Duke was the Nimrod of foxhunters. Even as a boy he was entrusted with his own pack of hounds and known for the rest of his life as 'Master'. Like the legendary Mr Jorrocks, he believed that 'all time is lost wot is not spent in 'unting.' He was in fact two men. In the hunting field he could become almost demented with rage at any check to his sport or breach of etiquette. As a host at Badminton or a rare guest in the houses of others, he was modest, friendly and considerate. Although proud of his possessions, he did not much care to discuss them. A guest once gushed over the Canalettos of Badminton: 'How perfectly lovely they are.' Master replied shortly: 'I don't know about their being lovely, but they are very like the house.'

Long days in the saddle kept him fit, except for the odd broken bone, into his ninth decade. He stood well over six feet and looked magnificent when mounted. Throughout his forty-six years as Master of the Horse, an office in the royal household held by his forebears in the reigns of Queen Elizabeth I and Queen Victoria, he was able to wear the same gold-encrusted coat.

He was disappointed to have no children. His heir was a cousin, David Somerset, who succeeded him in 1984 as 11th and present Duke of Beaufort. 'The boy is a picture dealer,' Master would say. 'Not sporting pictures, you know.'

Beaufort, Mary, Duchess of
(1897–   )

Widow of the 10th Duke of Beaufort (q.v.). She is the eldest daughter of Adolphus, Duke of Teck (1868–1927), and Lady Margaret Grosvenor, fourth daughter of the 1st Duke of Westminster. The Duke of Teck, the eldest of Queen Mary's three brothers, was educated at Wellington College and Sandhurst, served in the British Army in two wars and was Governor of Windsor Castle. In 1917 he relinquished his German styles and titles, and was created Marquess of Cambridge.

Lady Mary Cambridge, as she was known until her marriage in 1923, was brought up with members of the British royal family. She likes to recall how, as a child, she was at Buckingham Palace on the morning of Edward VII's Coronation, when the King came into the nursery wearing a gold tunic and said: 'Don't I look a funny old gentleman?' Suitably awed at the time, she has since added her own acerbic commentary: 'He was never funny, not old and by no stretch of the imagination a gentleman.' She adored King George V, however, who was always nicer to other people's children than to

his own. He would take her to the races at Goodwood or sailing in his yacht *Britannia*.

In 1939, Queen Mary left Marlborough House, in London, to spend the war years with her niece at Badminton. The Duchess wrote to a friend, Osbert Sitwell: 'Oh, how I longed for you to be there when she and about fifty-five servants arrived. Pandemonium was the least it could be called. The servants revolted and scorned our humble home. They refused to use the excellent rooms assigned to them. Fearful rows and battles royal fought over my body – but I won in the end and reduced them to tears and pulp.... The Queen, quite unconscious of the stir, has settled in well, and is busy cutting down trees and tearing down ivy.'

The most splendid and famous of all Badminton trees was saved from the royal axe only after another spirited engagement, this time between the Duchess and her aunt. It was a cedar, planted near the house by the fifth Duke at the end of the eighteenth century; his youngest son FitzRoy, who as Lord Raglan later commanded the British army in the Crimean War, was said to have leaped over it as a sapling. But the romance of history counted as nothing with Queen Mary when her own comfort was at stake. She had convinced herself that the tree bred insects which then swarmed into her bedroom, and demanded that it be cut down. 'Over my dead body,' the Duchess retorted. Instead she offered Queen Mary another room, but this was rejected. At length they reached a compromise: the tree remained and Queen Mary's windows were covered with insect-proof gauze.

Her war on ivy also caused the Duchess much vexation. The old Queen would motor round the estate stripping it from cottage walls; but it was of the ornamental variety much cherished by the villagers, who complained. Queen Mary thought the country most awfully untidy and insisted on collecting farm implements left out in the fields, under the delusion that they were valuable pieces of scrap metal. She was more usefully occupied in dragooning her household and visitors into clearing shrubberies so that they could be planted with young trees. Only

Archbishop Lang (q.v.) was brave enough to mutiny. 'I will *not* go into the woods to pick up sticks,' that Prince of the Church declared. Queen Mary also liked browsing in the muniment room at Badminton.

With the return of Queen Mary and her retinue to London, life at Badminton became more tranquil, but not for long. The annual three-day horse trials and the opening of the house to the public revealed the Duchess's instincts of hospitality on a wider scale. Small of stature and unpretentious in manner, she likes to boast of how often visitors have mistaken her for a housemaid. She loves dogs as her husband loved horses, and it is not always easy to find an unoccupied chair in her drawing-room.

Her conversation sparkles in any company. Before the annual luncheon at Windsor for Knights of the Garter and their wives, she saw that her neighbour would be that social crusader Lord Longford, whom she had never met. So she asked another Garter Knight what they could talk about. 'Pornography,' was the facetious answer. The Duchess thought he had said photography, and she and her new friend kept it up for two hours.

Sister Catherine Black, 1936

Bigge, Sir Arthur see Stamfordham, Arthur Bigge, 1st Baron

Black, Catherine

The nursing sister who, with three others, was called in to look after King George v during his serious illness of 1928–9. At the suggestion of Lord Dawson of Penn, she remained in the King's service for the rest of his life.

A few years after his illness, the King sent Sister Black to look at Dulwich Hospital, which had impressed him during an official visit. About a week later, two of the patients to whom she had spoken developed smallpox. To give the King the utmost protection, Sister Black was vaccinated and put into quarantine. The doctors wanted to vaccinate the King, too. He drove them from the room. 'Time enough for all that damned nonsense,' he said, 'when she or I get smallpox.'

Blacklock, Norman
(1928–   )

Surgeon Captain, Royal Navy, retired, and Professor of Urology at Manchester University. Although he does not appear in the official list of Her Majesty's Medical Household, he is an indispensable member of her entourage on overseas tours. Most of the Queen's doctors are distinguished in their profession and thus too busy in Harley Street or at teaching hospitals to travel abroad in attendance on her. Blacklock, however, manages to combine a Chair of Urology with a readiness to make himself available whenever required. Throughout the overseas tours he is never more than a few yards away from the Queen; invariably he carries a discreet bag containing all that may be needed in an emergency.

Blacklock is held in much esteem by the Queen's courtiers, who call him Hemlock. They take his advice on the virtues of a vegetable diet and some may even have read his published works, including 'Bladder Trauma in the Long-Distance Runner'.

Blunt, Anthony
(1907–1983)

Surveyor of the King's Pictures 1945–52, of the Queen's Pictures 1952–72, and Adviser for the Queen's Pictures and Drawings 1972–8. He was the youngest son of the Rev. A.S.V. Blunt, Vicar of Holy Trinity, Bournemouth, and later Chaplain to the British Embassy in Paris. It was during those early years in France that Anthony Blunt, under the guidance of his eldest brother, Wilfrid, later drawing master at Eton, developed an interest in pictures.

His academic career was of effortless distinction. From Marlborough College, where he was a contemporary of John Betjeman, he won a scholarship in mathematics to Trinity College, Cambridge. Although he took only a Second Class in Part I of the Mathematical Tripos, he went on to take a First in Modern and Medieval Languages. In 1932 he was elected to a Fellowship of Trinity with a dissertation on Nicolas Poussin. It was the first step in a career that led him to the very summit of his profession as an art historian.

Blunt travelled on the continent of Europe, joined the staff of the Warburg Institute and in 1939 was appointed Reader in the History of Art at London University and Deputy Director of the Courtauld Institute. Having served throughout the war in British intelligence, he was in 1945 appointed Surveyor of the King's Pictures in succession to Sir Kenneth Clark (q.v.). At once he stamped his knowledge and personality on the office with a memorable exhibition at Burlington House. 'The pictures looked lovely,' Queen Mary noted, 'and were well hung by Mr Blunt and the Committee.' Sir Oliver Millar (q.v.), historian of the royal picture collections and his successor as Surveyor of the Queen's Pictures, recorded 'the age of enlightenment that

Anthony Blunt's appointment ushered in.' He set in train the restoration and cleaning of the collections, wrote volume after volume of the definitive catalogue and became chairman of a small committee to acquire works of art by living British and Commonwealth artists. In 1972, on retiring as Surveyor at the age of sixty-five, he continued to put his knowledge at the Queen's disposal as special adviser on pictures and drawings. He was made CVO by George VI and KCVO by Elizabeth II.

On a wider canvas, Blunt meanwhile consolidated his reputation as the most admired British-born art historian of his generation and a world authority on Poussin. From 1947 to 1974 he was Professor of the History of Art at London University and Director of the Courtauld Institute, which under his influence became a celebrated nursery of art historians. He received several British and foreign decorations, and honorary degrees from four universities. Then came the fall.

In November 1979 the Prime Minister, Margaret Thatcher, astounded the House of Commons and in turn the country with a statement about Blunt's past life. As long ago as 1964, she revealed, he had confessed to spying for Soviet Russia while employed by MI5 during the war, but had been spared public exposure and prosecution in return for a promise to tell all he knew to our own intelligence service. What particularly shocked the nation was the disclosure that a known traitor had thus been

Anthony Blunt, 1979

employed in the Queen's household for the past fifteen years. Whether or not the Queen knew of his confession and subsequent absolution remains uncertain.

What did emerge, largely in Andrew Boyle's book, *The Climate of Treason*, was the story of his conversion to Communism at Cambridge and his readiness to supply his friend Guy Burgess with the names of other likely recruits. This he justified in the cause of anti-Fascism: a claim more plausible in the 1930s than half a century later. During his wartime years in MI5 he had access to much secret information which he surreptitiously passed to Russian intelligence. Several foreign agents of the Allies are said to have lost their lives through these disclosures. Although Blunt broke off contact with Soviet Russia after the war, he kept up his links with the defectors Philby, Maclean and above all Burgess. The tale of his treachery, or as much of it as he disclosed, was extracted from him only after prolonged cross-examination. Once the truth had been made public in 1979, Blunt was stripped of his knighthood and renounced most of his other honours.

At his death in 1983, Blunt left an estate valued at £850,000. Almost half of this was represented by Poussin's *Rebecca at the Well*. He had spotted the picture for sale in 1932 at £100. On asking his Cambridge friend Lord Rothschild to lend him the purchase price (about £2,000 in the currency of 1985), Rothschild had generously responded with a gift. Blunt, a bachelor, left the bulk of his estate to a companion of many years, who offered the Poussin to the Government in lieu of tax. The transaction was refused on grounds of public policy. Private donations later enabled the Fitzwilliam Museum, Cambridge, to acquire the picture.

Boyd-Rochfort, Captain Sir Cecil
(1887–1983)

Racehorse trainer to King George VI and Queen Elizabeth II. Born in West Meath, Ireland, and educated at Eton, he became stud and stable manager to Sir Ernest Cassel in 1913. During the Great War he served in the Scots Guards, was wounded and received the Croix de Guerre.

In 1924 he set up his own training establishment at Freemason Lodge, Newmarket, where he remained until his retirement forty-four years later. His skill and patience with horses won him thirteen English classics and well over £1 million in stake money for his owners. In 1946 he trained Hypericum to win the One Thousand Guineas for King George VI and in 1958 Pall Mall to win the Two Thousand Guineas for the Queen.

He had been disappointed, however, not to win the 1953 Derby for the Queen with Aureole, which was beaten into second place. The race was run at the end of Coronation week and is said to have prompted this conversation between a lady-in-waiting and the Queen on the day before the sacred ceremony:

'You must be feeling nervous, Ma'am.'
'Of course I am, but I really do think Aureole will win.'

Captain Boyd-Rochfort studies form. Newmarket, 1963

In the following year Aureole won both the Coronation Cup and the King George VI and Queen Elizabeth Stakes.

'The Captain', knighted on his retirement, was a handsome man, with stately, somewhat old-fashioned habits. His 6 feet 4 inches were crowned by a Homburg hat of the 1920s; he never drove a car; and he hardly ever graced the lesser racecourses. But he was one of the first trainers to take on stable girls in place of the traditional lads. Nor did he disdain a gamble on the unaristocratic handicaps. Dying in his ninety-sixth year, he left estate valued at almost £700,000.

Cambridge, Lady Mary see Beaufort, Duchess of

Carisbrooke, Alexander, Marquess of
(1886–1960)

He was born Prince Alexander of Battenberg, the eldest son of Prince Henry of Battenberg by his marriage to Princess Beatrice (q.v.), Queen Victoria's youngest daughter. Brought up at Windsor, he would later claim with some justice to have been the Queen's favourite grandchild. The party which she gave for him on his tenth birthday included a cinematograph show; and on his eleventh, both a cinematograph show and performing dogs.

The consciousness of royal birth also made him reluctant to relinquish his princely title and style of 'Highness' when in 1917 his cousin George V abolished all such German attributes. It gave him only moderate pleasure to exchange them for three new peerages of the United Kingdom: Marquess of Carisbrooke, Earl of Berkhamsted and Viscount Launceston.

'Drino' Carisbrooke, as he was known to family and friends, served in each of the three Services in succession: in the Royal Navy from 1902 to 1908, in the Grenadier Guards during the Great War (when he was mentioned in despatches) and in the RAF during World War II. Yet he failed to impress with his martial virtues. 'The completest dud I always think,' the Prince of Wales wrote of his fellow Grenadier in 1917, 'such an affected ass.' In the same year he married Lady Irene Denison, only daughter of the 2nd Earl of Londesborough. A few months later the Prince of Wales again wrote of him: 'I hear that Irene Carisbrooke has signs of a baby and that Drino has retired to bed for a month's rest cure!' The only child of the marriage was Lady Iris Mountbatten, born in 1920.

Between the wars he was not too proud to accept employment in a merchant bank and to sit on the boards of several companies. He also became senior steward of the National Greyhound Racing Club, a pastime which the great Lord Lonsdale described as fun but not sport.

Carisbrooke shared his mother's delight in music and enjoyed social life and gossip. A guest described him in his house at Kew: 'He was immaculately dressed in a well-pressed check suit, padded shoulders, and jangling gold bracelets and rings. He reminded me of an old spruce hen, cackling and scratching the dust in a chicken-run.'

He died in 1960, four years after his wife.

Cartland, Barbara
(1902–   )

She is the mother of Raine, Countess Spencer, second wife of the 8th Earl; and thus step-grandmother to the Princess of Wales. A prolific author of romantic novels, she writes twenty books a year and has sold three hundred million copies of them in seventeen languages. She claims to have rejected forty-nine proposals of marriage before accepting Alexander George McCorquodale in 1927. The marriage was dissolved in 1933, and three years later she was married to another member of the McCorquodale family. Miss Cartland is spectacularly addicted to pink clothes, feathered hats, pekineses and a white Rolls-Royce. She believes fervently in health foods; and her friend the late Lord Mountbatten used to swear by the pills she pressed on him containing vitamins and other more arcane substances.

Barbara Cartland did not attend the wedding of the Prince and Princess of Wales in St Paul's Cathedral in 1981, but appeared on television looking as smart as paint in the uniform of the St John Ambulance Brigade. The *Times Literary Supplement* paid her the compliment of reprinting this extract from her first novel, called *Jigsaw* and published in 1923:

'The usual overdressed and be-titled crowd filled the pews with their scented pampered bodies, rustling their silks, patting their dyed hair and surreptitiously powdering their noses, without a thought for the young couple embarking on the new and somewhat precarious craft of married life on to the uncharted sea of the future.'

Cassidy, Sir Maurice
(1880–1949)

Heart specialist and physician to successive

Sovereigns. In 1949, shortly before Cassidy's death, his patient King George VI made a pilgrimage of gratitude to his sick bed and personally bestowed on him the GCVO.

Cazalet, Peter
(1907–1973)

Racing trainer to Queen Elizabeth the Queen Mother from 1949 until his death. He came of a family that had fled from France as Huguenot refugees and prospered both in England and in Russia. His father lent his villa in the south of France to Queen Victoria, and Peter's godparents were Queen Victoria Eugénie of Spain (q.v.) and the King and Queen of Bulgaria.

Educated at Eton and Christ Church, Oxford, he showed skill at most ball games, playing cricket both for his school and his university. Enthusiasm for steeplechasing led him to set up his own training establishment at Fairlawne, the family estate in Kent. In 1932 he married Leonora, the step-daughter of P. G. Wodehouse. She died in 1944. Five years later he married Zara, daughter of Sir Harry Mainwaring.

Barbara Cartland

Sir Maurice Cassidy

The Queen Mother with her trainer, Peter Cazalet, at Newbury races, 1964.

He served during the war in the Welsh Guards with his friend and fellow amateur rider, Lord Mildmay (q.v.). It was Mildmay who in 1949 suggested that the Queen (later Queen Elizabeth the Queen Mother) should send her first steeplechaser to be trained at Fairlawne. Thus began a sporting partnership that lasted for almost a quarter of a century and saw Cazalet train more than 250 winners for his royal patron.

The most coveted prize eluded them. In the Grand National of 1956, the Queen Mother's Devon Loch led over the last fence, full of running and with the race apparently at his mercy. Fifty yards from the winning post, the horse collapsed. To this day there has been no conclusive explanation. The experienced jockey, Dick Francis, later to win fame of another sort as a writer of thrillers, believes that Devon Loch was terrified by the tremendous cheers heralding a royal victory: 'A wave of sound shattering intensity.' It was characteristic of the Queen Mother that her first thoughts were for the horse, the jockey, the trainer and the stable lads. 'The most perfect display of dignity I have ever witnessed,' the Duke of Devonshire told Harold Nicolson. 'I hope the Russians saw it.'

Few owners of steeplechasers and hurdlers show a profit over the years. After one lean season, it was whispered, the Queen asked to be allowed to pay Cazalet's account. The Queen Mother, gratefully accepting the offer, signed her name at the bottom of the bill. Before sending it on to Buckingham Palace, she had an afterthought. Under her signature she added an apologetic, 'Oh, dear.'

Cédard, Monsieur
(d.1935)

Chef de cuisine to King George v. Although the King was an abstemious man, plagued by dyspepsia and seasickness, he took Cédard with him even when visiting the troops in France throughout the Great War. The royal chef pursued his art under discouraging circumstances: not only wartime shortages of butter and cream, lamb and poussins, but also the King's patriotic banishment of wines and spirits from his table until victory had been won. The future Prime Minister, Neville Chamberlain, dining at Windsor in the third year of the war, noted 'a nasty sort of pink mould for a sweet.' And the wife of the Queen's Librarian described what she called 'a very plain little dinner.' It consisted of mulligatawny soup; turbot with shrimp sauce; vegetable cutlets, green peas and new potatoes; asparagus; cold baked custard in china cups; and dessert.

Channon, Sir Henry
(1897–1958)

Member of Parliament, diarist and friend of the royal family. He was born in Chicago, the grandson of a Somerset man who had emigrated to the United States, founded a prosperous business as a ships' chandler and acquired a fleet of his own. Educated in Chicago and in Paris, Channon returned to France in 1917 as a member of the American Red Cross and later became an honorary attaché at the United States Embassy. There he enjoyed the favour of both Proust and Cocteau.

In 1918 he settled permanently in England. He was an undergraduate at Christ Church, Oxford, then shared a house in London with Prince Paul of Yugoslavia, the future brother-in-law of Princess Marina, Duchess of Kent (q.v.), and Lord Gage, who became a Lord-in-Waiting to King George v. Henry Channon was known during his English years as 'Chips', apparently because of his friendship for someone called 'Fish'.

In 1933, the year in which he published the best-known of his books, *The Ludwigs of Bavaria*, he married Lady Honor Guinness, eldest daughter of the 2nd Earl of Iveagh. The marriage, which was dissolved in 1945, brought him many advantages and joys: a wife, a much-loved son, an addition to his private income, a directorship of Arthur Guinness, and in 1935 a safe Conservative seat. Southend-on-Sea could indeed have been mistaken for a pocket borough of an earlier age. It was held from 1918 to 1927 by Channon's father-in-law; from 1927 to 1935 by his mother-in-law; and since his own death in 1958 has been held by his son Paul, a Minister in the Governments of Edward Heath and Margaret Thatcher. 'Chips' adored the Commons, what he called 'this smelly, tawny, male paradise.' During his twenty-three years at Westminster, however, he made only four speeches, totalling twenty-one minutes in length, and asked no more than eighteen parliamentary questions. And although he yearned for office, he had to be content with three years as Parliamentary Private Secretary to the Under-Secretary for Foreign Affairs. He was knighted in 1957.

Channon's gifts were social rather than political. He had two splendid houses. In London there was No. 5 Belgrave Square, with its dining-room of blue and silver copied from the Amalienberg, near Munich; in Essex he bought Kelvedon Hall. There he entertained many friends, some of them unexpected; but with the exception of Mrs Ernest Simpson (q.v.), he did not seek the company of his compatriots. Those to be found in the present book include King Edward VIII, King George VI and Queen Elizabeth, Queen Mary, Queen Victoria Eugénie of Spain, the Duke and Duchess of Kent, Sir Cecil Beaton, Lord Carisbrooke, Lady Colefax, Lady Diana Cooper, Sir Noel Coward, Lady Cunard, Mrs Ronald Greville, the Mountbattens, the 16th Duke of Norfolk and Sir Philip Sassoon.

'Chips' Channon

These friendships he enshrined in his diaries, a selection from which was published in 1967. For all their faults of taste and revelation of artless ambition, they make compulsive reading and offer an important contemporary record of such episodes as Chamberlain's policy of appeasement and the Abdication of Edward VIII. During his short reign, the King twice dined with 'Chips' in Belgrave Square. Between the two dates, the diarist wrote: 'We were invited to eleven dinner parties tonight. The Iveaghs, while amused by our royal activities, are nevertheless impressed. Their gangster son-in-law from Chicago has put their daughter into the most exclusive set in Europe.'

Channon's diaries contain other memorable moments. In September 1935: 'It is very difficult to spend less than £200 a morning when one goes shopping.' (That sum, in the currency of half a century later, represents £4,000). On 11 March 1937: 'An unbelievable day, in which two things occurred. Hitler took Vienna and I fell in love with the Prime Minister.' At a dinner he gave for the Queens of Spain and Rumania two years later: 'I laced the cocktails with Benzedrine, which I find always makes a party go.' And on the death of Emerald Cunard in 1948: 'London society has had a horrible blow. There is only me left.'

Too much censoriousness would be misplaced. The foibles of a Boswell are of less concern than his recollections of Dr Johnson.

Charles, Prince of Wales
(1948–   )

Born at Buckingham Palace on 14 November 1948, the eldest of the four children of Princess Elizabeth, later Queen Elizabeth II, and her husband Prince Philip, Duke of Edinburgh. In February 1952, on the death of his grandfather King George VI and the accession of his mother, he became heir apparent and Duke of Cornwall. Not until 1958 was he created Prince of Wales, his Investiture following eleven years later. Prince Charles made his first ceremonial appearance at his mother's Coronation in 1953. A small boy in a white satin suit and brilliantined hair, he sat next to his grandmother, Queen Elizabeth the Queen Mother. Afterwards he appeared with other members of the royal family on the balcony of Buckingham Palace wearing his Coronation Medal: the first of a constellation of stars and ribbons he was to receive over the years.

Asked in later life how he had been trained for his royal role, Prince Charles replied: 'I learned the way a monkey learns: by watching its parents.' More formal lessons were the task of his governess, Miss Peebles, who also showed him the sights of London. For a few months in 1957 he attended Hill House, near Knightsbridge, one of a crocodile of small boys in a uniform of brown jersey, shorts, cloth cap and sandals. This fashionable establishment, with its emphasis on good manners and games, was a prelude to his first boarding school, Cheam, where his father had once been a pupil before it moved from Surrey to a wooded corner of Hampshire. Charles bore its spartan rigours with resignation, showing average ability both in the classroom and on the playing fields. But as the first heir to the throne ever to be sent away to school, he was perpetually under siege from the Press. Intrusive journalists and photographers, not all of them British, at times made life very unhappy for a nine-year-old boy whose only ambition was to resemble all other nine-year-old boys.

When the time came for the Prince to leave Cheam in the spring of 1962, there was a division of opinion about his future. Prince Philip wanted his son to follow him to Gordonstoun, in Scotland, where thirty years earlier he had been one of the first pupils of Kurt Hahn (q.v.). The Queen was thought to favour Eton, where she had once been tutored in constitutional history by Henry Marten (q.v.); if so, she had a fervent ally in the Queen Mother, all of whose brothers had been educated there. Charles, less of an extrovert than his father, would have been better suited to Eton, with its traditions of tolerance and personal choice and the privacy of a separate room for each boy. He would also have seen far more of his family at Windsor, scarcely ten minutes' walk from the school. What finally decided the issue was not only Prince Philip's preference for Gordonstoun, but also its remoteness; the hordes of journalists and photographers who could have been expected to infest Eton would find the open spaces of Morayshire less appealing.

Prince Charles, accompanied by his father, arrived at Gordonstoun in May 1962. Neither then nor later did he show dismay at the bleakness of both the landscape and the school regime. But more than twenty years on, his youngest brother Prince Edward, another old boy of the school, revealed on television that Prince Charles had 'hated' the place. The supposed triumph of character over intellect and the apotheosis of the cold shower were not the only miseries he endured. Affectionate by nature, he was lonely and homesick in a public-school world of totem and taboo that shrank from appearing to curry favour with the heir to the throne.

Two episodes of those years became public knowledge. On an expedition to Stornoway, on the Isle of Lewis, he took refuge from a crowd of goggling spectators in the bar of an hotel, where he ordered the only drink that came to mind: cherry brandy. By ill luck, this modest debauchery on the part of a boy of fourteen was witnessed by a freelance journalist, who sold the story to the newspapers. Their readers concluded that the Prince must be a high-spirited young fellow, cast in the mould of his popular ancestor, King Edward VII; the school took a dour view of the escapade, and Charles was demoted. The setback was temporary, and in time he rose to be guardian, or head boy. Meanwhile there was the theft, presumably by a fellow pupil, of the exercise book in which he wrote his essays. Its contents, published throughout the world, revealed him to be a well-balanced, liberal-minded boy; a magnanimous one, too, who after all he had suffered nevertheless extolled the virtues of a free Press.

He interrupted his final years at Gordonstoun to spend two terms at Timbertop, an outpost of Geelong Grammar School, sometimes called the Eton of Australia. He enjoyed the freedom of his new life that introduced him to tree-felling, gold-panning and sheep-shearing. Contrary to what some had expected, his Australian contemporaries proved less inhibited than Gordonstoun boys and welcomed him with rowdy good-nature; the only person consistently unpleasant to him at Timbertop, he later recalled, was an Englishman.

With A-levels in French and History, the Prince of Wales was accepted for a place at Trinity College, Cambridge, the *alma mater* of Edward VII, George VI and Prince Henry, Duke of Gloucester (qq.v.), none of whom had lived in college or stayed the full three years or sat for a degree. The Master of Trinity throughout his time in Cambridge was the retired Conservative statesman, Lord Butler: a man renowned for his formidable intellect, mercurial humour and worldly assessment of friend and foe alike. 'Rab' Butler, the only head of a college at either Oxford or Cambridge ever to be a Knight of the Garter, took a courtly as well as an academic interest in the young Prince. He allowed him such luxuries as a telephone and a small kitchen in his rooms, and winked at his infringement of the university rule that forbade a freshman to keep his own car in Cambridge. The Prince repaid the Master's trust. Examinations in Archeology and Anthropology at the end of his first year brought him a place in the upper division of Class II: a good Second Class. The Master urged him to continue with these subjects and to aim at a First in his finals. But the heir to the throne thought he ought to know more history, and he had his way.

Prince Charles made the most of Cambridge. He had first become stagestruck at Gordonstoun, where he took the title role in a haunting Shakespearean tragedy. Inevitably, however, it was the third witch who stole some of his glory with the line: 'All hail, Macbeth, that shall be King hereafter.' Now he exchanged a dagger for a dustbin in the most celebrated of his appearances in Cambridge revue. He also learned to fly, played the trumpet and the cello, won a Half Blue for Polo, and extended the social and political boundaries of his friendships. But the Master was irritated by the encroachment of public duties on an undergraduate's freedom. The Prince spent the whole of the summer term of 1969 in Aberystwyth, learning Welsh and enduring much uncouth abuse from the Principality's nationalist minority. Throughout these painful but instructive weeks he displayed a good-humoured restraint and modesty that disarmed criticism. In July, the Queen invested him as Prince of Wales in Caernarvon Castle: a colourful ceremony devised primarily to meet the demands of television and stage-managed by the Earl of Snowdon (q.v.), his uncle by marriage.

Similar diversions continued to obstruct his pursuit of the past: public engagements in Malta, a conference on conservation in Strasbourg, introduction into the House of Lords, a tour of Australia and New Zealand, followed by another of Japan. In his final exams in June he took a II.2 in History, a grade lower than his previous result, but achieved under severe handicap. Thirteen years later, when Oxford gave the Prince an honorary degree, he charmed the rival university by admitting to 'some East Anglian academic qualifications, even if on most occasions they do not show.'

Between the ages of twenty-two and twenty-seven, the Prince of Wales served successively in the RAF and the Royal Navy. He trained at Cranwell and Dartmouth. He flew every type of aircraft except a supersonic jet, sailed the world in every type of ship except a Polaris submarine. He descended from the skies by parachute and rose from the waves by escape-hatch. He grew a beard and a moustache in the Queen's service, but the Queen did not care for them; the beard came off on the first day of his return to Buckingham Palace, the moustache on the second. The Prince was at last given command of his own ship, HMS *Bronington*, a wooden-hulled minehunter of 360 tons with a complement of four officers and thirty-three ratings. He retired from the active list at the end of 1976 to take part in the ceremonies of the Queen's Silver Jubilee year and to raise a charitable fund of more than £16 million.

Even during those maritime years he was often recalled to undertake royal duties. He attended the Coronation of King Birendra of Nepal and the funerals of General de Gaulle, Sir Robert Menzies and President Jomo Kenyatta. He represented the Queen at the independence celebrations of Fiji, the Bahamas and Papua New Guinea, and toured other countries of the Commonwealth. He managed covetable holidays, too: shooting with the Duke and Duchess of Wellington in Spain, fishing with Lord and Lady Tryon in Iceland, swimming with Lord and Lady Brabourne in the Caribbean.

His life has since become more fragmented than that of any other member of the royal family: partly because of the many demands made on him, partly because of the energy and enthusiasm with which he responds. He encourages exploration and archeology; voluntary service and youthful enterprise; conservation and forestry; the restoration of cathedrals and restraint in modern architecture. As befits a descendant of Count Dracula and Leopold Lafontaine, the doctor of Stanislaus II, King of Poland, he is a Fellow of the Royal Colleges of Surgeons and of Physicians; but his regard for faith healing and other unorthodox practices is looked on with suspicion by both institutions. He is President of the Bach Choir and the

Friends of Covent Garden, delights in listening to music and invited Kiri Te Kanawa to sing Mozart at his wedding. Sadly he has parted with his cello, the favourite instrument of another, eighteenth-century, Prince of Wales; thus recalling the great Duke of Wellington, who burned his violin because it distracted him from his professional duties. The Prince succeeded his father as Chancellor of the University of Wales (as well as Colonel of the Welsh Guards) and from his uncle, Lord Mountbatten, has inherited responsibility for United World Colleges: a far-flung chain of Gordonstouns in spirit if not precisely in form.

The Prince of Wales is a fluent public speaker whose modesty and self-deprecating humour show to particular advantage on television. More even-tempered than his father, he did once explode after bathing from a beach near Melbourne: 'It's like swimming in undiluted sewage.' The enraged local mayor threatened to give him 'a good thump under the ear.' British audiences are more indulgent; but the Prince may well reflect that one scold in the family is enough, particularly when dwelling on the supposed shortcomings of Britsh industry.

For a whole decade, Press and public speculated on the Prince's ultimate choice of a wife. There was no shortage of candidates for his affection, and he acquired a reputation for treating even the successful with cavalier caprice. Name after name was canvassed, one or two from the other Royal Houses of Europe, most from the English aristocracy, a few of equivocal background. The years crept on, and the nation echoed the plaint of the Prince's favourite Shakespearean character: 'What, will the line stretch out to the crack of doom?' At last, in February 1981, his betrothal was announced to Lady Diana Spencer (q.v.), youngest daughter of the 8th Earl Spencer. He was thirty-two, she not yet twenty. His choice was greeted with universal delight. Less wilful than his great-uncle, the Duke of Windsor (q.v.), the heir apparent had not forgotten that the woman he married must one day be Queen. The wedding was solemnized in St Paul's Cathedral on 29 July

1981 by the Archbishop of Canterbury, Robert Runcie (q.v.).

The Prince and Princess have since performed the first duty of their role by producing two children in direct line of succession to the throne: Prince William, born in 1982, and Prince Henry, born in 1984. The family has a London house in Kensington Palace, which also shelters Princess Margaret and Princess Alice, Duchess of Gloucester; their nephew calls it the aunt heap. Some years before his marriage, the Prince was offered a rent-free tenancy of Chevening, a Palladian mansion in Kent, endowed and given to the nation by the 7th Earl Stanhope. He scarcely used it at all but instead bought Highgrove House, in Gloucestershire, from the late Maurice Macmillan, MP, son of the former Prime Minister, the Earl of Stockton.

It is but one indication of how well insulated from financial stress the Prince of Wales finds himself. His income is derived not from the parliamentary grant known as the Civil List, but from the revenues that the eldest son of the Sovereign traditionally enjoys as Duke of Cornwall. The Duchy estates, covering 130,000 acres and including much valuable London property, in 1983 produced a net surplus of £795,126; in 1984 it rose to £978,000. Of this sum, the Prince retains three-quarters, voluntarily remitting the rest to the Treasury. He is by long custom required to pay no income tax on Duchy revenue. There are thus the means to support a quietly sumptuous way of life, to build up a trust fund for the children and to give handsomely to charitable causes.

No computer could have devised so presentable an heir to the throne as Prince Charles. He has a wife, a family, widespread interests, a desire to please, an eccentricity or two but no obvious vices. As resolute a patron of the arts as of physical prowess, he has chosen the writer and explorer Laurens van der Post as godfather to one son, the portrait painter Bryan Organ as godfather to another. The Prince's consciousness of royal birth is tempered by modesty; his innate conservatism by social concern; his love of foxhunting by antipathy to both the shooting and eating of birds and beasts.

Only one problem clouds the Prince's horizons. What is he to do with himself for the next twenty years or more? For the Queen is not yet sixty, in robust health and as accomplished a constitutional monarch as any of her line. In the civil service, she would be pensioned off to make way for her designated successor: Buggin's turn, as the practice used to be called. It may be that in time the Queen will wish to be released from her golden treadmill; but there must be no pressure for her to do so. The purpose of monarchy is survival; and the habit of enforced abdication, once acquired, cannot be shed. Such a doctrine may perhaps squander the best years of an heir's life; the alternative is even more hazardous.

The Prince and Princess of Wales with Prince William, 1984

Charlotte

King George V's pet parrot. The King hated to be parted from this most privileged member of his household. 'Glad Charlotte is all right,' he wrote home to his private secretary while cruising in the Mediterranean in 1925, 'and that the housemaid is taking proper care of her.' At Sandringham he would come to breakfast with the bird on his finger, then let her forage over the table. If Charlotte disgraced herself by making a mess, the King would slide a mustard pot over it so that the Queen should not see.

The parrot was in the next room to the King's at his death in 1936, and travelled up to London with the funeral party. She was inherited by Prince Henry, Duke of Gloucester (q.v.).

Charteris, Sir Martin
later 1st Baron Charteris of Amisfield
(1913–   )

Sir Martin Charteris by David Poole, 1979

Private Secratary to the Queen, 1972–7. One of his grandfathers was the 11th Earl of Wemyss, the other the 8th Duke of Rutland; but he does not discourage the legend that Montague Corry, Disraeli's private secretary, is somewhere entangled in his family tree. Educated at Eton and the Royal Military College, Sandhurst, he was commissioned into the King's Royal Rifle Corps and served throughout the war. In 1946 he was head of military intelligence in Palestine, where he won the confidence of Chaim Weizmann, the Zionist leader and later first President of Israel.

Appointed Private Secretary to Princess Elizabeth in 1950, Charteris was with her in Kenya at the moment of her accession to the throne in 1952. For the next twenty years he served as Assistant Private Secretary to the Queen, then as Private Secretary from 1972 until his retirement in 1977. As dedicated to her person as to the concept of monarchy, he brought an imaginative lightness of touch to his work that must have made their daily business sessions the briskest and most exhilarating she has known. Others, too, delight in his company and seek his advice, punctuated as it is by pinches of snuff and quizzical glances over half-moon spectacles.

In 1978 he was created Lord Charteris of Amisfield. He took the title from the house in the Lowlands of Scotland that had once belonged to an eighteenth-century kinsman: Colonel Francis Charteris, who was dismissed from the Army for cheating, thrown out of the Dutch service for theft, convicted of rape (though pardoned), and enriched by gambling and usury. Reviving, if not honouring, the memory of that adventurous forebear is the sort of joke Martin Charteris enjoys.

In the same year that he became a peer, Charteris was installed as Provost of Eton, or resident chairman of the governing body. So eager was the college to secure him that it changed the ancient statute which required the Provost to be a university graduate: a qualification which the Sandhurst-educated Charteris did not possess. As amended by the Privy Council in 1977, the statute declares that the

Provost may be 'similarly qualified in the opinion of the Crown by experience or attainment.' In acquiring Charteris, Eton has gained more than a Provost. There is rarely a role at court for the wives of Private Secretaries, even the most talented of them. But Gay Charteris, daughter of the 1st Viscount Margesson, has now come into her own as a Provost's wife of exceptional grace and warmth.

Charteris's interest in the arts is reflected in his appointments as first chairman of the National Heritage Memorial Fund and as a trustee of the British Museum. He also sits on the board of Claridge's Hotel. His pastime is sculpting. While watching Oscar Nemon at work on a head of the Queen, he picked up a handful of clay and made a likeness of the sculptor, playfully adding a pair of horns. Nemon, impressed by his talent, begged him to do more. Charteris has since produced several portrait busts and some striking studies of dolphins and birds: also a decorative fireback for the Queen Mother's dining-room at the Castle of Mey. In 1981 he was elected an honorary Fellow of the Royal Academy. Entirely at ease in those Bohemian preserves, he turned up at one of its banquets wearing an evening tail coat, stiff shirt, butterfly collar, a constellation of stars and decorations: everything required of him, in fact, except that he had forgotten to put on a white tie.

Clark, Sir Kenneth
later 1st Baron
(1903–1983)

Surveyor of the King's Pictures, 1934–44. Born in Grosvenor Square, London, he spent a lonely and neglected childhood while his parents restlessly dissipated a family fortune founded on Paisley thread. In Monte Carlo, where his father more than once broke the bank, Kenneth's only friend at the age of seven was the Empress Eugénie. Thus began a lifetime of effortless intimacy with the great.

He hated his years at Winchester, a school which at that time equated conformity and cruelty with manliness. His housemaster detested him, perhaps with reason. Coming out of chapel one day, Clark was asked by a friend what he would like to do on leaving Winchester. 'Help Mr Berenson to produce a new edition of his book on the drawings of the Florentine painters,' he replied. The housemaster happened to be walking behind him. 'Bloody little prig,' he said. After an interlude at Trinity College, Oxford (with real pictures on the walls and not a Medici print in sight), there he was at I Tatti, demurely buttering Bernard Berenson's toast and sorting his photographs of old masters. The rapture did not last. Clark later wrote of his patron and mentor 'perched on the pinnacle of a mountain of corruption.'

At twenty-five he produced a remarkable book on the Gothic Revival; at twenty-six he was appointed to catalogue the King's collection

Sir Kenneth Clark

of Leonardo drawings at Windsor; at thirty he was director of the National Gallery. The roll of his subsequent achievements and honours was of monotonous distinction: head of the films division of the wartime Ministry of Information (someone had mistaken one sort of picture for another); chairman of both the Arts Council and the Independent Television Authority; knight, peer, Companion of Honour, member of the Order of Merit; author of a stylish autobiography, flecked with learning and imagination, with wit and malice; the televised exponent and arbiter of civilization itself. Even his misfortunes were exceptional; while lesser men could not sleep for the noise of cars or cats, Clark was awoken at Chartwell by the rise and fall of Winston Churchill's dictation.

In 1934 Clark declined an invitation to become Surveyor of the King's Pictures. George V, a proud and possessive owner, thereupon descended on the National Gallery in person. Having shaken his stick at a Cézanne and declared that Turner was mad, he turned on the reluctant courtier. Clark later described their conversation:

'Why won't you come and work for me?'
'Because I wouldn't have time to do the job properly.'
'What is there to do ?'
'Well, Sir, the pictures need looking after.'
'There's nothing wrong with them.'
'And people write letters asking for information about them.'
'Don't answer 'em. *I want you to take the job.*'

Clark could no longer resist; he was obliged to accept the post of Surveyor of the King's Pictures in addition to the burden of running the National Gallery. All he had feared then came to pass. 'The English,' he wrote, 'are not very fond of art but they are very fond of pedigrees. ... I should have spent my time reading the history of the Hanoverians and working in the National Portrait Gallery. But I was too obstinately committed to aesthetic values to give up my time to the second-rate limners of royalty.' He nevertheless stuck it out for a whole decade, until

relieved of his duties by Anthony Blunt (q.v.).

With King George V, Clark established an easy, even affectionate relationship. Queen Mary, however, he thought stiff and inarticulate; and her son King George VI seemed overwhelmed by the cares of an unsought crown. But in Queen Elizabeth, later the Queen Mother, he found both a friend and a pupil. He helped her to form an attractive if unadventurous collection of modern paintings; and in 1942 persuaded her to commission twenty-six sketches of Windsor from John Piper in case the Castle were bombed. These water-colours of delicately tinted stone and brooding skies were inspected by the King after church one Sunday. He said to the artist: 'You have been unfortunate with the weather, haven't you, Mr Piper.'

Neither fame nor a private income protected Clark from a querulous discontent with his lot. All his life, he confessed, he had suffered from 'an oppressive feeling of nimiety, or too-muchness: too many possessions, too many books, too much to eat and drink.' The last of these ordeals he would spare his guests, who marvelled at the wafer-thin slice of meat to which each was rationed; and his first wife liked to recall that the only present he gave her during their courting was a bag of peppermint bullseyes. Such was his reaction to the dyspeptic luxury of an Edwardian childhood.

An austere manner that could be mistaken for shyness brought him few intimates. He would put a glass screen (to borrow a phrase of Henry Moore) between himself and those he chose not to know. Yet he loved his friends and was capable of imaginative and generous gestures. He gave confidence and encouragement to young artists; and when Cecil Day-Lewis (q.v.) lay dying, Clark brought him a coveted first edition of Coleridge, pretending that he had had to dispose of his library on moving to a smaller house.

Clark's marriage to Jane Martin, which lasted from 1927 until her death in 1976, was marked by fitful happiness but no peace of mind, least of all during the years of her declining health. They had a daughter and two sons, one of whom,

Alan, became a Conservative MP and Minister in Mrs Thatcher's Government. In 1977, Clark married as his second wife Mme Nolwen de Janzé-Rice, the daughter of a French landowner. One half of the year they spent at his country house, Saltwood Castle, in Kent; the other at hers, Parfondeval, in Normandy. He died in May 1983, a few weeks before his eightieth birthday, leaving an estate valued at several million pounds. Some of his works of art he left to national museums; others were sold to meet death duties. One picture alone, Turner's *Seascape: Folkestone*, fetched £6,700,000 in the sale room.

Cobbold, Cameron, 1st Baron
(1904–   )

Lord Chamberlain of the Household, 1963–71. He comes of a family of brewers and bankers established in Suffolk for at least seven centuries. Educated at Eton and King's College, Cambridge, he joined the Bank of England as an adviser in 1933 and rose swiftly to the top. He was an executive director 1938–45, Deputy Governor 1945–9 and Governor 1949–61. Cobbold received a peerage in 1960. Two years after his retirement he agreed to become Lord Chamberlain, a post he described as 'part-time chairman of a large company with a single active shareholder' (see *Airlie, 13th Earl of*).

In 1967 a Joint Committee of both Houses of Parliament proposed the abolition of the Lord Chamberlain's ancient rights of censorship over stage plays. To this Cobbold gave his emphatic agreement, fearing that the exercise of such powers would continue to involve the Sovereign in embarrassing controversy. Four years later his grasp of finance helped to convince a House of Commons Select Committee that the Queen's Civil List should be regularly increased to match inflation.

Tall and handsome, 'Kim' Cobbold performed his ceremonial duties with dignity. At a reception held for the Diplomatic Corps at Buckingham Palace, a newly arrived foreign ambassador inquired of a courtier: 'Who is that godlike creature in the centre? He looks like Zeus.' The courtier replied: 'Why, the Lord Chamberlain, of course.' The ambassador: 'No, no, I was looking at the painted ceiling.'

He married in 1930 Hermione, daughter of the 2nd Earl of Lytton, Governor of Bengal and temporary Viceroy of India. On Lytton's death in 1947 she succeeded to the family house and estates at Knebworth, in Hertfordshire, where the Cobbolds made their home. In 1972 the property was handed over to their eldest son, David Lytton-Cobbold, who opens the house to the public and the park for pop concerts.

Colefax, Sibyl, Lady
(1874–1950)

Friend of King Edward VIII. She was the daughter of James Halsey, of the Indian Civil Service; a niece of Walter Bagehot, author of *The English Constitution*; and a granddaughter of James Wilson, founder of *The Economist*. In keeping with these professional antecedents, Sibyl Halsey was married to Sir Arthur Colefax, a successful patent lawyer. Kenneth Clark described him as 'a heavy man with a very large face who was thought by those who had never visited the provinces to be the biggest bore in London.'

Lady Colefax pursued the eminent in every walk of life with relentless dedication; and once she had lured them to Argyll House, in Chelsea, they were made to sing for their supper. When Edward VIII and Mrs Simpson dined there in June 1936, she persuaded Arthur Rubinstein to play the piano. But the King, disappointed that the *barcarolle* on the programme turned out to be by Chopin rather than by Offenbach, grew restless and soon after midnight remembered that it was bedtime. Lady Colefax at once replaced Rubinstein by Noel Coward, whose rendering of 'Mad Dogs and Englishmen' enticed the King back to the drawing-room. The evening was saved. During the last anxious weeks of the reign she was one of the few guests to be welcomed to the royal retreat of Fort Belvedere.

Having lost some of her money in the Wall Street crash of 1929 and been further impoverished by her husband's death, Sibyl Colefax courageously turned her hands to business. She became a successful interior decorator, at first on her own and later in partnership with John Fowler. After the sale in 1936 of Argyll House – Osbert Sitwell called it Lions' Corner House – she continued to entertain on a smaller scale in Lord North Street, near the Houses of Parliament.

Throughout the war, friends flocked to her suite in the Dorchester Hotel, although each was required to pay a share of the bill for dinner. These evenings were known as Sibyl's 'Ordinaries'. Small and bent, with little buttery eyes like a dolphin, she succeeded in charming every visitor except the shy and taciturn Field Marshal Wavell.

Colville, Lady Cynthia
(1884–1956)

Lady-in-waiting to Queen Mary. She was born Cynthia Crewe-Milnes, third daughter of the 1st and last Marquess of Crewe, the Liberal statesman. Her first experience of State ceremonial was at the age of nine, when her father held court

Lady Cynthia Colville

at Dublin Castle as Lord Lieutenant of Ireland. She spent four years of her youth at the Royal College of Music.

In 1908 she was married to George Colville, who had been called to the Bar but preferred carpentry. He made his own mahogany front door; also a sailing dinghy which he built in an upper room of a London house, then launched into the street below. Their third son was (Sir) John Colville (q.v.), private secretary to the Queen as Princess Elizabeth.

Lady Cynthia was a dedicated social worker and magistrate. In 1923 she received two letters by the same postal delivery. One asked her to become Liberal parliamentary candidate for Shoreditch, the other a woman of the bedchamber, or lady-in-waiting, to Queen Mary. She chose the second, and remained at court for the rest of her life. Her health was not always robust. Sir Bruce Bruce-Porter cured her of a duodenal ulcer with a diet of nearly raw meat mixed with cream, haemoglobin from horses' blood and glasses of hot water. Thereafter his patient was able to stand up to a regime which required her to answer Queen Mary's letters sometimes until one in the morning, occasionally throughout the night.

Her spirit was adventurous. When the King and Queen were away from Sandringham, Lady Cynthia once slipped into the King's room to test how hard his bed was. Jumping up and down on it, she later reported, was like jumping on the floor.

Colville, Sir John
(1915–   )

Private Secretary to Queen Elizabeth II when Princess Elizabeth, 1947–9. The third son of Lady Cynthia Colville (q.v.), he was educated at Harrow and Trinity College, Cambridge, and began his association with the royal household as a Page of Honour to King George V. He joined the Diplomatic Service in 1937 and two years later was transferred to No. 10 Downing Street

as an assistant private secretary to the Prime Minister, Neville Chamberlain. In May 1940, Winston Churchill took him over, as he put it, 'with the other livestock.'

Still in his twenties, Colville begged to be released after eighteen months to become a pilot. Churchill approved his intention. 'The RAF,' he said, 'is the cavalry of modern war.' But he was dismayed to hear that Colville would be enlisting in the ranks before sailing for South Africa to begin his training. 'You mustn't,' the Prime Minister warned him, 'you won't be able to take your man.' Colville nevertheless survived the next two years without a valet. In 1944 he was recalled to No. 10, where he served Churchill and his successor Attlee, then rejoined the Foreign Office.

In 1947 Colville agreed to become Princess Elizabeth's first official Private Secretary on the understanding that he would return to diplomacy after two years. For the circumstances of his appointment, see under *Elizabeth II, Queen.* He married in 1948 the Princess's lady-in-waiting, Lady Margaret Egerton, a daughter of the 4th Earl of Ellesmere. In the following year he resumed his career in the Foreign Service and was posted to Lisbon as First Secretary in the British Embassy. Then came the general election of October 1951 and Churchill's return to Downing Street. The new Prime Minister took one look at Attlee's private office, declared it (quite wrongly) to be 'drenched in Socialism', and retrieved Colville from Portugal to be principal private secretary throughout the whole of his second administration.

On Churchill's retirement in 1955, Colville divided his time between merchant banking and literature; his books include a biography of Field Marshal Lord Gort, Commander-in-Chief of the British Expeditionary Force in 1940. He also became one of the founding fathers of Churchill College, Cambridge, an achievement that in 1974 brought him a knighthood.

His strongest claim to fame may well lie in the copious diaries which he kept during his years of service under the Crown. Already he has generously put them at the disposal of Churchill's biographer, Martin Gilbert, and embodied extracts from them in his own published essays. They whet the appetite for the fuller edition now in preparation. Some of his anecdotes are droll, as when he asks the Prime Minister which he dislikes more, the Foreign Office or the Treasury. Churchill replies: 'The War Office.' Others are chilling. Churchill's doctor, Lord Moran, says of penicillin: 'It will make lust safe for democracy.' And Air Marshal Harris, asked at Chequers about the recent raid by RAF Bomber Command on Dresden, answers: 'There is no such place as Dresden.'

Colville is reputed to have Boswellized the Queen, too, during his years as her Private Secretary. Those intimacies, however, like the Palace diaries of Sir Alan Lascelles (q.v.), are unlikely to be unveiled for several decades.

Colville, Sir Richard
(1907–1975)

Press Secretary to King George VI and Queen Elizabeth II, 1947–68. The son of Admiral Sir Stanley Colville and cousin of Sir John Colville (q.v.), he was educated at Harrow, joined the Royal Navy as a paymaster and in 1943 was awarded the Distinguished Service Cross for gallantry. In 1947 he became Press Secretary at Buckingham Palace in succession to another sailor: Captain Lewis Ritchie, who under the pseudonym 'Bartimeus' wrote breezy tales of the sea.

There was nothing breezy about Colville, at least in the performance of his duties. Press inquiries were met at best with guarded courtesy, sometimes with impatient disdain, never with good humour. Colville was prepared to answer simple questions about the Queen's public engagements, but not to trespass on what he conceived to be her private life. He believed, as he wrote to the Press Council, that 'the Queen is entitled to expect that her family will attain the privacy at home which all other families are entitled to enjoy.' To this the Press Council

replied that although it shared his regret at occasional instances of journalistic bad taste, 'the private lives of public men and women, especially royal persons, have always been the subject of a natural curiosity. That is one of the consequences of fame or eminence or sincere national affection. Everything therefore that touches the Crown is of public interest and concern.'

It was particularly unfortunate that Colville's costive reserve coincided with a widespread quickening of interest in the monarchy: the marriage of Princess Elizabeth in 1947, the birth of her children, the accession and Coronation of a young and pretty Sovereign. Lacking previous knowledge of the Press, he seemed to make no distinction between journalists in search of scandal or sensation and those – the majority – who needed little encouragement to stimulate and strengthen loyalty to the Crown. All were made to feel that their questions were impertinent if not downright vulgar. A Canadian journalist who innocently asked Colville whether he could see round Buckingham Palace was told: 'I am not what you North Americans would call a public relations officer.'

Nor did Colville believe it to be his duty to notice or correct rumours about the royal family. Throughout the worldwide Press comment on Princess Margaret's romance with Group Captain Peter Townsend (q.v.) he had no comments to offer, no guidance for the reporter or even for the Group Captain himself, Townsend later wrote in his autobiography, *Time and Chance*: 'Since I was so closely bound up with Princess Margaret's future, it might have been better if Richard Colville, instead of leaving me to cope alone, had co-operated with me. But not once, during the whole affair, right up to the bitter end, did he contact me or attempt to evolve a joint front with me towards the Press.' In October 1955, two weeks before Princess Margaret declared that she would not marry Group Captain Townsend, Commander Colville varied his liturgy of 'no comment'. He issued a rare communiqué: 'No announcement concerning Princess Margaret's personal future is at present contemplated. The Princess has asked the Press Secretary to express the hope that the press and public will extend to Her Royal Highness their customary courtesy and co-operation in respecting her privacy.' That teasing phrase *at present* served only to drive the world's Press to a frenzy of speculation.

The exasperated comments on Colville's regime which appeared in the newspapers, particularly during the early years of the present reign, can scarcely have escaped the Queen's notice. She must therefore have approved of her Press Secretary's dedication to the Silent Service throughout his landlocked years in Buckingham Palace.

Connaught and Strathearn, Prince Arthur, Duke of
(1850–1942)

Queen Victoria's third son, was born at Buckingham Palace on 1 May 1850, the eighty-first birthday of his godfather, the great Duke of Wellington, and died in the year of El Alamein. More submissive to discipline than his elder brother, the future King Edward VII, he acquired an early and lifelong passion for soldiering. After two years at the Royal Military Academy, Woolwich, he was commissioned into the Royal Engineers. He later transferred to the Rifle Brigade, with whom he saw service in Canada.

Throughout his military career, the Duke of Connaught and Strathearn (as he was created in 1874) neither sought nor received special privileges, much less accelerated promotion. As a young staff officer he occupied a room so small that he could lie in bed and simultaneously open the window and poke the fire. The Duke commanded the 1st Guards Brigade during the Egyptian campaign of 1882, displaying what the Commander-in-Chief described as 'cool courage under extremely heavy fire.' Four years later he was entrusted with the important command at Bombay. Successive Governments, however, refused to sanction his promotion to

The Duke and Duchess of Connaught, 1890

be Commander-in-Chief either in India or, on the retirement of the old Duke of Cambridge, at home. Queen Victoria wrote:

'She cannot and will not submit to the *shameful principle* that Princes are to suffer for *their birth* in a monarchical country. Have a Republic at once, if that is the principle. She must *have an assurance* that such is *not* the case. Arthur was recommended *solely* on account of his peculiar *fitness*.

'It is very abominable that the Government, and a so-called Conservative one too, should wish to pander to the Radicals! Questions may and will be asked whatever is done; but the simple answer is that the Duke has gone through *every grade* from the lowest with honour and distinction, served in Canada, at Gibraltar, in the field in Egypt, and in India for five years where he earned golden opinions.'

The Duke was consoled with lesser commands in Aldershot, Ireland and Malta, and in 1902 was promoted to the rank of field marshal. Three years earlier he had renounced his right of succession to the Duchy of Saxe-Coburg-Gotha held by his elder brother, Prince Alfred, Duke of Edinburgh.

In 1911 the Duke of Connaught was appointed Governor-General of Canada. His five years in Ottawa were marred only by a bitter quarrel with Sam Hughes, the Canadian Minister of Militia and Defence. Hughes wrongly believed that the Duchess, who was born a Princess of Prussia and never lost her German accent, exerted an unpatriotic influence on Government House; and he refused to allow her husband to review Canadian troops. The Duke was further humiliated when the British Government, for political reasons and against the wishes of both the Duke and of King George v, bestowed on Hughes both a knighthood and the honorary rank of lieutenant-general.

Although the Duke retired from public life in 1928, he continued to interest himself in freemasonry (he was Grand Master from 1901 to 1938) and in all things military. His sunset years were passed in Clarence House, London; Bagshot Park, Surrey (today the headquarters of the Royal Army Chaplains Department); and a villa in the south of France.

It is surprising that a man trained in the profession of arms should have proved so untrustworthy with a sporting gun. At one pheasant shoot, when aiming at a low-flying bird, he put out an eye of his brother-in-law, Prince Christian of Schleswig-Holstein (q.v.); and some years later, as he blazed away at Windsor, the feathered hat of a royal spectator, the Queen of Italy, was seen to tremble unduly in the wind. But the Duke's eye was sharp enough to spot the most minute lapses in the wearing of uniform and decorations. 'My dear fellow, you are a Grenadier, are you not?' he once asked an officer. 'Sir,' the unsuspecting victim replied. 'Then why the devil,' the Colonel of the Grenadier Guards continued, 'are you wearing Coldstream spurs?'

'He is such a gentleman, so courteous and kind,' one of Queen Victoria's ladies-in-waiting wrote of the Duke. It was an opinion that won almost universal acceptance. Even Beatrice Webb, who thought the curtsey a demeaning compliment, laid aside her radical principles in his presence. 'As he hobbled up to me,' she wrote of a ceremonial occasion, 'I had not the heart to disappoint him.' The old Aga Khan dated the decline of British manners in India from 1890, when the Connaughts returned to England: The whole tone of relationships stiffened ... less and less did Europeans invite Indians to their houses, and soon it became rare for the races to meet around a luncheon or dinner table.'

The Duke of Connaught outlived not only his wife, who died in 1917, but also two of his three children: his only son, Prince Arthur of Connaught, and his elder daughter, Margaret, Crown Princess of Sweden. He was consoled by the love both of his younger daughter, Lady Patricia Ramsay (q.v.) and of Leonie Lady Leslie, who even during the Duchess's lifetime had been accepted as an indispensable though discreet partner in a *ménage à trois*. At his death in 1942, the Duke was succeeded by his grandson, the Earl of Macduff, on whose early death in the following year the dukedom became extinct.

Connaught, Prince Arthur of
(1883–1938)

Only son of the Duke of Connaught (q.v.). Born at Windsor, he was educated at Eton and the Royal Military College, Sandhurst. In 1901 he joined the 7th Hussars and served in South Africa. During King George v's tour of India in 1911–12, Prince Arthur was appointed a Counsellor of State. 'He was very pleasant,' the Clerk of the Privy Council noted, 'and most ready to sacrifice his convenience in order to be regular in attendance.' That was characteristic of the man: punctual, courteous and undemanding. During the Great War successive Commanders-in-Chief used him to look after distinguished

Prince Arthur of Connaught

visitors. He also undertook ceremonial missions abroad on behalf of the Sovereign.

In 1899 the Duke of Connaught had renounced both for himself and for his son the succession to the Duchy of Saxe-Coburg-Gotha, then held by another of Queen Victoria's sons, the Duke of Edinburgh. Prince Arthur thus missed the opportunity of becoming a minor constitutional monarch. From 1920 to 1923, however, he played a similar role as Governor-General of South Africa. He reverted on his return to the lesser office of chairman of Middlesex Hospital, helping to raise a building fund of £2 million. Prince Arthur received almost every honour in the King's gift except a peerage. Nor did he live to succeed to his father's dukedom.

The Prince married in 1913 Princess Alexandra (q.v.), elder daughter of the 1st Duke of Fife and his wife Princess Louise, the Princess Royal (qq.v.). They had one son, Alastair, born in 1914, who as heir to the dukedom of Fife, which his mother had inherited in 1912, bore the courtesy title of Earl of Macduff. He succeeded his paternal grandfather as the 2nd Duke of Connaught in 1942 and died in the following year.

Cooper, Lady Diana
(1892–   )

Friend of the royal family. Born Lady Diana Manners, third daughter of the 8th Duke of Rutland, she has been known to exclaim, 'Papa!' on seeing a photograph of Harry Cust, that writer of fitful brilliance and irresistible seductive powers. Her perennial beauty and wit have brought her the devotion of generation after generation of besotted admirers: Asquith and Beaverbrook, Chaliapin and Otto Kahn, Ernest Simpson and Ernest Bevin, together with a whole host of those gilded young men who died in the Great War.

In 1917 the Duke of Connaught (q.v.) declared that she was 'the only possible wife that could keep the Prince of Wales on the throne.' Two years later, however, Lady Diana chose to marry Duff Cooper, a clever but penurious clerk in the Foreign Office who as a young officer in the Grenadier Guards had won the Distinguished Service Order for exceptional gallantry. Both parents of the bridegroom had royal connections. His mother, a sister of the 1st Duke of Fife (q.v.), after two elopements and a divorce, had been ostracized by Edwardian society; his father, Sir Alfred Cooper, vice-president of the Royal College of Surgeons and a specialist in embarrassing ailments, was surgeon-in-ordinary to the Duke of Edinburgh and Coburg, a younger brother of King Edward VII; Cooper was once suspected of inadvertently poisoning his patient but claimed that a careless dispensing chemist was to blame.

Lady Diana loved her husband and he loved her. But both had passion to spare, and there have been more eternal triangles in their joint lives than in the whole of Euclid. The one child of the marriage is John Julius Cooper, Viscount Norwich, who has devoted much of his life to the history and preservation of Venice. Having overcome her family's prejudice against Duff Cooper, Lady Diana freed him from his financial shackles by taking to the stage. Curiosity drew King George v and Queen Mary to *The Miracle*, in which the Duke of Rutland's daughter achieved a *tour de force* in a silent role. But her laurels wilted when the King summoned her to the royal box and said: 'Of course, you've got no words to learn or say, and that's half the battle.'

Her earnings as an actress enabled Duff Cooper to resign from the Foreign Office and pursue an eighteenth-century career as politician, man of letters and rake. Having reached the Cabinet, he courageously resigned in 1938 as a protest against Neville Chamberlain's pact with Hitler at Munich. He was recalled to office by Winston Churchill two years later and retired in 1947 as British Ambassador in Paris. He died in 1954, having been created Viscount Norwich. His wife spelt it Norrich, believing that accuracy in such matters, like the new peerage itself, was slightly common; she asked to be known by her former style of Lady Diana Cooper.

It was not until Mrs Simpson entered the life of the Prince of Wales that the Coopers were

Lady Diana Cooper

drawn into his intimate circle and invited to the royal retreat of Fort Belvedere, near Windsor. Here is part of a letter written by Lady Diana about that outpost of Manhattan: 'I am in a pink bedroom, pink-sheeted, pink Venetian-blinded, pink-soaped, white-telephoned and pink-and-white maided. The food at dinner staggers and gluts. *Par contre* there is little or nothing for lunch, and that foraged for by oneself American-style. . . . The comfort could not be greater, nor the desire on his part for his guests to be happy, free and unembarrassed. Surely a new atmosphere for Courts?' But she found the servants 'a bit hobbledehoy because H.M. wants to be free of comptrollers and secretaries and equerries, so no one trains them.'

In the summer of 1936, King Edward VIII invited Duff and Diana Cooper to join him and Mrs Simpson for a cruise in the yacht *Nahlin* along the Dalmatian coast. Their host, she noted, wore 'spick-and-span little shorts, straw sandals and two crucifixes on a chain round his neck.' The Defender of the Faith was not alone in displaying the cross; Mrs Simpson wore two identical pieces on her wrist. As so often on cruises, there were bouts of ill temper and frayed nerves. Lady Diana resented the King's constant apologies for the boat, the food, the company and most of all himself. 'How he spoils everyone's fun,' she wrote. It also annoyed her when fellow passengers referred to Delphi as Delhi. The cruise confirmed her suspicion that Mrs Simpson would never do as Queen of England. After the Abdication, Lady Diana saw the Windsors from time to time; and as the wife of the British Ambassador in Paris disobeyed a Foreign Office edict that she should not curtsey to the Duchess. But there was no real friendship between them. At one post-war meeting she found the Duchess of Windsor 'slim and svelte as a piece of vermicelli'; as for the Duke, 'common, of course, and boring, but not so puppetish as I thought.'

The Coopers had never been intimate with the new King and Queen as Duke and Duchess of York, and in the months following the Abdication wondered whether they had literally put themselves out of court. In April 1937, however, they were summoned to dine and sleep at Windsor: though only because Duff was Secretary of State for War. His wife sat on the right of the King, who asked her: 'When did *you* know about it?' From then on, she wrote, it was jabber, jabber, jabber, and Lady Desborough (q.v.), on the King's left, got no conversation at all. Duff Cooper, too, basked in royal favour. Collared by the Queen after dinner for tea and talk, he was not released until 12.30 a.m. His wife welcomed the new regime. 'Fort Belvedere was an operetta,' she said. 'This is an institution.'

Well into her tenth decade, Lady Diana continues to enjoy a widowhood not so much merry as frenetic. Though bones grow frail, they are strong enough to carry her to dinner party, concert or opera; and though those bluest of eyes grow dim, they were alert enough one night to see that the friendly but faceless woman who had engaged her in conversation was wearing remarkable diamonds: so remarkable in fact that they could belong to only one person. Lady Diana, born in the reign of Queen Victoria, dipped in homage to her great-great-granddaughter.

Coward, Sir Noel
(1899–1973)

Playwright, actor and friend of the royal family. Born in the London suburb of Teddington, he was the son of Arthur Coward, who worked for a firm of music publishers. With little formal education, Noel took to the boards at the age of ten and played many juvenile roles. He served in the Artists Rifles at the end of the Great War and on demobilization joined Arthur Bourchier's company. Success as a playwright came in 1925 with a melodramatic piece, *The Vortex*. It was followed by *Hay Fever*, the first of his brilliant, mannered, heartless comedies. However much he relished the social adulation that engulfed him, Coward remained a dedicated and industrious professional, whether as writer, actor,

In Which We Serve: Noel Coward as Lord Mountbatten

composer, singer, dancer or director of plays and films.

In 1931 he received unexpected recognition from George V when the King celebrated the election victory of the National Government by taking his family to *Cavalcade*, a chronicle of upper-middle-class life from the death of Queen Victoria to the turbulence of the 1930s. Its sentimental patriotism exactly caught the mood of the hour and the audience spontaneously rose to sing the National Anthem.

A decade later, Coward repeated his triumph with the film *In Which We Serve*, a wartime tribute to the Royal Navy inspired by the exploits and character of his friend Lord Louis Mountbatten (q.v.) when in command of HMS *Kelly*. Coward wrote the script, directed the film and played the leading role. King George VI, who brought his wife and daughters to see some of the scenes being shot, later suggested that Coward should be rewarded with a knighthood; but his kindly wish was thwarted, perhaps by whispers of an unorthodox though discreet private life, or by Coward's technical infringement of the currency regulations during a visit to the United States. It was nearly thirty years before such official prejudice faded.

Coward's romantic devotion to the royal family was lifelong, but neither unselective nor always reciprocated. In youth he believed that he had made a firm friend of the Prince of Wales, later Duke of Windsor. He was disillusioned when, after a long evening at the piano helping the Prince to learn the ukulele, his pupil cut him dead in Asprey's the following day. It led Coward to suggest at the time of the Abdication that statues of Mrs Simpson should be erected throughout England for the blessing she had bestowed on the country.

Coward occasionally dined with the Windsors in France after the war; one night he even danced the Charleston and a sailor's hornpipe with the Duke. But when recording that bizarre entertainment in his diary, Coward noted 'a little sadness and nostalgia for him and for me a curious feeling of detached amusement, remembering how beastly he had been to me in our early years when he was Prince of Wales and I was just beginning.'

Feelings of a different sort were outraged when he watched an amateur performance of Edgar Wallace's *The Frog* put on in 1954 for charity by Princess Margaret and her friends. 'The whole evening,' he wrote, 'was one of the most fascinating exhibitions of incompetence, conceit and bloody impertinence that I have ever seen in my life. With the exception of young Porchester, who at least tried to sustain a character, the entire cast displayed no talent whatsoever.... Those high-born characters we watched mumbling and stumbling about the stage are the ones who come to our productions and criticise us! They at least betrayed no sign of nervousness; they were unequivocally delighted with themselves from the first scene to the last which, I may add, was a very long time indeed. In the dressing-room afterwards, where we went civilly to congratulate Porchy, we found Princess Margaret eating *foie gras* sandwiches, sipping champagne and complaining that the audience laughed in the wrong places.' When this severe passage from Coward's diary was published after his death, Princess Margaret said: 'I don't like *foie gras*.'

There were few royal houses which did not welcome Noel Coward with genuine warmth. He was always prepared, quite literally, to sing for his supper; and his quicksilver conversation was neither overbearing nor obtrusive. A fellow guest once quoted a Latin tag, adding pretentiously, 'Tacitus, you know.' Noel replied: 'I haven't read Tacitus since last Monday.' In pre-war days he won the friendship of the Duke and Duchess of Kent and in later years of Queen Elizabeth the Queen Mother (with whom at Sandringham he once sang as a duet 'My Old Man Said Follow the Van').

The apotheosis of Coward's intimacy with the royal family is described in his diary for December 1969: 'My birthday lunch was given by the darling Queen Mother at Clarence House, where I received a crown-encrusted cigarette-box from her, an equally crown-encrusted cigarette-case from the Queen herself, and some exquisite cuff-links from Princess Margaret and Tony. During lunch the Queen asked me whether I would accept Mr Wilson's offer of a knighthood. I kissed her hand and said, in a rather strangulated voice, "Yes, Ma'am".

Apart from all this, my seventieth birthday was uneventful.'

Sir Noel Coward died three years later of a heart ailment. This, his doctors had long told him, was aggravated by excessive smoking.

Crawford, Marion
later Mrs George Buthlay
(1909–   )

Governess to Princess Elizabeth and Princess Margaret Rose. Born in Kilmarnock, Ayrshire, she studied at Moray House Training College, Edinburgh, and was engaged to teach history to the children of the 10th Earl of Elgin at Broomhall, their house on the Firth of Forth. From there she would daily walk down to the naval base at Rosyth to give lessons to the small daughter of the admiral commanding the coast of Scotland whose wife, Lady Rose Leveson Gower, was a sister of the Duchess of York. One day, Miss Crawford later wrote, 'as I crossed the lawn there came over me an eerie feeling that someone was watching me. It made me look up towards the house. Then it was I saw there was a face at the window, and for the first time I met that long cool stare I was later to come to know so well.' It was the future Queen Elizabeth II, aged six.

The Duke and Duchess of York at once took to this tall, forthright Scots girl, not much older than twenty; and in spite of misgivings about her youth and lack of experience, engaged her as nursery governess to their two daughters. She too, ambitious to train as a child psychologist, had doubts about her task, but agreed to a trial period. She remained for seventeen years, until both her charges were grown up. One early sacrifice she felt obliged to make was her favourite colour of misty blue. She was not alone in her choice. There came a day when she, the Duchess and the two Princesses all appeared in the same shade. 'After that,' she wrote, 'I tactfully adopted brown.'

At Broomhall, the Bruce children had called

her Cuppie, because of the tea that heralded her arrival and departure. The little Yorks preferred Crawfie, and the name stuck. Sometimes feeling out of her depth when promoted from nursery to schoolroom, she gave the Princesses an adequate but undemanding education, with outside help for such subjects as French and constitutional history. Her life was sheltered and placid, relieved by traditional skirmishes with the children's nanny. Once, too, Crawfie was exposed to the wind of current events. A few days before the Abdication of King Edward VIII, she was standing on the steps of the Duke of York's house in Piccadilly, waiting for a taxi. A crowd gathered. Someone shouted, 'Mrs Simpson,' and someone else booed. Crawfie hurried indoors again.

Then came the move to Buckingham Palace, where only the annual garden parties failed to please: 'I had a far better time sitting in the window of my room with a tea tray and a pair of field glasses.' Windsor Castle, where she spent the war with her charges, was gloomy and isolated, with a routine that left her scarcely any life of her own. More than once she tried to return to Scotland and a fuller career, but agreed to remain in royal service until neither Princess had futher need of her instruction.

In September 1947, two months before Princess Elizabeth's wedding, Crawfie was herself married in Dunfermline Abbey. The bridegroom was Major George Buthlay, who worked in Drummond's Bank. Princess Elizabeth gave them a coffee set; Princess Margaret, three bedside lamps. From Queen Mary, who over the years had made many tactful suggestions about the children's education, came a complete dinner service. On Crawfie's retirement, the King provided the married couple with Nottingham Cottage, a grace-and-favour residence in Kensington Palace. Once more Queen Mary showed her appreciation by filling it with Victorian furniture and flower prints. Crawfie also received a pension and was appointed a Commander of the Royal Victorian Order.

Perhaps she thought these rewards inadequate; it is said that she would also have liked to become a Dame in the Order, as well as a lady-in-waiting to one or other of her former charges. What remains beyond dispute is that the publication in 1950 of a book entitled *The Little Princesses* shattered the confidence which the King and Queen and their daughters had placed in her. It was partly the content of her revelations that gave offence: scarcely a mention of the affectionate interest shown by the King and Queen in the upbringing of their daughters, and a distorted contrast between the regal virtues of Princess Elizabeth and the caprice of her younger sister. Far more wounding, however, was the breach of trust by one who had been taken into the family circle: a sense of outrage that their privacy had been purloined and sold for gain. There were nevertheless many loyal subjects who, while deploring the betrayal, found much to entertain and enlighten in Marion Crawford's simple prose.

In the wake of *The Little Princesses* appeared more of her recollections and a vapid but well-remunerated commentary on the life and work of the new Queen. Then came retribution. In the issue of *Woman's Own* for 16 June 1955, she assured her readers that 'the bearing and dignity of the Queen at the Trooping of the Colour ceremony at the Horse Guards' Parade last week caused admiration among the spectators.' As for Royal Ascot, she continued, 'it had an enthusiasm about it never seen there before.' Both statements were untrue. The magazine had gone to press before the events she purported to describe; owing to a rail-strike one had been cancelled and the other postponed. Her life of letters was at an end. But she lives on in a phrase that will one day enrich the English dictionary: 'To do a Crawfie.'

Cunard, Lady
(1872–1948)

Friend of King Edward VIII. Maud Burke, as she was known in her native California, later preferred to be called Emerald. In New York she married Sir Bache Cunard, grandson of the founder of the shipping line, who was twenty years her senior. His death in 1925 completed her release from a life of oppressive boredom in a Leicestershire country house. Thereafter she spread her wings in London to dazzling effect.

Most descriptions of Lady Cunard compare her to a bird. With yellow fluffy hair, a sharp little beak of a nose and a chirruping voice, she was said to resemble a canary of prey. To Harold Nicolson, however, she looked like 'a third-dynasty mummy painted pink by amateurs.' Her conversation flitted from theme to theme, displaying every device of wit and allusion, of parody and paradox. Kenneth Clark called it a diet of *hors d'oeuvres*. Well read and a patron of the opera, she was wooed in vain by George Moore and in turn loved Sir Thomas Beecham for thirty-four years until he deserted her.

Lady Cunard was the friend of the Prince of Wales whom as Edward VIII she hoped to see become the Roi Soleil of an English Versailles. He included her, together with Mr and Mrs Ernest Simpson, in the first official dinner he gave as King; and when the Channons entertained their Sovereign to dinner in Belgrave Square, they placed her on the King's left.

Emerald Cunard

After the Abdication, her enemies claimed, she tried to ingratiate herself with the new King by denying her friendship with the old. 'Maggie, darling,' she was said to have asked Mrs Greville (q.v.), 'do tell me about this Mrs Simpson. I have only just met her.' The story was an unworthy fabrication. Emerald Cunard was not a woman to seek royal favour by changing her tune. At a dinner party early in the reign of George VI, she startled Prince Friedrich of Prussia with the inquiry: 'Monseigneur, which do you think the most unfashionable, the Connaughts or the Gloucesters?'

During the war she was obliged to give up her house in Grosvenor Square and take rooms in the Dorchester Hotel. There she continued to maintain a salon on a smaller scale. Her wit remained uncomfortably mordant. At a wedding reception in 1946, 'Chips' Channon gazed at the rich, well-dressed assembly and observed with satisfaction: 'This is what we have been fighting for.' 'What,' Emerald replied, 'are they all Poles?'

Cust, Captain Sir Charles, 3rd Baronet, *Royal Navy* *(1864–1931)*

Friend and equerry of King George V. The close links between Cust and his future Sovereign went back to the days when both were young naval officers in the Mediterranean. Prince George wrote from HMS *Alexandra* in 1888: 'That brute Charles Cust is sitting on the deck of my cabin behind me, because I have not got another chair, abusing me and my cabin.' It was a habit which Cust retained even after the Prince, by then Duke of York, appointed him to be his equerry in 1892. He remained an outspoken but devoted friend until his death.

He once told the King at Balmoral: 'You haven't in the whole of this house got a book that's worth reading. Your so-called library is nothing but beautifully bound piffle.' The King gave orders for the presentation volumes to be

Sir Charles Cust (*right*) with Major Fetherstonhaugh and Prince Henry at the Epsom Derby, 1927

replaced by a library of sound Scottish books. At Sandringham, Cust alone was bold enough to complain when the King's parrot, Charlotte (q.v.), roaming at will over the breakfast table, dug her beak into the equerry's boiled egg.

Like all court favourites, Cust was determined that no outsider should usurp his privileged intimacy. When at a shooting party Lady Fingall addressed the King with familiarity, Cust led her aside. 'I have grown up on the steps of the throne,' he told her, 'and I can tell you that there are three kinds of people in the world: blacks, whites and royalties.' That aphorism does less than justice to Cust's master. Of all monarchs, George was most free from prejudices of race and colour.

Dalton, Canon John *(1839–1931)*

Tutor to King George V. The son of the vicar of Milton Keynes, he took First Class Honours in Theology at Cambridge, followed by Holy Orders. As curate at Whippingham, near Osborne, he attracted the notice of his parishioner,

Queen Victoria, who in 1871 approved his becoming tutor to her grandsons, the future King George V and his elder brother Prince Albert Victor, Duke of Clarence. Dalton was a firm disciplinarian with a booming voice which he bequeathed to his son Hugh, Chancellor of the Exchequer in the Labour Government of 1945. But he had his lighter moments, allowing the young princes to shoot at him with bows and arrows as if he were a running deer.

He accompanied them when they joined the training ship *Britannia* as naval cadets and during their cruise round the world in HMS *Bacchante*. Dalton was well rewarded. He became a Companion of the Order of St Michael and St George, a chaplain to Queen Victoria and a Canon of St George's Chapel, Windsor. He also married the sister of a shipmate, Catharine Evan-Thomas. An account of the voyage of the *Bacchante* in two thick volumes was published in 1886 and dedicated to the Queen. Although purporting to have been written by the young princes under Dalton's editorial direction, the work was a pious deception. Almost every one of its 750,000 words came from the tutor's pen. It was not his only service. When Prince George went to sea on his own, Dalton kept him supplied with cigarettes. Having thus aquired the habit, his pupil carried it to the grave.

King George V, as he became in 1910, maintained a lifelong affection for Dalton. He took him to India as his chaplain, invited him each summer to Balmoral, entrusted to him the religious education of his own children. He also used to enjoy Dalton's rumbustious reading of the lessons from the Old Testament, in which the Almighty was endowed with a thundering bass, Isaiah with a piping falsetto. But when the King tried to have him appointed Dean of Westminster and later Dean of Windsor, not even royal influence could overcome the unanimous hostility of his fellow clergy. Overbearing and cantankerous, Canon Dalton was a perpetual irritant in the otherwise tranquil life of the Windsor cloisters. On the appointment of a new Dean in 1917, the King's Private Secretary warned the unfortunate man: 'It is not too much

to say that Dalton has made your predecessor an unhappy man for a quarter of a century.' The new incumbent had to endure similar torment for only fourteen years: until Dalton's death in 1931 at the age of ninety-one. Even at his funeral, none could be sure how he would behave; he had threatened to jump out of his coffin and 'spoil the whole show.'

Dawson of Penn, Bertrand, 1st Viscount
(1864–1945)

Physician to four Sovereigns. The son of an architect, he was born at Croydon, Surrey, and educated at St Paul's School, University College, London, and the London Hospital. He qualified as a doctor in 1890 and became a Fellow of the Royal College of Physicians in 1903. Four years later he was appointed to the medical household of Edward VII. He subsequently included George V, Edward VIII and George VI among his patients. He was made KCVO in 1911, the first of many honours that came to him.

During the Great War he became consulting physician to the British Armies in France with the rank of major-general, and attended George V after the King had been thrown from his horse and seriously injured at Hesdigneul in 1915. In 1919 the Prime Minister, Lloyd George, another of Dawson's patients, recommended him for a peerage. The King hesitated. He thought that more senior doctors might feel aggrieved at being passed over; and that if war service were to count, surgeons had a stronger claim. Lloyd George persisted, and in 1920 the King approved a barony for Sir Bertrand Dawson; not so much a reward for past achievement as a recognition of the need for an authority on public health in the Upper House.

Lord Dawson of Penn, as he was gazetted, swiftly came to be regarded as the leading medical statesman of his day. From 1931 to 1938 he was President of the Royal College of Physicians. Sparely built but elegant, with dark hair, a neat moustache and eyes of penetrating

Lord Dawson of Penn, 1944

warmth, Dawson inspired infinite trust among his patients. Except for an habitual disdain of punctuality, he was thorough and methodical. That single failing he would explain away: 'I do one thing at a time.'

In 1928–9, Dawson attracted worldwide notice as the senior of the eleven physicians and surgeons who saved the life of George v. The King, laid low by a streptococcal infection of the chest, developed a septicaemia of the blood that affected his heart. It was characteristic of Dawson's foresight that he was able to assemble within a few hours a team of specialists trained for just such an emergency. Aware, for instance, that a pathologist might one day be required, he had already asked young Lionel Whitby (q.v.) to carry out a complete set of tests on himself, including such unpleasant procedures as drawing blood from the veins; Dawson had thus been able to judge whether Whitby possessed both the technique and the temperament to handle an eminent and sometimes irritable patient.

It was Dawson who, as the King lay comatose, halted the decline by plunging a

syringe into his chest and drawing off sixteen ounces of vicious matter. Later that evening, Sir Hugh Rigby (q.v.) operated to drain a concealed abscess and set the patient on the slow road to recovery.

The long, uneven course of both illness and convalescence exposed Dawson to disparagement and professional jealousy. The story went the rounds that for six weeks he had treated a man for jaundice before realizing that the patient was Chinese. Margot Asquith, in one of her more outrageous flights of fancy, used to say in old age: 'The King told me he would never have died if it had not been for that fool Dawson of Penn.' And the surgeon Lord Moynihan, after an angry exchange with Dawson about the treatment of a royal prince, taunted him to his face with the jingle:

> Lord Dawson of Penn
> Has killed lots of men.
> So that's why we sing
> God save the King.

Dawson shrugged off such malice. He was made a Privy Counsellor in 1929 and a viscount seven years later. By his marriage to a daughter of Sir Alfred Yarrow, the shipbuilder, he had three daughters but no son, and his peerages died with him.

Perhaps the most memorable of Dawson's contributions to history was in January 1936, as George v lay dying at Sandringham. He picked up a menu card and wrote on it in pencil a farewell of classic simplicity: 'The King's life is moving peacefully towards its close.'

Day-Lewis, Cecil
(1904–1972)

Poet Laureate 1968–72. Born at Ballintubbert, Ireland, the son of a Protestant parson, he moved to Worcestershire with his parents when eighteen months old. He made much of his Irish background and could drop easily into a convincing brogue. From Sherborne

Cecil Day-Lewis with his wife, Jill Balcon, receiving congratulations on being made Poet Laureate, 1968

School he went up to Wadham College, Oxford. Having found a First Class in Classics and Philosophy beyond him, he strove to achieve that greater rarity, a Fourth; his examiners thwarted his ambitions by awarding him a prosaic Third. From 1927 to 1935 he taught at a succession of schools. His pupils at Summer Fields, Oxford, included Benedict Nicolson (q.v.), who was conscious that he knew more French than his mentor.

Meanwhile Day-Lewis was writing poetry and is sometimes mentioned as an associate of W.H.Auden, Stephen Spender and Louis MacNeice. But his work was too conformist, too bland, to earn the esteem of pre-war critics; the briefness of his flirtation with Communism was also held against him. He was acclaimed more as a writer of detective stories under the pseudonym Nicholas Blake and a translator of Virgil. During the war he served in the Ministry of Information and afterwards became a publisher's reader, Professor of Poetry at Oxford and chairman of the Arts Council Literature

Panel. A handsome man with a melodious tenor voice, he was twice married: to Mary King in 1928 and to the actress Jill Balcon in 1951. Between these two events he enjoyed a long and affectionate relationship with the novelist Rosamond Lehmann.

In 1968 Day-Lewis was appointed to succeed John Masefield (q.v.) as Poet Laureate. He celebrated the Investiture of the Prince of Wales with some verses that began:

> Today bells ring, bands play, flags are unfurled,
>   Anxieties and feuds lie buried
> Under a ceremonial joy. You, sir, inherit
>   A weight of history in a changing world,
> Its treasured wisdom and its true
>   Aspirings the best birthday gift for you.

Unlike Masefield, whose odes were always published in *The Times*, Day-Lewis patronized the *Guardian*. The editor of *The Times*, William Rees-Mogg, declared himself 'undismayed'.

Day-Lewis had two memorable meetings with the Queen. At one he was mistakenly given the gold chain and badge of the Chancellor of the Order of St Michael and St George. At the other, a luncheon, he put his feet on what he thought was a well-placed footstool. It turned out to be a recumbent corgi.

Derby, Edward Stanley, 17th Earl of
(1865–1948)

Statesman and friend of King George v. He was the elder son of the 16th Earl and his wife, Lady Constance Villiers, eldest daughter of the 4th Earl of Clarendon. His political pedigree was thus impeccable; one grandfather had been three times Prime Minister, the other three times Foreign Secretary. Eddy, as he was known, spent an undistinguished boyhood at Wellington College before being commissioned into the Grenadier Guards. He retired from the Army in 1891 and in the following year was elected Conservative MP for Westhoughton, in his native Lancashire.

He became a Government Whip in 1895, Financial Secretary to the War Office in 1900 and Postmaster General, with a seat in the Cabinet, in 1903. Departing from his usual standards of courtesy, he denounced those postal workers who were pressing for higher wages as 'bloodsuckers' and 'blackmailers.' On the outbreak of the South African War he interrupted his parliamentary career to serve as Chief Press Censor, later as private secretary to the Commander-in-Chief, Lord Roberts (who also found employment for three dukes on his staff). He was defeated in the general election of 1906 and two years later entered the House of Lords on succeeding his father as 17th Earl.

During the Great War, Derby was successively Director of Recruiting and Under-Secretary at the War Office. When Lloyd George became Prime Minister in 1916 he appointed Derby to succeed him as Secretary of State, well knowing that he himself would continue to control the department. Derby proved an industrious but indecisive Minister. 'A very weak-minded fellow,' Field Marshal Haig said of him, 'and , like the feather pillow, bears the marks of the last person who has sat on him.' He showed to more advantage as ambassador in Paris from 1918 to 1920. Although he spoke scarcely a word of French, his *bonhomie* and his chef helped to overcome the suspicions that had developed between the wartime allies. He returned to the War Office under Bonar Law and Baldwin, finally retiring from national politics in 1924.

Derby was enormously rich, with a disposable income of about £100,000 a year when income tax was a mere shilling in the pound (five per cent) and money worth twenty times or more its present value. He and his wife, a daughter of the 7th Duke of Manchester, entertained on a scale almost matching that of the Sovereign. In the year George v came to the throne there were thirty-eight indoor servants at Knowsley, Derby's huge house near Liverpool, thirty-nine gardeners and thirty-seven keepers. When the King and Queen stayed there in 1913, no fewer than two hundred people slept under Derby's roof. The Minister in attendance wrote: 'Derby has personally worked out all the details himself of the routes to be traversed, the time to be taken, and has rehearsed the presentations to be made of various Mayors, Mayoresses and Councillors.' He was sometimes known as the King of Lancashire.

During another royal visit to Knowsley in 1921, he put on a display of boxing by Georges Carpentier and his sparring partner. The French newspapers wrote with delight of 'les deux Georges', but there were many in England who thought it an unseemly spectacle to lay before the Sovereign, his Consort and their daughter aged twenty-four. They were spared further indelicacy at the private film show on the last evening. Part of a nature film in which a duck laid an egg was obliterated.

Racing was a particular bond between the King and Derby, whose stable won a thousand races worth about £845,000 in stake money; three times he won the most celebrated race of all, established by the 12th Earl in 1780. He cherished his racehorses no less than his guests. When one promising animal fell ill, it was put on a daily diet of a bottle each of port and brandy, and three dozen eggs.

Lord Derby at ease

Desborough, Ethel, Lady
(1867–1952)

A lady-in-waiting to Queen Mary. It is strange to find this glittering bird of paradise at the staid court of King George v. One admirer called her the last of the great Whig hostesses; another claimed that she established the nearest English approach to a great Parisian salon. From her uncle, the 7th and last Earl Cowper, she inherited Panshanger, in Hertfordshire, with its splendid collection of pictures. Yet even at Taplow Court, the ugly overgrown villa on the Thames which came to her by marriage, she collected the Titans of politics and the arts leavened by a circle of high-spirited votaries young enough to be her sons.

Ettie Desborough's long life was marked by every triumph of fashion and wit and romance, but also by tragedy. Two of her sons were killed in the Great War and a third died in a motor accident. The eldest, Julian Grenfell, ensured his own immortality as a poet with

Lady Desborough with two of her children, Julian and Monica, and Nanny Wake, 1900

'Into Battle', written within a month of his death on the Western Front. Before allowing it to be published, his mother 'improved' the text in two or three places.

Her sweetness of character was more apparent to men than to women. Lord David Cecil wrote: 'There are those who will remember her not only as the sparkling queen of a brilliant, vanished world, but also as a lady of great age, lying half paralysed in a huge empty house and saying with the heart-rending ghost of a gay smile: "We did have fun, didn't we?"'

Margot Asquith was more censorious. 'Ettie,' she said, 'is an ox. When she dies she will be made into Bovril.'

Diana, Princess of Wales
(1961–   )

Wife of Charles, Prince of Wales (q.v.). She was born on 1 July 1961, the youngest of the three daughters of John Spencer, Viscount Althorp, by his wife Frances, daughter of the 4th Baron Roche. Their marriage was dissolved in 1969. Lord Althorp succeeded his father as 8th Earl Spencer (q.v.) in 1975.

Lady Diana Spencer was educated at Riddlesworth Hall, at West Heath, a girls' boarding school in Kent, and in Switzerland. Later she taught at the Young England Kindergarten, in Pimlico. Although brought up in a house on the Sandringham estate, she probably did not meet her future husband until he came to a shooting party at Althorp, her father's seat in Northamptonshire, in November 1977. They were betrothed in February 1981 and married in St Paul's Cathedral on 29 July of the same year. Prince William was born in 1982, Prince Henry two years later.

The Spencers have a long history of service at court. Lady Sarah Spencer, who married the 3rd Lord Lyttelton, was governess to Queen Victoria's children. Her days in the royal nursery at Windsor, she wrote, consisted of 'accounts, tradesmen's letters, maids' quarrels, bad fitting

The Princess of Wales with Harry, 1985

of frocks, desirability of rhubarb and magnesia, and, by way of intellectual pursuits, false French genders and elements of the multiplication table.' The Princess of Wales's father was an equerry to King George VI and to the present Queen; and both her grandmothers and four of her great-aunts have served in the household of Queen Elizabeth the Queen Mother.

The Princess of Wales is much admired for her beauty, her shy charm and her frivolous hats. There must also be a note of regret that she had so little time before marriage for either the carefree joys of girlhood or a more sustained education in the arts.

Digby, Kenelm, 11th Baron
(1894–1964)

Knight of the Garter and Lord Lieutenant of Dorset. Educated at Eton and the Royal Military College, Sandhurst, he served with the Coldstream Guards in the Great War, winning the DSO and the MC.

A large and genial man, he loved his garden and would sport a huge pink carnation of his own growing as big as a cabbage. He was no less an authority on the breeding of cattle and of horses. This he turned to advantage at the Grand National meeting of 1938, when he was the only winner of the Daily Tote Double. It paid £5,062 for a ten-shilling (50p) ticket.

Staying once with the Duke of Beaufort (q.v.) for the three-day horse trials at Badminton, Digby came down early to breakfast and unknowingly ate the dog's porridge. Nobody liked to tell him of his mistake, so he went on doing it.

Dimbleby, Richard
(1913–1965)

Broadcaster. On leaving Mill Hill Scool, in North London, he worked on *The Richmond and Twickenham Times*, which was owned by his family, first as an apprentice printer, then as a local reporter. In 1936 he joined the BBC, serving from 1939 to 1945 as a war correspondent. He reported much of the fighting in the Middle East, flew with the RAF on twenty operational missions and covered the Allied invasion of France in 1944.

It was as a commentator on ceremonial occasions that Dimbleby became a national institution. Seductive on radio and television alike, his silken sentences chronicled royal weddings and funerals, the Opening of Parliament and Trooping the Colour, State visits at home and abroad. Above all, his presentation of the Coronation of 1953 exactly caught the euphoria and expectancy of the new reign.

Malcolm Muggeridge intended no compliment in dubbing him Gold Microphone-in Waiting; others called him pompous and patronizing, unctuous and trite. Although Dimbleby affected to ignore such disparagement, which extended to his well-upholstered aplomb, it wounded him deeply. Yet his dignified, uncritical, almost reverent approach to the monarchy touched the hearts of less sophisticated millions the world over. The confident professionalism he brought to the programme 'Panorama' was also widely admired.

Dimbleby was honoured with an OBE in 1946 and a CBE in 1959. His friends deplored that he received neither a knighthood from the State nor any grade in the Royal Victorian Order, bestowed by the Queen for personal services. As he lay dying from cancer, however, a royal footman was despatched to his bedside with six bottles of champagne. His memorial service in Westminster Abbey was watched on television by more than eleven million people.

Richard Dimbleby outside Westminster Abbey, 1953

Disraeli

The Duchess of Windsor's favourite pug dog. 'We had one called Peter Townsend, too,' she said, 'but we gave the Group Captain away.'

Du Cros, Sir Arthur, 1st Baronet
(1871–1935)

Industrialist and royal benefactor. Born and educated in Dublin, he founded the Dunlop Rubber Company and pressed the military advantages of the pneumatic tyre on the Government. From 1908 to 1922 he sat as a Conservative in the House of Commons, where with equal patriotism he advocated the need for aeronautical development in the Army. He became a very rich man. In 1916 he was created a Baronet.

Arthur du Cros performed two services for King George V. The first concerned Frances, Countess of Warwick, wife of the 5th Earl and a former mistress of King Edward VII. During the early years of George V's reign, in desperate need of money to satisfy her creditors, she let it be known that she was prepared to sell the letters written to her by her royal lover for a price approaching £100,000. That, she claimed, was the sum she had spent entertaining him in the style he demanded of his friends. The letters contained such endearments as: 'Goodnight and God keep you, my own adored little Daisy wife, for ever yours, your only Love.' It was in every sense a hot property. Learning of her blackmailing intentions, du Cros felt that friendship for Lady Warwick and devotion to his Sovereign obliged him to act as an honourable though reluctant intermediary between the two. In the King's Private Secretary, Lord Stamfordham (q.v.), she met her match. He persuaded du Cros to keep the financial negotiations on the boil until the King's solicitor was ready to make a

sudden and stealthy application to the High Court. The judiciary declared that it would be illegal to publish the compromising letters, at least in Britain; and to ensure that Lady Warwick should not be tempted to sell them to an American publisher, du Cros generously paid £64,000 of her debts out of his own pocket.

In 1929, du Cros was able to demonstrate his loyalty more economically. The King, convalescing from a near-fatal attack of septicaemia, required a pleasant retreat by the sea. Du Cros had just such a property: Craigweil, overlooking the Channel near Bognor, which he offered for as long as it might be needed. 'Hideous house,' an earlier visitor had noted, 'but trees in the garden, splendid sea view; and comfortable Elsinore battlements to walk on.' There the King regained his health and after three months was allowed to return to Windsor.

Bognor will always be associated with his recovery. It has been alleged that when he again lay gravely ill seven years later, one of his doctors sought to soothe a restless patient with a whispered, 'Cheer up, Your Majesty, you will soon be at Bognor again.' To this the King is said to have replied, 'Bugger Bognor', and instantly expired. The tale carries a certain plausibility. The King was always emphatic in his language, not least when being fussed by his medical advisers. There is, however, a happier variant of the legend which rests on the authority of Sir Owen Morshead (q.v.), the King's Librarian. As the time of the King's departure from Bognor drew near, a deputation of leading citizens came

Arthur du Cros during his election campaign of 1908

to Craigweil to ask that their salubrious town should henceforth be known as Bognor Regis. They were received by Stamfordham, who, having heard their petition, invited them to wait while he consulted the King in another room. The Sovereign responded with the celebrated obscenity, which Stamfordham deftly translated for the benefit of the delegation. His Majesty, they were told, would be graciously pleased to grant their request.

Edward VIII, King
later Duke of Windsor
(1894–1972)

The eldest of the six children of the Duke and Duchess of York, later King George v and Queen Mary, he was born at White Lodge, Richmond Park, on 23 June 1894, and baptized Edward Albert Christian George Andrew Patrick David, the last four of his names being those of the patron saints of the United Kingdom. His family called him David.

Brought up at York Cottage, a modest house on the Sandringham estate, Prince Edward later convinced himself that he and his brothers had spent a largely unhappy childhood; but from the evidence of contemporary letters and diaries it seems often to have approached the idyllic. There were long hours exploring the countryside on bicycles; shooting and fishing and boisterous games; an undemanding regime in the schoolroom; lavish presents on birthdays and at Christmas. In 1903 the future Prime Minister, Lloyd George, met David and his seven-year-old brother Bertie (later King George VI) at Balmoral. 'The two little Princes,' he wrote, 'are splendid boys and chattered away the whole of their lunch-time, not the faintest shyness.'

Even by the stern standards of a Victorian papa, it is true, the future King George v was an exceptionally watchful and severe father who let no lapse of behaviour or dress go by default. His early years in the Royal Navy had trained him to

instant submission, and he saw no reason why his sons should not benefit from the same discipline. There was another constraint between the royal children and their father that sprang from circumstances of birth. The Duke of York was in direct line of succession to the throne; in 1901, the year of Queen Victoria's death, he became Prince of Wales and in 1910 succeeded his father as George v. Even for those brought up on the steps of the throne, 'There's such divinity doth hedge a King.' Or as a resentful Duke of Windsor wrote in later years: 'Kings and Queens are only secondarily fathers and mothers.'

If Prince Edward suffered from an anxious and overbearing father, he received little protection or even comfort from an uncommonly detached mother. The social conscience which Queen Mary inherited from her own mother embraced the welfare of children in general rather than the care of her own brood. She hated the routine of childbearing, and like all affluent parents of the Edwardian Age delegated the upbringing of her children to others. Even in York Cottage, a house no larger than a vicarage, she failed to discover that a nurse was physically ill-treating David and ruining Bertie's digestion for life. She remained, moreover, a spectator in the collision of wills between the King and his adolescent heir, believing that her first duty was to a husband invested with both the lonely burden and the mystique of monarchy. 'I always have to remember,' she said of her sons, 'that their father is also their King.'

Following the royal tradition of centuries, the early education of Prince Edward was entrusted to a tutor. Henry Hansell (q.v.) displayed every virtue of muscular Christianity; his intellectual talents were less obvious. He nevertheless managed, with some outside assistance, to prepare both David and Bertie for entry into the Royal Naval College, Osborne, at the age of twelve and a half. The inadequacy of that homespun teaching was revealed when David ended his first term 'not far from the bottom'. It was also something of an ordeal for the young princes suddenly to exchange the comforts of home life

The Prince of Wales by John St Helier Lander

for a long bare dormitory shared with thirty other boys. In May 1909 Prince Edward was transferred to the Royal Naval College, Dartmouth, to complete his training ashore. There, for the first time, he began to make friends from outside the royal circle and could scarcely wait to go to sea with his shipmates. This, however, was delayed by the death in May 1910 of his grandfather, Edward VII; it brought his father to the throne as George V and thrust the new King's sixteen-year-old heir into the glare of public life.

At the Coronation in 1911, all were moved when the golden-haired boy prince, newly invested with Garter robes, removed his coronet, knelt at the King's feet and spoke these ancient words of homage: 'I, Prince of Wales, do become your liege man of life and limb, and of earthly worship; and faith and truth I will bear unto you, to live and die, against all manner of folks. So help me God.' At Caernarvon Castle a few weeks later he was invested as Prince of Wales. Already impatient of medieval mummery, he grumbled at a 'preposterous rig' of white satin breeches and a surcoat of purple velvet edged with ermine. Lloyd George taught him a few words of Welsh, and the Principality took him to their hearts.

In 1912, accompanied by Mr Hansell, he spent four months in France attempting to master the language, learning something of art and architecture, and enjoying that elegant Parisian society which was to be the solace of his later life. There followed visits to Germany, where he stayed with the King and Queen of Württemberg and the old Grand Duchess of Mecklenburg-Strelitz. The memoirs he wrote as Duke of Windsor speak of 'the industry, the thoroughness, the discipline, the perseverance and the love of the Fatherland so typical of the German people.' At the time, however, he dubbed them 'fat, stolid, unsympathetic and intensely military.' But he took to the language, which in later life he spoke often, fluently and with relish.

Meanwhile he had become an undergraduate at Magdalen College, Oxford. The President was Sir Herbert Warren, a man too much

remembered for his social pretensions, too little for his classical scholarship and love of letters. The Prince discerned the first but failed to benefit from the second. It was with amused defiance that he would afterwards quote the unpromising prologue to Warren's report on him: 'Bookish he will never be.' The Prince joined the Officers Training Corps, played football, got drunk, was introduced to constitutional law by Sir William Anson and to foxhunting by an equerry. After eight such agreeable but desultory terms, he left Oxford in June 1914 to prepare for an attachment to the Army; with the outbreak of war in August, it was to last more than four years.

The Prince of Wales immediately joined the Grenadier Guards and began training as an infantry officer. Lord Kitchener at first refused to allow him to serve on the Western Front, fearing not so much the death of the heir to the throne as his capture by the enemy. By November, the Secretary of State had relented. Even then the Prince could not serve in the trenches with his regiment but was posted to staff appointments behind the lines. 'I feel such a swine,' he told a friend, 'having a soft comfortable time out here while the Guards Division is up at Ypres.' His emotional distress was reflected in an addiction to violent exercise and a sparse diet; in a pursuit of such danger as he could contrive to sample; in a reluctance to spend home leave with his family and a growing disobedience to his father. He resented the award to him of the newly instituted Military Cross as if it had been a badge of shame. 'I don't feel I deserve it in the least,' he wrote, 'never having served in the trenches.'

Emerging from the war at the age of twenty-four, the dejected Prince was within a year despatched on the first of those overseas tours which won him universal adulation. The handicap of shyness, uncertain stamina and bouts of nervous depression were outweighed by boyish good looks, charm, informality and a social conscience. Particularly in the presence of returned veterans, he seemed to reach out beyond the bunting and the red carpets into the hearts of his audience. Each successive journey served to renew and strengthen the links between Great Britain and her Empire; perhaps they also masked the impending disintegration of an imperialism that within a generation had all but vanished. Lloyd George called the Prince 'our greatest ambassador,' and even the King, so sparing of praise, wrote to him after his visit to Canada: 'I offer you my warmest congratulations on the splendid success of your tour, which is due in a great measure to your own personality and the wonderful way in which you have played up. It makes me very proud of you.'

The euphoria did not last. The Prince found much of his itinerary of a paralysing boredom, and said so. 'He seemed to think that he could alter his programme just as he pleased,' a British ambassador reported, 'and refuse to go on expeditions for which long and expensive preparations had been made.' He also shocked his overseas hosts by trying to procure informal companionship. The Japanese alone co-operated, but took appropriate precautions. 'There was nearly a terrible scandal,' the ambassador wrote home, 'because two missionary ladies who wished to present him with a Japanese Bible were hurried off by the police on the ground that they had not been inspected and disinfected.' On the same tour the Prince was contemptuous of a message from his father, warning him not to go to dances in Holy Week – 'Holy Week with a capital H and a capital W,' the Prince sneered, and had to be dissuaded from sending a rude reply. Even Lloyd George was disturbed by these lapses, and told the culprit: 'If you are one day to be a constitutional King, you must first be a constitutional Prince of Wales.'

Such episodes sharpened the conflict between an apprehensive George V and his wilful heir. The King believed that the survival of the monarchy depended upon impeccable standards of morality and manners, two facets of behaviour to which he attached equal weight. He thus rebuked peccadilloes of dress and deportment with a severity that should have been reserved for grave misconduct. There were absurd clashes over a forgotten pair of gloves, the wrong sort of hunting boots, a new fashion

in trousers with turn-ups that evoked the sarcastic inquiry, 'Is it raining in *here*?' When the newspapers showed the Prince with Lord Louis Mountbatten in a swimming pool, the King exclaimed: 'You might as well be photographed naked, no doubt it would please the public.'

He saw in his son's nonchalant attitude to clothes a deeper malaise: an unwillingness to prepare for his eventual role. Instead of cultivating those sober, domestic virtues that alone, the King thought, could repel revolution, the Prince of Wales embraced a world of night clubs and painted finger nails, of equivocal weekends and loose marriage ties. Even his more wholesome sport of steeplechasing was forbidden by the King, lest an accident should endanger the succession to the throne. The Prince took a spiteful revenge. Shooting with his father at Sandringham and having missed several birds, he put down his gun and called out: 'I think this is an old woman's game.'

What most distressed the King and Queen was their eldest son's refusal to marry. The Prince liked to maintain that there was no suitable foreign princess available; but as long ago as 1917, the King had told the Privy Council that he would allow his children to marry into British families. Since then he had permitted Princess Mary to marry Lord Lascelles (qq.v.) and the Duke of York to marry Lady Elizabeth Bowes-Lyon (qq.v.). Had the Prince of Wales produced a bride of similar background, there is no reason to think that the King would have withheld his consent. As it was, he remained in his small bachelor quarters in St James's Palace or at Fort Belvedere, his toy castle near Windsor, solaced by a succession of married or divorced women. The longest, happiest and least rackety of these liaisons was with Freda Dudley Ward, the wife of a Liberal MP. It lasted from 1918 until 1934, when he fell deeply in love with Wallis Simpson, a divorced and remarried American with two living husbands. A few weeks before his death, George V discussed his heir with a cousin. 'He has not a single friend who is a gentleman,' the King confided. 'He does not see any decent society. And he is forty-one.'

To later generations, those sentiments may seem narrow and old-fashioned. But there were other failings of temperament and judgment on the part of the Prince. As early as 1925, Henry Channon (q.v.) wrote in his diary: 'The Prince of Wales one feels would not raise his finger to save his future sceptre. In fact many of his intimate friends think he would be only too happy to renounce it.' It took more than a decade to fulfil the prophecy, during which he continued to enchant an Empire with boyish charm and to show a genuine though intermittent concern for unemployment and other social problems. Those close to him, however, were alarmed by his outspoken tenderness for Nazi Germany. A friend noted in 1933: 'The Prince was quite pro-Hitler, said it was no business of ours to interfere in Germany's internal affairs either *re* Jews or *re* anything else, and added that dictators were very popular these days and that we might want one in England before long.' A German intelligence agent later reported to Berlin: 'Nor did he hold his father's view that the King must blindly accept the Cabinet's decisions. On the contrary, he felt it to be his duty to intervene if the Cabinet were to plan a policy which in his view was detrimental to British interests.' Is it any wonder that the King told his last Prime Minister, Baldwin: 'After I am dead, the boy will ruin himself in twelve months'?

As the coffin of George v was carried through the streets of London in January 1936, a sudden flash of light danced across the pavement. It was the jewelled Maltese cross that surmounts the crown, loosened by the jolting wheels of the gun-carriage and now lying in the gutter. 'A most terrible omen,' Harold Nicolson (q.v.) wrote in his diary. Wits claimed that the accident had occurred opposite Simpson's restaurant in the Strand. In fact it happened, with equal portent, outside what was to be the graveyard of Edward VIII's reign: the Houses of Parliament.

Even as his father lay dying, the new King had ordered that the clocks at Sandringham, for many years kept thirty minutes fast to gain more time for winter shooting, should be put back. Archbishop Lang (q.v.), in attendance at George v's deathbed, wondered: 'What other customs will be put back also?' They were of the sort that gave Edward VIII an easily won reputation as a reformer. He abolished the frock coat at Court in favour of the morning coat; he dispensed with his car one rainy morning and walked a hundred yards from Buckingham Palace to the offices of the Duchy of Cornwall clutching an umbrella; he cut down the staff on the royal estates with what his biographer Frances Donaldson calls 'a small, compulsive stinginess and a lack of regard for men who had rendered long and faithful service.'

The King was capricious, too, in carrying out his official duties. At his best, as when addressing war veterans, he could still captivate. At his worst, as when holding a presentation party for debutantes, he failed to conceal his boredom and would even cut short the engagement. He neglected the essential paper work of a constitutional monarch, sometimes leaving his red despatch boxes unopened for days or even weeks on end. Unknown to the King, this particular burden was eased by the staff of the Foreign Office, who deliberately witheld from him certain sensitive papers, lest they be read by other eyes at Fort Belvedere or tempt the Sovereign into further pro-German indiscretions.

George v had several times intervened decisively in political questions, but only within the limits of the prerogative and after a close study of the documents. Edward VIII is best remembered for having told the unemployed of South Wales that 'something must be done.' That impetuous promise, often contrasted with the supposed sloth of his Ministers, was made on 18 November 1936, forty-eight hours after the King had informed the Prime Minister of his intention to abdicate in order to marry Mrs Simpson. Whoever else would help the miners, it was not to be their King.

'When I was a little boy in Worcestershire reading history books,' Stanley Baldwin used to say, 'I never thought I should have to interfere between the King and his mistress.' Had Mrs

Simpson been no more than Edward VIII's mistress, the Prime Minister might well have been spared his distasteful task. It was the King's irrevocable decision to make a divorced and remarried woman his wife that inflated a romantic friendship into the gravest of constitutional crises. Although many knew of his attachment, few suspected his intention: not least because for the past eight years she had been married to a British businessman, Ernest Simpson.

What did disturb the Court was the flaunting of his intimacy with her. Almost a resident of Fort Belvedere for the past two years, she was in May invited with her husband to a dinner party at St James's Palace; the names of all the guests, who included the Prime Minister and Mrs Baldwin, Lord and Lady Louis Mountbatten, Lord and Lady Wigram and Mr Duff and Lady Diana Cooper (qq.v.), were printed next day in the Court Circular. She accompanied the King, this time without Mr Simpson, on a much publicized summer cruise along the coast of Dalmatia. And in September she stayed with the King at Balmoral, where she is said to have assumed a proprietorial role when the Duke and Duchess of York came over from Birkhall.

Walter Monckton (q.v.), the King's legal adviser and confidant, was disturbed by such imprudence. Yet not even he suspected the depth of the King's passion. He later wrote: 'I thought, throughout, long before as well as after there was talk of marriage, that if and when the stark choice faced them between their love and his obligations as King-Emperor, they would in the end each make the sacrifice, devastating though it would be.'

Although the British Press continued to respect the King's private life, American newspapers were less inhibited. When their lurid reports of the royal friendship reached Downing Street, even the supine Baldwin wondered whether he should not discuss them with the King. What ultimately obliged him to do so was the knowledge that Mrs Simpson had begun divorce proceedings against her husband, alleging adultery. Once free of Ernest Simpson, there would be no legal obstacle to her marrying the

Supreme Governor of the Church of England as her third living husband, and emerging from the ceremony as Queen. It was a match which Baldwin's Government refused to condone.

The battle of wills between the Prime Minister and his Sovereign was joined on 20 October. Baldwin asked the King to persuade Mrs Simpson to withdraw her divorce petition. The King refused. The case was held a week later at Ipswich, a town near the east coast chosen to attract as little attention from the Press as possible. There, after evidence of Ernest Simpson's adultery had been heard, his supposedly wronged wife received a decree *nisi*; unless other circumstances intruded – such as her own possible misconduct – she would be free to remarry in April 1937.

Even in Baldwin's strait-laced Cabinet, the King had a friend: Duff Cooper, Secretary of State for War. Outside it he could depend on the most eloquent man of his generation, Winston Churchill. Both counselled him to sit tight. He had six months in which certain newspaper owners, Lord Beaverbrook and Lord Rothermere, could sway popular opinion in his favour; Edward VIII might yet marry Mrs Simpson and keep his throne. To the King's credit, he declined such a course. He wished neither to prolong a constitutional crisis nor to deceive his people by being crowned under false pretences. The date of the Coronation had already been chosen: 12 May 1937. 'For me to have gone through the Coronation service,' he later wrote, 'while harbouring in my heart a secret intention to marry contrary to the Church's tenets would have meant being crowned with a lie on my lips.'

On 16 November, Baldwin went again to the Palace. Having conferred with the Labour Opposition in the House of Commons, he was able to warn the King that his marriage to Mrs Simpson would be approved neither by the British Government nor by the Dominions. To this, Edward VIII replied that he would nevertheless marry; and that if he could not do so as King, he was 'prepared to go.' That in effect was the end of the conflict between two closed minds.

There were further meetings at Fort Belvedere, but to no effect. The King refused to renounce Mrs Simpson; Baldwin and the Dominions refused the compromise of a morganatic marriage, by which Mrs Simpson could have become the King's wife but not his Consort (see *Monckton of Brenchley, Viscount*). On 10 December, Edward VIII signed an Instrument of Abdication which within twenty-four hours had been approved by Parliament. On both days, prices rose sharply on the London Stock Exchange.

The former King expressed no sorrow at his departure. A courtier who witnessed those final hours wrote that everybody was immeasurably sad except 'the Chief Conspirator, who was honestly quite unmoved.' Perhaps it was an expression of relief after so long an ordeal; or perhaps it reflected an innate distaste for the burden of monarchy which he had now relinquished. The old King dined with the new, about to be proclaimed George VI; he sat with his grieving brothers, cheerfully drinking whisky while his toe nails were seen to; he broadcast a moving, dignified farewell composed with the help of Winston Churchill; he took leave of his family, then drove through the night to Portsmouth and exile. It is said that the Government had arranged for him to sail to France in the Admiralty yacht *Enchantress*; at the last moment they prudently substituted the destroyer HMS *Fury*.

To this day opinion on the Abdication remains sharply divided. Some would call the King's insistence on marrying a divorced woman a betrayal of the greatest of hereditary trusts, finding support for their view in the lines which Shakespeare put into the mouth of Laertes:

> . . . his will is not his own;
> For he himself is subject to his birth:
> He may not, as unvalued persons do,
> Carve for himself; for on his choice depends
> The safety and the health of the whole state.

Others, seeing the King's action as a challenge of the heart to an oppressive Government and an outmoded Church, gave it their blessing. It would, however, be idle to claim that the King was hustled off his throne by a wily Prime Minister against the inarticulate wishes of his subjects. During the weekend preceding the Abdication, Members of Parliament followed Baldwin's advice in meeting as many of their constituents as possible. They returned to Westminster on the Monday unanimous in the view that the King could not marry Mrs Simpson and remain on the throne. Against an almost unbroken wall of public opinion not even the romantic and outspoken championship of Winston Churchill could prevail. In the years ahead there were to be no toasts to the King over the Water.

The Abdication deprived Edward VIII of the styles and titles he had borne as King, but not those of his birth. He therefore emerged as His Royal Highness Prince Edward. The first act of the new Sovereign was to announce his intention of conferring a royal dukedom on his brother, although not until March 1937 was this formally gazetted as the Dukedom of Windsor. Such a gesture on George VI's part was prudent as well as gracious. For what if Prince Edward should try to recapture his popularity, perhaps even his throne, by embarking on a political career? Without a peerage, even a prince may seek election to the House of Commons; a non-royal duke, moreover, may sit and vote in the House of Lords; but by tradition, a royal duke was expected to hold his tongue on all contentious topics.

A financial settlement on the Duke of Windsor was less easily negotiated. He was far from destitute. Between 1910 and his accession in January 1936 he had accumulated private savings of at least £800,000, £20 million in the currency of 1985. They came largely from the revenues of the Duchy of Cornwall, the long-established income of the Sovereign's eldest son, on which he is required to pay no tax. At the death of King George V he had also inherited a life interest in Sandringham and Balmoral, the private property of the Sovereign. Even after his abdication, the Duke of Windsor was free to retain that life

LATE NEWS!
Yeast-Vite

The Evening News
LARGEST EVENING NET SALE IN THE WORLD
NO. 17,134 FIFTY-SIXTH YEAR LONDON: THURSDAY, DECEMBER 10, 1936
BROADCASTING PAGE 6
LATE EXTRA
ONE PENNY

RHINO-SOLE
SYNTHETIC PLASTIC LEATHER
6d
WOOLWORTHS

8 p.m. EDITION

THE KING ABDICATES

"My Final and Irrevocable Decision": The Duke of York Succeeds To The Throne at Once

"I CAN NO LONGER DISCHARGE MY HEAVY TASK WITH EFFICIENCY"

Abdication Instrument Signed To-day With The Three Royal Brothers as Witnesses

MESSAGE READ TO PARLIAMENT

"My Mind Is Made Up: Further Delay Cannot But Be Most Injurious"

King Edward the Eighth has abdicated his Throne. He announced his decision in the following message which he sent to Parliament this afternoon and which was read by the Speaker to the House of Commons:

After long and anxious consideration I have determined to renounce the Throne to which I succeeded on the death of my Father, and I am now communicating this My final and irrevocable decision.

Realising as I do the gravity of this step, I can only hope that I shall have the understanding of My peoples in the decision I have taken and the reasons which have led me to take it.

I will not enter now into My private feelings, but I would beg that it should be remembered that the burden which constantly rests upon the shoulders of a Sovereign is so heavy that it can only be borne in circumstances different from those in which I now find Myself.

I conceive that I am not overlooking the duty that rests on Me to place in the forefront the public interest, when I declare that I am conscious that I can no longer discharge this heavy task with efficiency or with satisfaction to Myself.

THE ABDICATION INSTRUMENT

I have accordingly this morning executed an Instrument of Abdication in the terms following:

"I, Edward the VIII of Gt. Britain, Ireland and the Dominions beyond the Seas, King, Emperor of India, do hereby declare my irrevocable determination to renounce the Throne for Myself and for my descendants, and My desire that effect should be given to this Instrument of Abdication immediately

"In token whereof I have hereunto set My hand this tenth day of December, nineteen hundred and thirty-six, in the presence of the witnesses whose signatures are subscribed.

(Signed) Edward R. I."

My execution of this Instrument has been witnessed by My three brothers, Their Royal Highnesses The Duke of York, the Duke of Gloucester and the Duke of Kent.

I deeply appreciate the spirit which has actuated the appeals which have been made to Me to take a different decision, and I have before reaching my final determination most fully pondered over them.

But my mind is made up. Moreover, further delay cannot but be most injurious to the peoples whom I have tried to serve as Prince of Wales and as King and whose future happiness and prosperity are the constant wish of My heart.

I take My leave of them in the confident hope that the course which I have thought it right to follow is that which is best for the stability of the Throne and Empire, and the happiness of My peoples.

"NO DELAY OF ANY KIND"

I am deeply sensible of the consideration which they have always extended to Me, both before and after my accession to the Throne, and which I know they will extend in full measure to My successor.

I am most anxious that there should be no delay of any kind in giving effect to the Instrument which I have executed and that all necessary steps should be taken immediately to secure that my lawful successor, My brother, His Royal Highness the Duke of York, should ascend the Throne.

EDWARD R.I.

The Duke of York.

The Duchess of York.

Their elder daughter, Princess Elizabeth.

The King To Go Abroad

The Press Association learns that King Edward will leave the country immediately after signing his Act of Abdication — probably tomorrow night.

King Edward will renounce with the Throne all his titles. It is probable that the Duke of York will confer a high peerage, probably a dukedom, on him.

• • •

King Edward's destination is being kept a close secret. But it is stated on what is described as good authority, that it is not a British Dominion or a British possesion.

• • •

It is believed that there will be no alteration in the Coronation date fixed for May 12.

Proclamation on Saturday

It is authoritatively stated that the Accession Council will be held on Saturday morning. The new King will be proclaimed on Saturday afternoon.

A change in monarchy is the one occasion upon which all the members of the Privy Council with the Lord Mayor, Aldermen and other representatives of the City are summoned to be present.

New King May Be George VI

It is understood that the Duke of York has not yet made a decision as to what title he will take. It is considered likely that he will choose to be known as George the Sixth rather than Albert the First.

Sensational Speech By Mr. Baldwin

"THE KING SAID: 'I AM GOING TO MARRY MRS. SIMPSON . . . I AM PREPARED TO GO'"

MR. BALDWIN made a sensational speech in the House of Commons after King Edward's message had been read.

Here are points from the speech which is reported fully on **Page Three**:

No more grave message has ever been received by Parliament.

His Majesty, as Prince of Wales, has honoured me with his friendship for many years, which I value.

When we said good-bye on Tuesday night at Fort Belvedere we both knew and felt and said to each other that that friendship, far from being impaired by the discussions of this last week, bound us more closely together than it ever had and would last for life.

"We Must Settle It"

I felt bound to speak to the King in view of the volume of correspondence which was coming to me in October.

I told the King that I wanted to talk it over with him as a friend to see if I could be of help to him.

He said: "You and I must settle this matter together. I will not have anyone else interfering."

I saw him the next time on November 16. I spoke to him on that occasion for twenty minutes on the question of marriage.

I told him that I did not think that a particular marriage was one that would receive the approbation of the country.

I pointed out to him that the position of the King's wife was different from the position of the wife of any other citizen in the country.

"I Am Prepared To Go"

Then His Majesty said to me, and I have his permission to repeat it. He said that he wanted to tell me something that he had long wanted to tell me.

He said: "I am going to marry Mrs. Simpson, and I am prepared to go."

I said: "Sir, that is most grievous news. It is impossible for me to make any comment on that to-day."

He sent for me again on November 21. In the meantime a suggestion had been made to me that a possible compromise might be arranged.

The compromise was that the King should marry and that Parliament should pass an Act enabling the lady to be the King's wife without the position of Queen.

When I saw His Majesty on November 25 he asked me if the proposition had been put before me and I said Yes.

I told him that I had not had a considered opinion, but if he asked me my personal reaction informally, my reaction was that Parliament would never pass the Bill.

Before The Cabinet

I asked him if he desired me to put forward the matter formally. He said he so desired. I told him it will mean my putting it before the whole Cabinet and communicating with the Prime Ministers of the Dominions.

He said that was his wish, and I told him that I would do it.

It is difficult to realise that His Majesty is not a boy. Although he looks so young he is a matured man with great experience of life and of the world.

He wanted to go in circumstances which would make the succession of his brother as little difficult as possible.

He stayed down at Fort Belvedere because he said he was not going to come to London while these things were in dispute because of the cheering crowds.

A Pencil Note

Mr. Baldwin then produced what he said was a pencil note sent to him by the King this morning.

The note said that the Duke of York and the King "have always been on the best of terms as brothers and the King is confident the Duke deserves and will receive the support of the whole Empire."

Continuing, Mr. Baldwin said: This crisis has arisen now rather than later from that frankness of His Majesty's character which is one of his many attractions.

This evening I shall ask leave to bring in the necessary Bill which will be available to members as soon as the House has ordered the Bill to be printed.

Mr. Baldwin said that last night, in reply to a minute which was sent to the King, the Cabinet received a message from him regretting that he was unable to alter his decision.

This Night Of History

Parliament heard to-night the most momentous pronouncement it has ever heard.

The House of Commons, filled as it has rarely been filled, heard afterwards Mr. Baldwin's sensational speech, reported in full on *Page Three*

Speeches in the House of Lords, including one by the Archbishop of York, are given on *Page Nine*.

Crowds scenes are described on *Page Four*.

At Fort Belvedere this night the Duke of York is dining with the King.

Mrs. Simpson Told By Phone

Mrs. Simpson was told the news over the telephone at Cannes tonight. It had earlier been announced on her behalf that the King was definitely not visiting Cannes or the Riviera. See Page NINE.

MR. ATTLEE'S TRIBUTE TO KING EDWARD

When Commons resumed tonight, Mr. Attlee, leader of Opposition, said:

"The King has decided that he can no longer continue on the Throne. The whole country will receive the news with deep sorrow, and his subjects will feel a sense of personal loss."

The personal affection which he had inspired in his people was greater than that given to any British Monarch.

"We can never forget how he felt for the miners in their time of trouble, how he showed his deep human interest in the unemployed and the people of the distressed areas."

They all tried to think of some way by which this conflict could have been resolved. They realised the great objection to every course. They hoped it would not have come to abdication.

"But the King has made his decision. He is resolved to abide by it, and we can do no other than accept it.

"The wish of all his people will be that he may have a long and happy life.

"We can all appreciate the strain of these events on the Prime Minister. The country has received a severe shock. It will take time to recover."

They would all try to do what they could to lighten the burden of the Prime Minister.

Mr. Attlee expressed on behalf of himself and his colleagues their deepest sympathy with Queen Mary and the other members of the Royal Family.

Mr. Attlee said he could not have supported a Morganatic Marriage Bill. He believed it to be an essential element in the monarchic principle itself that the lady whom the King married must become Queen.

"Such a Bill would have had to pass through all the Parliaments of the United Kingdom and the Dominions before it could have become valid in this country or any of the Dominions.

"The attempt to do so would have involved the throne in prolonged controversy which would have greatly impaired its prestige.

The Government had no option but to reject the proposals.

The Abdication Story, 10 December 1936

interest as well as the contents of the houses on the two estates, together valued at a little more than £250,000, or £6 million in the currency of 1985.

On 10 December 1936 there was a long meeting at Fort Belvedere between Edward VIII and his successor, their financial advisers and solicitors. It was agreed that the Duke of Windsor (as he would shortly become) should surrender to George VI his life interest in Sandringham and Balmoral, together with their contents. In return he was to receive an annuity of £25,000 (£600,000 in the currency of 1985). This sum was to come from the new King's private resources, unless the Government decided to make provision for the Duke in the Civil List: the vote of money for the Sovereign and other members of the royal family passed at the beginning of each new reign. In the event, the Government decided that the nation owed no obligation to the Duke of Windsor, who had voluntarily given up the throne and all that went with it. The burden of the annual payment thereupon fell on George VI.

That hasty agreement was subsequently altered in two ways, both to the Duke's disadvantage. He was required to bear part of the cost of pensions paid to retired retainers on the Sandringham and Balmoral estates, thereby reducing his allowance from £25,000 to £21,000. And the Government, although contributing nothing directly to the Duke's annuity, persuaded the King to attach a condition to its payment: that until further notice the Duke must not return to England without express permission. If the King did not comply, it was hinted, Parliament might be less generous than otherwise in fixing his own Civil List. Since no such condition had been imposed at the time of the Abdication, the Duke felt aggrieved. In an increasingly acrimonious exchange of letters, he threatened not only to have King George and his family evicted from Sandringham and Balmoral as trespassers, but also to lay claim to other valuable royal possessions. Although the Government may have been needlessly vindictive, the Duke was equally insensitive in failing

to realize the shock and contempt provoked by his Abdication. He was at length obliged to accept the altered terms of the settlement, but resentment lingered.

Meanwhile he tasted the bitterness of exile. On leaving England in the early hours of 12 December 1936, he had travelled to Schloss Enzesfeld, near Vienna, where he spent more than three months as the guest of Baron and Baroness Eugene de Rothschild. Then he moved to an hotel near Ischl. He did not dare join Mrs Simpson in the South of France until the decree *nisi* granted to her in October was made absolute in April; otherwise they risked an intervention by that guardian of public morals known as the King's Proctor and the withholding of her divorce. At the beginning of May they were reunited at the Château de Candé, near Tours, lent to them by a French-born naturalized American, Charles Bedaux. It was there, on 3 June 1937, that the Duke of Windsor married Wallis Simpson under French Law. The match was then solemnized according to the rites of the Church of England by the Rev. R.A.Jardine (q.v.) in defiance of his bishop. No member of the royal family attended the ceremony. But by the hand of Sir Walter Monckton, King George VI sent his brother an unamiable wedding present.

It was a letter informing the Duke that on his Abdication he had placed himself out of line of succession to the throne and was thus no longer entitled to the style of Royal Highness. Nevertheless, the King continued, it was his wish that the Duke should enjoy that style. To give effect to it, he had therefore declared by Letters Patent under the Great Seal, i.e. on the advice of his Ministers, 'that the Duke of Windsor shall . . . be entitled to hold and enjoy for himself only the title, style or attribute of Royal Highness, so however that his wife and descendants, if any, shall not hold the same title or attribute.' The Duke of Windsor was to be HRH; the Duchess of Windsor was not.

The only purpose of the declaration, it seems, was to exclude the Duchess from her husband's style. By George VI's express command, the director-general of the BBC, Sir John Reith, had announced his brother as 'His Royal Highness Prince Edward' before the ex-King's farewell broadcast on 11 December. On the following day, the new King told the Accession Council that his brother would be known as 'His Royal Highness the Duke of Windsor.' If, therefore, the Duke had not lost the style of Royal Highness on Abdication, why was it necessary to restore it to him? Again, Edward VIII had been told that he could not marry Mrs Simpson because she would then have to take his status and become Queen. So he gave up a kingdom and an empire to make her his wife. Now he was being told that she could not share even his reduced status. The declaration also contradicted an announcement made from Buckingham Palace in April 1923, when it was still unusual for princes to marry commoners: 'In accordance with the settled general rule that a wife takes the status of her husband, Lady Elizabeth Bowes-Lyon on her marriage has become Her Royal Highness the Duchess of York.' By 1935, when the Duke of Gloucester married Lady Alice Montagu-Douglas-Scott, the settled rule had been so accepted as to evoke no official announcement. Less than two years later it was broken. Chagrined by the ruling of May 1937, the Duke of Windsor consulted Sir William Jowitt, KC, who gave as his opinion that it was contrary to law. When Jowitt became Lord Chancellor in the Labour Government of 1945, the Duke reminded him of this, and hoped that he 'would now be able to see justice done.' Jowitt declined to act.

Resentment at the Duchess of Windsor's impact upon British history was not the only reason for the King's edict. The royal family and the Government shared a genuine doubt whether her marriage would last. If it had ended in divorce, as had her two previous marriages, she would have continued to be a Royal Highness and as such an embarrassment; for no machinery existed by which a person could be deprived of that style once it had been acquired.

To devote so ponderous a commentary to three words may seem excessive. But they blighted the Duke's life, although less so his wife's. 'This cold-blooded act,' he wrote thirty years later, 'in its uprush, represented a kind of Berlin Wall alienating us from my family.' Sometimes he pretended that the prohibition did not exist. Harold Nicolson was asked to meet the Windsors at Somerset Maugham's house in the South of France: 'Cocktails were brought and we stood around the fireplace. There was a pause. "I am sorry we were a little late," said the Duke, "but Her Royal Highness couldn't drag herself away." He had said it. The three words fell into the circle like three stones into a pool. Her (gasp) Royal (shudder) Highness (and not one eye dared to meet another).' More often the Duke would mull over the ancient insult to his wife and thus to himself. Perhaps the most memorable remark ever made to the present writer was when his former Sovereign confided to him: 'I served my country well for seventeen years, and all I got was a kick on the ass.'

Already homesick for England, the Duke tried to adjust to an expatriate life full of movement but empty of purpose. The man who had once caught the imagination of an empire now made do with golf and gardening, with clothes and cairn terriers. In the autumn of 1937 there came a sudden relief from boredom. Charles Bedaux, anxious to ingratiate himself with the Nazi regime for commercial reasons, arranged for the Windsors to visit Germany, ostensibly to study social conditions among the workers. The Duke, who had long shown an interest in the subject, saw two other reasons for accepting the invitation. Naïvely proud of his diplomatic talents, he hoped to ease the tensions between Great Britain and Germany. He also wanted the Duchess, who had been so humiliated by his own family, to experience the euphoria of a royal progress. (It was for just such a purpose that the Archduke Franz Josef took his morganatic and much-snubbed wife to Sarajevo in 1914.) The Windsors were well entertained and flattered by Goebbels, Goering, Hess and Ribbentrop, and on the final day had tea with Hitler at Berchtesgaden. The Duke, like so many foreign visitors, thought his hosts idealists with whom one could reach an accommodation. The Führer returned the compliment. 'She would have made a good Queen,' he said. The unfavourable publicity which the Duke and Duchess received in the British and American Press during their German visit obliged them to cancel a similar tour of the United States, also arranged by Bedaux.

The outbreak of war in September 1939 found them at the villa La Croë, Cap d'Antibes, on which they had taken a lease. At last, the Duke thought, the moment had come when he could return to England accompanied by his wife and resume the busy life of a prince. Having motored to Cherbourg they found that Churchill, recalled to office as First Lord of the Admiralty, had sent not only HMS *Kelly*, under the command of Lord Louis Mountbatten, but also his own son Randolph, in Hussar uniform, bearing a letter of welcome. The Duke's practised eye at once noticed that young Churchill's spurs were not only inside out but upside down: it made him feel that he himself was back in harness. On the same quay at Portsmouth from which he had sailed for France in darkness three years before, there was a guard of honour and a band, mounted at the order of the First Lord.

There the courtesies ended. No representative of the King was present to greet his brother; nor had any arrangements been made to put up the Duke and Duchess of Windsor in a royal palace or elsewhere. In London the Duke was briefly received by his brother at Buckingham Palace, neither of their wives being present. The invitation was not repeated, and six years were to pass before they met again. The Duke was offered a choice of posts: either Assistant Regional Commissioner for Wales, with responsibility for civil defence, or attachment to the British Military Mission in France. He chose the first, then was told he could have only the second; the Government, it seemed, wanted him out of the country lest that forty-five-year old Peter Pan should eclipse his hesitant brother. Accepting temporary demotion from Field Marshal to Major-General, he departed with his wife for Paris.

The Duke proved an unexpectedly useful member of the British Military Mission. The French High Command, suspicious of their allies, forbade visits to the Maginot Line throughout the winter of 1939. But they remembered the young Prince de Galles of another war, welcomed him back to France, invited him to go wherever he wished. In the guise of a liaison officer he was thus able to penetrate those doubtful defences against German armour; and with the help of a small intelligence staff to prepare reports on their inadequacy. For several months, however, he was forbidden to visit British troops, such was his supposed power of reviving old loyalties. Nor could he escape unpleasant little jealousies. The Duke was told to make himself scarce during the King's visit to the Front; and on another occasion rebuked for having inadvertently returned a salute meant for the Commander-in-Chief. With more justice he has been criticized for selfishly deserting his old equerry and friend, Major 'Fruity' Metcalfe, as the Germans advanced on Paris in May 1940.

To avoid capture or internment, the Duke and Duchess sought refuge in neutral Spain, then moved to Portugal. It has long been supposed that they were up to no good during their six-week Peninsular War. Captured German documents later revealed that the Duke had been the intended victim of a bizarre plot by Ribbentrop, the Nazi Foreign Minister. He was to have been held in Spain and used to undermine British morale, perhaps even supplant George VI and make peace with Germany. What has remained in doubt is the degree of encouragement, if any, which the Duke gave to those plans. Certainly he displayed a deplorable lack of judgment in forecasting Britain's probable defeat when talking to his Spanish and Portuguese friends, some of whom were German emissaries. But he made it clear that he would help to negotiate peace only if Britain were to be hopelessly beaten and his services requested by the British Government. It was also unseemly of him to use his Spanish connections to beg a favour of his country's enemies. Obsessed by possessions, he asked the German and Italian Governments to place a special guard on his two houses, one in occupied Paris, the other on the threatened French Riviera.

Even while Churchill was urging the people of Britain to brace themselves for a German invasion, he had to deal with a fractious Duke of Windsor, who announced by telegram from Lisbon that he would not return to England unless two conditions were met. The first was a promise that he be allowed to serve his country anywhere in the British Empire; the second that he and his wife be received by the King and Queen, if only for a few minutes, and the audience be made public in the Court Circular to demonstrate that they were not in disgrace. Neither demand was acceptable, and Churchill found it necessary to threaten Major-General the Duke of Windsor with a court martial unless he flew instantly to England. This proved unnecessary when the Duke agreed to become Governor of the Bahamas, albeit with much grumbling about travel arrangements and servants.

The appointment had to be made hurriedly and at the darkest moment of the war. There seems nevertheless to have been an element of spite in banishing the Windsors to so paltry a post. 'I dare say it is quite a good plan that they should go to the Bahamas,' the Foreign Secretary, Lord Halifax, noted, 'but I am sorry for the Bahamas.' An infertile chain of islands to the north of Cuba, it was among the least important of Britain's thirty-five colonial territories and the most unsuitable to be ruled by the ex-King. Members of the royal family had of course held the office of Governor-General of a Dominion such as Canada or South Africa; aloof from the strains of party politics, they performed the largely ceremonial duties of a constitutional monarch. As Governor of the Bahamas, however, the Duke embodied the roles of both Head of State and Prime Minister. He inherited an economy dependent on a winter tourist season; a strict colour bar; and a corrupt white oligarchy which regarded the colony as its private preserve.

Across four thousand miles of ocean, the new Governor was made to suffer pinpricks and restraints, imposed by Whitehall but often at the prompting of the Palace. The harassment began even while his future was under discussion in London. On 24 June 1940, two days after the fall of France, the King's Private Secretary, Sir Alexander Hardinge (q.v.), was not too busy to send a letter to the Foreign Office. The King, he wrote, had noted with extreme displeasure, that a telegram had referred to the Duke and Duchess as 'Their Royal Highnesses.' This appellation, Hardinge continued, was false and utterly impermissible, and such an error must never be made again. Similar instructions reached officials at Government House, Nassau, before the arrival of the new incumbent. 'You are no doubt aware,' the Lord Chamberlain telegraphed, 'that a lady when presented to HRH the Duke of Windsor should make a half-curtsey. The Duchess of Windsor is not entitled to this.' Such were the concerns of certain officials during what Winston Churchill called 'their finest hour.'

Without experience of either colonial administration or political manoeuvre, the Duke acquitted himself well. He saved the colony from starvation; he presided over the smooth transition of New Providence into a war base; he dealt firmly with civil disorder while attempting to remove social, political and economic grievances. His enemies have preferred to remember only his mishandling of the investigation into the murder of Sir Harry Oakes, the richest and most powerful man in the Bahamas; and his association with Axel Wenner-Gren, a Swedish industrialist of supposed Nazi sympathies.

After two years in Nassau, the Duke yearned to be rid of his Lilliputian realm and to serve his country on a wider stage; either as a Governor-General or in the United States, where he and the Duchess were invariably received with admiration as well as curiosity. But the only other post in prospect for him was the Governorship of Bermuda, a colony even smaller and more remote than the Bahamas. (Two years earlier, on being offered Bermuda, Lord De La

Warr had looked it up in an encyclopedia, then exclaimed, 'It is no larger than Bexhill' – the resort on the Sussex coast, most of which he owned.) So the Duke soldiered on to the end of the war. The Windsors received no public word of praise from the British Government; nor were they summoned to the customary farewell audience with the King, a courtesy accorded to all other retiring proconsuls and their wives.

For the remaining twenty-seven years of his life, he and the Duchess lived near Paris. The City of Paris offered them a lovely house in the Bois de Boulogne and the French Government relief from taxation. That weighed heavily with the Duke, whose fortune had been depleted by unsuccessful attempts to find oil on his ranch in Calgary, Alberta, bought when he was Prince of Wales. Those losses, as well as the perfection of clothes and jewels, of household management and entertainment demanded by his wife, led him to cultivate financiers and other men of business; without, however, any noticeable improvement in his bank balance. This he achieved by his pen, although with professional help. In 1951 he published a partisan but enticing volume of memoirs entitled *A King's Story*, followed by many ephemeral articles for the world's Press. So the coffers were never too bare for annual visits to New York and Palm Beach, and sometimes to Biarritz and Venice. It was a sadly self-indulgent routine in which there was little room for charitable causes or the arts.

Instead the Duke eked out his days with golf and gardening. At le Moulin de la Tuilerie, a country property of twenty-six acres near Gif-sur-Yvette, he laid out English lawns and herbaceous borders, a rock garden and waterfall. The Mill, within easy driving distance of Paris, rekindled something of his affection for Fort Belvedere. Both houses glowed with the retrieved treasures of his years as Prince of Wales and King: a Garter banner, royal portraits, a Welsh Guards drum, a clutter of jewelled boxes, the Chippendale table on which he had signed his Instrument of Abdication. He dressed his servants in royal livery. Lapped in domesticity, the Duke delighted to show off his command of

German and Spanish, even to startled guests who knew neither. He loved to reminisce with visitors from England: but not for too long, or the Duchess would briskly cut short the remembrance of things past. There were no regrets in those fading eyes: only happiness and pride.

In the drawing-rooms of Paris he was received with the deference once paid to his grandfather; and although age and failing health took their toll, neither seemed to touch that memorably handsome head or the simple courtesy of the *grand seigneur*. During brief but regular visits to England he stayed with his mother at Marlborough House; but both she and George VI went to the grave without receiving his wife. Queen Elizabeth II relented. She invited the Duke and Duchess to attend the dedication of a memorial to Queen Mary; she called on them when the Duke was receiving medical treatment in London; she and Prince Philip went to tea in the Bois during a State visit to Paris eleven days before his death from cancer of the throat.

His remains were flown to England, where they lay in state in St George's Chapel, Windsor. In the presence of his wife, a guest at Buckingham Palace, they were buried with the homage due to a King-Emperor. Then, and only then, was the most bitter of royal family feuds also laid to rest.

Edward, Prince
(1964–   )

Third son of Queen Elizabeth II and Prince Philip, Duke of Edinburgh. From Heatherdown, the preparatory school near Ascot, he followed his father and brothers to Gordonstoun, in Scotland. It had been popularly supposed that he was the most sensitive of the three brothers until, at the age of twenty, he gave his first television interview. He then revealed that the Prince of Wales had 'hated' his five years at windswept Gordonstoun; whereas he himself, it seemed, had cut rather a dash. 'Everybody thinks I was a proper little goody-good,' he said, 'but

Prince Edward: windsurfing at Cowes, 1980

they don't really know, do they? Just because I wasn't on punishment doesn't mean I was on the straight and narrow.' Prince Edward also declared his belief in corporal punishment. 'A beating or a thrashing, if used in the right context, is, I think, very valuable.'

On leaving Gordonstoun, he spent two terms as a junior housemaster at Wanganui Collegiate, New Zealand. He also became the first member of the royal family to walk round the world; as this feat took place at the South Pole it lasted no more than a few seconds.

Prince Edward is making his career in the Royal Marines, which he joined under the university cadet entrance scheme. He had already learned to fly and later spent five weeks at a commando centre. He will resume full-time training in 1986 on the completion of his University course. Before Prince Edward's arrival in Cambridge, there was a ritual display of indignation on the part of some undergraduates when they discovered through a leaked document that his three A levels were not of a particularly high grade. Both University and college, however, took the sensible view that an educated prince was better than a half-educated one. He was admitted to Jesus College – also the *alma mater* of Lord Snowdon (q.v.) – in the autumn of 1983. There he read Archeology and Anthropology before switching to History.

Uncomplicated and gregarious, he devotes his leisure to rugger and to the amateur stage, where he has produced his own much-applauded amateur revue. As Lord Butler, the Master of Trinity, used to say of the Prince of Wales when a Cambridge undergraduate: 'He should be encouraged to act. He will have to spend so much of his life as an actor.'

Elgar, Sir Edward
(1857–1934)

Master of the King's Musick. The son of a church organist in Worcester, he left school at fifteen and served a brief apprenticeship in a solicitor's office. He gave violin lessons in order to pay for his own advanced study of the instrument; but his skill as a composer was largely self-taught. A melodious flow of orchestral and chamber music, of songs and

Sir Edward Elgar

oratorios, had by the turn of the century established him in public favour as at least the equal of Sir Arthur Sullivan. *The Enigma Variations* (1899) and *The Dream of Gerontius* (1901) were followed in 1908 by the Symphony in A flat, the noblest in the history of English music. Three years later his Symphony in E flat, with its more restless themes, at first disturbed the audience. 'What's the matter with them?' the composer demanded. 'They sit there like a lot of stuffed pigs.'

Both Elgar and his music were welcomed at court through three reigns. He dedicated *Caractacus* to Queen Victoria and was commanded to conduct a concert at Windsor on her eightieth birthday. He adapted one of his *Pomp and Circumstance* marches to be sung at Edward VII's Coronation as *Land of Hope and Glory*. Having been knighted in 1904, he was made a member of the Order of Merit in George V's Coronation Honours of 1911: the only such distinction he valued. He wrote of the Royal Academy banquet in 1914: 'I went in, found they had *omitted* my O.M. and put me with a crowd of nobodies in the lowest place of all – the bottom table.' So he walked out and dined at his club off a herring.

On the death of Sir Walter Parratt in 1924, George V proposed that his office of Master of the King's Musick should remain unfilled; he had been similarly reluctant to appoint a successor to Alfred Austin (q.v.) as Poet Laureate. But the King and his advisers had second thoughts when Elgar protested that 'its suppression would have a very bad effect abroad where the effacement of the last shred of connection of the Court with the Art would not be understood.' The office went to the only possible candidate, himself; it has never since been allowed to lapse.

With his aristocratic features, military bearing and Edwardian elegance of dress, Sir Edward Elgar resembled the Duke of Connaught (q.v.). At heart, however, he despised the monarchy, or at least its trappings. 'Everything,' he wrote to a friend, 'seems so hopelessly and irredeemably *vulgar* at Court.' And in 1927: 'H.M. has offered me the wretched K.C.V.O. (!!!) which awful thing I must accept! Alas!' He was obliged to endure two further penances: a baronetcy in 1931 and the GCVO in 1933. He nevertheless did his duty as Master of the King's Musick. In 1929 he wrote a carol to celebrate George V's recovery from a grave illness; and in 1931 a *Nursery Suite* dedicated to the future Queen Elizabeth II and her sister Princess Margaret Rose.

'Rudyard Kipling translated into music,' was how Elgar's contemporary, Sir Charles Villiers Stanford, described *Land of Hope and Glory*. It remains the most popular of his melodies but does not truly reflect the composer's temperament. His was a troubled spirit that both scorned and craved worldly success; a genius that lay not in patriotic bombast but in darker and more latent themes.

No man owed more to the encouragement of his wife. She was Caroline Alice Roberts, the daughter of a major-general, whose family disapproved of the match. Neither before their marriage in 1889 nor after her death in 1920 did Elgar produce anything of substance.

Elizabeth II, Queen
(1926–   )

The elder daughter of the Duke and Duchess of York, later King George VI and Queen Elizabeth, she was born on 21 April 1926 at 17 Bruton Street, the London home of the Duchess's parents, the Earl and Countess of Strathmore. The house was destroyed by bombs during World War II and later rebuilt as a bank, where a plaque records the birth of the future Queen. The child's parents were then living at White Lodge, Richmond Park, but in the following year moved to 145 Piccadilly. In 1931 they acquired a country house: Royal Lodge, Windsor Great Park. Both residences were reassuringly near those of Princess Elizabeth's grandparents, King George V and Queen Mary, who melted with pleasure at her demure charm. A visitor to Sandringham described Lilibet at the age of one year and nine months:

'She perched on a little chair between the King and me, and the King gave her biscuits to eat and to feed his little dog with, the King chortling with little jokes with her – she just struggling with a few words, "Grandpa" and "Granny" and to everyone's amusement has just achieved addressing the very grand-looking Countess of Airlie as "Airlie". After a game of bricks on the floor with the young equerry Lord Claud Hamilton, she was fetched by her nurse, and made a perfectly sweet little curtsey to the King and Queen and then to the company as she departed.'

Later that year she accompanied her grandparents to Balmoral, where Winston Churchill was a fellow guest. 'There is no one here at all,' he wrote to his wife, 'except the family, the household and Princess Elizabeth – aged two. The latter is a character. She has an air of authority and reflectiveness astonishing in an infant.' Even in the nursery she was no stranger to royal duties. One morning at Windsor Castle, the officer commanding the guard strode across to where a pram stood, containing Princess Elizabeth: 'Permission to march off, please, Ma'am.' There was an inclination of a small bonneted head and a wave of a tiny paw. Nearly a hundred years earlier, the young Queen Victoria had emerged less well from just such an encounter. She wrote in her diary: 'Lord M. told me that he heard it had been remarked that I didn't bow to the Officer when the Escort changed; I thanked Lord Melbourne for telling me so, and I said I would take care and do so.'

Princess Elizabeth had a traditional upbringing. Her nanny was Mrs Knight, known as Alla, the daughter of a tenant farmer on Lord Strathmore's estate in Hertfordshire. She displayed the old-fashioned virtues of her breed: starchy discipline tempered by infinite kindness. There was a nurserymaid, too: Margaret MacDonald, known as Bobo, who was to continue in the Princess's service as dresser and devoted friend. They were joined by Marion Crawford (q.v.), the young nursery governess responsible for giving lessons to the six-year-old Lilibet and later to her sister, Margaret Rose, who was born in 1930. Crawfie, as she was known, at once noted Princess Elizabeth's passion for order, system and design. She wrote of her charges: 'The two little girls had their own way of dealing with their barley sugar. Margaret kept the whole lot in her small, hot hand and pushed it into her mouth. Lilibet, however, carefully sorted hers out on the table, large and small pieces together, and then ate them very daintily and methodically.' The elder Princess's obsession for tidiness at one time led her to hop out of bed several times a night to make sure that her shoes were quite straight, her clothes arranged just so. She was laughed out of the habit, but that early regard for order and routine has proved useful to the constitutional monarch.

Even for a Princess born out of direct line of succession to the throne, her education was far from exacting. At the age of ten she was spending only seven and a half hours a week in the schoolroom, although further periods were set aside for music, dancing and drawing. Queen Mary was disturbed to hear that such formative subjects as poetry, Bible reading and literature merited no more than half an hour each; she also urged more history and geography. But her granddaughter's education was not confined to what Crawfie taught her. She startled the Prime Minister one day with her greeting: 'I saw you in *Punch* this morning, Mr MacDonald, leading a flock of geese.'

The Abdication and her father's accession as King George VI unsettled all their lives. The family moved to Buckingham Palace, where they never quite recaptured the happiness of near-obscurity. Then came the war, and the two Princesses were first isolated in Scotland, then immured in a blacked-out Windsor Castle. The pace of Elizabeth's education quickened to match the duties that would one day fall to her as Sovereign. She crossed the river to Eton, where Henry Marten (q.v.) introduced her to constitutional history. She acquired another tutor in the Vicomtesse de Bellaigue, who not only instructed her in French, but also taught her history and literature in the language; Mme de Bellaigue's son, Geoffrey, became Surveyor of the Queen's Works of Art. For diversion there were tea parties given by the officers on guard and home-produced pantomimes, with Princess Elizabeth as a Prince Charming in tights; the King, however, insisted that the heir to the throne should wear nothing too short or unseemly. Queen Victoria had similarly instructed a *décolletée* granddaughter before going into dinner: 'A little rose in front, dear child, because of the footmen.'

Those who remembered the old Queen saw her regal qualities reflected in a great-great-granddaughter not yet sixteen. At her confirmation by the Archbishop of Canterbury in St George's Chapel, Lady Airlie (q.v.) noted that 'the carriage of her head was unequalled, and there was about her that indescribable something which Queen Victoria had.' Princess Elizabeth showed the same pride when, on her sixteenth birthday, she inspected the Grenadier Guards for the first time as their Colonel. It was an historic role. Her immediate predecessor had been the old Duke of Connaught (q.v.) whose godfather, the Duke of Wellington, was appointed Colonel of the Grenadiers in 1827. She assumed more active military duties in 1945 as a second subaltern in the Auxiliary Transport Service, learning to drive and maintain the heaviest military vehicles. Even in khaki she could not escape the past; her superior officer was Commandant Wellesley, descended from the Great Duke himself.

The Princess and Prince Philip of Greece (q.v.) had meanwhile fallen in love and wished to marry without delay. But the King was reluctant to lose a much-cherished daughter; there were political obstacles, too. The Prince, a serving officer in the Royal Navy, wanted to become a naturalized British subject at the very moment when the future of the Greek monarchy was to be submitted to a plebiscite. So a reluctant Princess Elizabeth was swept off with her parents and younger sister for a three-month tour of South Africa. She spent her twenty-first birthday in Cape Town and broadcast a moving message of dedication to the Imperial Commonwealth. Her heart remained elsewhere.

'There she goes,' the King remarked to Field Marshal Smuts, 'alone as usual, an extraordinary girl.'

Within two months of the family's return, she was allowed to announce her betrothal to Prince Philip. 'Anyone would think that she had travelled down from Scotland by herself,' the King said testily to a courtier one morning. The newspapers had not mentioned that her father was also on the train. There was another indication that the Princess had not yet achieved her complete freedom. The King, rightly deciding that his daughter ought now to have a private secretary, appointed a young man without either allowing his daughter to interview him or even troubling to do so himself. John Colville (q.v.) was in fact well qualified for the post by birth and experience. His mother was a lady-in-waiting to Queen Mary, and both his grandfathers had been at court. As for 'Jock' Colville himself, he had served King George v as a Page of Honour and three Prime Ministers as private secretary. But neither he nor the Princess had ever met since he saw her in her bath when she was six weeks old. Their reunion twenty-one years later fortunately turned out to be cordial.

In spite of the post-war austerity of 1947, the wedding in Westminster Abbey on 20 November recaptured both colour and pageantry. When it was realized an hour or two before the ceremony that the bride's pearl necklace was still on display with the other presents in St James's Palace, Colville demonstrated just how fast he could run. The wedding bouquet also went missing but was retrieved from a cooling cupboard. Princess Elizabeth, whom an indulgent Board of Trade had allowed an extra 100 clothing coupons, looked enchanting in white satin. Prince Philip, handsome and fair-haired, wore naval uniform and the newly bestowed star of the Order of the Garter; that morning he was also created Duke of Edinburgh, although too late for the title to be printed on the order of service. They spent their honeymoon first at Broadlands, the home of Lord and Lady Mountbatten (qq.v.), then at Birkhall, a few miles from Balmoral. 'Your leaving us has left a great blank

in our lives,' the King wrote, 'but do remember that your own home is still yours and do come back to it as much as and often as possible.'

Until 1949, Princess Elizabeth had no option. Without a London home of their own, she and her husband occupied a suite in Buckingham Palace, where their first child, Prince Charles, was born in November 1948. By August 1950, when she gave birth to Princess Anne, they had moved into Clarence House, a few hundred yards down the Mall. Those first years of marriage were not spent only in England. Prince Philip was able to resume his naval career with the Mediterranean Fleet and Princess Elizabeth to enjoy the carefree life of any sailor's family in Malta. Although the King's health continued to fluctuate, he seemed well enough for them to undertake a tour of Canada and the United States in October 1951 and to leave for East Africa, Australia and New Zealand three months later.

They got no further than Kenya. Early in the morning of 6 February 1952, King George vi died in his sleep at Sandringham. His daughter, who had spent the night watching wild animals at Treetops Hotel, a game reserve in the Aberdare Forest, at once left for home with her husband. It was as Queen Elizabeth II, a sad, slight figure in black, that she descended the aircraft steps at Heathrow and was received by her first Prime Minister, Winston Churchill.

She was not yet twenty-six, but already displayed the attitudes of a Sovereign. In the first months of the reign, an old court favourite asked her whether Churchill was treating her as Melbourne had treated the young Queen Victoria. 'Not at all,' she replied, 'I find him very obstinate.' One clash of wills was over the BBC's request to televise the Coronation of June 1953. Against the advice of the Prime Minister and the Cabinet, the Earl Marshal and the Archbishop of Canterbury, she insisted that her subjects had a right to join her in the most sacred ceremony of all. As a result, the service was seen by more than 20 million and heard by another 12 million. The ancient ritual unfolded with almost flawless dignity, although there was a moment of suspense when she dipped an old-fashioned pen in an old-fashioned inkpot, and it emerged dry; the second dip proved more rewarding. Richard Dimbleby (q.v.) clothed the occasion in a rich tapestry of words, but was shocked by the seedy appearance of the peers' benches after their occupants had left the Abbey: 'sandwich wrappings, sandwiches, morning newspapers, fruit peel, sweets and even empty miniature bottles.'

The youth and beauty of the Queen, extolled by an old and romantic Prime Minister, prompted some commentators to proclaim a second Elizabethan Age. Certainly it stirred the blood when in 1953–4 she became the first reigning Sovereign of any nationality to circumnavigate the globe; and in doing so, she scarcely ever set foot outside her own territory. Then came murmurings of discontent.

Some of her Scots subjects resented her being known as Elizabeth II in a kingdom where no Elizabeth I had ever reigned. South of the border, republicans called for the abolition of the monarchy; radicals for a more thrifty institution; Tory reformers for a Queen less identified with aristocratic conventions and a hidebound court. Of these three classes of critic, the last can claim most progress. Their standard bearer was the 2nd Lord Altrincham, who later renounced his peerage and is known as John Grigg. Reviled both for what he said and what he was wrongly supposed to have said, he has lived to see the abolition of presentation parties for debutantes and other quaint ceremonies.

Even when well-meant, much of that early criticism was cast in churlish language that cannot have failed to wound a woman doing her best in a role she had not sought. She showed no sign of it. Although the Queen smiles in public less easily than her mother, she has continued for thirty years and more to go about her duties with a serene self-confidence that evokes admiration and respect. In an age of increasing specializaton, no other woman in the world is required to display such diversity of talent. She is the annointed Sovereign, the senior civil servant, the Head of the Commonwealth. Nor, in the eyes of those who know her best, has she ever ceased to be the devoted wife and mother, the steadfast friend, the conscientious landowner.

The anthropologist who wishes to study tribal apotheosis need not go as far afield as the primitive peoples of Borneo or of Brazil. On the very edge of Pimlico he will find an hereditary chief invested, if not with divine right, at least with more than a touch of myth and mystery. It is true that the Queen reigns but no longer rules; the autocracy of Elizabeth I has given way to the parliamentary democracy of Elizabeth II. As Walter Bagehot put it: 'A Republic has insinuated itself beneath the folds of a Monarchy.' Yet the trappings of royal authority persist. The Queen drives to Westminster in a gilded coach and wears a diamond crown. She has at her command a Master of the Horse and a Mistress of the Robes, a Clerk of the Closet and a Yeoman Bed Hanger, a Lord High Almoner and a Poet Laureate, two Gold Sticks, a Serjeant Surgeon, several apothecaries and a coroner. Even her shopping list evokes an image of lordly profusion: she has granted her Royal Warrant to purveyors of shotguns and potted shrimps and soap; to manufacturers of angostura bitters and racing colours, lightning conductors and gold leaf; to window cleaners and harpsichord tuners, seedsmen and chiropodists.

Like all ancient creeds, monarchy cherishes its own arcane language in the most improbable circumstances. After the unseemly turmoil of a general election, the Court Circular announces that the Queen has been 'graciously pleased' to accept the resignation of a defeated Prime Minister; and that his successor has 'kissed hands' on appointment – as if he were a sixteenth-century Cecil decorously paying homage to an earlier Elizabeth. Ministers dependent on the ballot box still begin their letters to the Sovereign: 'With humble duty.' Buckingham Palace knows, as the Church of England has yet to learn, that to rewrite a litany in modish or populist language repels the faithful without seducing the agnostic.

The Church of which the Queen is Supreme Governor does, however, continue to pray for her with medieval regularity. As long ago as

1872, that sceptical scientist Francis Galton published a paper entitled 'Statistical Inquiries into Efficacy of Prayer.' He showed that in spite of such sustained supplications, the average age of death for English Sovereigns was 64.04, compared with 67.31 for the aristocracy and 70.22 for the gentry. Perhaps we should all pray harder. There is another practice which distinguishes even a constitutional monarchy from a republic. The Queen's subjects dream about her, and not only by night. Such unconscious tributes are less often paid to Presidents Reagan, Gorbachov and Mitterrand.

However little the forms of monarchy have changed, the Queen herself is the victim of a social as well as a political revolution. The Sovereign, it used to be thought, should be as protected from the common touch in public as in private, meeting only a handful of local grandees and a carefully rehearsed artisan or two. When Queen Victoria spent a day with Baron Ferdinand de Rothschild at Waddesdon Manor in 1888, she asked to have luncheon alone with her daughters, while her host ate with his other guests. George v was similarly advised to confine his sport in India to shooting tigers from the back of an elephant; to be seen splashing through a duck marsh in waders would diminish the respect of the Indian peoples for their King-Emperor.

Now the Queen goes on foot through the crowds, with here and there a little chat over the shopping basket; she has come to Coronation Street, and warmth of heart has displaced some of the magic of monarchy. Not everyone welcomes the change. Perhaps the way of life of a Sovereign should retain some element of mystery, of remoteness. If majesty descends to the market place, if she is to be here, there and everywhere, meeting her subjects on equal terms, only heredity separates a monarchy from a republic. Since Queen Victoria ascended the throne, that genetic lottery has given us a succession of prizes. The good princes and princesses have been crowned, the bad have died or abdicated or been born out of succession. That luck may not always continue (although it is

seemingly assured for at least one more reign). To expose the Sovereign to a perpetual public test is to challenge fate, to invite a day-to-day comparison between crowned head and elected politician; to initiate a competition in saloon-bar affability that may not always be won by the Lord's Annointed.

The day-to-day life of the Queen attracts both envy and pity. Certainly she is spared many of the discomforts and irritations of her subjects: the queue in the rain, the handle that comes off the suitcase, the cancelled train, the forgotten latchkey. She enjoys smooth transport, delicious food, exciting sport, smiling faces. She is positively enjoined to wear clothes of the utmost elegance. 'The consciousness of being well dressed,' an august lady confessed at the turn of the century, 'gives me an inward peace which religion could never bestow.' The Queen is always consulted, always humoured. During a State visit to France, she happened to mention to her host in the Louvre that she had never seen the Mona Lisa. A few minutes later, two attendants staggered in with the picture, which they exhibited to the Queen on bended knees.

There is another side to the coin. Here is part of the evidence given by her private secretary, Sir Michael Adeane (q.v.) to the House of Commons Select Committee on the Civil List:

'All these engagements are enjoyable – and there are many who would welcome the opportunity of attending them. But for the Queen, who can never enjoy them with the freedom of a holiday maker, the pleasure of attending them is bound to be tempered by the strain imposed on her as a public figure and by the knowledge that somebody is looking at her all the time and that she is being continually photographed, filmed and televised as well. The strain of a long day in a provincial town, taking a lively interest in everything, saying a kind word here and asking a question there, always smiling and acknowledging cheers when driving in her car, sometimes for hours, has to be experienced to be properly appreciated.'

Nor are the Queen's duties at an end when she returns from such a day. For she is also an official, highly respected and in some ways exceptionally privileged: nevertheless an official, who rarely has a complete holiday and who never retires. The precise limits of the royal prerogative wielded by that official are not to be found in the Statute Book. Bagehot claimed that the Sovereign, without consulting Parliament, could declare war on France for the conquest of Brittany and conclude peace by the sacrifice of Cornwall; make every man and woman in the kingdom a peer and every village a university; disband the Army and the Navy, dismiss the civil service and pardon all prisoners. Elizabeth II has put none of these powers to the test. She is the model constitutional Sovereign guided paradoxically by the doctrine that 'the Queen can do no wrong.' The dictum evokes a fantasy of royal licence unbounded and majestic misbehaviour unreproved. It has a drabber meaning: that although the Queen can do no wrong, her Ministers can. The Queen is permanent, Ministers are expendable. All acts of Government, in other words, are carried out in the name of the Sovereign; but the responsibility for them rests with Ministers dependent on a parliamentary majority. Conversely, the Sovereign must ultimately accept the advice of her Ministers on all matters of government policy. To reject it would be to provoke their resignation and a general election fought on the issue of Crown versus People.

While adhering punctiliously to this doctrine, the Queen has been at pains to shed certain prerogatives, the exercise of which could expose her to political controversy. Twice during her reign she has been obliged personally to choose a new Conservative Prime Minister from among rival claimants: on the resignation of Anthony Eden in 1957 and of Harold Macmillan in 1963. On both occasions she was without Ministerial advice: an outgoing Prime Minister cannot bind his Sovereign to his suggested choice of a successor, for at the very moment he resigns he ceases to bear parliamentary responsibility for that advice. Should such circumstances arise in future, the Conservative Party will present her with a single candidate elected by an agreed procedure, as is already the custom in the Labour Party. This has been designed to remove the Sovereign from the arena of political and personal rivalries. She will still have a duty to choose a Prime Minister acceptable to Parliament; but whether or not the *best* Prime Minister acceptable to Parliament will be the responsibility of others. The Sovereign will thus be spared the controversy that followed her choice of Lord Home rather than of Mr Butler in 1963. (see *Adeane, Sir Michael*)

What then remains to the Queen outside the bounds of Ministerial advice? Not power, but influence: the right to be consulted, the right to encourage, the right to warn. So that the Sovereign may be equipped to perform these constitutional duties, she receives a ceaseless flow of paper. There are minutes of Cabinet meetings, Ministerial submissions and memoranda, Foreign Office telegrams and despatches, copies of *Hansard*, reports from her Ministers and Governors-General in the Commonwealth overseas. Then there are the newspapers and a personal mail of well over a hundred letters a day. In that sense the Queen is never off duty.

There have been eight Prime Ministers during the present reign: Churchill, Eden, Macmillan, Home, Wilson, Heath, Callaghan and Thatcher. The first four were aristocrats, either by birth or marriage; the last four are of humbler origin. Those who suppose that the Queen is more at ease with one stratum than with another are mistaken; all are received with equal friendliness, though not friendship. From the elevation of the Sovereign, even Prime Ministers are much of a muchness. The Queen may discern a difference of function between a Lord Chamberlain and a footman, but scarcely any of social class. There is the same refreshing aloofness in her attitude to other trivia which disturb her subjects. It is said that Mrs Thatcher felt embarrassed at a public ceremony because her frock closely resembled that of the Queen. Afterwards, Downing Street discreetly asked the Palace whether there was any way in which the Prime Minister could know of the Queen's choice on such occasions. The reply was both

The Queen at her Birthday Parade, 1983

reassuring and dismissive: 'Do not worry. The Queen does not notice what other people are wearing.'

The Prime Minister of the day usually finds that the Queen is more interested in personalities than in policies: what an historian has called 'the endless adventure of governing men.' She is nevertheless impregnably well-informed on every aspect of government. Harold Wilson has declared: 'Any Prime Minister or other Minister who goes for audience not having read some of the Cabinet papers that he is saving for the weekend may well feel at a disadvantage.' That is not to imply a perpetual tension between the Sovereign and her advisers, a nagging challenge on this or that aspect of policy. To quote Bagehot, the greatest wisdom of a constitutional ruler lies in 'well-considered inaction.' But as the Queen's experience accumulates with the years, it would be a foolish Prime Minister who brushed aside her counsel.

A Dean of St Paul's Cathedral once asked the Queen what she could do if a Prime Minister submitted a name for an ecclesiastical appointment with which she was not happy. 'Nothing constitutionally,' she replied, 'but I can always say that I should like more information. That is an indication that the Prime Minister will not miss.' On at least two occasions in recent years the Queen has used this tactful technique when controversial names have been put forward for honours.

A flippant or evasive remark will evoke a Victorian response: she stares at the offender in silence. The Queen's rare display of anger is not always silent. During one of the Press campaigns which regularly erupt against the cost of the Royal Yacht *Britannia*, the Queen sent for the First Lord of the Admiralty. She did not ask him to sit down. He explained the faults in the original design, the need to install modern equipment, the humiliation if the vessel broke down. The Queen listened impassively. 'And who pays?' she asked. The Minister, thinking himself on firmer ground, replied with enthusiasm that it would of course be the Government, not the Queen. 'I see,' she said icily, 'you

pay and I get the blame.' He was then shown out.

Accusations of royal extravagance are a perennial irritant. It is never cheap to maintain a focus of national pride and reverence. As the wise Bagehot observed: 'There are arguments for not having a court, and there are arguments for having a splendid court; but there are no arguments for having a mean court.' One of the most persistent of critics, who complained that after twenty years the Queen Mother's Civil List had been raised from £70,000 to £95,000, omitted to add that his own parliamentary salary during the same period had more than quadrupled; or that a new car park for MPs at Westminster had cost £2½ million, more than twice the amount of the Queen's current Civil List. At the height of the controversy, the Duke of Bedford made his own memorable contribution: 'The royal family are very good value. What do they cost: a penny a month? a penny a day? When decimals come in, you won't even be able to pee for that.'

The Queen is also Head of the Commonwealth, a free association of nearly fifty independent States. It is an ingenious and civilized device by which Britain has exorcized the ghost of a no-longer fashionable empire. It also permits the Sovereign to remain Queen of some overseas territories and a welcome visitor to them all. To maintain touch with so many diverse nationalities and creeds, as she undoubtedly does, is a severe but heartening task. 'At home,' Elizabeth Longford has written, 'the Queen always has to be a senior civil servant. When abroad she can almost feel herself a Gloriana.' Yet this sometimes requires her to ignore if not to connive at much that is offensive to her British subjects: corruption, oppression, bloodshed.

What remains remarkable is how rarely the Queen has received conflicting advice from two of her Governments which possess equal constitutional rights. In 1964 her Canadian Ministers advised her not to cancel her visit to Quebec in the face of terrorist threats from the French-Canadian separatists. Although there were murmurs among her United Kingdom Ministers that she ought not to be exposed to such a danger, these misgivings were not pressed; the Queen, with characteristic courage, did visit Quebec and returned safely.

There was a tremor of a different sort when the Queen devoted her Christmas broadcast of 1983 not to any specifically Christian theme but to extolling 'the spirit of the Commonwealth' and in particular its economic role. The broadcast also included a televised conversation between the Queen and Mrs Gandhi. The Indian Prime Minister was to meet a tragic death within the year; but many of the Queen's British subjects felt that she was an inappropriate choice for the occasion. The Queen's Christmas broadcast of 1984 embraced the universal theme of the family and showed pictures of her grandchildren. It was received with rapture.

The Queen who belongs to all her subjects, irrespective of origin, creed and class, leads the private life of a rich and confident country landowner. Even as a child she was besotted by horses. Round the dome of 145 Piccadilly stood more than twenty of them, a foot high, made of wood and on wheels; each had to be fed and watered before the little Princess would go to bed. She turned Crawfie into a horse pulling a grocery cart; and when she was being taught to ride by Owen the groom, the King complained that he himself now counted as nothing in his daughter's life.

She grew up to be a skilled horsewoman; and such is her insistence on wasting no moment of the day, she has appeared for an unexpected Privy Council at Windsor wearing jodhpurs. The Queen's supposed attachment to racing is often misunderstood. Although she devotes a whole week of the year to Royal Ascot and attends a few other meetings, including the Derby, her interest lies largely in the breeding and performance of her own horses. The Queen is as knowledgeable as any trainer on pedigree and conformation. There may, however, be an element of exaggeration in a sporting sentiment attributed to her: 'If it were not for my Archbishop of Canterbury, I should be off in my

plane to Longchamps every Sunday.' The Queen names her own yearlings with the agility of a crossword addict. Thus a colt by Queen's Hussar out of Christchurch is called Church Parade; another by Halo out of Joking Apart becomes St Boniface, the patron saint of clowns. She delights in dogs, too; not only those bad-tempered corgis which disgruntled footmen seem forever to be carrying on and off aircraft of the Queen's Flight, but the black labradors which she trains as gundogs at Sandringham.

Not only in name does the Queen occupy four substantial houses. 'It is impossible to move a cushion from one chair to another,' a courtier has said, 'without her noticing it.' She cares for their works of art and has added to them with distinction. Sir Oliver Millar (q.v.), Surveyor of the Queen's Pictures, in a book notable for its absence of sycophancy, writes that her acquisitions have been the most fruitful and stimulating since the death of the Prince Consort in 1861. They include miniatures, portraits of the royal family and their servants, and a collection of works by modern artists: Graham Sutherland, Barbara Hepworth, L.S.Lowry, Roger de Grey, Ivon Hitchens. Australian painting is represented by William Dobell, Rex Batterbee, Russell Drysdale and Sydney Nolan. In 1962 the opening of the Queen's Gallery, reconstructed out of the bomb-damaged private chapel at Buckingham Palace, enabled the public to share her pride and pleasure in the royal treasures.

Although the Queen sometimes attends commemorative concerts and gala performances of opera and ballet, her favourite pastimes lie elsewhere. A Minister of the Crown who had been present on one such occasion and happened to be in attendance a few nights later, jauntily expressed the hope that she had 'got through it all right.' She replied sharply: 'Not so loud.' He likes to think that she was joking.

When another of her Ministers responsible for planning the Coronation of 1953 was congratulated on his stage management, he replied that he had been exceptionally fortunate in his leading lady – a remark which some thought in the worst of taste. But was he so very wrong?

The Queen is the current protagonist of a drama that stretches back to the dawn of history yet whose survival in a restive world can never be taken for granted. She has studied her role with professional care and invested it with dignity; she exemplifies both the duties of high office and the virtues of a happy family life. It is a calm, confident performance, as unaffectedly sincere after thirty-three years as it was in her youth.

Elizabeth, Queen Consort
of King George VI,
later Queen Elizabeth the Queen Mother
(1900–   )

The youngest and best-loved of Eminent Victorians was born in London, the ninth of the ten children of the 14th Earl of Strathmore and his wife, Nina Cecilia Cavendish-Bentinck. Lady Elizabeth Bowes-Lyon divided her childhood between St Paul's Walden Bury, a Queen Anne house in Hertfordshire, and Glamis Castle, the family seat in Scotland where nine centuries earlier King Duncan had spent his last troubled night as the guest of Lady Macbeth. Descended from that royal line, she can boast one of those rumbustious pedigrees not uncommon north of the border: a saga of brawls and battles, of rebellion and imprisonment and sudden death that has endowed her with strength and resilience.

Her upbringing at Glamis, for all its wide estates and rich soil, was never luxurious. An experienced old snob who yearly wended his way from castle to castle, described it as 'an average picknicky place: parlourmaids and that sort of thing.' The family creed was a simple Christianity buttressed by paternalism and local duty and love of the land. It is from Scotland rather than England, from the country rather than the town, that eighty years later the Queen Mother continues to draw inspiration. Not for her the hothouse seclusion that led Queen Mary

to exclaim at Badminton in old age: 'So *that's* what hay looks like!' Rather does she epitomize the convivial democracy of a Scottish Women's Rural Institute, less happy in pastel shades and ostrich feathers than in the stout shoes and tweeds of days on the hill.

A desultory education at the hands of governesses left Lady Elizabeth with a love of English poetry and a confident grasp of the French language. But even at Glamis she was not spared the realities of the Great War, which began on her fourteenth birthday. The castle became a military hospital whose patients long remembered the healing touch of her sympathy. Behind the cheer and comfort lay a private grief: the death in action of her brother Fergus, serving on the Western Front.

With the coming of peace she danced her way through the London season and was the prettiest of bridesmaids at the wedding of her friend Princess Mary to the future Earl of Harewood (qq.v.). Among her own suitors was the Princess's brother, the Duke of York, whom she met for the first time since childhood at a ball in Grosvenor Square. But her affection for that shy, frustrated young man did not at once turn to love; nor was she anxious to barter the freedom of a happy family circle for the stiff confines of King George V's court. The Press, however, was determined that she should be the next Queen of England. 'Chips' Channon (q.v.), a fellow guest of hers when staying with Lord Gage in the country, noted in his diary on 5 January 1923: 'The evening papers have announced her engagement to the Prince of Wales. So we all bowed and bobbed and teased her, calling her "Ma'am": I am not sure that she enjoyed it. It couldn't be true, but how delighted everyone would be! She certainly has something on her mind. . . . She is more gentle, lovely and exquisite than any woman alive, but this evening I thought her unhappy and distraite.'

Afterwards it emerged how uncomfortably near the mark her friends' mockery had been. The betrothal was announced of Lady Elizabeth Bowes-Lyon not to the Prince of Wales but to his younger brother, the Duke of York.

The Queen Mother in Venice, 1984

Channon's diary continues: 'I was so startled and almost fell out of bed when I read the Court Circular. . . . We have all hoped, waited, so long for this romance to prosper, that we had begun to despair that she would ever accept him. He has been the most ardent of wooers, and was apparently at St Paul's Walden on Sunday, when he at last proposed to her. He motored at once to Sandringham and the announcement is the result, the royalties allowing her no time to change her mind. He is the luckiest of men, and there's not a man in England today that doesn't envy him. The clubs are in gloom.'

King George V was delighted by the news. In a world of looming clouds, he wrote, 'this is the only gleam of sunshine.' A day or two before the wedding ceremony in Westminster Abbey, the former Prime Minister, Henry Asquith, was invited to a party at Buckingham Palace to see the presents. He does not seem to have enjoyed it: 'There were huge glass cases like you see in Bond St. shops, filled with jewels and every kind of gilt and silver ware: not a thing did I see that I would have cared to have or to give. The poor little bride, everyone says is full of charm and stood in a row with the King and Queen and the bridegroom, and was completely over-shadowed.' It must have been the last time that 'the poor little bride' was overshadowed, whether as Duchess of York, Queen Consort or Queen Mother. The King adored her at sight. 'The better I know and the more I see of your dear little wife,' he wrote to his son from Balmoral soon after the wedding, 'the more charming I think she is and everyone fell in love with her here.' The family marvelled at the response of that quarterdeck martinet when she appeared a minute or two late for a meal, and apologized. 'We must,' he said, 'have sat down a little early today.'

The BBC wanted to broadcast the marriage service from the Abbey on 26 April 1923, the first time for more than five centuries that a King's son had wed there; but the Chapter thought it would be irreverent and refused permission. After a wedding breakfast of eight courses at Buckingham Palace, the Duke and Duchess of York spent their honeymoon first at Polesden Lacey, lent to them by Mrs Ronald Greville (q.v.), then at Glamis, where the bride unromantically developed whooping cough. Their first home was White Lodge, Richmond Park, today the Royal Ballet School. It was here that Queen Mary's parents, the Duke and Duchess of Teck, had lived for many years, and where the future King Edward VIII was born. The house, however, had little more to offer a newly married couple than an historic past. It was large and expensive to maintain; too near London for privacy, too far for ease of travel. But three years went by before Lord Lee of Fareham, who had earlier given Chequers to the nation, could be persuaded to buy the lease. In 1927 the Yorks moved into their first London house, 145 Piccadilly, and in 1931 the King

offered them the Royal Lodge, in Windsor Great Park, originally a *cottage orné* of George IV: the Fort Belvedere, as it were, of that voluptuous monarch.

Except for a world tour in HMS *Renown* that occupied the first six months of 1927, these were years of content. Princess Elizabeth was born in April 1926 at the London house of the Duchess's parents; Princess Margaret Rose in August 1930 at Glamis. A programme of official engagements at home and occasional excursions abroad was punctuated by spacious holidays at Balmoral and Sandringham, where the Duke could perfect his shooting and the Duchess acquire skill with a salmon rod. As if by some miraculous reprieve, the Duke's stammer began to yield to the treatment of Lionel Logue (q.v.); this in turn helped him tame his virulent temper and so lighten the burden borne by his wife.

The death of King George V in January 1936 deprived the Duchess of a wise and understanding counsellor. 'I miss him dreadfully,' she wrote. 'Unlike his own children I was never afraid of him, and in all the twelve years of his having me as a daughter-in-law he never spoke one unkind or abrupt word to me, and was always ready to listen and give advice on one's own silly little affairs. He was so kind and dependable. And when he was in the mood, he could be deliciously funny too!' There was a more dejected side to the old King's nature, induced by the conduct of the Prince of Wales. During convalescence from a serious illness in 1929, he had more than once confided to other members of his family that his eldest son would never succeed to the throne: a puzzling conjecture that at the time could be put down to low spirits. Six years later, he broadcast his fears more widely. A lady-in-waiting heard him say: 'I pray to God that my eldest son will never marry and have children, and that nothing will come between Bertie and Lilibet and the throne.' And to his last Prime Minister, Baldwin, he said: 'After I am dead, the boy will ruin himself in twelve months.'

If the Duchess of York remembered those chilly valedictions at the outset of the new reign, she seems to have brushed them aside; nor did her husband brood over his fate as Heir Presumptive. The Prince of Wales had already confounded one of his father's prophecies by being proclaimed Edward VIII; and at forty-one he was young enough to marry, have children and thus spare his diffident younger brother the succession. In January 1936, none dared imagine that before the year was out, the Duke and Duchess of York would have become King George VI and Queen Elizabeth; but then none suspected that the new Sovereign, for all his past caprice, would 'ruin himself in twelve months.'

The course of King Edward VIII's love for Mrs Simpson bears only obliquely on the story of Queen Elizabeth the Queen Mother, although its outcome was to change her life. The two women met no more than half a dozen times in forty years, and neither chooses to recall the exact circumstances. One day Mrs Simpson was brought over to Royal Lodge by the then Prince of Wales when her unsolicited advice on how to improve the view failed to melt her green-fingered hosts. Her desire to please was again regarded as patronizing when in the autumn of 1936 she received the Duke and Duchess at Balmoral as if she were already its chatelaine.

Between these two encounters, Mrs Simpson, as yet undivorced from her current husband, was an unpaired guest at a much-publicized dinner given by King Edward VIII in St James's Palace on 9 July 1936. He also included the Duke and Duchess in the party: a gesture, it may be thought, more of defiance than of hospitality. Mrs Simpson noted that the Yorks were cool and remote. Another guest, Winston Churchill, also felt a chill of displeasure that evening when he spoke of King George IV's secret marriage to Mrs Fitzherbert. The Duchess said: 'That was a long time ago.' Churchill persisted with his mischief. Aware that their host was about to travel abroad incognito with Mrs Simpson as Duke of Lancaster, he dwelt on the conflict between the Houses of York and Lancaster during the Wars of the Roses. The Duchess did not yield: 'That was a *very* long time ago.'

The distaste of the Duke and Duchess of York

for the King's romance turned to despair when they learned in October of his determination to marry Mrs Simpson, even if it cost him his throne. From then until the Abdication eight weeks later, no plea could touch that closed mind. (See *Edward VIII, King,* and *George VI, King.*) On 11 December 1936, Edward VIII was succeeded by his brother the Duke of York, who on the following day addressed his Accession Council and was proclaimed King George VI. Throughout this ordeal the new Sovereign was denied the presence and encouragement of his Consort; Queen Elizabeth was confined to bed with influenza. Neither drew much comfort from a jaunty telegram which the Duke of Windsor despatched from France during his first hours of exile: 'Have had good crossing. Glad to hear this morning's ceremony went off so well. Hope Elizabeth better. Best love and best of luck to you both. David.'

On 14 December, the King's forty-first birthday, he made the first of those chivalrous gestures that were to punctuate his reign. He appointed the Queen to be a Lady of the Garter.

It has often been surmised that Queen Elizabeth ever afterwards maintained an implacable hostility to the Duke and Duchess of Windsor: the Duke for his selfish dereliction of duty, the Duchess for having supposedly lured the golden-headed Prince Charming from his throne. Certainly neither the King nor the Queen discouraged the Government's decision to withhold from the newly married Duchess of Windsor the style of Royal Highness borne by her husband from birth. Nor did the Queen wish to see them welcomed back to England in any capacity that might erode her own husband's slowly won confidence. Neville Chamberlain, who succeeded Baldwin as Prime Minister in May 1937, suggested that the Duke might in time come home to resume a share of the royal family's public engagements. The King agreed in principle, although doubting whether November 1938, the date favoured by the Duke, might not be too soon. The Queen, however, rejected the plan out of hand.

Walter Monckton (q.v.), the Duke of

Windsor's confidant, offered one explanation: 'I felt then, as always, that she naturally thought that she must be on her guard because the Duke of Windsor, to whom the other brothers had always looked up, was an attractive, vital creature who might be the rallying point for any who might be critical of the new King who was less superficially endowed with the arts and graces that please.' Monckton's somewhat theatrical view of royal relationships was surely of less concern to the Queen than the strain which Edward VIII's defection had imposed on her husband's nervous temperament and delicate physique. George VI, who by choice would have been no more than a conscientious country gentleman, had since youth painfully learned to master the royal arts of ceremonial and affability. But he had no experience of the statecraft demanded of a constitutional monarch: that he was obliged to acquire from scratch the day he ascended the throne. How unfeeling it would have been of his wife had she not resented the cause of the intolerable burden he bore; or, as the years went by, grieved over his dwindling reserves of strength and untimely death.

So it was not until the outbreak of war in September 1939 that the Windsors returned to England from France. Even then, such warmth of welcome they received came not from the King and Queen but from Winston Churchill, by now First Lord of the Admiralty. Although the King saw his brother briefly before he was packed off abroad in a minor military appointment, the Queen refused; nor would either receive the Duchess of Windsor. Queen Elizabeth's barrier of reserve was not lowered until as Queen Mother she greeted the Duchess at the dedication of a memorial to Queen Mary in 1967. Five years later she murmured words of sympathy to her at the Duke's funeral at Windsor. Thereafter, on the few occasions Queen Elizabeth has been to Paris, she has always sent flowers and a kind message to the ailing Duchess.

Meanwhile the King and Queen were crowned in Westminster Abbey on 12 May 1937: a service of dedication that erased many unhappy memories of the previous reign. At the

moment Queen Elizabeth was crowned as Consort, Churchill turned to his wife, his eyes full of tears. 'You were right,' he said. 'I see now that the "other one" wouldn't have done.'

Throughout World War II, the Queen symbolized both defiant resolve and the gentler gifts of sympathy and encouragement. When the German invasion seemed imminent in the summer of 1940, she had herself taught how to fire a revolver. No less characteristically, she refused to wear the unbecoming uniforms of the Women's Services; she would go down fighting in powder blue. With the King, she endured the enemy Blitz on London, driving out again and again to comfort the victims. After the first of the nine air raids that damaged Buckingham Palace, she said: 'I'm glad we've been bombed. It makes me feel I can look the East End in the face.' Her two daughters remained in the comparative safety of Windsor. She scorned all offers of a temporary home for them overseas. 'The children won't leave without me,' she explained, 'I won't leave without the King, and the King will never leave.' She could act swiftly and decisively when the occasion demanded. Hearing that the Duke of Wellington had gone abroad with his regiment leaving the treasures of Apsley House unprotected from air raids, she ordered the most valuable of them to be stored at Windsor.

Within the restrictions of wartime rationing, the Queen continued to entertain. Sir John Reith, the father-figure of the BBC, was among those bidden to dine at the Palace one night, wearing day clothes. He ate cold jellied soup, ham mousse and cold chicken, an ice with strawberries and cream. At 10 o'clock, when a tea tray appeared, the Queen poured out and handed round the cups herself. Mrs Roosevelt, wife of the American President, came to stay for a few days in 1942, impressed by sparse meals served on silver plate. She occupied a huge bedroom heated only by a small electric fire, its windows boarded up after the bombing. She returned to the United States with a warm heart and a streaming cold. Winston Churchill was a regular visitor. The Queen soon healed any lingering differences. 'We look forward to the future battles,' she wrote to Mrs Churchill after the Africa campaign of 1943, 'with the comfortable feeling that we've got the right man as Prime Minister.' And one day, Queen Elizabeth likes to recall, he arrived at the Palace proclaiming: 'I bring you victory.'

It was indeed peace . . . of a sort. That united little family was once more able to recapture the life and laughter of carefree years in Royal Lodge and 145 Piccadilly; to spend holidays together at Balmoral and Sandringham; to sustain each other through a gruelling tour of South Africa. There followed the bitter-sweet joy of losing Princess Elizabeth in marriage and the birth of two grandchildren. But the King, beset by the political cares of the post-war world, never regained his full strength. In February 1952, after three years of almost continuous discomfort and ill health, he died.

Beyond the reach of comfort, Queen Elizabeth withdrew from all but her closest family and friends. It was feared she might remain in seclusion for the rest of her life. Then Edith Sitwell sent the widowed Queen a copy of her own anthology, entitled *A Book of Flowers*. Queen Elizabeth replied from Scotland in a letter of haunting pathos and renewed hope:

'It is giving me the greatest pleasure, and I took it out with me, and I started to read it, sitting by the river, and it was a day when one felt engulfed by great black clouds of unhappiness and misery, and I found a sort of peace stealing round my heart as I read such lovely poems and heavenly words.

'I found a hope in George Herbert's poem –

Who would have thought that my shrivel'd heart
Could have recovered greenness? It was gone
Quite under ground.

'And I thought how small and selfish is sorrow. But it bangs one about until one is senseless and I can never thank you enough for giving me such a delicious book wherein I found so much beauty and hope, quite suddenly one day by the river.'

Her spirits revived, and with them a return to public service. She assumed a role never before seen in a Queen Dowager. The nation was familiar with the shy, starchy benevolence of Queen Mary; some could still recall the ageless beauty and impulsive kindness of Queen Alexandra. But with the deaths of their husbands, those two widows all but disappeared into private life. Queen Elizabeth the Queen Mother, by contrast, has for more than thirty years continued to carry out a calendar of engagements hardly less full than that of the Sovereign herself. There are in all more than three hundred institutions which have received her patronage; on each of them she could well pass a *viva-voce* examination. And although she has now retired from an occasional old favourite such as London University, she has acquired others: the office of Lord Warden of the Cinque Ports, for instance, which she wears as gaily as a feather in her hat.

The Queen Mother is a most polished performer, with a sense of timing and a command of expression and gesture which any actress must envy. Those who line her path are drawn into a radiant conspiracy; those who hear her speak on public occasions are imbued with a sober idealism; those to whom she talks more intimately feel that never before have *they* sparkled to such advantage. Yet it is a display of interest and concern untinged by cynicism. She likes people. She has a Whiggish regard for the rights of the individual and a cautious mistrust of the system. 'One cannot expect much mother-love from an incubator,' the late Lord Samuel used to observe. The Queen Mother would agree with him, devoting time and ingenuity to the personal problems of others, to cushioning the impact of a bureaucratic State on those who cannot help themselves.

Of her own welfare and comfort she takes a more cavalier view. Neither ailments nor heartaches are allowed to interfere with her public duties. 'These things,' she told a Foreign Secretary's wife when talking of children who faint in church, 'are largely of the mind.' Having been ordered into hospital one evening for an investigation, she insisted on first carrying out a long-arranged meeting with the Women's Voluntary Service. Nobody at the reception suspected for a moment that their most vivacious guest would within an hour or two knowingly face the prospect of the surgeon's knife or worse. That is courage. She finds humour, too, in her own misfortunes. 'Of course,' she said when recovering from an operation, 'the word *comfortable* has a different meaning to the surgeon and to the patient.' Day-to-day setbacks evoke the same calm reaction. When Princess Elizabeth's tiara broke on the morning of her wedding, the Queen Mother quelled any sense of panic. 'We have two hours,' she said, 'and more than one tiara.'

Giving so much to duty, Queen Elizabeth regards her private life as her own. No member of the royal family can expect complete relief from pursuit and scrutiny. But the Queen Mother is spared the grosser intrusions of camera and notebook during evenings at the theatre or ballet, fishing or picnicking in Scotland, tramping National Hunt racecourses in every caprice of winter weather. It was at Kempton Park that she drew a subtle distinction between her public and private lives. One of her party, wanting to look at a televised football match, switched on the set in the stewards' box just in time to hear the crowd singing the National Anthem. 'Oh, do turn it off,' the Queen Mother said. 'It is so embarrassing unless one is there – like hearing the Lord's Prayer when playing canasta.' She did, however, once relieve public solemnity with a teasing allusion to her favourite sport. Opening the new British Library of Political and Economic Science, she borrowed a quotation from John Ruskin: 'What do we, as a nation, care about books? How much do you think we spend altogether on our libraries, public or private, as compared with what we spend on horses?'

The Queen Mother is in fact a discerning but unpredictable reader, who first introduced Lord Halifax to *Mein Kampf* (he had then been Foreign Secretary for two years) and Winston Churchill to Koestler's *Darkness at Noon*. In return the Prime Minister sent her Fowler's *Modern English Usage*; it had, he explained, liberated him from many errors and doubts. She

likes poetry and the lighter classics and anything written by her friends. When at the age of ninety-three P.G. Wodehouse received a knighthood, the Queen Mother offered to fly the Atlantic to bestow the accolade; but he died a few weeks later.

A sure but eclectic taste governs her private collection of pictures. There is Monet's *The Rock* and Sisley's *The Seine near St Cloud*; a Matthew Smith flower piece and a Paul Nash landscape; a Drysdale and a Nolan from Australia. She has a special affection for Sickert's portrait of King George V with his racing manager, Major Fetherstonhaugh (q.v.). She has herself been painted many times and displays an unflattering Graham Sutherland and a scarcely recognizable Augustus John. 'Mr John is quite cross with me,' she told a friend during one of his innumerable sittings, 'because I have been away on holiday and changed colour.' Not even regular refreshment with brandy could revive the artist's genius; and the composition, although hung in Queen Elizabeth's London drawing-room, remains unfinished.

She occupies four substantial residences: Clarence House, a few hundred yards from Buckingham Palace; Royal Lodge, Windsor; Birkhall, near Balmoral; and the Castle of Mey, on the Pentland Firth, a haven of solitude rescued from ruin. Throughout the year, each in turn comes alive to greet Queen Elizabeth and her friends with firelight and flowers, with mousse and Mosel. In one she has performed her duties as a Counsellor of State with a robust self-confidence that in its day sustained the monarchy itself; in another she has persuaded a lame but game Lord Chancellor to throw away his sticks and dance the night through.

There we may leave that evergreen enchantress, with her warmth and gaiety of spirit; her all-embracing sympathies; her quizzical tilt of the head and self-deprecating smile; her pride in having borne and brought up a Sovereign of rare distinction; her calm enjoyment of being in every sense the Queen Mother.

Esher, Reginald Brett, 2nd Viscount
(1852–1930)

Deputy Constable, later Constable, of Windsor Castle. The son of an ambitious lawyer who rose to be Master of the Rolls and was ennobled in 1885, he was educated at Eton and Trinity College, Cambridge, where he acquired patrician tastes. He served as private secretary to Lord Hartington, later 8th Duke of Devonshire, then spent five years as a Liberal MP. In 1895 the Prime Minister, his Eton friend Lord Rosebery, gave him the coveted post of Secretary of the Office of Works, which carried responsibility for the royal palaces. He thus won the personal esteem of Queen Victoria. In 1901 King Edward VII appointed him Deputy Constable and Lieutenant Governor of Windsor Castle. There he rescued the royal archives from forty years of neglect and published an admirable edition of Queen Victoria's letters.

Lord Esher's ability and influence are to be measured not by the offices he held but by those he refused at the hands of successive Prime Ministers. Salisbury urged him to govern Cape Colony; Balfour invited him to be Secretary of State for War; Campbell-Bannerman proposed that he should be Viceroy of India. He preferred the self-effacing role of *éminence grise*, although he did agree to preside over the important War Office Reconstruction Committee of 1904.

As the confidant of Edward VII, with whom he would discuss the affairs of the day over breakfast at Buckingham Palace, Esher expected to become a no less indispensable adviser to George V. At first the new King did consult him on such burdensome constitutional problems as the Parliament Bill and Home Rule for Ireland. But his ingratiating ways did not please a monarch brought up in the Royal Navy; Professor Harold Laski was later to express wonder that a man of Esher's obvious capacity could live for some forty years in a state of constant genuflexion. Esher retained his minor offices at Windsor, but in place of statecraft had to be content with running little errands for the Queen: binding up her letters, matching the exact shade of silk for the walls of a picture gallery, seeking an elegant coal scuttle. He would flatter her shamelessly. 'If you were not Queen and came into a room,' he said, 'everyone would ask who you were.' Queen Mary replied that her mother used to say the same.

During the Great War, Esher put on a uniform that some suspected to be of his own design and flitted across the Channel on confidential missions to the French Government and Army. He asked for the rank of lieutenant-general but his request was turned down. In 1918 he wrote unkindly of his old colleagues at court: 'It was a Rip Van Winkle appearance upon the scene. Either the world has stopped still or Buckingham Palace remains unchanged. The same routine. A life made up of nothings – yet a busy scene. Constant telephone messages about trivialities.' In 1922 he took part in discussions at the League of Nations on the limitation of armaments and was sworn of the Privy Council. He is said to have refused an earldom.

In spite of his capacity for negotiation, even intrigue, Esher was at heart a romantic. When entertaining members of the royal family he would remove finger-bowls from the table lest some guest of unsuspected Jacobite sympathies might be tempted to drink to the 'King over the

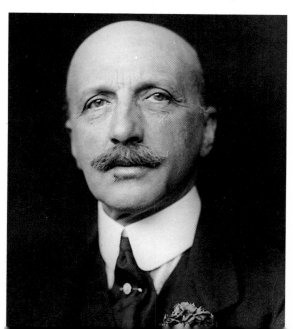

Lord Esher

Water.' And although he enjoyed more than half a century of marriage, it was his five years at Eton which lit a lifelong glow in his heart.

Farquhar, Horace, 1st Earl
(1844–1923)

Lord Steward of the Household and friend of the royal family. Descended from Sir Walter Farquhar, physician to the Prince Regent, he was well connected. One cousin married Charles Grey, Queen Victoria's private secretary, another Evelyn Ashley, the grandfather of Edwina Lady Mountbatten (q.v.).

Beginning his career in a Government office, Horace Farquhar worked for a firm of India merchants, then joined the banking house of Sir Samuel Scott, Bart & Co and married the widow of a partner. He made himself invaluable to the bank by persuading the Earl of Fife to invest considerable sums in its care. His own money he used astutely both to entertain the eminent and to contribute to political party funds. He was created a baronet in 1892, a baron in 1896, a viscount in 1917 and an earl in 1922. He also received a Privy Counsellorship and a constellation of stars on his breast. At no time did his record of public service alone seem to justify this cornucopia. He himself was not at all surprised to receive a peerage after only three years as a Conservative MP; he privately confessed that he had subscribed more than 'the accepted tariff.'

Farquhar had meanwhile been brought into the royal family circle by the Duke of Fife, as his friend became on marrying in 1889 Princess Louise (qq.v.), the eldest daughter of the Prince of Wales. On the death of Queen Victoria, Edward VII appointed Farquhar Master of the Household. Attendance at court did not require him to abandon either his banking business or his even more adventurous operations on the stock exchange. In 1907 he was at the centre of a scandal concerning a Siberian gold-mining company. After he had assembled an impressive board of directors that included Lord Knollys, the King's Private Secretary, and Lord Howe, the Queen's Lord Chamberlain, the shares soared, then fell with a rattle. Many investors lost money, but Farquhar was said to have netted £70,000.

If the future King George V knew of the episode, it did not affect his regard for Farquhar, a Norfolk neighbour with whom he had shot for the past twenty years. On ascending the throne in 1910 he reappointed him to be a Lord-in-Waiting, and on the day he was crowned accepted from him a portrait of the late King. Farquhar was always giving imaginative little presents. Even young Prince Henry, the future Duke of Gloucester (q.v.), received 'a nice box of soldiers with tents, both red and white.' The war was no curb to his opulence, and in 1915 the Prime Minister, H.H.Asquith, was shocked to be offered 'a regular banquet of many courses, of which I only partook of about two.'

In 1915 Asquith made him Lord Steward of the Household, at that time a political appointment. Farquhar held the same office under Lloyd George in 1919–22. Genial and open-handed, he was more splendidly housed than were most members of the royal family. There was Castle Rising, in Norfolk, which he leased from the King; White Lodge, Richmond Park, Queen Mary's old house; and No. 7 Grosvenor Square, where at a post-war ball Lady Elizabeth Bowes-Lyon met Prince Albert, Duke of York, for the first time since a children's party in 1905. His resources seemed inexhaustible.

Already, however, there were whispers of his involvement in the sale of honours by both the Conservatives and the Lloyd George Liberals. In 1923, when called upon as treasurer of the Conservative Party to account for large sums from more reputable sources, Farquhar could neither produce the money nor offer a satisfactory explanation of its disappearance. The new Prime Minister, Bonar Law, charitably put it down to Farquhar's increasing mental confusion, but nevertheless dismissed him as treasurer. The King gave his old friend the benefit of every doubt, continued to dine in Grosvenor Square, and visited him on his deathbed later that year.

Farquhar's Will was long and grandiose, his bequests many and generous, as befitted an estate provisionally sworn at £400,000 in the currency of 1923. The King was left two Louis Quatorze castors, together with anything he cared to choose from the contents of Castle Rising; the Queen, a Louis Seize commode, together with the contents of White Lodge. For Queen Alexandra there was a *sang de boeuf* vase, and for Princess Victoria two Dresden quails. The family of Farquhar's friend and business partner, the Duke of Fife, who had died in 1912, were remembered with especial bounty. The Duke's widow had been well provided for by her rich husband, so was left only two or three *objets d'art*. Her two children, both daughters, fared better. Princess Maud was to receive a diamond necklace as well as £50,000, unless she had already married, when the same sum would go to her husband. Princess Arthur of Connaught was also to have a diamond necklace, together with the contents of No. 7 Grosvenor Square and the residue of Farquhar's property not otherwise bequeathed. Nor were friends of lesser rank forgotten. Forty-eight of them, their names a roll-call of the aristocracy, were each to receive £200 with which to buy a memento. Among them were the King's two private secretaries Stamfordham and Wigram (qq.v.); Wigram was to have an additional £3,000.

Then came the most astonishing dénouement. The fortune made by banking and on the Stock Exchange; the proceeds of his philanthropic enterprises on behalf of Lloyd George and the Conservative Party (if indeed they had failed to reach their intended destinations); those lavishly bequeathed riches, those splendidly furnished houses: all were engulfed by huge and unsuspected debts. Rumour had it that Farquhar, always a patron of the stage, had invested recklessly in the theatres of London and Paris at a time of depressed conditions. Whether by speculation or extravagance, the net value of his estate was nil. Not one of his legatees received so much as a silver matchbox or a penny piece.

Even that was not the end of the matter. It

Horace, by Spy

emerged in the following year that Farquhar's trusteeship of the Fife estates had been exercised as irresponsibly as his guardianship of Conservative funds, and that £80,000 of trust money had disappeared. The law, unsentimental in such matters, required his co-trustee, the Duchess of Fife, to refund the sum.

Fermoy, Ruth, Lady
(1908–   )

The maternal grandmother of the Princess of Wales. She was married in 1931 to the 4th Baron Fermoy, of the ancient Irish family of Roche. One of Queen Mary's first thoughts on leaving the deathbed of her husband King George v was to inquire about Lady Fermoy's new-born baby who in 1954 was married to Viscount Althorp, later 8th Earl Spencer (q.v.).

Ruth Fermoy, a pianist of professional accomplishment, founded the King's Lynn Festival in 1951, remaining its chairman and principal fund-raiser for the next quarter of a century. From 1956 she has been a lady-in-waiting to Queen Elizabeth the Queen Mother, an assiduous patron of the festival.

Fetherstonhaugh, Major F.H.W.
(1858–1931)

Racing manager to King George v, 1922–31. He is immortalized in the portrait which Sickert painted of him with the King. Based on a newspaper photograph taken at the Grand National in 1927, it depicts two gloomy faces in billycock hats. Queen Elizabeth the Queen Mother, who owns the picture, has commented: 'You can see that *they* didn't back the winner.'

Under Fetherstonhaugh's management, the King won his only classic race, when the bay filly Scuttle took the One Thousand Guineas in 1928.

After Fetherstonhaugh's death in 1931, his widow took over the management of the breeding stud, which was divided between Sandringham and Hampton Court. She also looked after the King's betting transactions. His wagers became less adventurous with the years. Before coming to the throne, he would sometimes risk hundreds of pounds on a race. In 1924 he put no more than £1 on Master Robert, who won the Grand National at 25 to 1. The King clung to the comforting illusion that his sparse winnings were enough to subsidize his stamp collection.

Fielden, Air Vice-Marshal Sir Edward
(1903–1976)

First Captain of the King's Flight 1936–52, of the Queen's Flight 1952–62 and Senior Air Equerry 1962–69. The son of a doctor and educated at Malvern College, he joined the RAF in 1924 and was awarded the Air Force Cross. In 1929 the Prince of Wales, later King Edward VIII, selected him as instructor and personal pilot for his Gipsy Moth light aircraft. This innovation in royal transport aroused widespread anxiety not least in King George v, who detested those noisy machines and refused ever to take to the air.

In January 1936 the new King flew from Sandringham to London for his Accession Council and six months later appointed Fielden to be Captain of the King's Flight. King George VI renewed the appointment after the Abdication, as did Queen Elizabeth II in 1952.

During the war Fielden won the Distinguished Flying Cross for ferrying our secret agents in and out of enemy-occupied France. From one such mission he brought back a bottle of French wine of the 1941 vintage. This the King served to the Prime Minister, Winston Churchill, at one of their weekly lunches, teasing his guest by refusing to say how he had come by it.

Fielden's role after the war was largely administrative. Known inappropriately as 'Mouse', he was exuberant, warm-hearted and the best of company. But in pursuit of swifter and safer royal travel he could be authoritative, abrasive and cunning. He was feared in Whitehall, where he would not hesitate to beard the Chief of Air Staff in his efforts to prise more up-to-date machines for the RAF. 'Always deal with the organ-grinder,' he used to say, 'not with the monkey.' He was equally sharp with those who urged him to recruit men of expensive education and polished manners to the Queen's Flight. 'I would rather arrive on time with a sergeant-pilot,' he replied, 'than late with an Old Etonian.'

'Mouse' Fielden, 1932

Fife, Alexander Duff, 6th Earl and 1st Duke of (1849–1912)

The son of the 5th Earl of Fife, a Scottish landowner of independent mind who on sporting expeditions would invariably take with him what looked like a pair of telescopes; one was full of brandy, the other of whisky.

Lord Macduff, as he was known until succeeding to the earldom in 1879, sat for five years as Liberal MP and had a prosperous career as a financier. He was a founder and vice-president of the Chartered Company of South Africa and engaged in other enterprises with his friend Lord Farquhar (q.v.). Fife owned fourteen country houses and more than 100,000 acres, though not one in the county from which his title derived. In 1889, on his betrothal to Princess Louise (q.v.), eldest daughter of the future King Edward VII, Queen Victoria described him as 'immensely rich.' Before the wedding she created him Duke of Fife, although with some reluctance. Conceited and sometimes roughly spoken, he is thought to have taken advantage of a marriage that brought him so close to the throne.

On 13 December 1911, Fife, his wife and their two daughters Princess Alexandra and Princess Maud (qq.v.) were shipwrecked off the coast of Morocco while on their way to Egypt. The superstitious noted that the vessel in which they were travelling was the P & O liner *Delhi*; and that she foundered the very day after King George V had proclaimed Delhi the new capital of India. By their own wish, the Fife family were among the last of the passengers to leave the doomed ship. They jumped into a small boat personally commanded by Rear-Admiral Christopher Cradock, from HMS *Edinburgh*; and when it overturned, he carried them through the waves and surf to the rocky shore. For this courageous performance he was made KCVO by the Duchess's brother, King George V.

Having recovered from their ordeal, the Fifes left for Gibraltar in HMS *Hampshire* (the cruiser which in 1916 went down with Lord Kitchener on her way to Russia), then resumed their journey to Egypt. There the duke caught a chill which turned to pneumonia. He died in Assuan on 31 January 1912. The dukedom of Fife devolved by special remainder on his elder daughter, who in the following year married her cousin Prince Arthur of Connaught (q.v.).

Fisher, the Most Rev. Geoffrey
later Lord Fisher of Lambeth
(1887–1972)

Archbishop of Canterbury 1945–61. The youngest son of a Warwickshire parson, he was educated at Marlborough College and Exeter College, Oxford, where he took First Class Honours in Greats. He went on to read Theology, in which he also took a First; for each of his twelve papers he received an 'alpha' from each examiner.

He returned to Marlborough as an assistant master in Holy Orders. In 1914, when only twenty-seven, he was appointed headmaster of Repton. Here he followed William Temple, whom he was again to succeed in 1945 as Archbishop of Canterbury; and among Fisher's Repton pupils was Michael Ramsey, his successor as Archbishop in 1961. Throughout his eighteen years as headmaster of Repton he proved an able administrator and a fierce disciplinarian, unsparing of boys and teaching staff alike. One casualty was a radical-minded assistant master called Victor Gollancz who achieved later fame as a radical-minded publisher. Fisher had meanwhile married Rosamund Forman, daughter of a Repton master who had himself married his headmaster's daughter. Fortified by that apostolic succession, they had six sons, one of whom became Master of Wellington College and another President of Wolfson College, Oxford.

The tradition of making public school headmasters into bishops brought him to Chester in 1932 and to London seven years later. On the unexpected death of William Temple in 1945, Winston Churchill chose him to be the ninety-ninth Archbishop of Canterbury, although shocked to learn that the new Primate of All England had never read Renan's *Life of Jesus*. Fisher proved vigorous and businesslike, though never an inspiring leader. He began a revision of Canon Law designed to tighten ecclesiastical conformity, and moved cautiously towards an ecumenical understanding first with the Free Churches, then with the Protestant and Orthodox Churches overseas. In 1960 he travelled to Rome to see Pope John XXIII, the first such visit since 1397. It was only slightly marred by Fisher's incautious remark at the Press Conference which followed: 'There was no preliminary build-up, no theatrical staging; it was nothing like visiting Hitler or Mussolini.' As a shrewd man of business he raised the stipends of Anglican clergy. He also relished the annual chore of filling in his income tax return. 'I love it,' he told a friend, 'it is my Easter Monday recreation.' He liked detective stories and crossword puzzles, too.

In spite of a stocky figure that lacked the natural grace of Archbishop Lang, Fisher's presence was not unworthy of a royal occasion. He crowned Queen Elizabeth II with dignity and spoke the ancient ritual with clarity and conviction. He also prepared a small volume of meditation and prayer for the Queen's use in the months preceding her Coronation; as only seventeen carefully guarded copies were printed, the glow of its author's powerful intellect was concealed from all but a few. Some years earlier the Archbishop had no less discreetly received Prince Philip, a member of the Greek Orthodox Church, into the Church of England on the eve of his wedding.

Throughout the openly discussed romance between Princess Margaret and Group Captain Townsend (qq.v.) the Archbishop was sometimes pilloried as an obstructive opponent of true love; but that is perhaps the occupational

Archbishop Fisher and friends after a Coronation rehearsal, 1953

risk of all Anglican prelates, and it is difficult to see what other course he could have taken in the austere ecclesiastical climate of 1955. He showed a jaunty indifference to the hostility of the popular Press and enjoyed quoting two consecutive newspaper headlines. One read, 'The Archbishop Must Go'; the other 'The Archbishop Has Gone Too Far.' He also told the interviewer Richard Dimbleby (q.v.) that he did not care 'two hoots' what people might be saying and that much of it represented 'a popular wave of stupid emotionalism.'

Fisher was at pains to deny the truth of a supposed conversation with Princess Margaret which, touching a welcome chord of anti-clericalism, was widely repeated. When she came to see him at Lambeth Palace on 27 October 1955, the story ran, and found him surrounded by works on marriage and divorce, all carefully marked and cross-referenced, the Princess said: 'You can put away your books, Archbishop, I am not going to marry Peter Townsend.' Fisher, who was sometimes irascible but not vain, later told his biographer: 'I had no books of any sort spread around. The Princess came and I received her, as I would anybody else, in the quietness of my own study. She never said, "Put away those books," because there were not any books to be put away.'

On retiring as Archbishop of Canterbury in 1961 he was created Lord Fisher of Lambeth and retired to the rectory of a Dorset village. Until his death eleven years later he continued to follow Church matters with a critical scrutiny that found expression in two trenchant pamphlets and innumerable letters which reminded his correspondents of their least happy schooldays.

Ford, Sir Edward
(1910–)

Assistant Private Secretary to King George VI, 1946–52, and to Queen Elizabeth II, 1952–67. His father was the Very Rev. Lionel Ford, headmaster successively of Repton and Harrow, then Dean of York; his mother a daughter of the Rt Rev. E.S. Talbot, Bishop of Westminster.

Educated at Eton and New College, Oxford, and a scholar of both foundations, he was as a young man appointed tutor to Prince Farouk of Egypt, who lived in a house outside London, studying to enter the Royal Military Academy. Ford found him an unsatisfactory pupil who cared only for the sycophantic company of his domestic staff. 'It was a repellent sight,' he noted, 'to see him slapping his Italian valets on the back, or to find them meekly submitting to have their tongues painted with black ink before going in fancy dress to a servants' ball at Kingston.' The Prince returned prematurely to Cairo in 1936 on the death of his father, King Fuad, and subsequently ascended the throne. His later life betrayed few traces of an English education. Ford practised at the Bar until the outbreak of war. Already on the supplementary reserve of the Grenadier Guards, he rejoined the regiment, fought in France, North Africa and Italy, and was mentioned in despatches.

In 1946 he was appointed an Assistant Private Secretary to King George VI, continuing in the same role under Queen Elizabeth II. His quiet efficiency and good humour could well have brought him the senior post of Private Secretary. But as he was the same age as Michael Adeane (q.v.) and three years older than Martin Charteris (q.v.), there was no room at the top for all three. In 1967, therefore, he retired from the royal household. He has since been secretary of the Pilgrim Trust, High Sheriff of Northamptonshire and Prime Warden of the Goldsmiths' Company. He is also secretary and registrar of the Order of Merit; as that illustrious body is confined to twenty-four members, his duties are not onerous.

Ford married in 1949 Virginia, elder daughter of Lord Brand, the banker and public servant, and niece of Nancy Astor.

George V, King
(1865–1936)

Founder of the House of Windsor. He was born in London on 3 June 1865, the younger son of the Prince and Princess of Wales, afterwards King Edward VII and Queen Alexandra (qq.v.), and brought up in an affectionate and high-spirited family circle of an elder brother and three sisters.

Prince George and Prince Albert Victor received their early schooling from the Rev. John Dalton (q.v.), who accompanied the two boys throughout their naval training. This included a two-year cruise round the world in HMS *Bacchante*, a corvette of 4,000 tons, fully rigged but with auxiliary engines. By the age of fifteen, Prince George had faced both danger and death. Between South Africa and Australia, the *Bacchante* ran into a severe gale. Her sails in ribbons, her rudder almost torn off at the shaft, she drifted helplessly, out of touch with the other ships of the squadron and 400 miles from the nearest port. For three days and nights the senior officers had no sleep, until makeshift repairs allowed the corvette to limp on her way. Prince George's account of the storm is that of a seasoned professional, untinged by emotion. Earlier, however, on two successive days in the South Atlantic, a seaman had fallen to his death; one from the fore topsail yard of *Bacchante*, the other overboard from the flagship *Inconstant*. The Prince was deeply moved by the loss of a shipmate and drew a neat black border round his diary for that day.

It was not easy for Dalton to decide when the princes should be treated as grandsons of the Queen and when as humble midshipmen. Sometimes the change from one status to another could be abrupt. At the end of a ceremonial call in Alexandria the boys were returned to *Bacchante* in 'two tremendous state barges, in one of which there was a great blue velvet and gold sofa, beneath a heavy silk canopy, in thoroughly oriental style.' The diary entry for the next day begins: 'Got up at 5 a.m., had the morning watch.' Such was the code of discipline that sustained the future King throughout life.

A handsome and sturdy boy, though small for his age, Prince George swiftly overhauled his elder brother in all but inches. His spelling, it is true, remained premanently insecure, and well into manhood he called the greatest of poets 'Sheakspeare.' But he shone in seamanship; and as he climbed the ladder of his profession, there was every reason to suppose that he would achieve high rank on his own merits. In January 1892, however , shortly after Prince George had given up command of his gunboat, HMS *Thrush*, and was awaiting another appointment, his elder brother, recently created Duke of Clarence, died of pneumonia. At twenty-six, the shy, stolid naval officer found himself in direct line of succession to the throne. It was a daunting prospect.

Certain changes in his daily life helped to restore self-confidence. He was created Duke of York, he aquired quarters of his own: part of St James's Palace in London, and the Bachelors' Cottage (later known as York Cottage), a few hundred yards from Sandringham House. He was provided with a parliamentary income of nearly £30,000 a year and a small staff, including his shipmate and friend Charles Cust (q.v.) as equerry. He lacked only a wife.

Happily there was one to hand in the accomplished but heartbroken Princess May of Teck, who had been betrothed to Prince Albert Victor, Duke of Clarence, only a few weeks before his untimely death. There were discreet exchanges between the two families and more than a little pressure from Queen Victoria. The Duke of York embarked on a hesitant courtship which the future Queen Mary (q.v.) accepted with demure resignation. In May 1893 he proposed and was accepted. The nation rejoiced at so neat a solution to the demands of love, grief and dynastic need.

The wedding took place on 6 July 1893 in the Chapel Royal, St James's Palace, and the honeymoon at Sandringham. In a well-meaning attempt to spare his bride fuss and fatigue, the Duke himself chose new carpets, curtains and wallpaper for both their houses and filled them with modern furniture from Maple's emporium. For the first but by no means the last time in their married life, the dutiful Duchess of York held her tongue.

The Duke was relieved to find that eventual succession to the throne scarcely intruded on the life of a country gentleman. He had both the means and the leisure to pursue his two favourite pastimes, shooting and stamp collecting, and he excelled at both. A sharp eye and constant practice made him one of the half-dozen most lethal shots in the kingdom, although even his entourage would sometimes flinch at the extent of the slaughter. During one season at Sandringham, seven guns in four days killed 10,000 head of game; in a single day the Duke fired 1,700 cartridges and brought down 1,000 pheasants. Yet he would have been shocked had anyone questioned his love of beasts and birds. A niece, walking with him in the gardens at Windsor, noticed that when they came on a dead thrush, his eyes filled with tears.

It was not the Duke of York who founded the royal collection of postage stamps but his uncle,

Prince Alfred, Duke of Edinburgh. Pressed by debts, he sold his private collection to his brother the Prince of Wales, who in turn gave it to his son. On that foundation, the Duke of York built up the most comprehensive collection in the world devoted to the stamps of Great Britain and her dependencies. He enjoyed every advantage, for Colonial Governors and High Commissioners were instructed to watch for the appearance of new issues. Only once did they fail him. A British representative in the Middle East, hearing of a suspected case of smallpox in the local printing works, feared that the royal tongue might be contaminated; so he assiduously boiled his entire offering of 400 stamps in a saucepan before despatching them to London. 'Did Your Royal Highness hear that some damned fool has just paid £1,450 for a single stamp?' a courtier jocularly asked him one morning. 'I was the damned fool,' he replied. At his death in 1936 the collection consisted of 250,000 stamps in 325 large volumes: an investment of incalculable value that, like the royal library and picture collections, has become part of the national heritage.

Between 1894 and 1905, the Duchess of York bore her husband one daughter and five sons. They were Princess Mary, later Countess of Harewood and Princess Royal; Prince Edward, successively Prince of Wales, King Edward viii and Duke of Windsor; Prince Albert, later Duke of York and King George vi; Prince Henry, later Duke of Gloucester; Prince George, later Duke of Kent; and Prince John (qq.v.). All were brought up in the cramped little rooms of York Cottage, Sandringham. The Duke could well have afforded to lease a large country house in keeping with his rank; but he disliked entertaining. He grew fond of his ugly, sunless, rambling villa, its walls hung with reproductions from the Royal Academy, its furniture bought in the Tottenham Court Road, its passages haunted by the ghosts of ancient meals. A visiting preacher noted more with dismay than pride that the royal drawing-room was smaller than his own.

The publication of the Duke of Windsor's memoirs in 1951 gave widespread currency to the belief that he and his brothers had passed an unhappy childhood at the hands of a harsh father and an unfeeling mother. It is a myth which contains a grain of truth but much fantasy. The theme is discussed under *Edward VIII*. Here it suffices to say that the future King George v was an affectionate parent, albeit an unbending Victorian. He loved his children, was proud of their good looks and achievements, praised as readily as he rebuked. He brought them up with impeccable manners and a total absence of that high-born arrogance which permeated so many other royal houses; only thus, he believed, could his own line survive in an age of unrest. His concern centred largely on his eldest child, who showed a wilful disregard for his wishes not only in dress and deportment, but in graver matters of morality and constitutional duty. Separated by a gulf as much of temperament as of years, father and son were never reconciled.

Perhaps he did attach too much importance to what he wore; but then he grew up in an age that cared for such things. Endowed with neither inches nor a commanding presence, the King made the most of his modest attributes. His hair was always brushed with care, his beard neatly trimmed and annointed with lavender water, his manicured hands protected by gloves when shooting. Almost at death's door in 1928, he insisted on sending for a looking glass. He liked to have his family round him as he completed the ritual of dressing for dinner: the winding of the watch, the touch of scent on the handkerchief, the last adjustment to white tie and Garter Star. It was as if the centuries had rolled away and the Sun King reigned once more at Versailles.

On formal occasions he remained faithful to the frock coat and tall hat, their sombre glow relieved by a protrusion of starched cuff, a white slip under the waistcoat and perhaps a gardenia. For Ascot and other summer events, the entire ensemble might by grey. At a race meeting or at some such *rus in urbe* as the Chelsea Flower Show, the King wore a no less impeccably cut suit of the finest brown or grey cloth – he had seen enough of blue in the Navy – crowned by a hard, high, curly-brimmed bowler hat of black, brown or grey. His trousers were creased down the side, his overcoats generally long, his gloves ribbed in black. He pulled his ties through a ring rather than knot them, and kept them in place by a jewelled pin. He preferred boots to shoes and invariably carried a stick. On shooting days his valet laid out tweeds of a surprisingly bright check, eight-button spats that came almost up to his knees, and a Homburg hat. When sailing his yacht, the King wore a white flannel suit and flat cap without a peak. Scotland received the compliment of kilt, Inverness cape and feathered bonnet. It was as much a liturgy as a wardrobe.

The death of Queen Victoria in 1901 and the accession of King Edward VII placed few additional duties on the new heir to the throne: the Duke of Cornwall, as he was known, until in November the King conferred on him the title Prince of Wales. He was obliged to exchange his unpretentious corner of St James's Palace for the Wren grandeur of Marlborough House, where his parents had lived for the past forty years; this time he allowed his wife a free hand in its redecoration and furnishing. The new King arranged for his son to receive the more important Cabinet papers in preparation for the day when he too would succeed to the throne; and whenever the Duke stayed at Windsor, he was given a writing table next to his father's. Of more lasting benefit was the appointment of Sir Arthur Bigge, later created Lord Stamfordham (q.v.), as his Private Secretary.

Twice during Edward VII's reign, his son was obliged to abandon children, shotgun and stamps for a prolonged Empire tour. The first occasion, in 1901, took the Duke and Duchess of Cornwall to Australia, New Zealand and Canada in the *Ophir*, an Orient Line steamship of 6,900 tons. Preferring statistics to picturesque description, the Duke noted that he and his wife had been separated from home for 231 days; and that during those eight months they had covered 45,000 miles, laid 21 foundation stones, received 544 addresses, presented 4,329 medals, reviewed 62,000 troops and shaken hands with 24,855 people at official receptions alone. 'Wake up,

England!', the label which the Press affixed to the Duke's Guildhall speech on his return, exaggerated both his devotion to travel and his relish for the role of ambassador. He had done his duty and more. His true feelings were revealed in a letter to Queen Alexandra from Canada: 'Of course our tour is most interesting, but it is very tiring and there is no place like dear old England for me.'

The Prince of Wales, as he had now become, showed a deeper concern for India when with his wife he spent eighteen weeks in the winter of 1905–6 touring the sub-continent. It was an exhilarating and at times almost mystical experience which neither of them ever forgot. Eighty years later it is not easy to recapture the near unanimous satisfaction and pride with which Great Britain gazed upon her Indian Empire: more a sacred trust than an administrative or commercial union, a partnership in which the balance of advantage was held to lie less with the governors than with the governed. The notes which the Prince of Wales prepared for his father bear the mark of his own character: observant and kindly, with an entire absence of that colour prejudice which permeated every level of Edwardian society. 'I could not help being struck,' he wrote, 'by the way in which all salutations by the Natives were disregarded by the persons to whom they were given. Evidently we are too much inclined to look upon them as a conquered and down-trodden race and the Native, who is becoming more and more educated, realises this.' He was also astonished to learn that no Indian, whatever his birth or education, could be a member of the clubs frequented by Europeans. As King-Emperor, he later gave every encouragement to the founding of multi-racial clubs by his Viceroy, Lord Willingdon.

On paper the Prince could display statesmanship, particularly with Bigge at his elbow. In conversation, however, he was both garrulous and dangerously indiscreet. Shortly before H.H. Asquith became Prime Minister in 1908, the Prince of Wales was overheard at Windsor one night declaring that he thought him 'not quite a gentleman': a remark which Winston Churchill disobligingly repeated to Asquith. At another party, he leaned across the dinner table towards the Permanent Secretary of the Treasury and bellowed: 'I can't think how you can go on serving that damned fellow Lloyd George.' And by trumpeting his support for Admiral Lord Charles Beresford in the controversy that split the Royal Navy for a generation, he made a virulent enemy of Admiral Sir John Fisher.

On 6 May 1910, King George V entered upon his proud but dreaded heritage. 'At 11.45,' he wrote in his diary, 'beloved Papa passed peacefully away and I have lost my best friend and the best of fathers.' Like all hereditary institutions, monarchy is something of a lottery; and the student of affairs who read of Edward VII's death might have concluded that the nation's luck had at last run out. The new King, born out of direct line of succession to the throne and with only the limited education of a nineteenth-century naval officer, was further handicapped by an ingrained conservatism. On the eve of his forty-fifth birthday, his horizons did not stretch beyond the duties and pastimes of a Norfolk squire. He was ignorant of science and politics, indifferent to history and the arts, unmoved by distant horizons, except those of India. He spoke hardly a word of any foreign language. Public ceremonial affected his nerves and entertainment his digestion. Few could regard his accession with enthusiasm or even confidence.

His reign, moreover, was of unparalleled restlessness. He lived through the ordeal of one world war and died under the approaching shadow of another. He saw the downfall of the great empires of Russia, Germany and Austro-Hungary. He was embroiled in demands for Irish Home Rule and for Indian self-government: claims that presaged the dissolution of the British Empire itself. He mourned the increasing impotence of his country in the face of the dictators, and the shift of sea power westwards across the Atlantic. The scene at home was equally mercurial. The King was obliged to preside over the decline of the House of Lords and the rise of the Labour Party; to take

a watchful and sometimes active interest in those bitter disputes which culminated in the General Strike of 1926; to curb the trade in honours no less than the flight from the pound.

George V confounded every doubt. Under the tutelage of experienced private secretaries, he set about learning the trade of a constitutional monarch. To each of the problems which crowded in on him, day by day, he brought an inspired common sense and kindliness; and whatever the political complexion of the Government in office, he wielded his prerogatives – the right to be consulted, to encourage and to warn – with wisdom and restraint.

Few monarchs have been put to the test so swiftly; for within the first months of the reign he was the victim of two malevolent lies and a constitutional crisis. One slander labelled him a drunkard, the other a bigamist; and the Prime Minister, whom he had incautiously dubbed 'not quite a gentleman' two years earlier, took his revenge (or so the King believed) by extracting a dishonourable promise from him.

The myth of the King's addiction to alcohol was an aristocratic invention that attracted widespread belief. 'At pious meetings in the East End of London,' the Austrian Ambassador reported to Vienna, 'prayers are said for Queen Mary and the royal children, begging the protection of Heaven on their unhappy drunkard's home.' Except for a red face and a loud voice, the King betrayed none of the symptoms associated with intemperance. He was in fact an abstemious man, although he did like a glass of port after dinner. This he would fill to the brim, then lift to his lips with the same steadiness of hand and eye that had made him so commanding a shot. By continuing to excel at the sport he loved best, the King shamed some of his detractors into silence. The rest grew weary of the joke, and eventually the sniggers ceased.

It was in 1893, the year he proposed to Princess May of Teck, that the Duke of York (as he then was) first heard the rumour of his supposed bigamy. On 3 May, the very day of his betrothal, a London newspaper declared that he had lately contracted a secret but canonical

Coronation mug, 1911

marriage in Malta with the daughter of a British naval officer. At first he took it lightly. 'I say, May,' he told his fiancée one day, 'we can't get married after all. I hear I have got a wife and three children.' But as the lie persisted year after year, he grew enraged. Towards the end of 1910 there came an opportunity to destroy it once and for all. A republican paper called the *Liberator*, published in Paris but sent free to every British MP, asserted that in 1890 the future King George V had married a daughter of Admiral Sir Michael Culme-Seymour in Malta; that children had been born of the union; and that three years later the bridegroom 'foully abandoned his true wife and entered into a sham and shameful marriage with a daughter of the Duke of Teck.'

The Attorney-General of the day was Sir Rufus Isaacs, later Lord Reading, the future Lord Chief Justice and Viceroy of India; the Solicitor-General was Sir John Simon, the future Foreign Secretary and Lord Chancellor. In a joint opinion, those two astute and formidable lawyers doubted the wisdom of giving world-wide publicity to an article in an obscure paper with a small circulation. They nevertheless recognized that all the principal witnesses to the falsehood of the story were still alive: the eldest, Admiral Culme-Seymour being in his seventy-fifth year. That tipped the scales in favour of prosecution. The author of the article, E. F. Mylius, was arrested, charged with criminal libel and tried before the Lord Chief Justice and a jury on 1 February 1911. The defendant's bold move to have a subpoena served on the King as a witness was frustrated; the Sovereign, being the source of justice, cannot give evidence in his own court. But the prosecution produced convincing evidence to show that the King had met neither of the admiral's daughters nor even been in Malta during the time of the supposed marriage. Mylius was found guilty and sentenced to twelve months' imprisonment. The King's honour had been vindicated.

For an account of the indignity which George V suffered at the hands of his first Prime Minister, H. H. Asquith, see under *Lord Stamfordham*. It is a measure of the King's resentment that

twenty-one years after the audience at which Asquith had exerted unconstitutional pressure on him, the insult still rankled. In 1931, when talking to his friend Lord Crewe, who as another Liberal Minister had accompanied Asquith to the Palace in 1910, the King referred to the episode as 'the dirtiest thing ever done.' Crewe agreed that they had not treated him very well.

Those anguished months were relieved by the splendour of the Coronation. The King, a spectator noted, 'behaved throughout as those who knew him expected him to act: evidently profoundly impressed with the importance and sacredness of the occasion, but with the calmness and quiet dignity of a perfect English gentleman.' The guests in Westminster Abbey seem to have shown less decorum. A young gold staff officer, or usher, reported at the end of the day that he had picked up three ropes of pearls, three-quarters of a diamond necklace, twenty brooches, six or seven bracelets and nearly twenty balls knocked off coronets. He estimated his haul of debris to be worth £20,000; and there were about 200 such officials on duty.

In December 1911, the King-Emperor presented himself robed and crowned to the untold millions of his Indian subjects. 'It was,' he noted, 'entirely my own idea.' Most of his Liberal Ministers opposed so imaginative a spectacle as the Delhi Durbar. They objected to the Sovereign's long absence from England; and since the Crown of St Edward could not by law leave the country, they suggested that a new Crown be hired from Garrard, the jeweller. But the King had his way throughout and was able to announce two momentous administrative changes: the transfer of the Indian capital from Calcutta to Delhi, and the annulment of the recent and unpopular partition of Bengal. He was never to see India again; but for years to come he recaptured the memory of those jewelled weeks in the plans of Sir Edwin Lutyens (q.v.) for New Delhi.

Four uneasy years of peace gave way to the heavier strains of war. The King donned the mantle of Henry V with diffidence. He would always do his best but he was not a born leader.

The cheers outside Buckingham Palace on 4 August 1914 saluted the symbol rather than the man. 'The King came to see us this morning,' a soldier wrote from the Western Front, 'looking as glum and dyspeptic as ever.' Popularity he left to his Ministers and glory to the fighting men. His own role was unobtrusive but vital: to carry on the business of a constitutional monarch. He must know all yet relinquish ultimate responsibility; ease the path of the elected Government while safeguarding those prerogatives which in the stress of war could be lost forever.

'I cannot share your hardships,' the King told his troops, 'but my heart is with you every hour of the day.' He imposed an austere restraint on his public and private pleasures alike. He gave away most of his civilian wardrobe and ordered no new clothes except uniforms of khaki and navy blue. As long as the war lasted he rarely dined out and never went to the theatre. His only relaxation in London was to spend an hour or two each week with his stamp collection. Balmoral was closed, the gardens at Windsor turned over to potatoes planted during afternoons of strenuous digging. And although he continued to shoot during brief holidays at Sandringham, that too could be regarded as a patriotic contribution to the nation's larder.

A zealous Minister once assured the King that if Buckingham Palace were to be bombed by German aircraft it would have a stimulating effect on the people. He received the brisk reply: 'Yes, but rather a depressing effect on me.' Lloyd George risked precisely that answer when in the spring of 1915 he urged the King to set an example to the nation by abstaining from alcohol for the duration of the war. What might otherwise have been thought an impertinence on the Chancellor's part sprang from his alarm at the disruptive effect of heavy drinking by factory workers, particularly in the armament and shipbuilding industries. 'Drink is doing more damage in this war,' Lloyd George told a meeting of fellow Welshmen, 'than all the German submarines put together.'

Although a man of temperate habits, the King was accustomed to drink a little wine with his meals and a glass of port after dinner. He and the Queen nevertheless responded instantly to the call of patriotism. In locking his cellar doors, the King allowed himself a quiet grumble. 'It is a great bore,' he told his uncle, the Duke of Connaught. The King and Queen would have borne their self-imposed asceticism without complaint had it achieved its purpose and encouraged others to follow the royal example. Their gesture, however, was generally ignored and sometimes derided. The King did not hide his belief that Lloyd George had made him look foolish. And the Queen, who liked to flourish an occasional colloquialism, confided to a sympathetic Mr Asquith: 'We have been carted.'

The King toiled over his red boxes of papers, received Ministers in audience, toured factories, steeled himself to visit hospitals, suffered painful and lasting injuries when thrown from his horse during a visit to the Western Front. Yet amid the hysteria of those war years he was widely believed to harbour tender thoughts about the enemy. Lloyd George, receiving a summons to the Palace in 1915, remarked to his secretary: 'I wonder what my little German friend has got to say to me?'

In spite of an ancestry that for centuries had thrived on infusions of German blood, the King considered himself to be wholly and impregnably British. When H.G. Wells spoke of 'an alien and uninspiring Court', the King retorted: 'I may be uninspiring, but I'll be damned if I'm an alien.' Habits, opinions, pastimes, devotions, dress: all were indistinguishable from those of any other old-fashioned English country gentleman. He was therefore mortified by whispers that doubted his wholehearted support for the Allied cause. Such rumours were at first confined to a tiny minority: the malicious, the republican, the simple minded. But as the casualties of battle mounted year by year, they were joined by embittered victims of suffering or grief. The wartime conduct of the King and Queen, austere in private, tireless in public, should in itself have been enough to refute such slanders. Yet in 1917, with what seems to have been a momentary loss of nerve, the King determined to restore confidence by means of a theatrical gesture. He would rid the royal family of its Germanic taint by proclaiming his dynasty the House of Windsor.

The name, suggested by Lord Stamfordham, was inspired, recalling as it did the best-known and most beautiful of English silhouettes outside the capital: ancient, sturdy, benevolent. Yet the judgment on it by a Bavarian nobleman, Count Albrecht von Monteglas, was not without truth: 'The true royal tradition died on that day in 1917 when, for a mere war, King George v changed his name.'

A more practical and timely measure accompanied the proclamation of the House of Windsor. Members of the royal family were enjoined to relinquish all 'German degrees, styles, dignities, titles, honours and appellations.' That patriotic British admiral, His Serene Highness Prince Louis of Battenberg, accordingly assumed the anglicized surname of Mountbatten and was created Marquess of Milford Haven. His elder son, Prince George of Battenberg, acquired the courtesy title of Earl of Medina; his younger son, Prince Louis of Battenberg, that of Lord Louis Mountbatten, the style he bore until created Viscount Mountbatten of Burma in 1946 and Earl Mountbatten of Burma a year later (qq.v.). Another member of the Battenberg family, Prince Alexander, a captain in the Grenadier Guards, was created Marquess of Carisbrooke. The Queen's two surviving brothers, both senior officers in the British Army, assumed the surname of Cambridge, after their maternal grandmother's family, and each was created a peer. The Duke of Teck became Marquess of Cambridge; his younger brother, Prince Alexander of Teck, became Earl of Athlone (qq.v.). The King also made regulations to define and restrict the use of such princely styles and titles as survived, lest they proliferate like those of continental royalty. He deplored sweeping away so much of the past, yet was not ashamed of his handiwork. Cambridge and Carisbrooke, Milford Haven and Athlone: Shakespeare himself could not have composed a more resonant or patriotic call to arms.

Throughout Asquith's wartime premiership, the country endured an almost unbroken succession of reverses by land and sea. Dilatory and self-indulgent, he was obliged to resign in December 1916. The new Prime Minister was Lloyd George, the one man in national politics with both judgment and the resolution to achieve ultimate victory. The King did not welcome the change. Since their early collisions, he and Asquith had come to trust each other. Lloyd George, by contrast, displayed a nonchalance towards his Sovereign not far removed from contempt. He left letters unanswered, ignored a summons to a Privy Council without explanation or apology, made political, military and diplomatic appointments without informing, much less consulting the King. An acute difference of opinion on the conduct of the war inflamed their mutual dislike. Lloyd George was determined to curb Field Marshal Haig's costly and ineffective assaults on the Western Front; to hit the enemy at his weakest points, not his strongest. The King, convinced that military operations must be left to professional soldiers, deplored such political influence and did all he could to protect his friend the Commander-in-Chief.

Only once throughout four years of war did the King persuade Lloyd George to change course on an important matter of policy. It proved in retrospect to be the most perplexing act of his reign: the abandonment of the Tsar Nicholas II, a loyal ally and much-loved cousin, to degradation and death. It is undisputed that the Tsar, after his enforced abdication in March 1917, was first offered, then denied, asylum in England. The episode, however, has been obscured by a persistent myth: that it was the King who strove to rescue his cousin from the perils of the Russian revolution, only to be thwarted by a heartless and opportunist Lloyd George. The late Lord Mountbatten, with all the authority of close kinship and apparent omniscience, gave currency to the legend. A nephew of the Tsar – his mother and the Russian Empress were sisters – he continued to proclaim to the end of his life that Lloyd George's hands were stained with the

SILVER JUBILEE DAILY MAIL, May 6, 1935.

SILVER JUBILEE
Daily Mail
FOR KING AND EMPIRE

We Georgian Women
by Margaret Lane . . Page 4

The Queen's Work
by the Hon. Mrs. Francis Lascelles . . P.6

25 Years of Progress
by Sir-Malcolm Campbell P. 7

The Human Scene
in Pictures . . . Page 8

MONDAY, MAY 6, 1935

Price One Shilling

GEORGE V.—King and Emperor of "teeming millions in distant lands no less than of those who lodge within the four seas of Old England"

TO-DAY all ranks and classes in this country and the peoples of the whole Empire will join in loyal and affectionate congratulations to the King and Queen. The twenty-five years of the reign have been among the most momentous in history, and through all their dangers, sorrows, and vicissitudes, whether in peace or in the most agonising of wars, their Majesties have known how to command their subjects' devotion and love.

The story of those troubled years with their tremendous events is graphically told by Major-General Sir Frederick Maurice, one of our ablest historians and soldiers, in this special *Daily Mail* Silver Jubilee issue.

After twenty-five years the Throne stands secure—a rock on which the waves of time and revolution have beaten in vain. The contrast of its position with that which it held a century ago is extraordinary indeed. Then the Monarchy was unpopular and the general opinion was that it was not destined long to survive, and that republicanism was a preferable form of government. To-day its authority is firmly rooted in the hearts of the people, and General Hertzog's declaration, that he has done with republicanism, correctly represents the trend of modern thought throughout the Empire—and indeed the world.

The King is regarded everywhere as one of the greatest world-figures of our time, and his wisdom, statesmanship, and exalted sense of duty have won the admiration of his contemporaries. *The Daily Mail* is maintaining its attachment to Britain's eternal past and all that in it is beautiful and noble by producing in this special number a unique souvenir of the reign, recalling in pictures and words its most memorable events and portraying in the broadest outline the social aspects of that stormy, heroic age.

THE REIGN
and the MAN

by Maj.-Gen. Sir Frederick Maurice
K.C.M.G., C.B.

The acts, the wishes, the example of the Sovereign in this country are a real power; the Sovereign is the symbol of law and the source of honour and power.

Parliaments and Ministers pass; but the Sovereign abides in lifelong duty and is to them as the oak in the forest to the harvest in the field

SO mused a great Victorian statesman at a moment when Victoria was disposed to frown rather than to smile on him.

On this high holiday, with the guns thundering their Jubilee salute, William Gladstone's wise words will lose nothing of their weight.

Especially is this true if we reflect that the Whig and Tory controversies which alternately depressed and irritated a truly great Sovereign were as child's play compared to the problems of Imperial and international importance which, at times, have been almost a daily dish to set before the King.

The Great Test

NOR does it need more than a superficial view of events during the last quarter of a century to be sure that the single test that King George has applied to every proposal submitted to him is how far the scheme to be set afoot will enhance the safety, honour, and welfare of his people and their country.

If destiny did not at first point to the second son of Albert Edward Prince of Wales as a future King-Emperor, no wiser training could have been devised for him than the discipline which marks a sailor's life. No other curriculum, fortified as it was by later experience, would have enabled him to command as he climbed the steps of his throne that he was one of the few Englishmen in his wide-world Empire who had seen the whole of that Empire.

The thought may well have been burned into his mind that there now devolved on him the constant care for teeming millions in distant lands no less than for those who lodged within the four seas of Old England.

In August 1891, Prince George, who had worked hard and worried about nothing outside his professional duties, was promoted, strictly according to routine, to the rank of Commander, and his career as a sailor seemed settled.

But there was impending a shattering event which would compel him to alter abruptly his whole outlook on life and settle him as successor, in the third generation, to the Crown.

A Sudden Change

HE himself that winter was barely to recover from a fierce attack of typhoid fever, but his elder brother, a Prince of peculiarly amiable disposition, was fated to succumb to a specially vicious form of influenza then prevalent.

Those who watched Prince George closely at this time must have witnessed in a sudden change, a sudden spring, as it were, from the ladder of youth to the level of manhood.

Grave responsibilities lay ahead; there were onerous duties to be undertaken, and to fulfil them to the utmost of his power—for nothing less would satisfy him—a Prince still in his early twenties, must go into self-imposed training.

In a moment, almost, there had to be a complete readjustment of his outlook. Life up to that time had been mainly concerned with the careless joys of youth and the tasks connected with work which he loved. Now, the horizon of his future was immeasurably widened.

He would, in time, be called to the leadership of an Empire. He must look closely into the recesses of his character and see how far that character would lend itself to such a great rôle.

The way would be long and difficult, that he knew; but he was determined so to master his part that when it should be put into his hands he could interpret it faithfully, wisely, and well.

Then came the marriage with the Princess who had been his childhood's playmate—a union over which no cloud has ever cast a shadow—the quiet family life punctuated by service to the State and wide travel, the country pursuits, in one of which he was already (almost without rival) and the (early) apprenticeship as Heir to his father's Throne.

The temptation to compare George V. with Edward VII. is at times difficult, if not impossible, to resist. Suffice it here to say that their very difference in outlook and method only seemed to deepen their mutual affection and trust.

For the first time since the accession of the House of Hanover a British Sovereign of to-day was on terms not only of perfect harmony but of closest amity with a British Sovereign of to-morrow.

Such was the confidence existing between father and son that King Edward frequently instructed his Ministers to let the Prince of Wales know the contents of confidential despatches while informing no one else.

Fashoda was rather uncomfortably on the table when Mr. M. Delcassé, who had taken over the portfolio for Foreign Affairs, wisely decided to send Paul Cambon as French Ambassador to the Court of St. James's.

Two Peoples

THE Envoy, who was at once a man of the world, a diplomatist and steady thinker, asked for nothing better, and was prompt to form with the future King of England ties of serious friendship which later, through long years of blood and agony, were to be tested again and again and never be found to fail.

Early in 1902, M. Cambon took his courage and his pen in his hands and unfolded to Lord Lansdowne a proposal for an Anglo-French agreement. "Excellent," was King Edward's comment, while his son hastened to express to the Ambassador his hearty approval of the idea, which, put into effect, was to knit with ties of amity two peoples whose interests were largely common, and eventually to range alongside one another in battle order, two nations—who through two centuries had often faced one another in honourable warfare—against a common foe.

The Entente with our nearest neighbour across the Channel was the pièce de résistance in a menu which King Edward bent himself to draw up. And in the nine short years of his reign he succeeded in chasing the frown from the foreheads of all the rulers in Europe except those of the Central Powers.

He had been busy—and every detail of his business carried the careful endorsement of his son—with agreements not only with France and Russia but with Japan and the Scandinavian countries and Afghanistan.

He forged a bond with Japan.

which King George, with some reluctance, permitted Mr. Balfour's delicate fingers to sever. He brought the Sultan of Muscat and other minor Asiatic and African potentates to his side, and he was bold to send his congratulations to the President of the United States on his election.

Edward VII. left his Empire on terms with foreign Powers such as had been wholly outside the achievements—or even the thoughts—of any of his predecessors, but unhappily as regards domestic politics he must bequeath to his successor a legacy which was as formidable as it was complex in character.

The trumpeters had scarcely heralded his accession when King George V. was confronted with a great constitutional encounter in which his fingers (at both Houses of Parliament would be engaged) and of which the issue was largely problematical.

A Liberal Government found ranged against them not only the House of Lords but a strong party in the House of Commons helped by considerable social influence and tradition. And while the Prime Minister and his followers could not prevail without something more than the consent of the King, their opponents must rely on his active sympathy to win their cause.

Although such a compromise was scarcely in the air at the King's suggestion, if not at his command, a Conference was held—but yet in vain—between representatives of the Government and of the no less sturdy Opposition.

The Prime Minister repaired to Sandringham to expose his hand, the King hurried to London to receive him in audience with Lord Crewe.

(Turn overleaf)

QUEEN MARY.. "quiet family life punctuated by service to the State."

Silver Jubilee tribute, 1935

blood of the Imperial family. Correspondence between the King and his Ministers in March and April 1917 reveals a different chain of events leading to the murder of the Tsar and his family fifteen months later. It shows that the British Government would willingly have offered them asylum but for the fears expressed by Buckingham Palace; and that at the most critical moment in their fortunes they were deserted not by a radical Prime Minister seeking to appease his supporters, but by their ever affectionate Cousin Georgie.

In retrospect, the King's refusal to help his Russian cousins seems wholly out of character; it becomes intelligible only in the context of an England burdened by war-weariness and discontent. The first principle of an hereditary monarchy is to survive; and never was King George v obliged to tread the path of self-preservation more cautiously than in 1917. He felt himself doubly manaced: by a whispering campaign that doubted his patriotism, and by an upsurge of republicanism. At just such a time of insecurity, his Government urged him to endorse their offer of sanctuary to the Imperial family, a gesture that would have identified him with Tsarist autocracy and imperilled his own repute as a constitutional monarch. Kings are more sensitive to the spectre of revolution at home than abroad; and in March 1917 George v failed to foresee the descent of Russia into Bolshevik barbarism.

'Very often I feel in despair,' the King told his wife, 'and if it wasn't for you I should break down.' In the fourth year of war, the strain began to show. A Minister noticed that 'the little man's stumpy beard is getting quite white at the point.' It was disheartening for the King to practise virtue yet be identified with tyranny; to live austerely, hand over savings of £100,000 to the Treasury and drive himself to the limit of endurance with State papers and public appearances, yet be reminded by Ramsay MacDonald that 'it is the Red Flag which now floats over the Imperial Palace in Petrograd.' Then suddenly the tide of battle turned. The German offensive faltered and the Allied armies struck back.

Throughout August and September 1918, the enemy were on the run, leaving no fewer than 350,000 of their men as prisoners. Turkey surrendered on 30 October, Austria on 4 November, Germany a week later. 'Today,' the King wrote on 11 November, 'has indeed been a wonderful day, the greatest in the history of the Country.'

The coming of peace allowed the King to resume a familiar routine. He and his family spent Christmas and the New Year at Sandringham, returning to London in February. The court moved to Windsor in April, then back to the capital until the call of Ascot in June. He raced at Goodwood in July, sailed at Cowes in August, shot grouse in Yorkshire and at Balmoral for the rest of the summer. Sandringham beckoned him back in the autumn for the partridges and pheasants. He scarcely ever went abroad; from the end of the war until his death seventeen years later he spent no more than eight weeks overseas, five of them on an enforced Mediterranean cruise recovering from a bout of bronchitis.

However exacting the demands of sport and philately, he never neglected his red boxes. To the problems of the post-war world he brought industry, common sense, compassion and a growing self-confidence. Having failed to reconcile an Ireland divided by the Home Rule controversy in the early reign, he tried again in 1921, and by a visionary speech in Belfast helped to patch up a temporary settlement. He curbed the sale of honours, a practice not confined, as is sometimes thought, to the henchmen of Lloyd George; other political parties were scarcely less culpable. In 1923, when required to select a new Prime Minister from the Conservative ranks, he prudently chose the unregarded Mr Baldwin rather than the experienced Lord Curzon: not on grounds of superior character but because the growing strength of the Labour Party required Government policy to be deployed and defended in an elected House of Commons, rather than an hereditary House of Lords.

The King's prescience was recognized when in the following year Britain elected her first

Labour Government. 'Today 23 years ago dear Grandmama died,' he wrote in his diary. 'I wonder what she would have thought.' Certainly Queen Victoria would have approved of the kindly paternalism and consideration with which her grandson welcomed Ramsay MacDonald and his untried colleagues; although doubtless she would also have shared his detestation of Socialism in theory and practice. He made a close friend of MacDonald and in 1931 saved the country, as he believed, by persuading him to form a 'National' Government in defence of the pound. Between those events lay the General Strike of 1926. Here the King again ran true to form; he was not unsympathetic to the demands of miners and other aggrieved workers, but insisted that violence was an unacceptable political weapon.

George V's conservative temperament did not exclude a lively and imaginative mind. He suggested the creation of life peerages almost half a century before they came into being. He authorized generous redundancy payments for servants at the Palace who had lost their jobs as a post-war economy: a far from common bounty in those days. He was similarly before his time in asking that ex-Prime Ministers should receive a statutory pension. Jostling these enlightened items in the Royal Archives, it must be said, are an equal number of trivialities. Should women factory workers remove their gloves before being presented to the Queen? May the Governor-General of Canada continue to use a red crown on his writing paper – the colour reserved for the Sovereign – or must he change to gubernatorial blue? Would the King object if the United States Ambassador came to court in evening trousers instead of the obligatory knee breeches? The King was indeed upset when he saw a newspaper photograph of his Lord Chancellor arriving at Downing Street in an old soft hat, and instructed Stamfordham to rebuke him for not wearing a tall hat. An unrepentant Lord Birkenhead replied with what his Sovereign called 'a very rude letter.'

The reign drew to its end in gathering cloud and fitful sunshine. The rise of the dictators threatened not only peace but civilization itself. 'The bomber', Baldwin assured the Commons in 1932, 'will always get through.' Widespread unemployment, particularly in Wales and north-east England, touched the conscience of the nation without evoking a remedy. Yet it was against these darkening horizons that the monarchy displayed a new-found strength and the gruff old King submitted to deification. He had almost died in the winter of 1928–9 from an infection of the lung that turned to general septicaemia. 'It was his bloody guts that pulled him through,' the Labour Minister, J.H. Thomas, declared. Lord Dawson of Penn and Sir Arthur du Cros (qq.v.) also played their parts: one by assembling a skilful team of doctors, the other by providing a salubrious house at Bognor for the royal convalescence. Then came the death of Stamfordham; and although Clive Wigram (q.v.) proved an able successor, the King mourned a friend as well as an incomparable Private Secretary. Foreign affairs oppressed him, too. He had no illusions about the greed and wickedness of Mussolini and Hitler, but his morale sagged. 'I am an old man,' he said, when not yet seventy. 'I have been through one world war. How can I go through another?'

The marriages of his remaining sons, all except the eldest, delighted him. But as the scandalmongers feasted on the reputation of the Prince of Wales, the King grieved for a wayward child and a threatened monarchy. It was with anger and despair that he learned of his heir's attachment to Mrs Simpson (q.v.), a divorced, remarried woman with two living husbands. He thought her unsuitable as a friend, disreputable as a mistress, unthinkable as a Queen. He was no less dismayed by the Prince's tenderness towards Nazi Germany and the imprudence of his letting these views be known.

Mistrustful of all modern inventions except the telephone, the King was persuaded late in life to deliver an annual Christmas broadcast. He proved a master of the art, and year by year would reach out into the hearts of his people. It was, however, through no wish of his that the Government decided to make a national festival of his Silver Jubilee. He disliked any conscious pursuit of popularity; and although moved by the affection which greeted him and the Queen during their progress through the streets of London, he deplored the fuss and expense. 'A wonderful service,' he said on leaving St Paul's Cathedral, 'just one thing wrong with it: too many damn parsons getting in the way.'

King George v spanned the centuries. At his christening in 1865, the Minister in attendance on his grandmother, Queen Victoria, was Lord Palmerston. In the last weeks of his life he handed the seals of office to a new Foreign Secretary, Anthony Eden. Then his strength ebbed away; but dutiful to the end, he did not die until he had held a Privy Council in his bedroom at Sandringham and attached a wavering signature to parchment. On 20 January 1936, an Empire waited for the last message of all: 'Death came peacefully to the King at 11.55 p.m.' Three days later, as his remains left for burial at Windsor, the stillness of the morning was broken by the crow of a cock pheasant.

George VI, King
(1895–1952)

The second of the five sons of the Duke and Duchess of York, later King George v and Queen Mary, he was born at York Cottage, Sandringham, on 14 December 1895, the anniversary of the death of the Prince Consort, and baptized Albert Frederick Arthur George. Bertie, as he was known in the family, spent a shy and tearful childhood. His digestion was impaired for life by an incompetent nurse; his legs were encased in splints to cure him of knock-knees; he grew up in the shadow of a much-admired elder brother and a heavy-handed father. 'Now that you are five years old,' the Duke of York told Bertie in 1900, 'I hope you will always try and be obedient and do at once what you are told, as you will find it will come much easier to you the sooner you begin.' At the

age of eight he developed a stammer.

Although accepted in 1909 for the Royal Naval College, Osborne, Prince Albert had been inadequately prepared by his tutor, Henry Hansell (q.v.), and in his final examinations came sixty-eighth out of sixty-eight. He did scarcely better throughout the more advanced course at Dartmouth, his final position being sixty-first out of sixty-seven. Yet he was beginning to gain confidence. During one holiday at Sandringham, he watched in ecstasy as the spoon with which his father was stirring his tea dissolved before his eyes; made of an alloy with a low melting-point, it came from a joke-shop. He showed the same bravado as a midshipman in the battleship HMS *Collingwood*. 'On Friday night after I was turned in,' he wrote to his father, by now King George v, 'I fell out of my hammock, with the help of someone else, and hit my left eye on my chest.' The King's advice to his son was of biblical simplicity: 'I should do the same to the other fellow if I got a chance.'

Prince Albert's naval career, the traditional royal vocation of a second son, was clouded by seasickness and ill-health. An operation for appendicitis in the early months of the Great War failed to cure persistent bouts of nausea and pain which preyed on his nerves. Much against his will, he was obliged to spend periods of sick leave in a hospital ship or ashore. But he extracted a promise from his father that, should his ship be ordered into action, he would be summoned to rejoin her. The eve of the Battle of Jutland found him in the sick bay of HMS *Collingwood* suffering from a surfeit of soused herring. He at once left his bed and fought throughout the engagement in his gun turret. In 1917 he was operated on for an inflamed duodenal ulcer which had remained undiagnosed for two weary years. Thereafter his health improved, although it was never to be robust. He spent the last months of the war in the Royal Naval Air Service, then in the newly constituted Royal Air Force. From duty rather than enthusiasm he learned to fly and was the only member of the royal family to become a fully qualified pilot.

Even while her two eldest sons were naval cadets at Osborne, Queen Mary had tried to have the curriculum modified to include more history and French for the future King Edward VIII. She added with prophetic insight: 'Albert ought to be educated also. Look at William IV. He was a long way from the throne yet he succeeded.' George V disagreed. It was not until 1919 that Prince Albert was able to study constitutional history during the uneventful, sadly remote year he spent at Cambridge with his brother Prince Henry. He had another history lesson in 1920 when the King gave him 'that fine old title of Duke of York which I bore for more than nine years and is the oldest Dukedom in the country.' A few weeks later the new Duke, partnered by Louis Greig, the former naval doctor who had become his equerry, won the RAF tennis doubles. It was a triumph not at all marred by his losing to Greig in the semi-final of the singles.

In 1923 the Duke of York took the wisest decision of his life. He wooed and wed Lady Elizabeth Bowes-Lyon, youngest daughter of the 14th Earl of Strathmore (see *Elizabeth, Queen Consort of King George VI, later Queen Elizabeth the Queen Mother*). King George V, who had already made him a Knight of the Garter on his twenty-first birthday, gave him the Order of the Thistle on his wedding day as a tribute to the bride's Scottish ancestry. Her role can hardly be exaggerated. Sir John Wheeler-Bennett (q.v.) later wrote: 'The Duchess was not only to be the partner of his happiness but his inspiration and encouragement in the face of adversity, his enduring source of strength in joy and sadness. Hers was the ability to sustain or reward him by a single smile or gesture in the public battles which he waged with his stammer; hers the capacity to calm with a word that passionate temper which ever and anon would burst its bounds.' In the absence of suitable royal residences, the newly married couple had to make several temporary homes for themselves before settling down to unbroken domestic happiness in 145 Piccadilly and Royal Lodge, Windsor Great Park. There they raised a family.

Princess Elizabeth was born in 1926, Princess Margaret Rose four years later.

In 1926 the Duke experienced yet another blessing. He became a patient of Lionel Logue (q.v.), who taught him how to overcome his speech defect and so dispel much of the terror which turned each public appearance into a private nightmare.

With his wife he carried out a full programme of royal engagements at home and abroad. Alone he made himself an authority on industrial affairs: a vocation which led his brothers to dub him The Foreman. The most imaginative of his efforts to bridge the gap between social classes was the Duke of York's Camp: an annual gathering of boys between the ages of seventeen and nineteen, nominated in equal numbers by public schools and industrial firms. The Duke, who never enjoyed Cowes Week with the same delight as did his father, would slip away each year to spend a day with them by the sea. In shirt and shorts, he played games, he chatted, he led the singing of what became both the *leitmotiv* of his venture and almost a national institution: 'Under the Spreading Chestnut Tree.'

So the busy but undemanding years rolled by, disturbed only by the economic crisis of 1931 which required the Duke to give up his stable of hunters. He found consolation in laying out a garden of exceptional beauty at Royal Lodge and learning almost all there was to be known about rhododendrons. In January 1936 the death of his father and the accession of his elder brother as Edward VIII brought him to the very steps of the throne as Heir Presumptive. Even then, the likelihood of his succeeding to the Crown seemed remote; for although the new King was still unmarried at forty-one, he was not more than eighteen months older than the Duke of York and in good health.

Then came the blow that changed his life. On 17 November the King told his brother that he was determined to marry Mrs Simpson, whatever the consequences. The Duke's ordeal was made all the more painful by what he called in his diary 'the awful and ghastly suspense of waiting.' Day after day he tried to plead with his brother, but each successive appointment was cancelled at the last moment. On the evening of 7 December he took Fort Belvedere by storm, but by then it was too late to reason with the King. 'I found him pacing up and down the room,' the Duke noted, 'and he told me his decision that he would go.' The Duke dined there on the following night. The Prime Minister, Stanley Baldwin, was a fellow guest; he too had failed to persuade Edward VIII to renounce Mrs Simpson and keep his throne. 'My brother,' the Duke wrote, 'was the life and soul of the party, telling the P.M. things I am sure he had never heard before about unemployed centres, etc.' He whispered in despair to Walter Monckton (q.v.): 'And this is the man we are going to lose.'

On 9 December the Duke again confronted his brother, then returned to London to give an account of their fruitless talk to Queen Mary. 'I broke down and sobbed like a child,' he wrote. The next day he witnessed the signing at Fort Belvedere of the Instrument of Abdication. It was followed by a discussion about the King's finances, 'a terrible lawyer interview which terminated quietly and harmoniously. . . . I later went to London where I found a large crowd outside my house cheering madly. I was overwhelmed.' On 11 December, at Royal Lodge, he dined with his brother for the last time. 'When David and I said goodbye we kissed, parted as freemasons and he bowed to me as his King.' The reign of George VI had begun.

That choice of name was significant. Bertie, as he remained to his family, was in every way his father's son. 'You have always been so sensible and easy to work with,' George V had written at the time of his marriage, 'and you have always been ready to listen to my advice and to agree with my opinions about people and things, that I feel that we have always got on very well together (very different to dear David).' Now his name itself proclaimed that fickle brilliance had given way to tradition; that the winter of discontent was to be followed, if not by glorious summer, at least by the glow of domestic virtue. Those who did business with the new King

noted that even his handwriting resembled that of his father.

They were reassured too by the resilience of the monarchy and the speed with which the new Sovereign assumed the industrious habits of his father. Few of those who served Edward VIII had in their hearts accepted him as King. Sir Kenneth Clark (q.v.), summoned to Fort Belvedere during the brief reign, commented on the poor quality of the china and suggested that the King should use some of the fine services kept at Windsor. So they drove over together after dinner and chose both china and silver from its immense store. The next day a courtier telephoned Clark and said: 'Do you know what that fellow has done? He came over here by night and stole some china and silver.' The new King and Queen, by contrast, were welcomed into their inheritance with warmth as well as relief.

During the first years of his reign, George VI was nevertheless haunted by insecurity. He told a Minister: 'All my ancestors succeeded to the throne after their predecessors had died. Mine is not only alive, but very much so.' In retrospect he seems to have exaggerated the danger of his brother's seeking to become a King over the Water. Even during the Abdication crisis, Edward VIII had found few champions. There were the Communists and the Fascists, each hoping to exploit the Government's embarrassment for political ends; Winston Churchill, who did not take long to regret his romantic impulse; and Lord Beaverbrook, who confessed that his interest was not to keep the King but to 'bugger Baldwin.' As the nightmare receded, most of his former subjects concluded, albeit with sadness, that they were well rid of a monarch so capricious as to barter an empire for a woman's love.

Yet George VI's apprehension was understandable. In spite of all he had done for his brother, the former King simply would not leave him alone; night and day he telephoned Buckingham Palace from his exile in Austria. Within hours of his accession the new King had promised to create him Duke of Windsor; bestowed on him the Grand Cross of the Order of the Bath, the only great order of chivalry he had not received as Prince of Wales; made an ample financial settlement in his favour. What George VI would not tolerate was the torrent of advice and objurgation from Schloss Enzesfeld that cast him in the role of surrogate monarch. At length he ordered Walter Monckton to tell the Duke that his telephone calls must cease.

The Queen's resentment at the burden placed on her husband by the Abdication also stiffened the King's attitude towards his brother. He refused to attend the Duke's wedding to Mrs Simpson in June 1937, much less resist the decision of his Ministers that the style of Royal Highness borne by the bridegroom be withheld from the bride. When the tide of war brought the Windsors back to England in September 1939, the King received the Duke briefly and without affection, the Duchess not at all. Nor would he countenance any public appointment for the Duke that might rekindle the popular acclaim of earlier years; banishment to the Bahamas was to be his lot. Between 1940 and the King's death twelve years later, the brothers scarcely met or even corresponded except in glacial terms.

The King and Queen had meanwhile been crowned in Westminster Abbey on 12 May 1937. 'I could eat no breakfast,' he wrote, 'and had a sinking feeling inside.' But both acquitted themselves to perfection. Others did less well. Archbishop Lang (q.v.) not only juggled with the crown before depositing it on his Sovereign's head; while holding the printed oath for the King to read, he also managed to obscure the vital words with his thumb. The Lord Great Chamberlain nearly put the hilt of the Sword of State under the royal chin while attaching it to its belt. And turning to leave the Coronation Chair, the King noted, 'I was brought up all standing, owing to one of the bishops treading on my robe. I had to tell him to get off it pretty sharply as I nearly fell down.'

King George VI would have liked to follow his father's example by holding a Durbar for his Indian subjects. But in 1937 he felt that he still had too much to learn at home. 'I do need time

to settle in,' he told the Secretary of State. By the following year, when he had gained experience, there were both political and financial objections from the Indian Government, and the plan was postponed indefinitely. Towards the end of the war he suggested that a visit to his troops in South East Asia 'would buck them up.' Again his Ministers proved obstructive. He is said to have complained, perhaps jocularly, that Churchill grudged him the Burma Star, a decoration for which he but not the Prime Minister would then have qualified. The last King-Emperor went to the grave without having set foot in India.

In the summer of 1939, however, the King and Queen were able to visit Canada and the United States. At Hyde Park, the Roosevelt family estate, the President greeted them with a tray of cocktails. 'My mother,' he told them, 'thinks you should have a cup of tea. She doesn't approve of cocktails.' 'Neither does mine,' the King said, and took one. The two Heads of State discussed world affairs until 1.30 in the morning. In their talk, of which the King later made an impressively detailed record from memory, lay the seeds of close wartime co-operation.

George VI's first Prime Minister, Stanley Baldwin, had retired soon after the Coronation. It took the King some months to warm to the less avuncular Neville Chamberlain, although he readily supported the Government's policy of appeasing Hitler and Mussolini. Indeed he had more than once to be restrained from sending personal messages to the dictators in the cause of peace. The King nevertheless believed that diplomacy should be buttressed by vigorous rearmament. Here he may have been deceived into optimism when the Royal Navy mounted a demonstration at sea to show the ease with which anti-aircraft fire from a warship could bring down a radio-controlled target plane. As the guns failed to score a single hit, secret orders were given for the plane to be flown into the sea as if it had been destroyed by accurate marksmanship.

In the autumn of 1938, when Chamberlain was staying at Balmoral, the King tried to persuade him to remain for an extra day's shooting, even offering to fly him down to London in a royal plane in time for a Cabinet meeting. Chamberlain refused; he had never flown before, disliked the sound of it, and hoped he would never have to take to the air. A fortnight later he flew to Berchtesgaden: the first of his three journeys to meet Hitler that culminated in the Munich agreement. In retrospect it seems perhaps unwise of George VI to have identified himself with an ignoble surrender; to have invited the Prime Minister on his return to appear with him and the Queen before the cheering crowds that flocked to Buckingham Palace. In those hysterical hours, however, few failed to share the King's relief or to endorse Chamberlain's claim that he had brought back 'Peace with Honour.' Less than a year later, Hitler marched against Poland and Britain was at war with Germany.

George VI was not a born leader. He could seem shy and harassed, aloof and even morose. Yet when put to the test of war he displayed nobler qualities: resolution and dignity and the chivalry of an earlier age. He was fortunate in being spared the relentless scrutiny of the television camera; and although he never ceased to find public speaking or broadcasting a hateful task, his simple, confident words lifted many hearts.

Politically, however, his touch was less sure. Regard for Chamberlain as a man of peace blinded him to the Prime Minister's inadequacy in war. When in May 1940 the Government's conduct of the Norwegian campaign provoked a revolt against his leadership, the King wrote angrily in his diary: 'It is most unfair on Chamberlain to be treated like this after all his good work. The Conservative rebels like Duff Cooper ought to be ashamed of themselves for deserting him at this moment.' The country now demanded an all-party Government to wage war with vigour; and when Labour refused to serve under Chamberlain, the Prime Minister was obliged to resign on 10 May. 'We then had an informal talk over his successor,' the King noted. 'I, of course, suggested Halifax, but

he told me that H. was not enthusiastic, as being in the Lords he could only act as a shadow or ghost in the Commons, where all the real work took place. I was disappointed over this statement, as I thought H. was the obvious man, and that his peerage could be placed in abeyance for the time being. Then I knew that there was only one person I could send for to form a Government who had the confidence of the country, and that was Winston.' And about time, too, it may be added. Nor did the King readily abandon his preference for Halifax, the austere former Viceroy of India and Foreign Secretary throughout the most humiliating years of appeasement. 'I cannot yet think of Winston as P.M.,' the King wrote on 11 May. 'I met Halifax in the garden and I told him I was sorry not to have him as P.M.' Churchill, after all, had been the only leading statesman of the day to embrace the cause of Edward VIII in December 1936.

It was several weeks, perhaps months, before the King felt at ease with his new Prime Minister. Churchill had hardly returned to Downing Street from the Palace on 10 May when he received a handwritten letter from the King. It contained no message of encouragement but a warning against the Prime Minister's proposed appointment of Lord Beaverbrook to be Minister of Aircraft Production. Churchill, immersed in forming his new Government while simultaneously following the German invasion of the Low Countries and France, did not reply. On 30 May, however, he did respond to an even more trivial exercise of the royal prerogative: an objection by the King to the appointment of Brendan Bracken, the Prime Minister's Paliamentary Private Secretary and friend, to the Privy Council. 'I should have thought,' Churchill wrote to Sir Alexander Hardinge (q.v.), the King's Private Secretary, 'that in the terrible circumstances which press upon us, and the burden of disaster and responsibility which has been cast upon me after my warnings have been so long rejected, I might be helped as much as possible.' The King had the grace at once to withdraw his opposition.

Together the King and his Prime Minister

Philatelic souvenir, 1937

endured the Battle of Britain, and in the ordeal drew closer. Either could have said after the fall of France: 'I feel happier now that we have no allies to be polite to and to pamper.' In fact it was the King. By the end of September their formal weekly audiences had been replaced by a regular Tuesday luncheon at the Palace, when their talk ranged over the whole field of war. At Christmas, Churchill gave the King one of his celebrated siren-suits. 'I could not have a better Prime Minister,' George VI wrote a few days later. Churchill responded by entrusting the King with every secret. He was among the few Ministers and military commanders to receive the Enigma intelligence decrypts; and one of only four who knew the complete plans for the use of the atom bomb.

Such confidential exchanges did not preclude an occasional scrap. In June 1944 the Prime Minister made plans to watch the Allied landings in Normandy from a warship. The King, who would also have enjoyed the scent of battle, failed to dissuade Churchill from such self-indulgence until the last hour. He also brought a draught of cold common sense to some of the Prime Minister's more bizarre notions: what he once called 'another of Winston's damned 2 a.m. decisions.' John Colville (q.v.), Churchill's private secretary, noted that both the King and the Queen were: 'a little ruffled by the offhand way he treats them – says he will come at six, puts it off until 6.30 by telephone, then comes at seven.' Directing a World War is not the most punctual of enterprises.

Nine times Buckingham Palace was hit by enemy bombs during the war. An equerry who had won the Military Cross in the trenches a generation earlier described one night in 1941 when 'this great house continuously shook like a jelly . . . for two or three hours it was like a front line trench under bombardment.' It was while touring the battered streets of London and other cities, talking to the survivors and their rescuers, that the King conceived the George Cross and the George Medal: awards for civilian heroism which he personally designed and instituted. With another imaginative gesture, he presented

a Sword of Honour to Stalingrad as a token of homage from an ally. In November 1943 it was brought by Churchill to a meeting of war leaders in Teheran, and presented to Stalin. Having raised it to his lips and kissed it, Stalin passed the sword to Marshal Voroshilov, who dropped it.

Twice the King went overseas to visit his troops. In 1943 he flew to North Africa; for security reasons he was referred to until his safe arrival as General Lyon. In spite of suffering from severe sunburn and a rebellious tummy, he was heartened by those thousands of cheering men; then he sailed across to Malta and thanked its people for the sustained courage under siege that had already earned the island a unique George Cross. In 1944 he spent nearly two weeks inspecting the Allied Armies in Italy. Field Marshal Alexander welcomed his Sovereign with a luncheon that included caviar and turtle soup, tournedos and peach Melba. The BBC reported that the King had 'sat down to his first meal of Army rations.'

Victory brought George VI no repose. He was depressed beyond measure when the General Election of July 1945 robbed him of Winston Churchill. The new Labour Government contained many unknown faces and a Prime Minister as shy as himself. Even during its first hours in office, the by now experienced King displayed his judgment. When Clement Attlee told him of his intention to send Ernest Bevin to the Treasury and Hugh Dalton to the Foreign Office, he suggested that the Prime Minister would do better to reverse their roles. This Attlee accepted, although he afterwards claimed that the King's advice had not been 'a decisive factor.' Certainly the distinctive temperament of each Minister matched his ultimate office: a robust Foreign Secretary and a wily Chancellor of the Exchequer.

Dalton was stung to hear that the King had described the Treasury as 'only an accountant's job' and believed that he himself was disliked by the court. That may well have been so. The son of Canon Dalton (q.v.), George v's old tutor, he had been brought up at Windsor and educated at

Eton and King's College, Cambridge. For a man of such background to become a Socialist cannot have endeared him to the King. Lord Longford, another Etonian member of the Labour Party, has described his first audience at the Palace as a Junior Minister in the Attlee Government. The King looked quietly at Frank Pakenham (he had not yet succeeded his brother as 7th Earl of Longford) and after a pause said: 'Why did you . . . join them?' George VI felt much more at ease with men such as Bevin who, on being asked where he had acquired his great knowledge of the world, replied that it had been 'plucked from the hedgerows of experience.' The Queen, too, was enchanted when the Foreign Secretary, invited to a banquet at the Palace, gazed on the gold plate and said: 'I like your crockery.'

The King's suspicion of public-school Socialists was reciprocated. They identified him with a grasping, or at best thoughtless upper class. When Dalton laid his Budget proposals before the King in 1945, he wrote: 'I noticed in the course of my explanation that it was when I said that I was going to increase the surtax that His Majesty showed most interest.' A few years later, another Labour Chancellor, Hugh Gaitskell, had an audience at the Palace to explain his imposition of National Health charges and Nye Bevan's threat to resign. The King said: 'He must be mad to resign over a thing like that. I really don't see why people should have false teeth free any more than they have shoes free.' And he waved his foot at Gaitskell as he said this. The Chancellor recorded the scene in his diary, and added: 'He is, of course, a fairly reactionary person.'

Such an epithet cannot be measured with accuracy. The King was no blind opponent of change. He supported the Attlee Government in bringing Independence to India through the instrument of his own cousin, Lord Mountbatten, however much it saddened him to be the last of the King-Emperors. But he did think that Labour's proposals for nationalization were too sweeping, too bureaucratic and too elaborate to be enacted during the life of a single Parliament. What others denigrated as privilege he saw only

as a traditional, ordered way of life. When in 1948 he invested the poet Vita Sackville-West with the insignia of a Companion of Honour, he asked about Knole, her family home. She told him that the house had gone to the National Trust. The King raised his hands in despair. 'Everything is going now,' he said. 'Before long, I shall also have to go.'

If the fabric of society was crumbling, at least he would preserve its outward forms. Like his father, he cared for those minutiae of ritual and custom which symbolize continuity and permanence. For George VI, a knighthood was more than a social rank or a political reward. 'It is,' he told one on whom he had bestowed the accolade, 'a rededication of you to God's service and to mine.' He felt intense satisfaction when in 1946 the Prime Minister agreed to his suggestion that appointments to the three senior Orders of Chivalry, the Garter, the Thistle and the St Patrick, should no longer be on Ministerial advice. Like nominations to the Order of Merit they would in future be made on the Sovereign's own volition. The King celebrated the change by summoning the first Chapter of the Garter to be held since 1911 and addressing the Knights Companion on the Christian foundation of the Order.

A few weeks later, during his tour of South Africa, he was correspondingly incensed by Ministerial advice on the presentation of medals to blacks. These, he was told, he must not personally pin on; nor must he shake hands with the recipients. Instead he was to hand each medal to an official of the Native Department, so that at no point did he come into physical contact with a black. Such advice, coming from his Ministers in what was then a self-governing country within the Commonwealth, the King of South Africa could not constitutionally defy. When, as King of Great Britain, he moved on to the British Protectorates of Basutoland, Bechuanaland and Swaziland, the South African Government hoped that he would follow the same course. He refused. Both blacks and Europeans received their medals personally from the King, who then shook hands with each.

George VI had as obsessive an eye as his father for correctness of dress, particularly if it happened to be the King's uniform. He himself presented a flawless appearance to which he devoted both care and ingenuity. Each year, as the State Opening of Parliament approached, he would work at his desk day after day with the Imperial Crown on his head: so that on the morning of the ceremony he could wear it with comfort and dignity. He similarly accustomed himself to the weight of a Brigade of Guards bearskin cap by gardening in it before each annual Trooping the Colour.

It was the King who as a wartime economy put his footmen into blue battledress with the royal cipher on the breast pocket. He was less happy with the introduction of battledress into the Army, fearing lest Other Ranks should take to wearing collars and ties (as they eventually did) and so resemble officers. But officers, however senior, also had to be on their guard when the King was about. His first act on returning from Princess Elizabeth's wedding in 1947 was to inquire why a certain admiral had not been wearing his sword in Westminster Abbey. Nor did he hesitate to rebuke his fellow Sovereign, King Peter of Yugoslavia, for wearing a slender gold watchchain between the two breast pockets of his uniform.

There were pitfalls in the wearing of plain clothes, too. After the war, when it was difficult to have evening shirts starched, the King allowed soft ones to be worn at Sandringham. But when Queen Mary was staying, guests were expected to wear stiff butterfly collars with their soft shirts as a mark of respect. Not even the King's schoolgirl daughters escaped the cares of haberdashery. On their joining the Girl Guides, he forbade them to wear the regulation long black stockings because they were so unbecoming.

The King's tongue was as sharp as his eye, his jokes usually at someone's expense. At its most attractive, his humour struck a whimsical, self-deprecating note. Shortly after the so-called 'Mayfair Men' had lured a jeweller from Cartier to a London hotel, then beaten him unconscious and robbed him of his diamonds, the King needed to choose some jewellery as a present. 'And would you believe it,' he said, 'Cartier insisted on sending *two* men to the Palace, *two* of them. They don't trust me.'

More often he resorted to heavy banter. A slip of the tongue, a wrong weather forecast, a solecism of dress or etiquette: if these were sometimes forgiven, they were never forgotten. 'Do you remember being fast asleep when a snipe came over you here?' he would ask a fellow gun. 'No, Sir, certainly not.' But year after year the culprit would be reminded of his lapse. It could be crueller than that. 'We are very glad to know that you have some ideas,' the King once said to a young guest whose suggestion for the improvement of the day's sport had proved unsuccessful, 'but have you any better ideas?' Such ritual and reiterated witticisms, a courtier wrote, were received with sour glee.

Both those examples of royal badinage are drawn from the sport he loved best. He shot at Sandringham for the first time on 23 December 1907, a few days after his twelfth birthday, killing three rabbits; he shot there for the last time on 5 February 1952, a few hours before his death, killing three hares with his last three shots. At his best he was as fine a marksman as his father, for whom no grouse could fly too fast, no pheasant too high. But he lacked the equable temperament of George V that could shrug off an easy shot missed, a minute error in adding up the bag, a setback to a well-laid plan. In a way much appreciated by his guests, George VI surpassed his father's generosity as a host; he abandoned the tradition by which the King took the best place at every stand throughout the day. Nor was he a fair-weather sportsman. 'Snow and very cold east wind,' he wrote in his game-book one January. 'I spent four hours in a hide in a kale field.'

If he found refreshment in the pursuits of a countryman, it was from his family that he drew strength. The love and support of his wife, the serene devotion of his elder daughter and the spirited affection of the younger: these sustained him throughout a reign of darkening shadows.

'I feel burned out,' the King wrote at the end of the war. The tour of South Africa, with its long sea voyage there and back, spared him an exceptionally cruel English winter; but the programme devised by the Union Government left him once more exhausted and seventeen pounds lighter in weight. Throughout 1948 he suffered increasingly from cramp in the legs which, in November, Sir James Learmonth (q.v.) diagnosed as arteriosclerosis. Although cheered by the birth of his first grandchild, Prince Charles, he spent an anxious winter and in March 1949 was obliged to undergo an operation to restore the blood supply to his left leg. The doctors suggested that it should be carried out in the Royal Masonic Hospital. 'I have never heard of a King going to a hospital before,' was his regal response. So the operation was performed by Learmonth in Buckingham Palace, and proved effective.

Thereafter the King led a reasonably full and active life. Throughout 1951, however, his health again deteriorated. In September he underwent an operation for the removal of his entire left lung, in which a malignant growth had been detected. With characteristic grit, he made yet another apparent recovery. In October he presided over the Privy Councils required by the return to office of a Conservative Government led by Winston Churchill; and on 31 January 1952 he stood on a windswept airport waving goodbye to Princess Elizabeth and Prince Philip as they left on a tour of East Africa, Australia and New Zealand. In the early hours of the morning of 6 February, King George VI died in his sleep at Sandringham.

Churchill said of him: 'During these last months the King walked with death, as if death were a companion, an acquaintance, whom he recognized and did not fear. In the end death came as a friend.' His remains lay in State at Westminster and then were carried to Windsor for burial. The Prime Minister's wreath of white lilac and carnations was in the shape of a George Cross. It bore the inscription: 'For Valour.'

Gilliat, Sir Martin
(1913–)

Private Secretary to Queen Elizabeth the Queen Mother since 1956. His grandfather was a Governor of the Bank of England and Member of Parliament; his father a barrister who won the DSO in the South African War; his elder brother, serving in India as a young officer, died after being mauled by a tiger.

Martin Gilliat was educated at Eton and the Royal Military College, Sandhurst, commissioned into the 60th Rifles and captured by the German Army while defending Calais in 1940. As a prisoner of war in Colditz he showed courage and ingenuity in trying to escape and on his release was mentioned in despatches and awarded the MBE. In 1947 he became Deputy Military Secretary to Lord Mountbatten (q.v.) as Viceroy of India and was wounded when fired upon in Delhi during communal riots. He served successively as Comptroller to Malcolm Mac-Donald when United Kingdom Commissioner-General for South East Asia and as Military Secretary to Field Marshal Lord Slim when Governor-General of Australia.

In 1956 Colonel Gilliat was summoned home for a trial period as Private Secretary to Queen Elizabeth the Queen Mother; nearly thirty years later he claims he is still waiting to hear whether his appointment will be made permanent. Tall, bald and beetlebrowed, he is the most convivial and emollient of courtiers, a member of many clubs, a dispenser of jokes and dewdrops and pink gin. At a drawing-room recital of modern music, his voice has been heard proclaiming: 'I don't mind what I have to listen to, as long as I get fed.' Another evening he seized a pudding spoon to eat the last of a particularly succulent sauce served with the meat. 'Not allowed to do this where I work,' he explained.

Behind the geniality lies a meticulous planner and a shrewd judge of character. It is a measure of his success at Clarence House that he has been made an honorary Bencher of the Middle Temple and an honorary Doctor of Laws of London University, two institutions with which the Queen Mother has long been associated. He was appointed KCVO in 1962 and GCVO in 1981.

Gilliat also acts as the Queen Mother's racing manager and has a prodigious knowledge of *Sporting Life* in every sense. Although he has himself owned the occasional horse, his racing colours of Etonian blue and black have rarely caught the judge's eye. An exception was the victory of Royal Tournament at Cheltenham; but that infuriating animal, having long disappointed, ran unbacked that day, and the Tote paid 150 to 1 on a winning ticket. Sir Martin tries his luck at the bridge table, too, and as a backer of theatrical productions.

Gilliat lives in a charming little manor house in Hertfordshire, is Vice-Lieutenant of the county, sits regularly as a magistrate and supports many charities. He is unmarried.

Gloucester, Prince Henry, Duke of
(1900–1974)

Third son of King George V and Queen Mary. He was born on 31 March 1900 at York Cottage, Sandringham. Among his godparents were the Kaiser William and Field Marshal Earl Roberts, hero of the Boer War. He was the first son of a British Sovereign to be sent away to school rather than educated by tutors. He went in 1910 to St Peter's Court preparatory school, Broadstairs, then on to Eton, where he boarded in the same house as the future King Leopold III of the Belgians. The experiment allowed him to mix with boys of his own age but failed to galvanize an unbookish mind. Queen Mary wrote to him with unusual sharpness: 'Do for goodness sake wake up and use the brains God has given you. All you write about is your everlasting football, of which I am heartily sick.'

Nor did his father make allowances for the peccadilloes of a schoolboy. The King was furious to learn that Harry (as he was known in the family) had damaged his knee 'while playing French cricket whatever that is – I should think a very silly game.' And when the Prince wished to see some German prisoners of war at a camp near Eton, his father thought the expedition 'in very bad taste.' He asked his son how he would like it 'if you were a prisoner for people to come to stare at you as if you were a wild beast.' Prince Henry, an amiable but highly strung boy, never overcame the nervous strain caused by his father's quarter-deck discipline.

From Eton he passed into the Royal Military College, Sandhurst, then spent a year at Cambridge with his elder brother Prince Albert, later Duke of York. But instead of sharing the full life of their fellow undergraduates at Trinity College, they were made to live in a house of their own. Prince Henry later confessed that during this university interlude he had never once entered the Fitzwilliam or any other museum. In middle age, however, he formed two fine collections: one of Chinese porcelain and other oriental objects, the other of sporting prints and drawings.

Commissioned into the King's Royal Rifle Corps, the Prince then transferred to the 10th Hussars, where he could combine his duties as a professional soldier with a love of field sports. In pursuit of the fox he suffered more than his fair share of riding accidents. 'Why can't you stick to croquet?' one of his brothers chided him when Prince Henry broke a collarbone and was unable to represent his father at a royal funeral. Queen Mary, too, was displeased by his thoughtlessness. 'I told Harry not to hunt,' she complained, 'until Aunt Maud had been buried.'

In 1928 the King created him Duke of Gloucester, Earl of Ulster and Baron Culloden. Neither those honours nor the Orders of the Garter, the Thistle and St Patrick diverted him from his chosen career as a soldier. But he was disappointed not to be able to serve abroad with his regiment in certain sensitive stations; Ireland, Egypt and India were all at various times forbidden him lest the presence of the King's son should arouse political resentment. In 1929 he led a mission to Japan to confer the Garter on the

The Duke of Gloucester on safari in East Africa

Emperor Hirohito; and in 1930 he was in Addis Ababa for the Coronation of the Emperor Haile Selassie, a ceremony which left its mark on a novel written by another British visitor, Evelyn Waugh's *Black Mischief*.

The Duke of Gloucester married in 1935 Lady Alice Montagu-Douglas-Scott, a daughter of his father's old friend and shipmate, the 7th Duke of Buccleuch. Neither that nor the death of King George V in January 1936 interfered with his plans for a two-year course at the Staff College. But the prospect of completing the course and ultimately of commanding the 10th Hussars was shattered by the Abdication of King Edward VIII in December. With the accession of the Duke of York as King George VI, only three lives stood between the Duke of Gloucester and the throne. Two of them, moreover, were children; Princess Elizabeth, the heir presumptive, was eleven and a half, Princess Margaret Rose four years younger. In the event of the King's death, the Duke would become Regent for the young Queen Elizabeth II and remain so until she came

of age (in the royal sense) on 21 April 1944. Even if the King were merely out of the country on State visits or other business, the Duke would have to be at hand to act as a Counsellor of State. George VI therefore concluded that it would be neither fitting nor practicable for his brother to continue as a regimental officer. At the age of thirty-six, an embarrassed and reluctant major found himself promoted to major-general.

On the outbreak of war in 1939, the Duke was appointed chief liaison officer to Lord Gort, Commander-in-Chief of the British Expeditionary Force in France. He served throughout the Battle of Flanders in 1940 and was injured by falling masonry during a German air raid. Returning to England, he assumed liaison duties on the staff of the Commander-in-Chief, Home Forces. More than once he tried to divest himself of high military rank in order to command a regiment or a brigade on active service. Instead he was promoted to lieutenant-general and despatched on worldwide tours of inspection.

In July 1942 his name achieved brief but

humiliating prominence in the national Press. Defeats in Africa and the Far East provoked a motion of censure in the Commons on Churchill's conduct of the war. It was proposed by a senior Conservative backbencher, Sir John Wardlaw-Milne. A fellow MP, 'Chips' Channon (q.v.), left this account of the speech:

'He was fair, calm and dignified, and he was listened to with respect, until he made the unfortunate suggestion that the Duke of Gloucester should be made Commander-in-Chief of the forces. The House roared with disrespectful laughter, and I at once saw Winston's face light up, as if a lamp had been lit within him, and he smiled genially. He knew now that he was saved, and poor Wardlaw-Milne never quite regained the hearing of the House.'

The Duke was in India when the report of the debate reached him. He wrote to his wife: 'What impertinence on the part of Wardlaw-Milne without asking anybody and me in particular.' Neither Sir John's inept proposal nor the boorish way in which the Commons received it diminished the Duke's distaste for politicians.

From 1944 to 1946 he was Governor-General of Australia, an appointment that was to have gone to his younger brother the Duke of Kent, killed in an air crash in 1942. Neither he nor the Duchess spared themselves, visiting every corner of the Commonwealth by air, often in discomfort. The Duke would afterwards complain that he had been driven too hard, and it was with relief that he returned with his family to England.

Until his death nearly thirty years later, he dutifully accepted whatever tasks were required of him, but without enthusiasm. Once when the memoirs of Princess Marie Louise (q.v.) were being discussed, he said jocularly: 'I am thinking of writing my own. And do you know what I shall call them? *Forty Years of Boredom*.' Public speaking did not come naturally to him; nor had he a fund of amiable small-talk with which to engage strangers. At the opening of a fruit and flower show, he spoke only once. 'What a bloody big marrow,' he said, 'glad I don't have

to eat it.' He had inherited a Hanoverian or perhaps a Teck temper. In Malaya the rain clattering on the tin roof woke him at 2 a.m. 'Who's having a bath at this hour of the night?' he roared. Mismanaged ceremonial could be sure to detonate just such an explosion. Even occasions which some would find enticing were a burden to him. At a performance of *Tosca* during a State visit, he watched dispassionately as Maria Callas plunged over the battlements; then his distinctive high-pitched voice rang round the opera house: 'Well if she's really dead, we can all go home.'

There were, however, three loves in his life: his family, his farm and the Army. Having himself suffered an unhappy childhood, he was a devoted and understanding father to his two sons, Prince William and Prince Richard (qq.v.). The family home was Barnwell Manor, a sixteenth-century house in Northamptonshire which had once belonged to the Buccleuchs. The Duke of Gloucester bought it in 1938, together with four tenanted farms, for £37,000, part of the legacy left him by his father. On returning from Australia he built up the home farm by his own efforts, never more content than when driving a tractor or stooking corn; he was proud, too, of his Guernsey herd. Each summer he took the family to Farr, in Inverness-shire, a delightful property with its grouse moor and deer forest.

In his dedication to the Army, its traditions and history, the Duke of Gloucester recalled those royal Field Marshals of another age: York, Cambridge and Connaught. Some thought him an anachronism; but the men he commanded – and wished he could have led into battle – looked to him with affection and respect. Queen Mary was among those who thought her son's abilities too little recognized. On her deathbed she sent a message to the Prime Minister, Winston Churchill, begging him to find 'something for Harry to do – like being Ranger of Richmond Park.' In 1955 he was promoted Field Marshal.

While driving himself and his wife back to Barnwell after Churchill's furneral service in

1965, his car left the road and overturned. Although he appeared unharmed, it is likely that the Duke had suffered the first of several strokes that by 1968 had left him almost totally paralyzed. Death released him from his suffering in 1974. He was buried at Windsor as a prince and a soldier.

Gloucester, Princess Alice, Duchess of
(1901–   )

Wife of Prince Henry, Duke of Gloucester (q.v.). She was born Lady Alice Montagu-Douglas-Scott, third daughter of the 7th Duke of Buccleuch. Her father, a fellow midshipman of the future King George v during the cruise round the world of HMS *Bacchante*, might never have survived to marry and raise a family but for a remarkable escape. Prince George described in his diary how one day in the Mediterranean his shipmate 'fell from under the maintop, nearly 40 feet, but was providentially brought up by the leg within a few feet of the deck by a couple of crossed side ropes, or he must have been killed.'

With her parents, three brothers and four sisters, Alice spent a childhood migrating by special train from one splendid family house to another. There was Boughton, a Versailles set down in the heart of Northamptonshire; Drumlanrig, a dream castle of pink sandstone dominating a wooded prospect of almost Hibernian green; Dalkeith, another Scottish stronghold, known locally as 'The Palace', from which General Monck plotted the restoration of King Charles II; Bowhill, of less architectural merit but sited in beautiful country between two tributaries of the River Tweed; and Montagu House, since demolished, that overlooked the Thames at Westminster and harboured sixty-eight inhabitants and one bathroom. The cellars at Drumlanrig and Bowhill each contained two 54-gallon barrels of whisky which were never allowed to be less than half full. York House and Barnwell Manor must have seemed to her like cottages after her marriage in 1935 to Prince Henry, Duke of Gloucester, the third son of King George v.

It was not in fact until the eve of her thirty-fourth birthday that Lady Alice succumbed to matrimony. She loathed débutante dances and other tribal gatherings of the London season, preferring the thrill and camaraderie of fox-hunting in Scotland, skiing in Switzerland and shooting big game in Africa. One visit to Kenya, during which she learned Swahili, lasted more than a year. On safari she gradually relinquished the rifle for the camera and the paintbox, and later held a successful exhibition of her African water-colours at a Bond Street gallery.

After an undemonstrative courtship, Lady Alice was betrothed to the Duke of Gloucester in August 1935. The death of her father a few weeks later caused the cancellation of elaborate plans for a wedding in Westminster Abbey. The ceremony was instead held in the privacy of the chapel at Buckingham Palace. For almost forty years the Duchess of Gloucester proved the ideal partner of a dedicated soldier but unwilling Prince of the Blood Royal. It was a marriage that required unexpected sacrifices on her part. As the wife of a serving officer in the 10th Hussars,

Princess Alice at Sandown Park, 1980

albeit a son of the Sovereign, she could look forward to a life similar to that she had always known. It would embrace the close-knit society of a regiment into which two uncles and two brothers had also been commissioned; the prospect of country pursuits at home, more exotic sport in India or other overseas stations where the British flag still flew.

These hopes lasted little more than a year. The Abdication of King Edward VIII in December 1936 placed the Duke third in line of succession to the throne and brought the Duchess as well as her husband an exacting programme of public duties many of which she carries out to this day. Throughout the war, while her husband served in the Army, she became Air Chief Commandant of the Women's Royal Auxiliary Air Force (WAAF) and Colonel-in-Chief of the King's Own Scottish Borderers, a regiment she later visited in the Malayan jungle, taking with her a sprig of heather for each man to wear in his bonnet. She also ran Barnwell, their recently acquired country house in Northamptonshire, and in 1941 gave birth to their first child, Prince William (q.v.). Her mother-in-law, Queen Mary, offered practical advice: 'Fortnum and Mason are *so expensive* that I think you had better go elsewhere for the cradle.' A second son, Prince Richard (q.v.), was born at a Nursing home in Northampton in August 1944.

Less than four months later, the entire family were on their way to Australia, where the Duke was sworn in as Governor-General, the first member of the royal family to hold the appointment. For the mother of two small children the Duchess's years in Canberra were something of a penance. Government House, she later wrote, was plagued by rats, mice, spiders and poisonous snakes; exposed to cruel winds; and almost bare of furniture, pictures and even light fixtures. 'Poor Nannie was aghast at the miserable nurseries awaiting her and the children,' she told Queen Mary, 'no electric kettle, no frigidair, nothing we had asked for.' The Duchess disapproved of other aspects of Australian life. There were the dockers who, because it was raining, refused to load Red Cross parcels for

Australian prisoners of war in Japanese hands; the gross meals on official occasions, 'served always on one's plate like a dog's dinner'; the Governor of South Australia 'who kept Prince Henry up late at night by his passion for silly games.' In spite of these and other hazards, the Gloucesters did their best to represent the Crown in a sometimes unappreciative Commonwealth.

Returning to England in 1947, the Duke and Duchess resumed their happy, unpretentious country life punctuated by official engagements and overseas tours. In 1965, however, the clouds began to gather. The Duchess suffered broken bones and required fifty-seven stitches in her face after a motor accident; the Rolls-Royce which her husband was driving to Barnwell after Sir Winston Churchill's funeral service in London swerved off the road, somersaulted three times and ended upside down in a field of cabbages. In spite of her injuries, the Duchess refused to cancel a tour of Australia three weeks later. The Duke seemed to have emerged unscathed but his health declined rapidly. From 1968 until his death in 1974 he was a complete invalid, deprived of both speech and movement. The family suffered another tragedy in 1972 when the elder son Prince William was killed in a flying accident.

It is not in the Duchess's nature to allow private grief to intrude on public duty. Before long she had once more picked up the threads of a royal routine. And there was consolation in the marriage of her younger son, who with his Danish wife and their three children made his home at Barnwell.

Born in the last year of the Victorian era, Princess Alice (as she is now styled) continues to display the qualities by which the old Queen herself is best remembered: industry, resilience, a shy charm, even a taste for authorship. The volume of memoirs she published at the age of eighty-one would not discredit a more professional pen. It is also livelier and less discreet than Queen Victoria's *Leaves from the Journal of our Life in the Highlands*.

Gloucester, Prince William of
(1941–1972)

The elder son of Prince Henry, Duke of Gloucester, and of Princess Alice, Duchess of Gloucester (qq.v.). He was born in Lady Carnarvon's Nursing Home at Hadley Common, Hertfordshire, evacuated from London to avoid wartime bombing. Among his godparents were Field-Marshal Lord Gort, vc, on whose staff his father had recently served; and Princess Helena Victoria (q.v.), who at her death left Prince William a legacy which he spent buying a racehorse called Adventurous.

After a happy childhood at Barnwell, the family home in Northamptonshire, and later in Australia, where his father was Governor-General, he was sent to a preparatory school at Broadstairs. 'My dear Papa,' he wrote, 'I arrived at Wellesley House at 6 o'clock. I found that you had given me two 10-shilling notes, did you mean it?' At Eton he generally did well at both work and games, and made an imaginative film of the new roof constructed by Sir William Holford for College Chapel.

Between school and university he was briefly attached to the 10th Hussars, to discover whether he would like to follow his father into the regiment as a professional soldier. He came out firmly against it. 'I am simply not interested in peace-time boy-scout activities,' he wrote to a friend. In any case, he continued, 'I am going to have a bloody good shot at showing that although I am just a rather junior appendage to this extraordinary institution called the Monarchy, I can also do as well as anyone else in some capacity or other in which I shall have no privileges or advantages.' It was to be a recurrent theme throughout the remaining years of his short life.

At Magdalene College, Cambridge, he played most games, took a respectable degree in History and made friends with whom he shared the first of several enterprising safaris to Ethiopia. He then spent a year at Stanford University, California, reading American history, political science and business studies. Back in England, Prince William worked for a few months in the private clients investment department of Lazards, the merchant bank in the City of London. It was thought that this introduction to high finance might help him in running the Barnwell estate he would one day inherit.

Prince William had meanwhile twice failed the Civil Service examination for permanent entry into the Commonwealth Relations Office, each time by a narrow margin. In 1965, however, he joined the service as a special entrant on short contract, and was posted to Lagos as a Third Secretary in the British High Commission. Even at twenty-five his royal background and skill at polo brought him the confidences and friendship of Nigerian Ministers denied to more senior British officials. That was sometimes resented in the High Commission, as was the detached view he took of British policy throughout the Nigerian civil war. 'I am becoming increasingly aware,' he wrote, 'that there is no room for my type within the slow moving and claustrophobic atmosphere of the Civil Service.' And a little later: 'Dear old Britain does nothing, tries to be neutral, looks damn silly and gets no thanks from either side!' While in Nigeria he bought his own aircraft, a Piper Twin Comanche, in which he made several transcontinental flights.

It was in his own plane that Prince William arrived in Tokyo in 1968, having been promoted to Second Secretary (Commercial) in the British Embassy, still only temporarily attached to the service. Although he was bored by paperwork, his warmth of manner and utter lack of pomposity appealed to visiting British businessmen; and he had no inhibitions in promoting, as he said, 'plastic shoes, ladies underwear and button badges.' In two ways he displayed his independence. With the permission of an understanding ambassador, Sir John Pilcher, he declined to live in the British Embassy compound, cheek by jowl with his colleagues. Instead he took a charming traditional Japanese house and garden; and he invited a decorative and intelligent Hungarian lady, rather older and more experienced than himself, to share it with him. Later she accompanied him to England, where his family received her politely but discouraged matrimony.

The increasingly precarious health of the Duke of Gloucester prompted his son to resign from the Diplomatic Service in 1970 in order to look after the Barnwell estate and to undertake a limited programme of public duties. For recreation he continued to fly his own aircraft, by now a Piper Arrow, in international rallies; he came seventh in the King's Cup Air Race, the premier event in the United Kingdom. It was in August 1972, while competing for a lesser trophy in Staffordshire, that his plane crashed soon after take-off, killing both himself and his co-pilot, Commander Vyrell Mitchell.

Prince William of Gloucester was endowed with many enviable qualities. He was handsome and intelligent, dashing and courageous and kind. Yet not even by the age of thirty had he quite found a role. He was too restless, too

Prince William boards his Piper Twin Comanche aircraft

resentful of privilege to be royal; too haunted by his upbringing, too loyal to his family to fight for the glittering prizes of another world. Such tensions left him discontented and sometimes depressed. He told a friend: 'It looks as though I shall spend the rest of my life shooting small birds and sleeping with larger ones.' Had Prince William survived but a year or two more, he would have come to terms with his inheritance: married, raised a family, farmed, exhorted boys' clubs in Leeds and encouraged exports to Lima. Such security of the spirit was denied him. He died young; but his memorial is to be found in many hearts.

Gloucester, Prince Richard, Duke of
(1944–   )

Younger and only surviving son of Prince Henry, Duke of Gloucester, and Princess Alice, Duchess of Gloucester (qq.v.). He was born at St Matthew's nursing home, Northampton. His godparents included Princess Marie Louise (q.v.), who made Prince Richard her heir, and Field Marshal Lord Alexander. After Eton and Magdalene College, Cambridge, he felt free to settle down as a practising architect in the belief that his elder brother Prince William (q.v.) would one day inherit their father's royal and family responsibilities. It was not to be. Less than two months after Prince Richard's marriage to Birgitte van Deurs, the daughter of a Danish lawyer, Prince William was killed in an air crash. In 1974, on the death of the Duke of Gloucester, Prince Richard succeeded to both the dukedom and the family estate of Barnwell, in Northamptonshire, with its 5,000 acres of farmland.

The Duke and Duchess with their three children have made Barnwell their home. They also occupy part of Kensington Palace. According to Princess Alice, 'they cannot afford a chauffeur, a lady's maid or a valet.' And in spite of having become president of the Institute of Advanced Motorists, the Duke prefers to use a motor bike. He is a trustee of the British

Prince Richard, Duke of Gloucester, with his wife and children, 1980

Museum, Colonel-in-Chief of the Gloucestershire Regiment and patron-in-chief of the New Islington and Hackney Housing Association. A photographer as well as an architect, he has published illustrated books on the buildings and statues of London. The Duke's interest in history has led him to become patron of the Richard III Society; he is disposed to believe that his namesake was guiltless of most if not all the crimes with which he has been associated.

Unlike his father, who was at his most convivial with a glass in his hand, the Duke is a teetotaller. Against smoking he wages a relentless crusade. In 1984, ten years after succeeding to a seat in the House of Lords, he made his maiden speech on the subject: a diatribe shorter but no less fervent than the *Counterblaste to Tobacco* written by his ancestor King James I nearly four centuries earlier. He attacked not only the habit of smoking but also the industry that spends £100 million each year on advertising and the Government which seemingly cares more for tobacco revenue than for the nation's health. The Duke thus broke with tradition twice over. The royal family are advised at all times to avoid provoking political controversy; and members of either House of Parliament about to make a maiden speech are similarly urged to abstain

from unconsidered or contentious themes.

The Duke, however, has history on his side. Many members of the royal family during the present century, including every Sovereign except Elizabeth II, have been heavy smokers; according to medical opinion, they have thus shortened their lives. Edward VII and George V both died of heart failure caused by bronchial weakness or narrowing of the arteries, as did the late Duke of Gloucester. Edward VIII died of cancer of the throat, George VI of cancer of the lung. The only senior member of the royal family who today continues to smoke is Princess Margaret.

Greville, the Hon. Mrs Ronald
(1867–1942)

Friend of King George VI, Queen Elizabeth and other members of the royal family. Baptized Margaret but more often called Maggie, she was the illegitimate daughter of the Rt Hon. William McEwan, Liberal MP and brewer, by his cook. 'That,' the child of the liaison would claim, 'is why I understand the people so well.' In 1891 Miss McEwan was married to the Hon. Ronald Greville, son of the 2nd Baron Greville, who died in 1908. On her father's death five years later, she inherited more than £1½ million. Small, stout and untouched by beauty, she harnessed money to intelligence and climbed relentlessly to the topmost pinnacles of social ambition.

Mrs Greville dispensed hospitality at her London house in Charles Street, Berkeley Square, (which later became the premises of the Guards Club); and in the country at Polesden Lacey, near Dorking, once the home of the playwright Sheridan and since her death the property of the National Trust. She allowed herself what Kenneth Clark (q.v.) called 'the slight fantasy of cultivating royalty,' and liked to boast that in a single morning three Kings had been sitting on her bed: presumably not all at the same time. She lent Polesden Lacey to the Duke of York and his bride for their honeymoon in 1923. When in 1936 he was called to the throne as King George VI, she felt a little sad. 'I was so happy,' she sighed, 'in the days when they used to run in and out of my house as if they were my own children.'

Like many of those who entertain acquaintances as well as friends, she incurred the disparagement of both. Cecil Beaton (q.v.) called her 'a galumping, greedy, snobbish old toad who watered at the chops at the sight of royalty.' No less unchivalrous, Harold Nicolson (q.v.) dismissed his hostess as 'a fat slug filled with venom.' Mrs Greville did indeed have a sharp tongue. On the outbreak of war in 1939 she said of Mrs Keppel, the former mistress of King Edward VII: 'To hear Alice talk about her escape from France, one would think she had swum the Channel with her maid between her teeth.' While the nation applauded Winston Churchill's oratory in the dark days of 1941, Mrs Greville observed: 'If only the Prime Minister could have permanent laryngitis, we might win the war.' She annihilated one persistent enemy, Lady Cunard (q.v.), with a single blow: 'You must not think that I dislike poor Emerald. I am always telling Queen Mary that she isn't half as bad as she is painted.'

At her death in 1942, Mrs Greville left an estate of more than £1½ million. Her bequests included all her jewels, 'with my loving thoughts,' to the Queen; £20,000 to Princess Margaret; £12,500 to Queen Victoria Eugénie of Spain; £10,000 to Sir Osbert Sitwell; and a like sum to resist vivisection.

Hahn, Kurt
(1896–1974)

Founder of Gordonstoun School. He was born in Berlin, the son of a well-to-do Jewish family, and read Classics at Christ Church, Oxford, before continuing his studies at Heidelberg and other German universities. During the Great War he worked for the German Foreign Office

Kurt Hahn at Gordonstoun

as a reader of English newspapers. He was private secretary to Prince Max of Baden, the last Imperial Chancellor of Germany; then to Dr Melchior, during the peace negotiations leading to the Treaty of Versailles.

After the war, Hahn helped Prince Max to found a co-educational boarding school at Salem, the Prince's estate near Lake Constance, and ultimately became its headmaster. Outspoken opposition to the Nazi regime led to his arrest in 1933. He was released by the intervention of Ramsay MacDonald, among others, emigrated to Scotland and in 1934 founded a new public school near Elgin, in Morayshire. Gordonstoun had once been the home of Sir William Gordon Cumming, disgraced after allegedly cheating at cards while a fellow guest of the future King Edward VII at Tranby Croft. Hahn exorcized any lingering traces of Edwardian decadence with an educational system designed, it was said, to curb 'the poisonous passions of puberty.' Its ideals owe something to Sparta, more to Plato and not a little to Dr Arnold of Rugby; its virtues are self-discipline and a healthy outdoor life. 'My best schoolmaster,' Hahn would say, 'is the Moray Firth.' And he liked to contrast his school of embryo coastguards with the 'jaded voluptuaries' nurtured by Eton.

If Gordonstoun too often develops character

at the expense of intellect, that handicap has been overcome by the most celebrated of its early pupils. Prince Philip, Duke of Edinburgh, one of whose sisters married the son of Prince Max of Baden, has since paid tribute to the system by sending his three sons there. He has also publicly praised Hahn's visionary and effervescent mind while sorrowing over his failings as an administrator. Certainly the headmaster lacked a sense both of proportion and priorities. The chairman of the school governors once wrote: 'The search for a missing sixpence was carried out as if it were a murder hunt; the careless disposal of a biscuit wrapping treated as if it were the placing of a pound of gelignite.'

Like other great headmasters, Hahn cultivated his own legend. He expressed his philosophy in striking aphorisms. 'You look for faults,' he told a pupil, 'I look for pure gold and I usually find it.' Or: 'I loathe a quarrel but I love a fight.' He would offer to cut up the meat of his neighbour at dinner whose arm was in a sling, then absent-mindedly eat it himself. Late for an appointment, he leaped into a London taxi, shouting his Gordonstoun telephone number at the driver. One day he came on four of his boys who were loafing away the afternoon. The first was Metcalf, which he pronounced Medcuff. 'You are Medcuffing,' he began. 'Stop Medcuffing.' He turned to the second boy: 'You are Beaumonting. Stop Beaumonting.' A third boy was likewise enjoined to stop Jacksing. Hahn then unexpectedly withdrew, to the disappointment of the fourth boy, who was called Hore.

Hankey, Sir Maurice, 1st Baron
(1877–1963)

Public servant and confidant of King George V. It is a measure of Hankey's ability that when he retired in 1938 as Secretary of the Cabinet, Secretary of the Committee of Imperial Defence and Clerk of the Privy Council, three men were required to relieve him of his triple burden.

Educated at Rugby School, Hankey joined the Royal Marine Artillery in 1895 as a second-lieutenant. In 1912, having by the age of thirty-four risen to no higher rank than captain, he was selected by the Prime Minister on the recommendation of Lord Haldane to be Secretary of the Committee of Imperial Defence. Having proved his genius for administration during the early years of the Great War, he became the first Secretary of the Cabinet in 1916. Asquith called him 'the organizer of victory.' Lloyd George said he was as essential as any man to ultimate success. Balfour believed that without him Britain would have lost the war.

These tributes were all the more remarkable in that Hankey lacked a commanding personality. He was below middle height, frugal in his tastes, humourless in conversation and numbingly verbose on paper (when he published his 600,000-word memoirs in 1961, the work sold only 1,599 copies and brought its author no more than £300). King George V nevertheless valued his judgment and used him as a trusted link with successive Governments, particularly when the antipathetic Lloyd George was Prime Minister.

Hankey recognized the King's qualities of industry and common sense. Reporting to him on a tour of the Commonwealth, he noted: 'There was hardly a scrap of information, whether of a material or political kind, with which the King did not seem to be familiar.' With tongue in cheek, he accepted his Sovereign's 'command' to vote for the National Government in the general election of 1931. As Clerk of the Privy Council, Hankey saw George V at Sandringham during the last hours of his reign. 'I caught the King's eye,' he wrote, 'and was profoundly touched by the smile which he gave me, such as I have often seen in his eye in better times.' He had earlier received, among his many honours, a GCVO personally bestowed by the King. One of Hankey's few administrative lapses occurred in February 1938, when George VI learned of Anthony Eden's resignation as Foreign Secretary from neither the Prime Minister nor the Secretary of the Cabinet but from a BBC broadcast. By the time Hankey took leave of the King on retiring from the public service later that year, the royal anger had abated. 'I can't think what we shall all do without you,' he was told.

On the outbreak of World War II in 1939, however, Hankey (by now a peer) was once again enjoying confidential talks with the King, this time as Minister without Portfolio and a member of Chamberlain's War Cabinet. In the following year Churchill demoted him, and he left the Government in 1942. Hankey continued to further the war effort in more unobtrusive ways. An admiring subordinate, C.P. Snow, enshrined him in his novel, *The New Men*, as Thomas Bevill.

Hansell, Henry
(1863–1935)

Tutor to the future King Edward VIII and King George VI. The son of a Norfolk squire, he was educated at Malvern College and Magdalen College, Oxford, where he excelled at cricket and football, and took Second Class Honours in

History. He became a schoolmaster, and as a private tutor ensured that Prince Arthur, son of the Duke of Connaught (qq.v.), passed the undemanding examination for Eton. In 1902 the future King George V appointed him to take charge of his two elder sons.

A handsome but humourless bachelor of forty, Hansell displayed many manly virtues but lacked the imagination of the inspired teacher. The Duke of Windsor, whose own educational standards were never exacting, later wrote of his tutor:

'I am appalled to discover how little I really learned. . . . Although I was in his care on and off for more than twelve years I am today unable to recall anything brilliant or original that he ever said.'

Hansell himself recognized the inadequacy of private tuition as preparation for a naval career. So did Queen Mary, who was disturbed by his personal limitations and wanted the boys to be taught more history and languages. But George V refused to allow them to be sent away to school. Only when he discovered that his ten-year-old eldest son could not calculate the average weight of the stags shot by his father at

Sir Maurice Hankey by Orpen, 1919

Alexander Hardinge

Balmoral did he engage a special mathematics tutor.

Both young princes, David and Bertie, passed into the Naval College · at Osborne under Hansell's guidance, but neither did him credit. George v was then persuaded to send the next two boys, Harry (later Duke of Gloucester) and George (later Duke of Kent) to St Peter's Court, a fashionable preparatory school on the south coast. This change of direction in the princes' education did not show any immediate improvement.

Hansell remained touchingly devoted to his royal pupils, and when the Prince of Wales departed on his post-war tours he would· be on the dock to wave him goodbye.

Hardinge, Sir Alexander
later 2nd Baron Hardinge of Penshurst
(1894–1960)

Private Secretary to King Edward VIII and King George VI. The son of the 1st Lord Hardinge of Penshurst, diplomatist, confidant of King Edward VII and Viceroy of India, he was educated at Harrow and Trinity College, Cambridge, served in the Grenadier Guards during the Great War and was awarded the Military Cross. In 1920 he was appointed an Assistant Private Secretary to George v, on whose death in 1936 he became Private Secretary to Edward VIII.

An early difference over emoluments clouded the relationship between the two men. It deteriorated swiftly towards the end of the short reign when the King made known his intention of marrying Mrs Simpson. Sir Walter Monckton (q.v.) later wrote: 'Hardinge took too pessimistic and critical a view of the King's conduct; I am sure that he expressed his opinion too emphatically and widely to have any hope of retaining the King's confidence when the crisis came.'

In November 1936, before the King's dilemma had become public knowledge,

Hardinge wrote him a sternly worded letter, warning of the constitutional perils that lay ahead and urging that Mrs Simpson should leave the country 'without further delay.' Although the King claimed to be 'shocked and angry' by this unpalatable advice, Hardinge was doing no more than his duty in seeking to keep his master on the throne. It later emerged, however, that before laying the letter before the King, he had shown it both to a member of the Prime Minister's staff and to the editor of *The Times*: an indiscretion which in retrospect would seem to justify the King's mistrust. During the remaining weeks of the reign the King refused to employ Hardinge in the negotiations with the Government that culminated in the Abdication; instead he called on the services of his old friend Sir Walter Monckton.

On the accession of George VI in December 1936, Hardinge was confirmed in his office and rewarded with two high honours: the GCVO for services to the Sovereign and the KCB for services to the State. He remained Private Secretary in peace and war until 1943, when at the age of only forty-nine he resigned on the advice of the royal physician, Lord Dawson of Penn (q.v.). Although his health was never robust – he had been obliged to take three months' sick leave soon after the Abdication – his early retirement may also have been prompted by a clash of personalities in the Palace. Oliver Harvey (later Lord Harvey of Tasburgh), at the time private secretary to the Foreign Secretary, Anthony Eden, wrote in his diary that the resignation of the 'strong, sensible, progressive-minded Private Secretary' had been 'largely caused by the Queen who was determined to get him out.'

Another contemporary view of Hardinge is less idyllic. Harold Macmillan, Minister Resident in North Africa during the visit of George VI to his troops in June 1943, was not a man to disparage a Grenadier. But he wrote: 'Alec Hardinge seems to me beyond the pale. He is idle, supercilious, without a spark of imagination or vitality.' It was also said that Hardinge had paralysed the routine at Buckingham Palace during his absence from London with the King by refusing to leave the office keys with the Assistant Private Secretaries.

In spite of Dawson's verdict in 1943, Hardinge lived for another seventeen years, having succeeded his father as 2nd Baron Hardinge of Penshurst in 1944.

Harewood, Henry Lascelles, 6th Earl of
(1882–1947)

Husband of Princess Mary (q.v.), the only daughter of King George v. Viscount Lascelles, as he was known until succeeding his father as Earl of Harewood in 1929, was educated at Eton and the Royal Military College, Sandhurst, and commissioned into the Grenadier Guards. But he did not intend to make the army his career, and from 1905 to 1907 served as honorary attaché at the British Embassy in Rome, when he acquired a knowledgeable interest in Italian painting. On the outbreak of war in 1914 he spent some months with the Yorkshire Hussars before rejoining the Grenadiers, eventually commanding a battalion of the regiment on the Western Front. During one battle a brother officer came on him imperturbably smoking an Egyptian cigarette which he held in the very tips of his fingers. 'Really,' he said, 'a most unpleasant and unfortunate afternoon. We have captured the village, but I have had quite a few casualties, and now they won't leave my H.Q. alone.' And as another salvo of shells exploded round him: 'There you are. What did I tell you?' He was wounded three times, gassed once and awarded the DSO and bar.

In 1922 he married Princess Mary, the only daughter of King George v and Queen Mary, who several years earlier had decided not to insist on her making a traditional match with a foreign prince. Although Lascelles was fifteen years older than his bride, he was tall and distinguished in appearance, heir to substantial estates in Yorkshire and already a rich man in his own right. On leave during the war he had made

The Princess Royal and Lord Harewood with their children, 1931

himself agreeable in the St James's Club to his great-uncle, Lord Clanricarde, whose eccentric habits and parsimony caused him to be shunned by most members of his family. On the old peer's death a few months later it was found that he had recently made a new Will, leaving to Lascelles almost his entire fortune of £2½ million.

It was sometimes said that Lord Harewood (as he became in 1929) was too domineering a husband to ensure a happy marriage; but this has been denied with vehemence by his elder son. He shared some of his wife's public duties and assumed others of his own. He was Lord Lieutenant of the West Riding of Yorkshire, Grand Master of the United Grand Lodge of England and a trustee of the British Museum. He was made a Knight of the Garter by King George v but refused a marquessate. Harewood enjoyed the responsibilities and recreations of a landowner; he also liked opera, and while learning his masonic ritual would stitch away at embroidery and *petit-point*.

Some of his fortune he spent on a large collection of Italian pictures under the tutelage of Tancred Borenius. More was probably lost on the racecourse, for he was an unsuccessful owner and a constant though unwilling benefactor of the bookmakers. At his death in 1947 he left a diminished estate of about £1½ million that was further depleted by heavy death duties. There were two sons of the marriage: George, Viscount Lascelles, who succeeded his father as 7th Earl of Harewood and Gerald Lascelles (qq.v.).

George Lascelles, 7th Earl of Harewood

Harewood, George Lascelles, 7th Earl of (1923–   )

Grandson of King George v and operatic director. The elder son of the 6th Earl of Harewood and Princess Mary, only daughter of King George v (qq.v.), he was known by the courtesy title of Viscount Lascelles until succeeding his father in 1947. He spent his childhood in Yorkshire, where he and his brother had the

good fortune to be coached at cricket by Wilfred Rhodes and Herbert Sutcliffe. King George vi appointed him a Page of Honour at his Coronation in 1937. Lascelles was educated at Eton and King's College, Cambridge, then commissioned into his father's old regiment, the Grenadier Guards. He fought in Italy, was wounded and taken prisoner by the Germans, incarcerated in Colditz and released in 1945. He spent some months as ADC to his great-uncle the Earl of Athlone (q.v.), Governor-General of Canada.

The rest of his career has been devoted to the study and administration of opera, a consuming interest which prompted his uncle the Duke of Windsor to exclaim: 'It's very odd about George and music. You know, his parents were quite normal.' George Lascelles in fact received no discouragement from his father; and his earliest operatic recordings were played on a gramophone presented to his mother by King Amannullah of Afghanistan.

Harewood, as he will now be called, worked at the Royal Opera House, Covent Garden, in various capacities in 1951–60 and as a director in 1969–72. He was artistic director of the Leeds Festival 1958–74 and of the Edinburgh International Festival 1961–5; adviser to the New Philharmonia Orchestra 1966–77; and managing director of the English National Opera 1972–85. He has edited the 1953 and 1976 editions of *Kobbe's Complete Opera Book* and written a volume of memoirs entitled *The Tongs and The Bones*. Among his public offices have been the Chancellorship of York University and the presidency of both the Leeds United Football Club and the British Board of Film Censors.

In 1949 he sought the hand of Maria Donata (Marion) Stein, the daughter of Erwin Stein, the Viennese music publisher who had fled to England to escape the Nazi persecution of the Jews. A woman whose dark beauty is matched by considerable gifts of intellect and character, she has made her own name as a musicologist and author of a standard primer on the pianoforte. It is a tribute to her musical ear that, having arrived in England with her parents at the age of twelve speaking not a word of English, she swiftly acquired a complete command of the language without a trace of foreign intonation.

As a descendant of George II, Harewood was obliged by the Royal Marriages Act of 1772 to seek the King's permission before entering into matrimony. This George VI refused to give as long as Queen Mary opposed the match. Under her grandson's persuasion she gave way and the ceremony took place at St Mark's, North Audley Street, Mayfair, in September 1949. Benjamin Britten, who had first introduced Miss Stein to Harewood, wrote an anthem for the occasion. Another friend, the novelist E.M. Forster, courtly but myopic, bowed to the cake at the wedding reception, thinking it was Queen Mary.

Lady Harewood bore her husband three sons; but in 1967, after some years of unhappiness, the marriage ended in divorce. In the same year Harewood married as his second wife Patricia Tuckwell, the Australian violinist and sister of the horn soloist, Barry Tuckwell. Once more he had to seek the Sovereign's permission under the Royal Marriages Act. Her decision was announced by the Government in a form that dissociated the Queen from personal involvement: 'The Cabinet have advised the Queen to give her consent and Her Majesty has signified her intention to do so.' That was not the end of the difficulty. As a divorced person, Harewood could not be married in a church; and the Act of Parliament which authorizes marriages in a registry office specifically excludes anyone subject to the Royal Marriages Act of 1772. He and his second bride were therefore obliged to be married by a judge in Connecticut, USA.

What scandalized the royal family and others was not so much the divorce as Harewood's public declaration that three years before his marriage to Miss Tuckwell she had borne him a son. His own defence of such conduct may be found in the pages of *Kobbe's Complete Opera Book*, where he writes of *The Marriage of Figaro*: 'Who nowadays bothers their heads with the uncomfortable fact that Beaumarchais's Countess had a baby by Cherubino?'

The episode affected Harewood in both his private and his public life. He was not invited to the funeral of the Duke of Windsor; he lost the friendship of Benjamin Britten, for whom he cherished a regard 'only just this side of idolatry'; and he was denied the post of chairman of the board of Covent Garden which had been half-promised him, on the improbable assumption that the opera house might thereby lose its royal patronage.

Six years after divorcing her husband, Marion Harewood was married to the Rt Hon. Jeremy Thorpe, MP, Leader of the Liberal Party, 1967–76.

In spite of his dedication to operatic management, Harewood has devoted much energy and enterprise to running Harewood House, his home near Leeds, in Yorkshire. Heavy death duties on his father's estate and other obligations have forced him to sell about 19,000 of its original 29,000 acres, as well as many of its works of art. Among them was Titian's masterpiece, *The Death of Actaeon*, which in 1971 fetched £1,680,000 at Christie's. Now opened to the paying public, Harewood House never-theless remains one of the great treasure troves of England. Lord Harewood's youngest son, whom his father sent to the village school for his primary education, was once asked by a fellow pupil whether he lived in a cottage. The boy tactfully replied: 'It's more like three knocked together.'

Hartnell, Sir Norman
(1901–1979)

Couturier to Queen Elizabeth II, to the Queen Mother and to other members of the royal

Norman Hartnell reveals his designs for the Queen's Coronation.

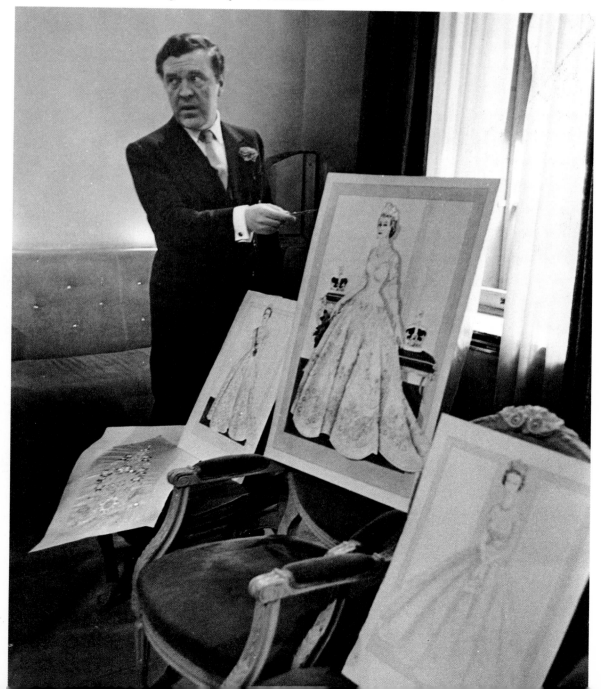

family. His first royal commission was his most troublesome: to design the dresses of the brides-maids, who included Princess Elizabeth and Princess Margaret, for the wedding of the Duke of Gloucester and Lady Alice Montagu-Douglas-Scott in 1935. He was proud of his drawings of long Kate Greenaway frocks, but King George V ordered Hartnell to shorten them: 'I want to see their pretty little knees.'

In 1937 he made the dresses of the Queen's Maids of Honour at the Coronation, but not that of the Queen herself. In the following year, however, he brought off a memorable coup when the Queen was suddenly bereaved by the death of her mother on the eve of a State visit to France. Recalling that black was not the only colour of mourning, Hartnell turned disaster into triumph by dressing her entirely in white: a dazzling display which evoked the admiration even of Paris.

He designed the dresses in which Queen Elizabeth II was married and crowned. Both reflected his sumptuous style and his distinctive use of embroidery with pearls and other lustrous decoration. One seamstress alone, Edith Aulay Read, did 3,000 hours of embroidery on the Queen's Coronation dress. At the Silver Jubilee in 1977, Hartnell was personally honoured by the Queen with the KCVO, the first couturier to be knighted.

Hartnell's art was not confined to the royal family. He made the dress of Barbara Cartland (q.v.) for her first wedding; and during the war he combined comfort with elegance in designing mass-produced 'utility' clothes.

Haskins, Marie Louise
(1876–1957)

She was the author of some lines in King George VI's Christmas broadcast of 1939 which instantly caught the public imagination and have been much quoted since:

'I said to the man who stood at the Gate of the Year, "Give me a light that I may tread safely into the unknown." And he replied, "Go out into the darkness, and put your hand into the Hand of God. That shall be to you better than light, and safer than a known way."'

The passage comes from *The Desert*, a collection of verse privately printed in 1908. It was sent to the King a few days before his broadcast, and he at once embodied it in his text. But it was not identified until after the broadcast.

Miss Haskins, a tutor and lecturer in the social science department of the London School of Economics, spent the Great War in a factory, supervising industrial welfare and the employment of women.

Marie Louise Haskins, 1940

Helena, Princess
later Princess Christian
of Schleswig-Holstein (1846–1923)

She was the third daughter of Queen Victoria and, in her mother's view, the least satisfactory. 'Poor dear Lenchen,' the Queen wrote, 'though most useful and active and clever and amiable, does not improve in looks and has great difficulties with her figure and her want of calm, quiet, graceful manners.'

In 1865, when only nineteen, she was married to Prince Christian of Schleswig-Holstein, a level-headed, well-read but dullish German, fifteen years her senior. 'His manners and movements are so old,' the Queen complained, 'it is such a pity.' Others noted that he did little except eat, smoke cigars and shoot other people's pheasants. This was not his fault. The poor man had none of his own. For although the Queen found him some slight employment as Ranger of Windsor Park, she insisted that it should 'make no difference *whatever* to the shooting which remains entirely in my hands and under my direction.' As a final humiliation, Prince Christian lost an eye when his brother-in-law, the Duke of Connaught, mistook him for a low-flying pheasant. Thereafter he would take his pick from a series of glass eyes, including a bloodshot one when he had a cold.

With the years, Prince and Princess Christian grew to be an imposing couple: he tall with a patriarchal white beard, she stout and animated. Princess Christian took an energetic interest in nursing and, like all Queen Victoria's daughters, loved music.

There were four children of the marriage: Princess Helena Victoria and Princess Marie Louise (qq.v.), Prince Christian Victor and Prince Albert. Prince Christian Victor (1867–1900), a captain in the King's Royal Rifle Corps, died of fever while serving in the South African War. His younger brother, Prince Albert (1869–1931), as heir to great estates in

Silesia, was then obliged to make his home there and to receive a commission in the German Army. Although on the retired list at the outbreak of the Great War in 1914, he felt in honour bound to serve his adopted country; but he asked to be spared the anguish of fighting against his English cousins on the Western Front and was instead given a staff appointment in Berlin. He succeeded to the Dukedom of Schleswig-Holstein in 1921 and died ten years later. His father, Prince Christian, died in London in 1917, and his mother in 1923.

Princess Helena

Princess Helena Victoria breakfasts with her grandmother. On the Queen's left is Princess Beatrice.

Helena Victoria, Princess
(1870–1948)

The third child and elder daughter of Prince Christian of Schleswig-Holstein and his wife Princess Helena (q.v.), Queen Victoria's third daughter. Born at Frogmore and brought up at Windsor, she was known in the family as Thora and by others as 'The Snipe', an affectionate allusion to the prominence of her nose. Unlike her sister Princess Marie Louise (q.v.) she never married.

Much of her life was devoted to the encouragement of music. During the Great War she arranged for the despatch of concert parties and musical instruments to entertain those fighting on the Western Front; and between the wars she made Schomberg House, in Pall Mall, which she had inherited from her parents and shared with her sister, one of the last private musical centres in London.

In King George V's purge of German styles and titles in 1917, the two sisters retained the title of Princess but lost the territorial designation of 'Schleswig-Holstein'. They were also obliged to abandon the style of 'Royal Highness' and adopt that of 'Highness'. In this they did better than their male Battenberg and Teck cousins, who were deprived of all their royal attributes.

Princess Helena Victoria accepted the demotion with good humour. Arriving at a luncheon party one day in 1937 after attending a rehearsal of King George VI's Coronation, she addressed the table at large: 'My dears, the seating arrangements in the Abbey are terrible, but *terrible*. Those poor peeresses. They have only twenty-four inches to sit on. Thank God I am a Highness and get thirty-two.'

Horder, Sir Thomas
later 1st Baron
(1871–1955)

Physician to each successive Sovereign from Edward VII to Elizabeth II. The son of a draper, he climbed the ladder of his profession with determination, independence and an inspired gift of diagnosis. He cared little for convention and would outrage his staid colleagues at St Bartholomew's Hospital by wearing a straw boater with a morning coat. His vigorous support for birth control, noise abatement and cremation provoked more widespread controversy. Horder's caustic tongue cost him the Presidency of the Royal College of Physicians; from 1941 to 1949 he was consistently defeated in the annual election for the office by Lord Moran, Sir Winston Churchill's doctor. But his own patients included three Prime Ministers: Bonar Law, Ramsay MacDonald and Neville Chamberlain. He had particular cause to remember two others: the newspaper owner,

Lord Northcliffe, who threatened him with a revolver, and the future Edward VIII, who would demonstrate his fitness by standing on his head. He fought the establishment of the National Health Service by the Labour Minister, Aneurin Bevan, who responded by calling him 'an incontinent romantic'. Small, dark and perpetually alert, Horder relished oysters and champagne, smoked pipes and cigars. He died in his eighty-fifth year.

Howlett, Mr

Valet to George V from 1901 until the King's death in 1936. He was entrusted with one of the most extensive and discreetly elegant wardrobes in Europe, every item of which he scrutinized and if necessary replaced at least once a year.

That was not Howlett's only care. He would also accompany George V when he went shooting, and cock the old-fashioned hammer guns which the King retained to the end. The valet had a memorable turn of phrase. When a hare suddenly crossed the King's path one day, Howlett warned him not to shoot. 'There are some peasants over there,' he said. And he did not mean pheasants.

Hua, Gabriel
(d. 1909)

A worldly, witty Frenchman with a black beard and a bald head who taught French to George V as a naval cadet, and later to his children: none of whom, however, acquired more than a hesitant command of the language. During a State visit to Paris, President Poincaré noted the King's 'slight British accent', adding generously: 'He seeks for the right word, but in the end he finds it.' George V certainly knew enough French to appreciate a performance of *Occupe-toi d'Amélie* to which Hua took him. He wrote in his diary: 'The hottest thing I have ever seen on the stage.'

For several years Hua taught French at Eton. It was noted that neither the Head Master, Dr Warre, nor Hua could pronounce the name of the other, although each made the same sound in the attempt. He taught the boys to gossip in French and they loved him. In spite of the *entente cordiale*, Hua was sometimes the victim of unseemly insular jokes. A foolish Eton beak called Booker struck a match on his bald head; and the royal children knowing of their tutor's relish for frogs' legs, persuaded the chef to prepare for a him a dish of tadpoles on toast.

Innes of Learney, Sir Thomas
(1893–1971)

Lord Lyon King of Arms, Scotland's leading authority on genealogy and heraldry from 1943 to 1969. The son of an ancient family and holder of an awesome office, he carried his learning lightly, even with a childlike exhuberance. Although his relish for fine distinctions and tortuous argument sometimes led him into perversity, he loved colour and ceremony, and insisted that heraldry should be the preserve neither of the rich nor the well born.

Sir Thomas Innes of Learney, Lord Lyon King of Arms

On State occasions at Holyrood or in St Giles's Cathedral he was an unforgettable master of ceremonies: his lanky stiff-gaited figure clad in scarlet and gold tabard, his alert mischievous eyes shielded by a velvet cap that had seen better days. His voice was high pitched, and he was almost the last of the Scottish aristocracy to use those Doric inflections which in others have succumbed to an English public-school education. In 1928 he married Lady Lucy Buchan, daughter of the 18th Earl of Caithness.

A guardian of conventional morality, he frowned upon divorce. When a peccant Scottish nobleman pleaded that he should not be excluded from the Queen's presence as he had been remarried in church, Lyon's reply was magisterial: 'That may well admit him to the Kingdom of Heaven but it will noo get him through the gates of the Palace of Holyroodhouse.'

Sir Thomas's son, Malcolm Innes of Edingight, having served as Lyon Clerk from 1966, was in 1981 appointed Lord Lyon King of Arms.

Jardine, the Rev. R. A.

Vicar of St Paul's, Darlington. In 1937 he read in the newspapers that Mrs Simpson, as a divorced person, could not be married to the Duke of Windsor according to the rites of the Church of England. Rejecting this doctrine as cruel and outmoded, Jardine wrote to the Duke of Windsor in France offering his services. These the bride and bridegroom accepted with gratitude, although both the Bishop of Durham, in whose diocese Jardine had a parish, and the Bishop of Fulham, whose jurisdiction extended over the Church of England in North and Central Europe, publicly declared their disapproval.

In June 1937, Jardine arrived at the Château de Candé, near Tours, which had been put at the disposal of the Duke and Mrs Simpson by Charles Bedaux, a French-born naturalized American. The priest had brought his prayer-book and vestments, but it did not prove easy to furnish a room as a chapel. First there had to be an altar. 'What about the table with the drinks on it, or the chest from the hall?' it was suggested. The chest was preferred, but part of it had to be draped to conceal a row of fat carved caryatids, or female figures acting as supports. There was no shortage of candlesticks, but on the night before the ceremony these were temporarily retrieved for the dining-room table. Finally, it was discovered that the Château had no crucifix, and the Duke appealed by telephone to the British Embassy in Paris.

Having overcome these sacerdotal difficulties, Jardine solemnized the marriage on 3 June 1937 in the presence of scarcely half a dozen English guests. One of them described him as 'a large-nosed red-faced little man.' He may well have offered his services out of Christian charity, but Sir Walter Monckton (q.v.) noted 'a marked weakness for self-advertisement.' Jardine later undertook a lecture tour of the United States on the subject of the Duke's wedding and is said to have opened a Lilliputian church in Los Angeles called Windsor Cathedral.

John, Prince
(1905–1919)

Fifth and youngest son of King George v and Queen Mary. At the age of four he developed epilepsy and was obliged to lead a secluded life in a house on the Sandringham estate, looked after

Prince John

lovingly by the family nanny, Mrs Bill. He grew up to be a handsome boy but died in his sleep at the age of thirteen.

'For him it is a great release,' Queen Mary wrote to a friend, 'as his malady was becoming worse as he grew older and he has thus been spared much suffering. I cannot say how grateful we feel to God for having taken him in such a peaceful way, he just slept quietly into his heavenly home, no pain, no struggle, just peace for the poor little troubled spirit.'

Prince John was buried in the graveyard of Sandringham Church, near the lych gate bearing the Latin inscription: 'Hodie mihi cras tibi' – 'I today, you tomorrow.'

Kelly, Sir Gerald
(1879–1972)

Painter and President of the Royal Academy of Arts. The son of a Vicar of Camberwell, he was educated at Eton. Although he did not enjoy his years there, he was intensely proud of his Eton connection and almost always wore his old school tie. On his election as President of the Royal Academy in 1949, he asked the Head Master whether the school could be given a whole holiday in his honour. 'No,' came the reply. Kelly studied painting in Paris, where he formed a lifelong friendship with Somerset Maugham.

Having by 1938 established his reputation for reliable likenesses, he was recommended by Kenneth Clark (q.v.) to paint the State portraits of King George VI and Queen Elizabeth: two huge canvases, each measuring nine feet by six. He had almost completed them by the outbreak of war in 1939, and came down to Windsor for a few days to add the final touches. There he remained, on and off, for the next five years. It was said that to prolong his stay he would steal down to the studio at dead of night to erase the previous day's work. Certainly he found it convivial to spend the war years in Windsor Castle; and the royal household, with whom he was invited to eat, enjoyed his Irish wit. The State portraits were eventually ready to go on show in the Royal Academy summer exhibition of 1945. When in the same year he received his knighthood, the band at the investiture played: 'Has anybody here seen Kelly?'

Small, ebullient and energetic, Gerald Kelly proved an enterprising President of the Royal Academy. In 1946 he suggested an ambitious public exhibition of pictures from the King's collection, and entrusted its planning to Anthony Blunt (q.v.).

Sir Gerald Kelly by Powys Evans, c. 1926

Kent, Prince George, Duke of
(1902–1942)

The fourth son of King George v and Queen Mary. He was born at York Cottage, Sandringham, on 20 December 1902. The diarist Lord Crawford described his first public appearance with his elder brother Prince Henry in 1911: 'One of the great successes of the Coronation was a standup fight between the two kilted princes after the ceremony in Westminster Abbey. By some imprudence the Prince of Wales and his sister were sent in a State coach with the younger brothers, but without a controlling prelate or pedagogue. When fairly started from the Abbey, a free fight began to the huge delight of the spectators in Whitehall. The efforts of Princess Mary to mollify the combatants were sincere but ineffectual, and during the strife she nearly had her sweet little coronet knocked off! Peace was ultimately restored after about fifty yards of hullaballoo.'

Prince George, who went to St Peter's School, Broadstairs, before following the Prince of Wales and Prince Albert into the Royal Navy, showed the same spirited behaviour in later life. Alone of his brothers, he was not cowed by the quarter-deck discipline of George v. At Balmoral, when the King was rebuking one of his sons for not wearing the skean-dhu in Highland dress, Prince George remarked disarmingly that he never knew what to do with the knives and forks and other odds and ends demanded by the kilt. He was devoted to his eldest brother, whom he more than once accompanied on overseas tours.

When an equerry of George vi referred to an uncle as the black sheep of the family, the King replied: 'All my family are black sheep.' His brothers, it is true, were always getting into scrapes, and none more than the tall, fair and handsome Prince George, some of whose entanglements recalled an earlier generation of royal rakes. He was exceptionally attractive to women, and his liaison with one unsuitable partner required his father to make a secret visit to Chequers to consult the Prime Minister. Another friend briefly tempted him into experimenting with drugs, an escapade that swiftly taught him to abandon such dangerous ground for all time.

In 1934 he found happiness and stability in his marriage to Princess Marina of Greece (q.v.). Shortly before the ceremony in Westminster Abbey he was created Duke of Kent, Earl of St Andrews and Baron Downpatrick. There were three children of the marriage: Prince Edward, who was born in 1935 and succeeded to the dukedom in 1942; Princess Alexandra, who was born in 1936; and Prince Michael, who was born in 1942 (qq.v.). On the death of his aunt Princess Victoria (q.v.), the Duke of Kent inherited Coppins, near Iver, a sprawling but comfortable gabled villa built in the last century. The Duke and Duchess also had a London house in Belgrave Square.

He was an anguished spectator of the Abdication, pleading in vain against the departure of a favourite brother. Then and later, there were rumours that the Duke of York felt himself unfitted to succeed to the throne, and that both he and his next eldest brother, the Duke of Gloucester, wished to renounce the Crown in favour of the Duke of Kent. There is no evidence, however, to support this speculation. It is true that in December 1936 he alone of the brothers had a male heir; but the nation that within living memory had celebrated the Diamond Jubilee of Queen Victoria would not readily have upset the line of succession in order to exclude the future Queen Elizabeth II.

The Duke of Kent was the only one of Queen Mary's sons to share her interest in pictures and furniture, books and bibelots. He also had the means to satisfy it. On marriage, his Civil List income had risen from £10,000 to £25,000: perhaps £500,000 in the currency of 1985. He had also inherited money from his father. The Duke bought prodigiously but with taste and discrimination. When in November 1938 he was nominated to be the next Governor-General of

Prince George, Duke of Kent, as a naval cadet

Australia, his friend 'Chips' Channon (q.v.) said that as there was no Cartier in Melbourne or Sydney, the appointment would save him half a million pounds. 'How *gemütlich* Coppins is,' Channon noted a year or two later, 'and how full of rich treasures, and gold boxes, *étuis* and pretty expensive objects always being exchanged or moved about. The Duke adores his possessions.' His spontaneous love of pictures led him to buy the Altieri Claudes, brought to England by Nelson; with other pieces from his collection they were sold after the war by his impoverished widow. Sir Oliver Millar (q.v.) has described him as the most distinguished royal connoisseur since George IV.

He was a good-natured man, too. David Herbert, the brother of the Duke's equerry, has recalled an evening in Belgrave Square when a nervous guest laughed so loudly at his host's jokes that he shattered the back of his chair, one of a rare and beautiful set made by Chippendale. The culprit was too desolate, too embarrassed even to apologize. But the Duke showed no chagrin. 'How fortunate that it was *your* chair,' he said. 'You see, there were only eleven of the original set, so I had one copied to make up the dozen. It was yours.' Royal hagiography abounds in such felicitous tales; and even if its author was not on oath when telling the story, it well matches its subject's character. During the war, for instance, the Duke risked personal unpopularity by doing all he could to ease the lot of Prince Paul of Yugoslavia, his wife's brother-in-law, interned in Kenya on the mistaken grounds of his being unfriendly to the Allies.

The war prevented the Duke of Kent from taking up his appointment as Governor-General of Australia. Instead he served first in the naval intelligence division of the Admiralty, then as an Air Commodore in the RAF. On 25 August 1942, the Sunderland flying boat which was taking him to Iceland for a tour of inspection crashed into a mountain in the north of Scotland. The Duke and all but one of his fellow passengers and crew died instantly. He was not yet forty and the nation mourned a Prince of many gifts and high promise.

Kent, Princess Marina, Duchess of
(1906–1968)

Wife of Prince George, Duke of Kent (q.v.). She was born in Athens on 13 December 1906, the youngest of the three daughters of Prince and Princess Nicholas of Greece. Her father was the third son of the Danish prince who became King George I of the Hellenes; she was thus a great-niece of Queen Alexandra and a first cousin of Prince Philip, Duke of Edinburgh (qq.v.). Her mother was the Grand Duchess Helen of Russia, the last of those entitled to bear the resounding style of Imperial and Royal Highness.

Princess Marina's upbringing, by contrast,

was of a disciplined simplicity at the hands of an English governess, Miss Fox. As is still customary, the Greek royal family spoke among themselves in English, which was the first of her several languages. The whirligig of Greek politics improved her French, too, by twice sending the family into exile, once in 1917 and again in 1922; and since there was not much money to spare during those early years in Paris, she acquired a practical knowledge of dressmaking that was to inspire a generation of couturiers. Some regarded Princess Marina as a suitable bride for the Prince of Wales, but the future Duke of Windsor was already besotted by Mrs Simpson. In August 1934, during a holiday with her brother-in-law and sister, Prince and Princess Paul of Yugoslavia, she was betrothed to Prince George.

Her wedding to the newly created Duke of Kent took place in Westminster Abbey on 29 November. George v was enchanted by his daughter-in-law. 'The King was a perfect angel to her,' the bride's mother told a friend. And the King himself cheerfully reported to his Prime Minister, Ramsay MacDonald: 'She has not a cent.' He was even prepared to alter his otherwise immutable shooting programme to accommodate the wedding celebrations.

They made a memorably handsome couple. The Duchess endowed her new role with grace and beauty, intelligence and style. Yet she was never quite absorbed into her husband's family; they did not share her consciousness of royalty as a caste apart, or of a Europe composed more of dynasties than of nations. Her friendships, however, were eclectic. They included such Tolstoian names from her past as Galitzine and Bagration, but also men of creative talent and wit from the arts and politics: Noel Coward and Malcom Sargent, Cecil Beaton and 'Chips' Channon (qq.v.). The private life of the Kents was intensely happy. The filled their two houses with beautiful objects; yet neither Coppins nor Belgrave Square ever ceased to be a family home for their children.

The war shattered this idyll. One of the Duchess's sisters was married to a German,

Princess Marina with her three children at Coppins, 1943

Count Toerring, the other to Prince Paul of Yugoslavia, exiled from his own country and degraded by the Britain he loved. In August 1942 there came the most crushing blow of all. Her husband, serving in the RAF, was killed when the plane carrying him to Iceland crashed in Scotland. Queen Mary characteristically drove up from her wartime home in Gloucestershire to comfort her widowed daughter-in-law; the Duke of Windsor, by contrast, immersed in his own affairs in the Bahamas, sent never so much as a line of sympathy.

One of the least expected misfortunes of her husband's death was a comparative poverty. The income from his parliamentary Civil List died with him, and his private fortune was held in trust for his three children. The Duchess was granted only the pension of an Air Commodore; and although in time she received part of the discretionary Civil List at the disposal of the Queen, that did no more than pay for the expenses of her public duties. She was therefore obliged to send some of her treasured possessions to the saleroom. In war and peace she continued to carry out a full programme of engagements. She brought a new elegance to the uniform of the Women's Royal Naval Service, and was no less devoted to the Royal National Lifeboat Institution, the All-England Lawn Tennis Club and the newly established University of Kent. As Colonel-in-Chief of the Royal West Kent Regiment she journeyed to the Far East to encourage them in their anti-guerilla operations in the Malayan jungle.

The loss of her husband never loosened for one moment the ties of duty to which she was born; but it increasingly separated her from an intimate relationship with the family into which she had married. She found solace in the love of her children and of two devoted sisters. She also kept alive the traditions of her childhood by celebrating the Greek Orthodox Easter with eggs dyed red and loaves of spiced bread. She enjoyed music and ballet and the theatre; history and biographies and novels; portrait painting and paper games, tennis and talk.

Her beauty, like that of her great-aunt, Queen Alexandra, scarcely diminished with the years; it was as if another of those romantically regal portraits by De Laszlo had stepped out of its frame. In the summer of 1948 a diarist wrote of an evening at the dream palace in Northamptonshire of the Duke and Duchess of Buccleuch:

'Coming down early for dinner I glanced onto the terrace and the long view and was overcome once more by the beauty of Boughton: and then I saw the Duchess of Kent in her blue Greek dress slowly advancing, and looking more lovely than ever. It was Shakespearian. A masque.'

In 1961, on the marriage of her elder son Prince Edward, Duke of Kent (q.v.), she abandoned Coppins to the young couple and made her home in an elegant corner of Kensington Palace. Princess Marina, as she was henceforth known, died there on 27 August 1968 after a short illness. She was buried at Frogmore, near Windsor, next to the remains of her husband.

Kent, Prince Edward, Duke of
(1935–　　　)

Elder son of Prince George, Duke of Kent, and Princess Marina, Duchess of Kent (qq.v.). He was born at No. 3 Belgrave Square, the London house of his parents, on 9 October 1935. 'He has fine blue eyes,' a family friend noted, 'golden curls and looks like all four Georges rolled into one.' The fifth George also thought well of him. 'Saw my Kent grandson in his bath,' the old King wrote with satisfaction a week or two before his death. Eddie, as he was called in the family, must indeed have been a pretty child. Thirteen years later, the Labour Party published a propaganda leaflet bearing the photograph of an attractive but unnamed baby supposedly flourishing under post-war socialism. The features, however, were recognized as those of the infant prince, who had, as it happened, been born under pre-war capitalism. The Labour Party apologized for its imposture and withdrew the pamphlet.

Edward, Duke of Kent with his mother and sister, 1956

Prince Edward was not yet seven when he succeeded to the dukedom on the death of his father in a wartime air crash; and for all the love his mother gave her three children, his boyhood suffered from the absence of paternal guidance. He went to Ludgrove, a fashionable preparatory school, then to Eton. Plagued by sinus trouble in that damp climate, he left after three years to breathe the crisper air of Le Rosey, in Switzerland, also the *alma mater* of the Aga Khan.

On leaving school, the young Duke joined the Army, did well at Sandhurst, qualified as an interpreter in French and was commissioned into the Royal Scots Greys, a mechanized cavalry regiment. He served in Germany, Hong Kong and Cyprus; became adjutant; passed high out of the Staff College. Then, to his chagrin, he was withdrawn from operations in Northern Ireland lest he should become too tempting a target for the IRA: an occupational hazard that similarly infuriated Edward Prince of Wales and Henry Duke of Gloucester (qq.v) in their military careers. Although the Duke of Kent would have risen high in the Service as a professional soldier, he disdained continuing under such a handicap. After holding staff appointments at the Ministry of Defence, he retired from the Regular Army in 1976 as a lieutenant-colonel.

In the same year he was made Vice-Chairman of the British Overseas Trade Board. To those who did not know him, it seemed a grotesque appointment: a royal duke and a cavalry officer, rather a shy man, too, in the role of salesman? Until recent years, the attitude of the royal family to the task of capturing overseas markets was distant, even disdainful. When in 1901 a wellwisher suggested that the future George v should address himself to 'trade and commerce' during his imperial tour, Edward vii referred to the theme as 'trade and commerce (!)'. Now his namesake and great-grandson was to devote much of his life to just such a mission.

His role is threefold. He visits British companies to see their problems for himself, from shop-floor to boardroom. He addresses conferences on the strategy and tactics of exporting. And he makes regular tours abroad, sometimes

with teams of businessmen, to fly the flag and bring home orders. Other members of the royal family also make spasmodic incursions into the industrial scene. Unlike the Duke of Kent, however, they do not always manage to avoid the pitfalls of such a vocation: the misplaced pleasantry that rankles, the facile denigration of Britain's methods and achievements.

The Duke was introduced to the complex world of electronics by Lord Mountbatten (q.v.) and is now chairman of the National Electronics Council. He puts his knowledge of the subject to good use not only on the Overseas Trade Board but also as a non-executive director of BICC, the manufacturers of electrical and electronic equipment.

His other roles cover a wide spectrum. He continues the royal attachment to freemasonry as Grand Master of the United Grand Lodge of England, an office held by his father from 1939 until his death. He also honours his father's memory as president of the RAF Benevolent Fund; and his mother's by succeeding her as president both of Wimbledon and of the Royal National Lifeboat Institution. As a soldier he has acquired the plumed hat of a major-general and the bearskin of Colonel of the Scots Guards. He is Chancellor of Surrey University and Grand Master of the Order of St Michael and St George.

In music he finds not only some of the most rewarding of his duties but also a sustained private delight. He brings a sensitive ear and much methodical study to his love of opera, particularly the works of Wagner. He first sat through *The Ring* at Bayreuth as a Sandhurst cadet in 1954, and has several times returned. He is also a familiar visitor to the London opera houses and concert halls, sometimes using the royal box, but equally content in a public seat. He has a large collection of recorded music and solaces his journeys by car with Radio 3.

Music is a shared joy of his family. He married in 1961 Katharine Worsley, the daughter of a Yorkshire landowner, who as Duchess of Kent (q.v.) is the patron of many melodious occasions. There are three children of the marriage:

George, Earl of St Andrews, born in 1962, who won a scholarship to Eton, then read History at Downing College, Cambridge; Helen, known as Lady Helen Windsor, born in 1964, who works in Christie's, the London auction house; and Nicholas, known as Lord Nicholas Windsor, born in 1970, who is at Westminster School. Nicholas has the distinction to being the first member of the royal family to appear professionally on the stage of Covent Garden; in 1980 he had a walk-on part in a crowd scene of Mozart's *Magic Flute*.

In London the Kents live in an unexpectedly small corner of St James's Palace, with a tiny staff. In the country they have Anmer Hall, on the Sandringham estate, in Norfolk, a comfortable but unpretentious house; it belonged once to E. T. Hooley, the share-pusher, but would not be out of place in the demure pages of a Jane Austen novel. With so much travel in the Duke's official life, he and his family generally prefer to spend their holidays here, enlivened by an occasional winter break in the French Alps or the Caribbean. He enjoys tennis and is a reliable shot; he listens to music with ferocious concentration, reads solid works of history and biography, writes his own speeches.

There was a time when he would scowl at the sight of a camera and freeze at the approach of a journalist; or, meeting strangers, switch off through shyness or boredom. Today he is at ease in any company: smiling and debonair, interested and informed, always dignified yet never overbearing. Of all members of the royal family, he is among the nicest and certainly the most underestimated.

Kent, Katharine Worsley, Duchess of
(1933–   )

Wife of Prince Edward, Duke of Kent (q.v.), with whom she shares a common descent from King Edward I. She is the only daughter of the late Sir William Worsley, 4th Baronet, Lord Lieutenant of the North Riding of Yorkshire

and captain (later president) of the Yorkshire County Cricket Club.

Originally a Lancashire family, the Worsleys have owned land at Hovingham, near York, since the reign of Queen Elizabeth I. The Duchess also has the distinction, unique in the royal family, of being descended from Oliver Cromwell: his great-granddaughter married Thomas Worsley of Hovingham, Surveyor of the Board of Works and Riding Master to King George II. Her own brother, Sir Marcus Worsley, the present Baronet, has also sat in the Commons and is a Church Commissioner. The Duchess's mother was Joyce Brunner, whose great-grandfather, the Rev. John Brunner, emigrated from Switzerland; and whose grandfather, Sir John Tomlinson Brunner, went into partnership with the German-Jewish chemist Ludwig Mond to establish the firm of alkali manufacturers out of which grew ICI.

On 8 June 1961, after several years of friendship, Katharine Worsley was married to the Duke of Kent in the splendour of York Minster. The Queen and her entire family were present at what was the first royal marriage to be solemnized there since that of King Edward III to Philippa of Hainault in 1328. The Worsley family has close links with the Minster. Its precious stained glass, nearly one-third of all the medieval glass in Britain, was stored for safety at Hovingham throughout the war; and as a girl, the bride had received lessons on its organ, a memorable but daunting privilege.

Music has long been one of the mainsprings of the Duchess's life and a passion she shares with her husband. She is an active patron of the Royal Northern College of Music in Manchester and of the Leeds International Pianoforte Competition founded by those inspiring teachers Fanny Waterman and Marion Thorpe. As a member of the Bach Choir she also sings the great choral masterpieces of Bach, Handel and Beethoven, as well as the lesser but sometimes more demanding works of later composers. Only after stringent tests are even the most eminent amateurs admitted to its ranks. And its musical director, Sir David Willcocks, has a

The Duchess of Kent with her younger son Nicholas arriving at St Paul's Cathedral for a rehearsal of the Prince of Wales's wedding, 1981.

tactful formula for weeding the Bach Choir of those who have become mere passengers. 'I fear,' he says, 'you have too delicate a voice for chorus work.' The Duchess of Kent, unsparing of herself in all she undertakes, has yet to receive that bouquet of thistles.

In 1966 she succeeded as Chancellor of Leeds University, Princess Mary, Countess of Harewood (q.v.). That too is an institution to which she never gives less than her best. Busy Vice-Chancellors do not always appreciate Chancellors who take too close an interest in the machinery of higher education, much less in its politics. But during the eleven years that the late

Lord Boyle was at Leeds, they established as harmonious a partnership as any; and his untimely death at fifty-eight brought her much sorrow.

No less becoming than her Chancellor's robes is the major-general's uniform she wears as Controller Commandant, Women's Royal Army Corps. Yet at heart the Duchess of Kent is neither an academic nor an Amazon: more a Good Samaritan whose words of comfort and sunlit smile have cheered many a soul on public and private occasions. There is courage too in the determination with which she has overcome ill health and exhaustion to undertake a relentless programme of engagements. The Court Circular speaks for itself, and that does not tell the whole story.

Such leisure as is left to her, she devotes to her family. 'Kings and Queens,' the Duke of Windsor observed, 'are only secondarily fathers and mothers.' Dukes and Duchesses, even royal ones, redress the balance.

Kent, Prince Michael of
(1942–   )

Younger son of Prince George, Duke of Kent, and Princess Marina, Duchess of Kent (qq.v.). He was born at Coppins, the country house of his parents, on 4 July 1942, American Independence Day. President Roosevelt therefore agreed to be a godfather, and Franklin was added to the infant's other names. Only three weeks after the baptism at Windsor, the Duke of Kent was killed in an air crash, leaving his widow to bring up their three young children.

Prince Michael was educated at Eton and Sandhurst, and commissioned into the 11th Hussars, subsequently amalgamated to form the Royal Hussars (Prince of Wales's Own). He served with his regiment and in the Ministry of Defence, showing a talent for languages, including Russian. He was also a successful competitor in the bobsleigh championships held each winter in Switzerland.

Prince Michael, 1984

On 30 June 1978, in Vienna, he married Baroness Marie Christine von Reibnitz, whose earlier marriage to Tom Troubridge, merchant banker and member of a distinguished family of sailors, had been annulled earlier that year. In the eyes of the Roman Catholic Church, to which the Baroness belongs, an annulment (unlike a divorce) is no impediment to remarriage; it is as if the annulled marriage had never taken place. Nor would the Baroness's remarriage to a member of the Church of England necessarily have debarred her from a Roman Catholic religious ceremony, although such 'mixed' marriages do require the specific permission of the Pope. Here, however, there was a complication. By the Bill of Rights of 1689 and the Act of Settlement of 1701, Prince Michael, sixteenth in line of succession to the throne, was obliged to forfeit that right on marriage to a Roman Catholic. Not wishing to deprive any children of his marriage of their right of succession, however remote, he announced that he would wish them to be brought up as Anglicans. This provoked the Pope to withhold permission from Prince Michael and his bride to marry in a Catholic Church. Instead there was a civil ceremony in the City Hall of Vienna. Not until June 1983 did the Pope relent and allow the marriage to be validated. The Vicar-General of the Diocese of Westminster then held a short service for the couple in the private chapel of the Archbishop, Cardinal Hume.

There are two children of the marriage: Lord Frederick Windsor, born in 1979, and Lady Gabriella Windsor, born in 1981. By a declaration of King George V, now operative for the first time, they are styled as if they were the children of a duke. Prince Michael has not changed his mind about wishing them to be brought up as Anglicans; but he has said that he would not attempt to influence them if ultimately they decide for themselves to become Roman Catholics.

In 1981 Prince Michael retired from the Army with the rank of major. He is now a director of two public companies: Standard Telephones and Cables and Aitken Hume, a merchant bank. One colleague says of him: 'Prince Michael is like his grandfather, King George V: not particularly quick, but he does save us from doing stupid things.' Another says: 'He does not say much. But when everybody else has finished talking, he comes up with the right answer.' The Prince also devotes much of his time to charitable causes and to freemasonry.

Since his marriage, Prince Michael has concealed his dark good looks behind a greying beard that gives him an eerie resemblance to his distant cousin, the Tsar Nicholas II. Like his uncle the Duke of Windsor, he may also be identified by the excessive size of the knot in his tie. He and his family live in a grace-and-favour apartment in Kensington Palace, but do not receive a Civil List. Out of their own means they have bought Nether Lypiatt Manor, in Gloucestershire, an early eighteenth-century house of outstanding beauty.

Kent, Marie Christine von Reibnitz, Princess Michael of
(1945–   )

Wife of Prince Michael of Kent (q.v.). She was born in Czechoslovakia on 15 January 1945, the only daughter of Baron Günther von Reibnitz, an officer in the German Army by his Hungarian wife, Countess Maria Szapary. Soon afterwards, her parents separated and were later divorced. The father went to farm in Portuguese East Africa; his wife took their young son and daughter to Australia. Marie Christine was brought up in a convent school in Sydney, spent nearly a year with her father in Mozambique, studied the history of art in Vienna, found work in London as secretary in an advertising agency and was apprenticed to an interior decorator.

In 1971 she married Tom Troubridge, the merchant banker son of Vice-Admiral Sir Thomas Troubridge. In April 1978 she succeeded in having the marriage annulled; three months later she married Prince Michael of Kent in Vienna. They have two children, and spend their time between a grace-and-favour apartment in Kensington Palace and a manor house of their own in Gloucestershire.

Princess Michael is a commanding figure on any occasion. Tall and elegant, she brings a daring sense of style to hair, clothes and jewels. Her talk is vivacious and informed, her knowledge of the arts recognized by her appointment as a trustee of the Victoria and Albert Museum. She is completing a book about twelve princesses who over the centuries have left their own countries for marriage. Nor is she altogether a bluestocking. She hunts the fox with the same zeal displayed by the Empress Elisabeth of Austria: yet another comforting comparison.

For all her strength of character, intellectual gifts and ability to captivate, Princess Michael remains something of a stranger in England. She can be formidable in defence of her acquired rank, displaying a Central European concern for precedence and protocol that is alien to the English temperament. It is no less quaint to find her denying in a newspaper interview that she is disliked by other members of the royal family; that the Queen refers to her as 'Our Val,' short for 'Valkyrie'; or that she and her husband have ever asked for a Civil List – a particularly persistent myth. Here perhaps some may detect injustice, for Prince and Princess Michael of Kent perform many public engagements without receiving the financial support given to other members of the royal family. The Prince and Princess, however, make almost all their public appearances not at the request of the Queen but by their own wish; and at a moment in the reign when there happen to be a dozen more senior members of the royal family available to represent the Sovereign.

That is not to deny the exceptional effort which Princess Michael puts into her charitable work or the benefit she brings to good causes. An American admirer was so moved by her record of public service that in 1984 he presented her with a racehorse. Perhaps he is not alone in showing his appreciation.

Princess Michael with her children, Frederick and Gabriella, 1984

Knollys, Miss Charlotte
(1835–1930)

Lady-in-waiting and lifelong friend to Queen Alexandra. The sister of Viscount Knollys, private secretary to Edward VII and George V, she was appointed to the household of the young Princess of Wales in 1872. For the next fifty-three years, Miss Knollys scarcely had a life of her own. She never took a holiday and dealt in longhand with much of Alexandra's personal correspondence.

Even after Queen Alexandra's death in 1925, she had one last, deplorable duty to perform. At the age of ninety she carried out the wishes of her dead mistress and confidante by burning the old Queen's papers. Fifteen years earlier, her brother had similarly been commanded from the grave to make a bonfire of Edward VII's papers, including letters from his wife. Thus did those busy royal correspondents try to ensure that their labours and thoughts should go unrecorded by history.

Lang, the Most Rev. Cosmo Gordon
later Lord Lang of Lambeth
(1864–1945)

Archbishop of Canterbury 1928–42. He was born at Fyvie Manse, Aberdeenshire, the third son of the Rev. John Marshall Lang, a Minister of the Kirk who later became Principal of Aberdeen University. From Glasgow University, where he enrolled at the age of fourteen, Cosmo went up to Balliol College, Oxford. There he helped to found the Oxford University Dramatic Society and was elected President of the Union. He took a Second Class in Greats followed by a First in History. In 1888 he won a Prize Fellowship at All Souls College which brought him a small income and the acquaintance of such eminent Fellows as the Prime Minister, Lord Salisbury. Both were much

Archbishop Lang with Princess Marie Louise, 1942

coveted by a young man who, as he confessed to a friend, had no prospects, little influence and a consuming ambition.

He began to read for the Bar as a prelude to politics, then felt an overwhelming urge to take Holy Orders. Having been ordained into the Church of England, he worked as a curate in Leeds but was soon lured back to Oxford as Dean of Divinity at Magdalen College. Oxford ran through Lang's life like a golden thread.

'Balliol,' he would say, 'was my mother, to whom I am bound by ties of filial gratitude; All Souls is my wife, who gave me a home and most generously received me back after a temporary residence with ... Magdalen, my very beautiful mistress, for whom during three years I forsook my wife.'

If that daring metaphor fell oddly from the lips of a lifelong bachelor, it at least reflected his delight in the society of an Oxford common room; whatever the pressures of his public career, he returned again and again. Raymond Asquith, the Prime Minister's son who was to die in battle during the Great War, described an evening at All Souls in 1903 which he shared with Lang, by now Bishop of Stepney, and Randall Davidson, the newly enthroned Archbishop of Canterbury: 'I was up till 4 this morning watching Stepney and Cantuar – both drunk – trying to cheat one another at poker; it was a very even match for tho' Stepney was far more cunning, Cantuar was far less drunk. Such is All Souls Day.' A generation later, Geoffrey Fisher (q.v.) was disturbed to hear his predecessor as Archbishop of Canterbury singing a ribald college song; but Lang, it must be said, was equally shocked by an Archbishop who allowed himself to be photographed with a pipe in his mouth.

Lang's association with the royal family began a year or two after he had left Magdalen to become Vicar of Portsea: a parish of 40,000 souls to whom he ministered with the help of thirteen curates. In 1898 he was summoned across the water to the Isle of Wight to preach before Queen Victoria at Osborne. 'The Queen has taken a great fancy to Mr Lang,' a lady-in-waiting noted. 'How soon will he be a bishop?' The answer came in 1901, when he was appointed Bishop of Stepney. His effortless ascent through the hierarchy of the Church continued. In 1909 he was enthroned as Archbishop of York.

King Edward VII took no deep interest in ecclesiastical matters; his short and simple charge to the new Archbishop was 'to keep the parties in the Church together and to prevent the clergy from wearing moustaches.' Nor did Lang at once establish an easy relationship with George V. Preaching before the future King at Portsmouth in 1898, he had insisted on commending Christian missions overseas, a practice which the Duke of York was known to abhor as both intrusive and futile. After the sermon they had a set-to. Lang maintained that being a Christian carried with it a belief in the worldwide mission of Christianity. 'Then you tell me that with my

views I can't be a Christian?' the Duke demanded. Lang replied that he could only state the
premises; it was for the Duke to draw the
conclusions. 'Well,' said the Duke, 'I call that
damned cheek.' Later they became friends and
Lang was invited to Balmoral and Sandringham.
'It might have been a curate and his wife in their
new house,' he wrote of life at York Cottage.

During the Great War, Lang fell victim to
anti-German hysteria when he innocently referred to his 'sacred memory' of the Kaiser
kneeling side by side with Edward VII at the
coffin of Queen Victoria. The phrase was long
quoted against him; and the vituperation to
which he was exposed helped to undermine his
health. Until 1916 dark-haired and youthful, he
emerged at the age of fifty-two an elderly man
with a bald head and a fringe of white. The
King, he noted, greeted his changed appearance
'with characteristic guffaws.' But by then their
friendship could bear such tremors. On succeeding Davidson as Archbishop of Canterbury in
1928, Lang became as much a personal chaplain
as Primate of All England. It was he who wrote
all but one of George V's Christmas broadcasts;
the exception, of an inspired simplicity that even
Lang could not emulate, came from the pen of
Rudyard Kipling. And as the reign drew to a
close, Lang was at the deathbed of his friend and
Sovereign.

Even as George V lay dying, Lang felt the chill
of the new reign. The Prince of Wales, about to
succeed as Edward VIII, resented the intrusion of
the Archbishop, whom he described as slipping
in and out of his father's room, 'a noiseless
spectre in black gaiters.' He also affronted Lang
by asking that there should be no religious
service when George V's coffin arrived at Westminster Hall for the lying-in-state; but the
Archbishop had his way, and with a touch of the
theatrical borrowed a purple cope which had
been worn at the funeral of Charles II.

King Edward afterwards wrote of Lang: 'The
mannerisms that had appeared to a youthful
mind as being kind and unfeigned were later to
give the impression of an over anxiety to please
. . . I was to decide that for a prelate he was almost

too polished, too worldly . . . more interested in
the pursuit of prestige and power than the
abstractions of the human soul.' The King,
however, was not altogether immersed in the
abstractions of the human soul. He suspected
that George V had discussed his son's shortcomings with Lang, particularly his liaison with Mrs
Simpson; and this inhibited the King in his
relationship with the Archbishop. But Lang's
part in the Abdication crisis has been much
exaggerated. Although concerned – as any
Churchman might be – by the prospect of
his Sovereign's marriage to a twice-divorced
woman, he was scarcely consulted by the
Prime Minister, Stanley Baldwin, and neither
influenced nor tried to influence events.

What did arouse widespread anger, even
among those who did not sympathize with the
King, was the broadcast made by Lang two days
after the Abdication. It has since been forgotten
that he praised Edward VIII's 'most genuine care
for the poor, the suffering, the unemployed; his
years of eager service both at home and across
the seas.' Those generous words were over-
shadowed by a passage as ill received as had been
his 'sacred memory' of the Kaiser:

'Even more strange and sad it is that he should
have sought his happiness in a manner in-
consistent with the Christian principles of marriage, and within a social circle whose standards
and ways of life are alien to all the best instincts
and traditions of his people. Let those who
belong to this circle stand rebuked by the
judgment of the nation.'

The judgment of the nation, however, was
that Lang had displayed a lack of Christian
forbearance. Retribution came in a cruel little
poem which spread by word of mouth throughout the kingdom:

My Lord Archbishop, what a scold you are.
And when your man is down how bold you
  are.
Of charity how oddly scant you are.
Old Lang swine, how full of Cantuar.

In the same broadcast, the Archbishop also
embarrassed his audience by a clumsy reference

to the stammer which the new King was courageously learning to overcome. If George VI and Queen Elizabeth were irritated by his patronizing words they did not show it. After calling on them to discuss the arrangements for their Coronation, he wrote that 'it was indeed like waking after a nightmare to find the sun shining.'

Both his piety and his gift for stagecraft found expression in the Coronation of 1937. The service was broadcast to the world, although it was not until the Coronation of Elizabeth II in 1953 that television cameras were allowed into Westminster Abbey. Even the newsreels, limited to certain parts of the ceremonial in 1937, were not released until Archbishop and Earl Marshal had scrutinized them for impropriety. Lang might have been tempted to suppress one sequence, except that it was taken at the most sacred moment of all. It showed him juggling with the crown before placing it on his Sovereign's head. He was the victim of misplaced zeal. As the Crown weighed seven pounds and so had to fit the royal head exactly, the King had suggested that a thread of red cotton should be inserted under one of the jewels to mark the front. But some officious person must have removed it just before the service began. Not finding it on one side, Lang turned the crown to see if it was on the other. His fumbling went down to history.

In 1942, at the age of seventy-six, the Archbishop retired and was created Lord Lang of Lambeth; he was thus able to continue attending the House of Lords. The King put a pleasant house on Kew Green at his disposal. Other financial problems were solved by Pierpont Morgan, who gave him £15,000, and by other friends who raised £2,000 to pay an impending claim for surtax. Those benefactions did not prevent Lang from referring in his resignation statement at the Convocation of Canterbury to the 'very slender means' he would have in retirement. His pension alone was £1,500 a year, compared to the £200 that awaited most of those he was addressing. Lang collapsed and died in December 1945 while hurrying to catch a train at Kew Station. His ashes were placed in Canterbury Cathedral, near the tomb of his predecessor Henry Chichele, the founder of All Souls College.

Our interest in Cosmo Lang lies less in his achievements as an ecclesiastical statesman than in the complexity of his character. During his thirty-three years as an Archbishop he failed to solve, indeed he scarcely touched, any of the pressing problems of the Church: conformity, liturgy, reunion, finance. Even his sermons, so lapidary in phrase and silver tongued in delivery, struck no note of leadership. What continues to fascinate is the contrast between his enamelled public dignity – throughout his years at York he never once entered a shop – and the sense of unworthiness which haunted him to the grave. He loved living in his own palaces and being entertained in others; yet he would spend part of each annual holiday ministering to his own soul in a humble Scottish retreat.

Once when Lang was showing some visitors a new painting by Orpen, he made the plaintive comment: 'They say that in that portrait I look proud, pompous and prelatical.' Hensley Henson, Bishop of Durham and the most waspish of his critics, was not the man to return a soothing answer. 'And to which of those epithets,' he inquired, 'does your Grace take exception?' There is, however, a lesser-known story about that picture. When it was first presented to Lang by a party of friends, he told them: 'It is a portrait of a very hard-working, very well-meaning, very lonely and very disappointed man.'

Lascelles, Sir Alan
(1887–1981)

Private Secretary to King George VI and to Queen Elizabeth II. He was a grandson of the 4th Earl of Harewood and cousin of the 6th Earl, Princess Mary's husband. Educated at Marlborough and Trinity College, Oxford, he numbered among his closest friends the war poet

Julian Grenfell. Lascelles himself served throughout the Great War in the Bedfordshire Yeomanry and won the Military Cross. In 1919 he spent a year as ADC to his brother-in-law, Sir George (later Lord) Lloyd, the Governor of Bombay. In 1920 he married Joan Thesiger, eldest daughter of the 1st Viscount Chelmsford, Viceroy of India.

For the next nine years Lascelles served as assistant private secretary to the Prince of Wales, later King Edward VIII; but as the Prince became increasingly capricious in the performance of his public duties and indiscreet in his private affairs, the affection of Lascelles cooled. He would later describe his MVO, which he was awarded in 1926, as 'hard-earned.' In 1929 he was glad to escape to

Sir Alan Lascelles by David Poole

Canada as private secretary to the Governor-General, the Earl of Bessborough.

Shortly before the death of George V in January 1936, Lascelles returned to royal service as the King's assistant private secretary. He retained the appointment in the short reign of Edward VIII, but was not taken into the King's confidence during the events leading to the Abdication.

On the accession of George VI he felt once more at home, and in 1943 he was appointed Private Secretary on the retirement of Sir Alexander Hardinge (q.v.). He had meanwhile accompanied his new master on a visit to Canada and the United States, during which he became the first British subject to be knighted by his Sovereign on American soil. The King, who had acquired little experience of statecraft as Duke of York, depended much on Lascelles, particularly during the strains of World War II. But the Private Secretary's relations with the Queen, later Queen Elizabeth the Queen Mother, were never more than formal. He found her a rival and sometimes obstructive counsellor in all that touched the Sovereign; and she perhaps found him too bleakly intellectual in his approach to both the frailty and the variety of the human spirit.

In May 1940, when the fall of Neville Chamberlain pointed to Winston Churchill as his likeliest successor, Lascelles shared the King's misgivings. He said after hearing one of Churchill's most memorable speeches of that perilous summer: 'It is too early to judge whether he will be a great Prime Minister. What I am certain is that he will go down to history as a great poet.' In spite of occasional clashes of opinion, the two men came to trust each other. It is curious that although Lascelles was never called anything except Tommy by family, friends and close colleagues, Churchill alone persisted in addressing him as Alan.

The coming of peace in 1945 did little to ease the burden of a Private Secretary. George VI was less well able than his father to appreciate the ways of a Labour Government. To these cares were added increasing anxieties about the King's health and a deep personal sorrow: the death of Sir Alan's only son, John Lascelles, at the age of twenty-nine. After the death of the King in 1952, Lascelles remained at the Palace only long enough to ensure continuity from one reign to another. He retired in 1953.

There was a strain of austerity in Lascelles which detested pretentiousness. 'Look at that Theudas,' he would observe of some self-important personage. The allusion was to Acts v, verse 36: 'For before these days rose up Theudas, boasting himself to be somebody.' He refused the peerage customarily offered to a retiring Private Secretary and was annoyed that, without warning, Churchill had recommended him for the Grand Cross of the Bath. Lascelles disliked excessive public display no less, and rightly denounced a proposal that a national observance of prayer before the invasion of German-occupied Europe in 1944 should include the parading of the Coronation regalia in St Paul's Cathedral. But during his last months of office, his instinct for once played him false. When the newly crowned Queen visited her Scottish kingdom in June 1953, Lascelles advised her to wear day clothes for the most solemn ceremony of all: the presentation of the Honours of Scotland – Crown, Sceptre and Sword – in St Giles's Cathedral. The congregation, robed and jewelled in all their finery, saw it as a Sassenach snub.

Lascelles lived on in retirement for nearly thirty years, occupying a secluded grace-and-favour house converted from the old stables of Kensington Palace. He read widely, listened to music, grew a beard. He also became chairman of the Historic Buildings Council and of the Pilgrim Trust, as well as a director of the Midland Bank. He was always willing to help historians and biographers, many of whom will treasure his incisively phrased and drily humorous letters written in a fine italic script on whatever scraps of paper came to hand. At his death, Lascelles left a modest fortune of £63,000 and a diary of his years at court. That literary mine, however, will be neither exploded nor exploited until the next century.

Lascelles, Hon. Gerald
(1924–   )

Younger son of the 6th Earl of Harewood and Princess Mary, the Princess Royal (qq.v.). Educated at Eton, he served in the Rifle Brigade during the war and sits on the boards of many companies, some of them connected with the motor racing industry.

He has experienced marital complexities similar to those of his brother the 7th Earl of Harewood (q.v.). When his marriage to Angela Dowding was dissolved after twenty-six years in 1978 he found that under the Royal Marriages Act of 1772 and other legislation he could not remarry in England. It was therefore in Vienna that he married his second wife, Elizabeth Colvin, in November 1978.

For more than twenty years, Lascelles and his first wife lived at Fort Belvedere, on the edge of Windsor Great Park. From 1930 until the Abdication in 1936 it had been the private residence of the Duke of Windsor as Prince of Wales and King: it was in the drawing-room that he signed the Instrument of Abdication in favour of his brother, King George VI. Lascelles occupied Fort Belvedere not as a grace-and-favour residence bestowed by the Sovereign but on a lease from the Crown which has since passed through many hands.

Bearing a quaint resemblance to a toy fort, complete with turret and a semicircle of eighteenth-century guns, it was designed for William, Duke of Cumberland, in about 1750 and transformed by Wyattville for King George IV in 1827–9. A century later the Duke of Windsor restored the fabric, cleared the undergrowth and laid out a fine garden and swimming-pool. A stained-glass window on the spiral staircase bears the Prince of Wales's feathers. But by some mischance his motto appears not as 'Ich Dien' (I serve) but as 'Hic Dein', which might mean anything. Lascelles

Gerald Lascelles

inherited some of his mother's books which in turn had belonged to his grandmother. They included a three-volume work on Marie-Antoinette and a recipe book marked by a strip of paper in Queen Mary's handwriting: 'Veal for when the Queen comes.'

Learmonth, Sir James
(1895–1967)

Scottish surgeon and authority on vascular diseases. In 1949 he operated on King George VI for arteriosclerosis of the right leg, thus saving the limb from amputation. At a subsequent examination in the King's bathroom, George VI, wearing only a dressing-gown and slippers, said to Learmonth: 'You used a knife on me, now I'm going to use one on you.' He then produced a hitherto concealed sword, told him to kneel and bestowed on him the accolade of knighthood.

Leicester, Thomas Coke, 3rd Earl of
(1848–1941)

Friend and neighbour in Norfolk of King George V. There was much rivalry between the two men. The King liked to boast that although Sandringham was only half the size of Leicester's estate at Holkham, he killed twice as many partridges. Leicester, however, did his best. To a complaint that one of his churchyards was disgracefully overgrown, he replied: 'Nonsense, best breeding ground for partridges in England.'

He also resented the generosity with which the King raised the agricultural wages at Sandringham, thereby obliging his less affluent neighbours to follow his lead. Lady Leicester said to her husband during this period of strained friendship: 'It is a long time since the King and Queen have been to Holkham. Shall I ask them to luncheon?' Leicester replied: 'No, Alice, don't encourage them.'

The Coke family has nevertheless continued to provide equerries and ladies-in-waiting to the royal family.

Ley, Dr Henry
(1887–1962)

Organist at the Coronations of successive Sovereigns. His early years were spent as a chorister at St George's Chapel, Windsor, where he was regarded as a prodigy. He was elected organist at Christ Church, Oxford, even as an undergraduate, then spent nearly twenty years as precentor of Eton College. There his pupils included the 7th Earl of Harewood (q.v.) and Humphrey Lyttelton, the jazz trumpeter.

One of Ley's memorable anecdotes was of his early days at Windsor, when a fellow chorister got his finger stuck in a hole in the carved pew. After a desperate struggle, the boy burst into tears, and the second male tenor was sent out for help. He came back with the verger, who in turn called in a carpenter to saw off part of the pew. When the operation was complete, a little procession moved off down the nave: the verger in front, the tenor and the carpenter in the rear, and in the middle the diminutive weeping chorister, with a piece of carved pew and a candle half as big as himself still stuck on the end of his right index finger.

Lichfield, (Thomas) Patrick Anson, 5th Earl of
(1939–   )

Cousin of the Queen and photographer. He is the son of the late Viscount Anson, who did not live to succeed his father, the 4th Earl, and Anne Bowes-Lyon, a niece of Queen Elizabeth the Queen Mother, who married as her second husband Prince Georg of Denmark. Educated at Harrow and the Royal Military Academy,

Patrick Lichfield

Sandhurst, he served for five years in the Grenadier Guards before setting up as a professional photographer. In 1975 he married Lady Leonora Grosvenor, elder daughter of the 5th Duke of Westminster.

Patrick Lichfield's kinship with the royal family and his lively sense of publicity smoothed the way to the summit of his career; but he would never have climbed beyond the foothills without professional skill. (His sister, Lady Elizabeth Shakerley, shows the same determination running a successful catering business.) One of his first assignments was to photograph the Danish royal family. Although they were cousins by marriage, his hands shook so violently that he had to refuse a cup of tea. 'I had done a very strange thing,' he later wrote, 'and turned into a tradesman.' Yet few tradesmen have received so many royal warrants. In a single year, 1971, he sailed across the Indian Ocean with the Queen in *Britannia* to take photographs for her forthcoming Silver Wedding; was invited to shoot at Balmoral in every sense; and spent Christmas as a guest at Windsor, where he snapped the entire family watching a Marx Brothers film on television.

His best-known photographs are of the wedding of the Prince and Princess of Wales. He has also shown himself intrepid in the face of massed corgis. Scarcely any royal face has escaped his candid but kindly camera. Sometimes, however, he has had to pay a bizarre forfeit. When he went to Paris to photograph the Windsors, the Duke remembered that he was a fellow Grenadier. 'Before I fully realized what was happening,' Lichfield recalls, 'I found myself, sword in hand, marching with him up and down the lawn doing regimental sword drill.'

Logue, Lionel
(1880–1958)

Speech therapist to King George VI. Born in Adelaide, South Australia, he was trained as an engineer before discovering his remarkable gifts for correcting and curing speech defects. In 1924 he set up his practice in London. Two years later the Duke of York, later King George VI, consulted him about the stammer which had afflicted him since boyhood, making even the shortest public utterance a penance. Logue wrote of his patient: 'He entered my consulting room at three o'clock in the afternoon, a slim, quiet man, with tired eyes and all the outward symptoms of the man upon whom habitual speech defect had begun to set the sign. When he left at five o'clock, you could see that there was hope once more in his heart.'

For the next ten weeks the Duke visited Logue almost daily and carried out the prescribed exercises. Sometimes there was the encouraging presence of the Duchess, too. After one month the Duke noticed a vast improvement in his speech. 'I am sure I am going to get quite all right in time,' he told his father, 'but 24 years of talking in the wrong way cannot be cured in a month.' The essence of Logue's treatment was to instil self-confidence in his patient; then to teach him how to breathe correctly and to control the rhythm of the diaphragm. With so willing a pupil, he had a startling success. The Duke never lost his distaste for public speaking. But with Logue at hand to coach and rehearse him for occasions such as the Opening of Parliament, he was able to read a text with only momentary hesitation.

What might have been a serious check to his progress occurred in December 1936, when he succeeded to the throne on his brother's Abdication. The mental strain and physical exhaustion which he suffered made it more difficult than ever to control his breathing. Then came a well-meaning but inept public reference by Archbishop Lang (q.v.) to the new King's speech impediment: a *bêtise* which could not fail to increase the nervousness of both the monarch and his subjects. Logue was justly furious at Lang's intrusion on such delicate ground, and correspondingly relieved when the King rose above his emotional distress.

For his incalculable services, Logue was made MVO in 1937 and CVO in 1944.

Lorne, John Campbell, Marquess of
later 9th Duke of Argyll
(1845–1914)

The eldest son of the 8th Duke, he bore the courtesy title of Lorne until succeeding his father in 1900. Technically a commoner, he was thus able to sit in the House of Commons. Elected Liberal MP for Argyllshire in 1868, he also acted as private secretary to his father, a Cabinet Minister in successive Liberal Governments.

In 1871 he married Princess Louise (q.v.), the fourth daughter of Queen Victoria, in St George's Chapel, Windsor. Although bride and bridegroom were distant cousins, each descending from King James I of Scotland (1394–1437), some members of the British and German royal families frowned on a match between a sovereign's daughter and a subject. Queen Victoria, with her deep affection for all Scots, took a more realistic view. 'Small foreign Princes are very unpopular here,' she replied to one such complaint. Sir Henry Ponsonby, her private secretary, put it more robustly: 'No use talking now of this or that Seidlitz Stinkinger. They are out of the question.'

The Queen did not require her son-in-law to relinquish his political career; and although he rarely spoke in the Commons, he retained his seat until appointed Governor-General of Canada in 1878. He made heavy weather of the task. 'It is no easy thing,' he said. 'You must have the patience of a saint, the smile of a cherub, the generosity of an Indian prince and the back of a camel.' During those years in Canada the marriage is thought to have foundered in all but name. Denied the remedy of separation, much less of divorce, the unhappy, childless couple performed their public duties together but in private went their separate ways. The Queen, believing that idleness aggravated most ills, tried to find further employment for Lorne. In 1886, three years after he and Princess Louise returned from Canada, she made the extraordinary suggestion that Gladstone might include him in his newly formed Liberal Government as Under-Secretary for the Colonies. But the Prince of Wales strenuously objected. 'I hardly think the Queen's son-in-law should form part of her Government,' he wrote, 'no matter what party is in power; and how could he form part of a "Home Rule" Government?' A few days later, Gladstone asked the Queen whether she would approve of Lorne's appointment as Viceroy of Ireland. 'I declined its being offered on account of expense ostensibly,' the Queen noted, 'but really on political grounds.'

Lorne parted from Gladstone on the issue of Irish Home Rule and in 1895 was re-elected to the Commons as Liberal Unionist MP for South Manchester. He held the seat until succeeding his father as the 9th Duke of Argyll in 1900. Lorne was more industrious as a man of letters than as a parliamentarian. He wrote fiction, verse, reminiscences, several works on Canada and an operatic libretto. His publication in 1892 of a eulogistic biography of his mother-in-law's *bête noir*, Lord Palmerston, did not prevent his appointment in the same year as Governor and Constable of Windsor Castle, an office he held until his death in 1914.

Louise, Princess,
Duchess of Fife and Princess Royal
(1867–1931)

The eldest daughter of King Edward VII and Queen Alexandra, she was married in 1889 to Alexander Duff, 1st Duke of Fife (q.v.), a rich Scottish landowner eighteen years her senior. They had two daughters, Princess Alexandra and Princess Maud (qq.v.); one was married to her cousin Prince Arthur of Connaught, the other to the 11th Earl of Southesk. In 1905 King Edward granted the Duchess of Fife the additional title of Princess Royal. Her husband died in 1912.

Although shy and withdrawn, the Duchess

John Campbell, Marquess of Lorne

was not without spleen. Like her sisters, Princess Victoria and Princess Maud (later Queen of Norway). she disdained the morganatic blood of her sister-in-law, Queen Mary. 'Poor May, poor May,' she would sigh, 'with her Württemberg hands.'

The tranquillity of her life as a middle-aged widow was much disturbed when, after the death in 1923 of Earl Farquhar (q.v.) an intimate friend of her husband and a co-trustee of the Fife estates, large sums of money were found to be missing. Obliged by law to make good the deficiency, she was, a contemporary noted, 'open-mouthed in consequence.' In 1924 she raised part of the imposition by selling some family pictures at Christie's.

The Tsar Nicholas II, Queen Victoria, Princess Louise Duchess of Fife, the Tsarina, the Duchess of Connaught, Princess Margaret and Princess Patricia of Connaught (with cat), Balmoral, 1896

Louise, Princess, Marchioness of Lorne
and later Duchess of Argyll
(1848–1939)

The fourth and most beautiful daughter of Queen Victoria, she was married in 1871 to John Campbell, Marquess of Lorne (q.v.) elder son and heir of the 8th Duke of Argyll. Educated on more practical lines than her new sisters-in-law, she delighted in teaching one how to sew on a button and transformed the life of another by giving her a pair of spectacles.

In 1878 she accompanied her husband to Canada on his appointment as Governor-General. There she suffered a terrible sleigh accident, being dragged by the hair and losing an ear. In spite of the unhappiness of their marriage, Victorian convention required the couple to

(*Overleaf*) The Marriage of Princess Louise to Lord Lorne, 1871, by Sidney Hall

Princess Louise, Marchioness of Lorne

conceal the rift. They had no children.

Princess Louise's uninhibited tongue did not add to her popularity. One of the Queen's ladies-in-waiting wrote of her: 'She is fascinating but oh, so ill-natured I positively dread talking to her, not a soul escapes.' And a little later: 'Never have I come across a more dangerous woman, to gain her end she would stick at nothing. One would have given her a wide berth in the sixteenth century, happily she is powerless in the nineteenth.' On the death of her brother-in-law, Prince Henry of Battenberg, she offended her widowed sister, Princess Beatrice (q.v.) by a heartless assertion that she alone had been his confidante and that Beatrice had been nothing to him. This, wrote another member of the family, she indicated by a shrug of her shoulders.

An accomplished sculptress, Princess Louise executed the memorial to Prince Henry in Whippingham Church, near Cowes, as well as the marble statue of Queen Victoria at Kensington Palace, overlooking the Round Pond. She wrote magazine articles under the *nom de plume* of Myra Fontenoy, patronized artists and encouraged higher education for women.

Having been born in 1848, the year that saw Louis-Philippe and Metternich tumble from power, she survived to deplore the invasion of Poland by Hitler in 1939.

Lutyens, Sir Edwin
(1869–1944)

Architect and President of the Royal Academy of Arts. In 1912, the year after George V had proclaimed Delhi as the new capital of India, Lutyens was entrusted with designing Viceroy's House, the focal point of the new city. His palace of courts and colonnades proved to be among the most magnificent in the history of architecture. 'Sloping gently upward,' Robert Byron wrote, 'runs a gravel way of such infinite perspective as to suggest the intervention of a diminishing glass; at whose end, reared above the green tree-tops, glitters the seat of govern-

ment, the seventh Delhi, four-square upon an eminence – dome, tower, dome, tower, dome, red, pink, cream and white, washed gold and flashing in the morning sun.'

The King-Emperor followed its construction with interest and pride. Yet the Versailles of the British Raj was also its Valhalla. According to legend, every new city built at Delhi foretold the end of a dynasty. In 1929, Lord Irwin became the first Viceroy to occupy the new seat of government; less than twenty years later, Lord Mountbatten became the last.

A more restrained example of the genius of Lutyens is the Cenotaph, in Whitehall, unveiled by George V in 1920 as a memorial to the dead of the Great War. Its inspired simplicity is deceptive: it does not contain a single vertical or horizontal line. The 'verticals,' if extended, would meet at a point 1,000 feet above ground; and the 'horizontals' are radials of a circle whose centre is 900 feet below ground.

Lutyens was also responsible for designing the Dolls' House presented to Queen Mary after the war and now on permanent display at Windsor Castle. Built in the style of Wren to a scale of one inch to the foot, exactly as Swift depicted Lilliput in *Gulliver's Travels*, it is a marvel of the diminutive. There is a garden, a garage containing a Rolls-Royce and a Daimler, well-stocked cellars and larders. Crown jewels in the strong room, gold frying pans in the kitchen, toys in the nursery: nothing has been forgotten. The leading artists of the day adorned its walls and ceilings. Celebrated authors wrote books the size of postage stamps for its library. Only George Bernard Shaw refused to contribute, 'in a very rude letter,' Princess Marie Louise noted.

Edwin Lutyens was a big man, scarcely ever seen without a small pipe in his mouth. His wit was irrepressible. After a bitter and protracted quarrel with Herbert Baker, architect of the Secretariat buildings in New Delhi, he confessed: 'I have met my Bakerloo.' In the bedroom of the Queen's Doll's House, one pillow was embroidered with the initials MG, the other with GM. They meant, he explained, 'May George?' and 'George May.'

Appointed to the Order of Merit in 1942, he had earlier been knighted. Just before the ceremony at Buckingham Palace began, a very nervous man next to him asked about the procedure. 'Quite simple,' Lutyens told him. 'The Lord Chamberlain will call out your name and lead you up to the throne. You must then go down on one knee and sing *God Save the King*.' 'But I don't even know the words,' the terrified new knight replied. 'Don't worry,' Lutyens assured him, 'the King will help you out with them.'

Mackworth-Young, Sir Robert
(1920–   )

Librarian of Windsor Castle, 1958–84. The grandson of a Governor of the Punjab and son of another senior Indian Civil Servant, he was educated at Eton and King's College, Cambridge. He served in the RAF during the war, then in the Foreign Service before succeeding Sir Owen Morshead (q.v.) at Windsor. He is a tall, thin, unobtrusive man, courteous of manner and drily humorous.

Although it is the Queen's Private Secretary who bears the title of Keeper of the Archives, the effective guardian of that rich hoard is the Queen's Librarian. During his years at Windsor, Mackworth-Young was noted for the generosity of his guidance to scholars and the tact with which he preserved the reputation of past Sovereigns from unseemly revelation.

'Robin' Mackworth-Young also possesses the ingenious mind of the scientist. Having bought a fine harpsichord made for him by Sir Michael Cary, Permanent Secretary to the Ministry of Defence, he found that the slightest change in the weather would throw it out of tune. So he used his knowledge of electronics, picked up as a wartime signals officer, to construct a device for tuning every sort of musical instrument from a cinema organ to the human voice. This he has developed commercially, finding a ready market for it both at home and abroad. Among those who have bought his increasingly sophisticated models are a manufacturer of concertinas, the Glyndebourne Opera and the restorer of the Queen's State Trumpets.

Maclean, 1st Baron and 11th Baronet
(1916–   )

Lord Chamberlain of the Queen's Household from 1971 to 1984. Charles Maclean, or Chips as he is known to his intimates, was educated at Canford School, in Dorset, a public school established as recently as 1923 but on traditional lines. He served throughout the war of 1939–45 in the Scots Guards, a brother officer in his battalion being Robert Runcie, later Archbishop of Canterbury (q.v.). From 1959 to 1975 he was Chief Scout of the Commonwealth and left his mark on the movement by introducing long trousers as an alternative to the once ubiquitous bare knees of Baden-Powell.

Lord Maclean, 1975

Sir Edwin Lutyens presents a model of the Viceroy's House, New Delhi, to its first occupant, Lord Irwin.
Watercolour by Marjorie Shoosmith, 1931

Lord Maclean, 27th Chief of the Clan Maclean, devotes much of his life to good causes on both sides of the Scottish border; is a director of the Distillers' Company; cherishes Duart Castle, his thirteenth-century family seat on the Isle of Mull; and has written a story book for children. In 1969 he was made a Knight of the Thistle, Scotland's premier Order of Chivalry.

As Lord Chamberlain he has organized the weddings of Princess Anne and the Prince of Wales, the funerals of the Duke of Windsor and Lord Mountbatten, and innumerable garden parties and investitures. An imperturbable man whose expressionless gaze masks a dry wit, he does not always see human nature at its most attractive. He emerged from a diplomatic reception a few weeks before the Prince of Wales's marriage. 'A very nice party,' he said. 'Only three people asked me for invitations.'

In his semi-retirement he has been appointed Chief Steward of Hampton Court Palace, which stands on the banks of the Thames about fifteen miles from the centre of London. Built by Cardinal Wolsey and acquired by King Henry VIII, it has not been occupied by the Sovereign for the past two centuries. The Palace, however, continues to house many old royal servants and their families in grace-and-favour apartments.

Mann, the Rt Rev. Michael
(1924–   )

Dean of Windsor and Domestic Chaplain to the Queen since 1976. Educated at Harrow and the Royal Military College, Sandhurst, he was commissioned into the 1st King's Dragoon Guards and served during the war in the Middle East, Italy and Palestine. After nine years in Nigeria as a member of the Colonial Service and a spell at the Graduate School of Business Administration, Harvard, he studied at Wells Theological College and took Holy Orders in 1957. From 1962 to 1967 he was Vicar of Christ Church, Port Harcourt, Nigeria, and later a Canon of Norwich Cathedral. After only two

The Dean of Windsor and the Queen Mother

years as Bishop Suffragan of Dudley, he was chosen by the Queen to be Dean of Windsor: an appointment which by the tacit consent of successive Prime Ministers remains in the personal gift of the Sovereign.

The Dean, who bears himself with military precision, is a pellucid preacher. His spiritual guidance of the royal family is reflected in the letters he has exchanged with Prince Philip, published in 1984 under the title *A Windsor Correspondence*. They illuminate a fundamental difference in the attitude of each man to Christianity. Prince Philip wrote to Mann: 'Whether "God became man in Jesus Christ" is a philosophical question; what is a matter of fact is that Jesus tried to show us how to live so that the world would become a better place.' The Dean, a skilful Christian apologist even when arguing on his knees, replied: 'The belief that "God became man in Jesus Christ" is not, in the Christian view, a philosophical question; it is a matter of faith. And to say that "Jesus tried to show us how to live so that the world would

become a better place" is to be selective of the evidence and to ignore the main thrust of the New Testament. If Jesus was merely a fine ethical teacher, I doubt whether the New Testament would have been written, and certainly not in the way it has come down to us.'

Michael Mann is a devoted curator of St George's Chapel and its attendant Tudor buildings. To ensure that they should be repaired with only the finest timber for many years to come, he first secured some of the Queen's oak trees from Windsor Great Park. Then he wrote to all the Knights of the Garter, whose banners hang in St George's, asking for trees from their own estates. Of the full complement of twenty-four Knights, several of whom live overseas, ten each felled an oak and sent it to be stored at Windsor. It is a striking comment on how far England's premier order of chivalry, founded in 1348, remains the preserve of substantial landowners. The ten, in Garter seniority, were the Duke of Beaufort (q.v.), Lord De L'Isle, Lord Ashburton, Lord Cobbold (q.v.), Sir Edmund

Bacon, Sir Cennydd Traherne, Lord Waldegrave, Lord Abergavenny and the Duke of Grafton.

A student of military history, the Dean has hung the walls of his Deanery with swords and accoutrements, pictures and prints. He is a trustee of the Imperial War Museum, and has written a history of the Waterloo campaign as seen through the eyes of his old regiment. It is dedicated to the memory of his only son, Captain Philip Mann, killed in action in 1975 while serving with the army of the Sultan of Oman.

Margaret, Princess
(1930–)

Sister of Queen Elizabeth II. The younger daughter of the Duke and Duchess of York, afterwards King George VI and Queen Elizabeth, she was born on 21 August 1930 at Glamis Castle, the Scottish house of her mother's parents, the Earl and Countess of Strathmore. In those days the Home Secretary was required to be present at royal births, and the Labour Minister J.R.Clynes had to kick his heels until the infant put in an appearance. The Duke and Duchess wanted to call her Ann, but her grandfather King George V insisted on Margaret. Her parents added Rose, after her godmother and aunt, Lady Rose Leveson Gower. 'I think that it is very pretty together,' her mother wrote to Queen Mary. The double name caught the public imagination and clung to her through childhood; but it was not used in the family.

She was a pretty and amusing little girl who on her fifth birthday captivated the playwright James Barrie, a guest at Glamis. 'Is that really your very own?' he asked, pointing to a present by her plate. She said: 'It is yours and mine.' Barrie was so pleased by this graceful response that he put it in his play, *The Boy David*, promising her a penny for every performance of it. By the time it was staged two years later, he had forgotten his debt; but the King had not, and sent a message that if Barrie did not at once pay his daughter her royalties, he would hear from the royal solicitors. A contrite Barrie drew up a mock-solemn agreement which was engrossed on parchment: the last thing, as it happened, he ever wrote. He died before the sack of pennies could be delivered and his executors discharged the debt.

Among the many confidences committed to print by the children's governess, Miss Marion Crawford (q.v.) is this vignette of sisterly love:

'Neither was above taking a whack at her adversary, if roused, and Lilibet was quick with her left hook! Margaret was more of a close-in fighter, known to bite on occasions. More than once have I been shown a hand bearing the royal teeth marks.'

Adored nevertheless both by her parents and her sometimes patronizing sister, she spent a happy childhood, even after the accession of her father in 1936 required the family to move from the intimacy of 145 Piccadilly to the vast gloomy spaces of Buckingham Palace. If there was a shadow in her life, it was her grandmother Queen Mary, whose own shyness made her seem more formidable than she was. She also earned Princess Margaret's lifelong dislike by her tactless refrain: 'How small you are! Why don't you grow up?' The old Queen, through her lady-in-waiting, Lady Cynthia Colville (q.v.), wrote to 'Crawfie' in April 1940: 'Her Majesty is rather sorry to hear that Princess Margaret is so spoilt, though perhaps it is hardly surprising. I dare say, too, she has a more complicated and difficult character, and one that will require a great deal of skill and insight in dealing with. But perhaps in a year or two her general outlook and attitude to life may improve out of all recognition.'

Crawfie, too, had her say: 'Though Lilibet, with the rest of us, laughed at Margaret's antics – and indeed it was impossible not to – I think they often made her uneasy and filled her with foreboding.' It is difficult to see how else a high-spirited child should behave when, with an elder sister, she was immured in Windsor Castle throughout five years of war, as securely as if she had taken the veil. Those were scarcely the

circumstances in which either girl could best develop her character.

It has sometimes been surmised that Princess Margaret was jealous of her sister's superior status as heir presumptive to the throne. There is a simpler explanation for any supposed resentment: the four years' difference in age which in any small family establishes coveted privileges for the elder, a sense of exclusion in the younger. To this day Princess Margaret regrets that she was not allowed to accompany, or even follow, the future Queen to Eton for tutorials on history from Henry Marten (q.v.). Instead there was a disagreeable history lesson from Queen Mary. Coming on her granddaughter playing with the cords of the window blinds, she reminded her how King George of Hanover had lost his sight when a chain purse he was swinging hit his eye. It must also have aroused envy in a precocious girl to see her elder sister in love and commissioned into one of the Women's Services.

Soon, however, she was embarking on her own programme of public engagements, followed in 1947 by the tour of South Africa with her parents and sister. In the same year she was a bridesmaid at Princess Elizabeth's wedding; and almost overnight, it seemed, the newspapers were tipping this young man and that as her future husband. At Windsor one evening, standing by Gainsborough's portraits of the thirteen children of King George III, Princess Margaret observed to a guest: 'Look at all those poor girls, waiting to be sold into captivity.' Such, she determined, would not be her own fate; slim, vivacious and exceptionally pretty, she would not necessarily make her choice from the young aristocrats summoned to Balmoral for her inspection.

Romance, when it came, was indeed unconventional. She fell in love with Group Captain Peter Townsend (q.v.). Sixteen years her senior, he was a handsome and much-decorated fighter pilot who had been appointed an equerry to the King in 1944 and later Master of the Household. Throughout the distress of her father's failing health and untimely death, the Princess found solace in Townsend's gentleness and sympathy.

Princess Margaret by Annigoni

And as his own marriage disintegrated, he too drew consolation from her mercurial charm. The reorganization of the royal households in the new reign conspired to further their friendship. Townsend relinquished his post at Buckingham Palace to accompany the widowed Queen Mother and Princess Margaret to Clarence House as Comptroller.

In the early months of 1953, Princess Margaret confided to the Queen that she and Townsend loved each other and wished to marry. The Queen was immersed in preparing for her Coronation; and while neither encouraging nor opposing the match, she begged her sister to wait a year before making up her mind. There the matter might have rested. But as a member of the royal household, Townsend felt it his duty to inform the Queen's Private Secretary, Sir Alan Lascelles (q.v.), of his wish to marry the Sovereign's sister. He received the celebrated rebuke: 'You must be either mad or bad.' For Lascelles instantly realized that what the Queen had apparently taken to be no more than a romantic attachment could be the cause of a constitutional crisis.

At the root of the matter lay the Royal Marriages Act of 1772, instigated by King George III to prevent his sons from contracting unsuitable alliances. Still on the statute book two centuries later, it required all members of the royal family to seek the Sovereign's consent before marriage; failure to do so was to infringe the law and provoke its penalties. By 1953, moreover, the Sovereign was no longer a free agent in such matters. As a constitutional monarch, the Queen was obliged to accept her Ministers' advice; and Lascelles was experienced enough to know that the Cabinet of Sir Winston Churchill would never approve the marriage of Princess Margaret to Group Captain Townsend: of the Queen's sister, third in line of succession, to a man who had been through the divorce courts, albeit as an 'innocent' party. Whatever the personal beliefs of her Ministers – and they included men who had been divorced – they could not advise the Supreme Governor of the Church of England to sanction a match which

flouted the doctrine on divorce and remarriage she had sworn to uphold.

Princess Margaret had agreed to wait a year before once more pleading for permission to marry Peter Townsend. She now discovered that by waiting for yet another year, she would be beyond the reach of the Royal Marriages Act; for it appeared to allow members of the royal family to marry at will once they had reached the age of twenty-five and given formal notice to the Privy Council. Lascelles did not dissuade her from such a course, and she resigned herself to a two-year vigil: until her twenty-fifth birthday on 21 August 1955.

Both Lascelles and the Prime Minister did, however, suggest to the Queen that Townsend ought to be sent abroad lest his presence at court caused a scandal. The Queen refused. It would be enough, she said, if he were to move from Clarence House to Buckingham Palace as one of her own equerries. But after only a few weeks, that tolerant arrangement collapsed. Princess Margaret's glow of happiness as she talked to Townsend at the Coronation alerted the world's Press to their shared secret. This time the Government insisted that the Group Captain be banished, and he was packed off to Brussels as Air Attaché at the British Embassy. His exile lasted for the next two years, broken only by a brief visit to London in 1954. The Princess meanwhile carried out her public duties at home and abroad with exemplary poise.

She spent her twenty-fifth birthday at Balmoral amid intense speculation; but there was no announcement and she did not return to London until eight weeks later. The Princess arrived back at Clarence House on 13 October 1955; so, a few hours later, did Group Captain Peter Townsend. Pursued and besieged by the Press, they spent the next two weeks discussing their future. Only then, after two years of faithful separation, did they discover the bitter truth about the Royal Marriages Act. Princess Margaret, having reached the age of twenty-five, believed that she was free to marry. What nobody had told her was that her proposed match would still require the sanction of the

Government; and that if she persisted in marrying a divorced man, the Government would ask Parliament to pass a Bill depriving her of all rights of succession to the throne, certain other royal attributes and her Civil List, or annual income.

The material sacrifice would be considerable. At the beginning of the new reign, Parliament had voted her a Civil List of £6,000, which would rise to £15,000 if she made a suitable match. On marriage to Townsend, however, neither of those sums would be paid: a loss to her of £120,000 a year in the currency of 1985. Even terms as harsh as those were to be granted reluctantly. One member of the Cabinet, Lord Salisbury (q.v.), let it be known he would resign rather than countenance a Bill subverting the Canon Law of the Church. Such was the Christian fervour of a Government led during the past four months by Anthony Eden, who in common with some of his colleagues had remarried after divorce.

The harassed couple meanwhile continued their heart-searching. On Wednesday 26 October, *The Times* threw its weight against their marriage in a long leading article of majestic admonition. When a member of the newspaper's staff asked the editor whether it was not needlessly severe, he replied: 'No. Otherwise Princess Margaret might think herself free to marry Group Captain Townsend with the approval of *The Times*.' It was one of the few comic moments during those agonizing days. Nor did the leading article affect the Princess's decision which, with Townsend's agreement, she had reached forty-eight hours earlier. As a matter of courtesy, she drove to Lambeth Palace on 27 October to inform the Archbishop of Canterbury, Geoffrey Fisher (q.v.). When she had finished, he replied: 'What a wonderful person the Holy Spirit is.' Four days later, Princess Margaret issued this public statement:

'I would like it to be known that I have decided not to marry Group Captain Townsend. I have been aware that, subject to my renouncing my rights of succession, it might have been possible for me to contract a civil marriage. But mindful of the Church's teachings that Christian marriage is indissoluble, and conscious of my duty to the Commonwealth, I have resolved to put these considerations before others. I have reached this decision entirely alone and in doing so I have been strengthened by the unfailing support and devotion of Group Captain Townsend. I am deeply grateful for the concern of all those who have constantly prayed for my happiness.'

Although the Church's teachings that Christian marriage is indissoluble had not apparently deterred her from waiting two years to marry Peter Townsend, it would be cynical to suggest that material factors alone had led her not to marry him. She would have lost not only her Civil List but also the mainspring of her life. The daughter of George vi had been brought up to think of herself as one of a team, of what her father had whimsically called The Royal Firm. That dutiful concept did not accord with life in a cottage on a Group Captain's salary. To borrow Elizabeth Longford's striking image: 'Princess Margaret shares the artistic, even bohemian vein; but it is firmly embedded in Windsor Rock.'

She and Townsend, having separated at the end of October 1955, met only once more: in March 1958, on his return from a prolonged journey round the world. In the following year he married a young Belgian girl and now lives in France.

Looking back on the whole episode, Princess Margaret still has reservations about the conduct of Winston Churchill; in contrast to the chivalrous champion of King Edward viii's romance with Mrs Simpson in 1936, he proved himself as conformist as any bishop seventeen years later. But the person she has never brought herself to forgive is the austere and yet irresolute Sir Alan Lascelles. By inference if not implicitly, he led her to believe that by waiting two years she would be able to marry Peter Townsend; but having done her penance she found herself cruelly cheated. By 1955, Lascelles had retired as Private Secretary to the Queen, who gave him the use of a small grace-and-favour house at

Kensington Palace. A few years later, Princess Margaret also acquired a house there. Although he lived on until 1981, the neighbours never spoke. But sometimes she would see him walk by, and observe: 'There goes the man who ruined my life.'

The Princess showed resilience in picking up the pieces. Less than a year later, it seemed likely that she would marry an earlier suitor and close friend, Billy Wallace. The only surviving son of Captain Euan Wallace, Neville Chamberlain's Minister of Transport, and a grandson of Sir Edwin Lutyens (q.v.), he shared many of her interests, including the theatre. In 1954 he had taken the lead role in the charity production of *The Frog* which had so outraged Noel Coward (q.v.). Now, on the point of being betrothed to its assistant director, he admitted to a passing escapade in the Bahamas. Princess Margaret was not amused, and their understanding was at an end.

Antony Armstrong-Jones, afterwards Lord Snowdon (q.v.) came into her life at a dinner party given in 1958 by one of her ladies-in-waiting, Lady Elizabeth Cavendish. Five months older than the Princess, he had already made enough of a name for himself as a professional photographer to incur the envy of Cecil Beaton (q.v.). He was small, fair-haired, attractive and alert; and although he had been to school at Eton and coxed the Cambridge boat to victory over Oxford, his house in Pimlico, his cosmopolitan choice of friends and his skill with a camera qualified him as a genuine bohemian in the eyes of an admiring and artistic Princess.

She visited him at his retreat on the river in the East End of London; he was invited to Balmoral, then to Sandringham, where he sought her hand. The Queen gave her approval, the Privy Council did not demur and the betrothal was announced in February 1960. They were married at Westminster Abbey three months later. The bride looked ethereal in a dress of virginal severity made from thirty yards of white silk organza. As for Mr Armstrong-Jones, the official souvenir programme declared: 'The beauty and vigour of the many pictures in these pages which

are the product of the bridegroom's own camera justify the thought that today's ceremony involves the symbolic recognition that photography as one of the fine arts has come of age.' Those fulsome words were written by the same hand that in *The Times* of 26 October 1955 had sought to teach the Princess her duty.

On returning from their honeymoon, a six-week cruise of the Caribbean in the Royal Yacht *Britannia*, the Princess and her husband settled down in a small house at Kensington Palace, vacant since the death of Lord Carisbrooke (q.v.). It proved too cramped, however, for a growing family; and after the birth of their first child, David, in May 1961 they were promised 1A Clock Court, a whole wing of Kensington Palace last occupied by Princess Louise, Duchess of Argyll (q.v.). Since her death in 1939, it had been allowed to decay and now needed £85,000 of renovation to make it habitable. The parliamentary vote for the work provoked hostile questions about the Princess's supposed extravagance: a recurrent theme in her life. In this episode she was ill-served by the Government, which did not have the courage to explain to the Commons that much of that sum would in any case have had to be spent on restoration to preserve so fine but neglected an example of Wren's architecture. Instead they allowed the taxpayer to assume that its sole purpose was to provide another royal residence.

Princess Margaret's unconventional match with a photographer aroused both the interest and the malice of the Press. Armstrong-Jones was exposed to derision when created Earl of Snowdon a month before the birth of his first child, who was thus able to bear the courtesy title of Viscount Linley. He was denounced with equal fervour when, in a laudable effort to resume his professional career and so earn his own living, he became artistic adviser and photographer to *The Sunday Times*.

The marriage nevertheless began serenely. Princess Margaret was stimulated by her introduction to the more presentable exponents of journalism and the modern arts, flattered to be admitted to the hinterland of film and theatre and ballet; and how adventurous it seemed to visit houses where nobody dressed for dinner and the plates did not always match. Snowdon, too, was adaptable to the shibboleths of the royal family circle. He walked demurely in his wife's wake; he won the affection of both the Queen and the Queen Mother; he wore the blue and scarlet coat of the Windsor uniform with panache; and although he refused to exchange his motorcycle for a polo pony, he did take lessons at the West London shooting school.

Then cracks began to appear in the marriage, and not only behind closed doors. Their shared interest in the arts turned out to be superficial. He pursued them with a knowledge and professionalism that did not exclude commercial acumen. She, to her regret, felt ill equipped to follow her husband into a world of confident appreciation and criticism. There is a disconcerting entry in the diaries of Cecil Beaton after he had lunched with the Princess and her fiancé at the house of friends:

'One of the painters present had given them a large picture of a great number of hysterical-looking naked figures milling together in what appeared to be a blue haze or an earthquake or a trench scene of the 1914–18 war. Princess Margaret said, "They're all dancing." I took a gulp of champagne and said, "Oh, I'm so glad it isn't a disaster." Princess Margaret laughed so much that she had to lie flat in an armchair.'

The butt of Beaton's flattering, philistine wit was Anthony Fry, a talented painter whose work has been acquired by many leading galleries and private collectors, not least the late Lord Clark (q.v.), Sir John Sainsbury and Lord Snowdon himself.

'I have been misrepresented and misreported since the age of seventeen,' the Princess complained during a recent radio interview. After her marriage had ended in separation and divorce, she attempted to put the record straight by authorizing a biography of herself and co-operating with the author. Published in 1983, Christopher Warwick's book lays bare every distressing detail of mutual destruction: quarrels and silences, furtive romances and spoilt

holidays, nervous breakdown and physical collapse. The reader is spared neither the retreats to Mustique nor Roderic Llewellyn's clumsy incursion into her life (though neither Queen Elizabeth I nor the Empress Catharine would have thought her conduct unregal). Even the most cherished of all royal taboos, the sanctity of the bank balance, is broken; Princess Margaret, her biographer reveals, 'agreed to settle a six-figure sum' on her former husband. The book also places on record that in the performance of her public duties Princess Margaret is industrious, dedicated and compassionate. But how dear the price she has paid to establish those truths: no less than the sacrifice of privacy, and perhaps decorum. That her former husband has neither written nor inspired such an apologia in itself gives him a certain moral advantage.

When Princess Margaret was only eighteen, 'Chips' Channon (q.v.) noted 'a Marie Antoinette aroma about her.' Many have since echoed the sentiment with exasperated affection. They recall the thoughtlessly late hours; the monopolizing of a particular guest to the exclusion of all others; the swift, unsettling changes of mood, from whispered confidences to a blue, transfixing stare. 'Just when you think you are getting on famously with her,' a victim remarked, 'she hops back on to her twig.' Others have more endearing memories – the quicksilver mind that can complete a crossword between cigarettes; the laughter and mimicry and delight in the quirks of human behaviour; a knowledgeable love of ballet and gardens; courage in adversity and loyalty in friendship. Monarchy, like all hereditary institutions, is a gamble, and in Princess Margaret it has turned up a card.

Marie Louise, Princess
(1872–1956)

She was the youngest child of Prince Christian of Schleswig-Holstein and his wife Princess Helena (q.v.), Queen Victoria's third daughter. Born at Cumberland Lodge, Windsor, she was named after the Empress Marie Louise, Napoleon's second wife, whom Prince Christian at the age of eleven had once taken into dinner and ever afterwards revered. During a holiday in Germany, Princess Marie Louise met Prince Aribert of Anhalt, and with the encouragement of her cousin, the Emperor William II, married him in 1891. The Prince proved an unwilling husband. After nine distressing years, the childless marriage was annulled by a decree of Prince Aribert's father, exercising his medieval right as a sovereign prince. The Princess, a devout churchwoman, believed her marriage vows to be binding and never remarried.

Returning to England, she devoted the next half century to charitable and social causes. She stood above average height and had imposing features (although it was her sister Princess

Helena Victoria who came to be known as 'The Snipe'). If her broken heart never quite healed, Princess Marie Louise found solace in convivial friendships. She smoked and drank with evident relish, and her speeches on formal occasions were as lively and sometimes as startling as her private conversation. Foreign travel in particular stimulated her gifts of humour and mimicry. 'If I should be so inconsiderate as to die,' she told the captain of a ship in which she was bound for South Africa, 'don't put me in the fridge. Just wrap me up in a Union Jack and pop me in the sea.'

The Princess spent some years living in a bed-sitter of a London club; there she felt no less at home than in Schomberg House, Pall Mall, which she later shared with her sister. She inherited her mother's love of music. Sung to in

The marriage of Princess Marie Louise to Prince Aribert of Anhalt in St George's Chapel, Windsor, 1891

the nursery by Jenny Lind, she had politely inquired: 'Must you always make such a noise?' But the experience did not deter her from a devotion to the operas of Wagner and the friendship of his wife Cosima, Liszt's daughter. She collected Napoleonic relics; mastered the delicate art of enamelling in precious metals; planned the construction of Queen Mary's celebrated dolls' house, now at Windsor; and in her eighty-fifth year wrote her memoirs, a volume of confiding intimacy which within a month or two had sold 40,000 copies.

Princess Marie Louise died a few weeks later at her grace-and-favour residence in Mayfair. Her funeral in St George's Chapel, Windsor, was attended by 'pearly kings' and 'pearly queens', come from the East End of London for a farewell salute to their friend and patron.

Marten, Sir Henry
(1872–1948)

Provost of Eton College and private tutor to Princess Elizabeth, later Queen Elizabeth II. Except for his early years as an Oxford undergraduate, Marten's entire career was spent at Eton. He was the first master there appointed to teach only history, which he established as a thriving specialist study. With Townsend Warner he also wrote a well-known textbook that has oppressed generations of schoolboys. He encouraged his pupils to browse at will in his huge private library, but preferred them to choose some large or important work. 'Guedalla?' he would say, 'fireworky stuff.'

During the war, Princess Elizabeth came down from Windsor Castle for regular tuition in general history with an emphasis on those constitutional themes that concerned the heir to the throne. Marten would receive her alone in his study, but from force of habit would invariably begin: 'Now, gen'lemen.' In 1945 King George VI knighted him on the steps of College Chapel before the whole school. His death was described as the fall of an old tree.

Mary, Princess
later Princess Royal
and Countess of Harewood (1897–1965)

The third child and only daughter of King George V and Queen Mary. She spent a contented childhood at Sandringham, wielding over her five brothers what one of them called 'a sweet tyranny.' Educated by governesses, she showed promise at music and needlework and made a collection of seaweeds from the Norfolk coast. She also acquired a lifelong love of horses and skill in managing them. 'My sister,' King George VI said, 'was a horse until she came out.'

As early as 1912, when the Princess was fifteen, Queen Mary planned her daughter's future. She would be betrothed to Ernst August of Hanover, heir to the Duke of Brunswick and the only descendant in the male line of King George III. What Queen Mary proudly called the 'old' royal family (she herself, through her mother, was a great-granddaughter of George III) would thus be reunited with her husband's upstart dynasty of Saxe-Coburg-Gotha, soon to be renamed the House of Windsor. 'He will have a great fortune,' Queen Mary confided to a friend, 'and could be in England a lot.' Less than a year later, however, Ernst August married the only daughter of the German Emperor. The Great War put an end to further matchmaking; and it was not until 1922 that Princess Mary was married in Westminster Abbey to a middle-aged Yorkshire landowner, Viscount Lascelles, later 6th Earl of Harewood (q.v.).

The King mourned the departure of his only daughter from the family nest. In 1932 he bestowed on her the style of Princess Royal, until recently borne by his late sister, Princess Louise (q.v.). The Queen showed her continuing affection by making regular visits to Harewood, from which she would sally forth to pillage the antique shops of Harrogate.

Princess Mary's elder son has described his mother's character as compounded of shyness,

Princess Mary with Prince Albert, Prince George and Prince Henry, *c.* 1920

gentleness and kindness, with in later life a little Hanoverian spleen. Her dread of public appearances, never deterred her from a crowded calendar of engagements, especially when they involved nursing and the Women's Services. She was a fluent and copious letter-writer, too, who never forgot a friend or a good cause. But she found small talk a burden and discussion an ordeal. For months she endured the reek of tobacco in her car rather than ask a new lady-in-waiting not to smoke. Among her endearing quirks were thriftiness and superstition. The chatelaine of a mansion built by John Carr, decorated by Robert Adam and set in a park designed by Capability Brown would stuff her Chippendale furniture with every scrap of used wrapping paper and string. She would bow to a magpie three times; and if she chanced to see a piebald horse, would remain silent until the vision had been exorcized by the sight of a dog. Although abrupt of speech, she had a lovely voice. Her complexion, too, was strikingly beautiful.

The Princess's shy temperament, accentuated by ill-health, was sometimes mistaken for unhappiness and the blame attributed to an autocratic husband. If there were strains in the marriage, they did not extend to a shared enthusiasm for horses and horseracing. Within three weeks of Harewood's death in 1947, his widow went to watch the Derby at Epsom because his horse Tite Street was a runner. She also continued to keep her own horses in training. Another of the Princess Royal's pastimes was foreign travel. She and her husband were the first members of the royal family to visit the Duke of Windsor at Schloss Enzesfeld, near Vienna, just after the Abdication.

Throughout nearly twenty years of widowhood, the Princess Royal continued to live at Harewood with her elder son and his wife. She died there of a sudden heart attack in May 1965 while walking by the lake.

Mary, Queen Consort of King George V
(1867–1953)

She was born in London on 26 May 1867. Her father was Francis, Prince (later Duke) of Teck, grandson of the King of Württemberg and the only son of Duke Alexander of Württemberg by his morganatic marriage with Claudine, Countess Rhédey. The infant's mother was Princess Mary of Cambridge, a granddaughter of King George III and sister of the Duke of Cambridge, for almost forty years Commander-in-Chief of the British Army.

By the pedantic standards of the German monarchies, the morganatic taint inherited by Prince Francis disqualified him from a royal marriage. Queen Victoria, however, took a more robust view of dynastic niceties, and had summoned him to England in 1866 to marry her

first cousin, Princess Mary of Cambridge, for whom it had proved difficult to find a husband. At thirty-two, four years older than the Prince, she was good natured but excessively stout. 'Alas,' Lord Clarendon, the Foreign Secretary, wrote ungallantly of her, 'no German prince will venture on *so vast an undertaking.*' Teck, rightly considering himself fortunate to marry into the English royal family, was less particular. The wedding took place in Kew Church in 1866; and because the bridegroom was almost penniless, the Queen set up the couple in Kensington Palace. It was there that their first child was born, in the same room which had seen the birth of Queen Victoria.

The infant was baptized Victoria Mary, followed by six other names. Her mother would refer to her as 'my May-flower' and it was as Princess May that she was known until her husband became King in 1910. She then assumed the more majestic style of Queen Mary. Although Princess May retained a slight guttural accent to the end of her life, she was never allowed to think of herself as anything but English. She was joined in the nursery by three brothers: Prince Adolphus of Teck, later Marquess of Cambridge; Prince Francis of Teck (q.v.); and Prince Alexander of Teck, later Earl of Athlone (q.v.). All went to English public schools and served with distinction in the British Army.

The financial distress of the Tecks which cast a shadow over Princess May's youth was largely self-inflicted. The Duke had brought nothing more to the marriage than a fine profile and a shapely figure. His wife, however, received an annual parliamentary grant of £5,000 and a similar sum each year from her mother. In an age of plentiful servants and low wages, that should have sufficed to live comfortably and to raise a family. But the Duchess had generous instincts of hospitality; and her proud, touchy husband feared that any apparent economy in his establishment would detract from his already uneasy status. Not only were there lavish entertainments at Kensington Palace. In 1870 the Tecks persuaded the Queen to let them have the additional use of White Lodge, Richmond Park, ten miles from Kensington. This substantial house belonging to the Crown doubled their household expenses.

They were soon grievously in debt. Baroness Burdett-Coutts added her royal friends to the long list of charitable causes on which she spent her immense banking fortune; she lent them £50,000, with scant hope of ever seeing it again. But the more the Duchess of Teck received, the more she spent. At a time when tradesmen were pressing her for the payment of bills amounting to almost £20,000, she was invited to open a new church hall in Kensington, to which John Barker the grocer had contributed handsomely. 'And now,' she told her amused audience, 'I must propose a special vote of thanks to Mr Barker, to whom we all owe so much.' When it became apparent that even the most patient and loyal of creditors were about to issue writs, the Tecks took the traditional course of those who, to use their daughter's own evocative phrase, were in Short Street. They went abroad.

Between 1883 and 1885, Princess May shared her parents' temporary exile in Florence, living first at an hotel and later in a villa lent by friends. Whatever the failings of the Tecks as practical economists, they ensured a far better education for their daughter than ever the Prince of Wales's children received. Already well-grounded in English, French and German, she now studied Italian and the history of art, took lessons in singing and painting, learned to name the wild flowers of Tuscany. When the family returned to England in 1885, settling permanently at White Lodge, Princess May continued her education with an inspired governess. Madame Hélène Bricka introduced her pupil to the perspectives of history and to the problems of a rapidly expanding industrial society; she also instilled habits of concentration and order in a world of royal dawdlers. From her mother, May acquired a lifelong interest in philanthropy that was not confined to committee work. Dutifully, but without enjoyment, she became accustomed to visiting the poor, the sick and the distressed in the institutions devoted to their care; no dripping tap or recalcitrant lavatory ever escaped those watchful blue eyes.

Princess May could hardly have been expected to spend the rest of her life in ragged schools and asylums. Yet when the desires of this attractive, well-educated and serious-minded girl turned to marriage, she found herself almost an outcast. The reason was neither her parents' insolvency nor her own shyness; both could have been accommodated in an age of arranged matches. What made her an apparently unsuitable consort for even the smallest reigning houses of Europe was her morganatic blood. Her only remaining hope, marriage to a British commoner, seemed equally elusive. Neither her consciously royal mother nor her querulous semi-royal father would have encouraged Princess May's necessary descent in rank. Nor would an English or Scots suitor of ancient line relish being treated with condescension. The most recent example was discouraging. In 1871 the Queen's fourth daughter, Princess Louise (q.v.), had been married to the Marquess of Lorne. It proved an unhappy childless match. The heir to the dukedom of Argyll and to a score of other splendid titles had to accustom himself to an inferior place in the royal family circle. As James Pope-Hennessy (q.v.), wrote in his incomparable biography, *Queen Mary*: 'Princess May thus had the worst of both worlds: she was too Royal to marry an ordinary English gentleman, and not Royal enough to marry a Royalty. Or so, in the late eighteen-nineties, it seemed.'

She was rescued from her dilemma by the one person in Europe who possessed both the will and the means. Queen Victoria did not share the antipathy of her continental cousins to morganatic blood. Sweeping aside their stiff, traditionalist arguments, she determined that Princess May would make an admirable wife for first one and then another of her own grandsons. So it came about that a young woman without a fortune, seemingly condemned to spinsterhood by a flawed pedigree, found herself destined to be Queen Consort of Great Britain.

Queen Victoria's first choice of husband for Princess May was Prince Albert Victor, known as Eddy, the elder son of the Prince and Princess of Wales and thus in direct line of succession to the throne. He was less lively minded than his brother, the future King George V, indeed almost torpid; yet he was quiet, modest, well mannered, popular in his regiment and adored by his family. In 1890 his grandmother created him Duke of Clarence. Then his moral fibre seemed to deteriorate, although allegations that he used to visit the notorious homosexual brothel in Cleveland Street rest on unconvincing evidence. The Prince of Wales wrote to the Queen: 'His education and future have been a matter of some considerable anxiety to us, and the difficulty of rousing him is very great. A good sensible wife with some considerable character is what he needs most, but where is she to be found?'

Queen Victoria had the answer: Princess May of Teck. It was an arranged match, for the young pair, although cousins, scarcely knew each other. The early negotiations were entrusted to courtiers. 'Do you suppose Princess May will make any resistance?' one wrote to another. 'I do not anticipate any real opposition on Prince Eddy's part if he is properly managed and told he must do it – that it is for the good of the country.' In November 1891, the Queen summoned Princess May to Balmoral for a visit that lasted ten days. Neither her parents nor her intended fiancé were invited. At the beginning of December, while staying with the Danish minister and his wife at Luton Hoo, Princess May wrote in her diary: 'To my great surprise Eddy proposed to me in Mme. de Falbe's boudoir – of course I said yes – We are both very happy.'

The Prince and Princess of Wales were taking no chances with their wayward son; the wedding was arranged for February. Princess May and her parents meanwhile arrived at Sandringham in time to celebrate Prince Eddy's twenty-eighth birthday on 8 January 1892. He returned from shooting on 7 January feeling unwell, and retired early to bed. Next morning, suffering from influenza, he could barely struggle downstairs to look at his presents. On 9 January he developed inflammation of the lungs and sank into delirium. Five days later he was dead.

In the royal archives for that tragic month, the arrangements under discussion for the Duke of Clarence's marriage change with hardly a break in sequence to those for his funeral. It took place in St George's Chapel, Windsor. On the coffin lay Princess May's unworn bridal wreath of orange blossom.

It seems in retrospect as if a spontaneous and all-embracing conspiracy ensured that the bereaved Princess, a widow even before she had married, should become the wife of Prince Eddy's surviving brother. Queen Victoria once more brought the experienced, irresistible touch of the matchmaker to two young lives. The Duke of York, as Prince George was created in 1892, shyly pressed his suit; and Princess May, already bound to him by ties of affection and grief, as shyly responded. In May 1893 the nation learned with immense satisfaction of their betrothal. They were married in the Chapel Royal, St James's, on 6 July.

The Duchess of York's first years of matrimony undermined her confidence. Her mother-in-law, the Princess of Wales, torn between pleasure at her son's happiness and the loss of his undivided devotion, could scarcely conceal her jealousy of the intruder. Her three daughters were even more resentful of their new sister-in-law. Envious of her superior talents and mistaking her shyness for arrogance, they waged a campaign of sly disparagement. The Duchess, starved of reassurance even by her loving but inhibited husband, felt as if she were on permanent probation. Her oldest friend, Mabell Countess of Airlie (q.v.), once wrote after an emotional reunion: 'As a girl she had been shy and reserved, but now her shyness had so crystallized that only in such moments of intimacy could she be herself. The hard crust of inhibition which gradually closed over her, hiding the warmth and tenderness of her own personality, was already starting to form.'

Almost alone of the royal family, the old Queen showed affection and appreciation. 'Each time I see you,' she told May, 'I love and respect you more and am so truly thankful that Georgie has such a partner – to help and encourage him in his difficult position.' Yet her kindly but unnerving flow of questions and advice left its mark on Princess May for life. In 1934 Queen Mary was invited to visit an exhibition of historic clothes in a London house. Placed in a corner by itself was a plain black dress of silk once worn by Queen Victoria. As Queen Mary entered the room and suddenly caught sight of that alarming dumpy shape, she started and exclaimed: 'How on earth did they get that?' For a fleeting moment she was once more a frightened young woman facing her formidable grandmother-in-law.

The Duke and Duchess of York were required to make few public appearances, a fraction of those undertaken by members of the royal family a century later. During the forty years spent by the Queen in near seclusion, the Prince and Princess of Wales assumed almost all the ceremonial and social functions of the monarchy. In the eyes of the world, however, the Sovereign was sovereign, her heir a stylish substitute and the rest mere reflections of a distant effulgence. Even after the old Queen's death in 1901, when Prince George and Princess May became briefly Duke and Duchess of Cornwall, then Prince and Princess of Wales, their official duties were undemanding. They toured Australia, New Zealand and Canada in 1901 and India four years later; they attended the marriages of their European cousins and other family reunions. Otherwise they were satellites of King Edward VII and Queen Alexandra. In London they lived at Marlborough House, a few hundred yards from Buckingham Palace; in the country, York Cottage, a dark and poky villa almost on the doorstep of Sandringham House. So the tranquil years went by, while they raised a family of one girl and five boys (see *King George V*).

On the death of King Edward VII in 1910, all seemed likely to change. Until then the new Queen had been known as May, using her first two names, Victoria May, for her official signature. She wrote to an aunt a few days after her accession: 'I hope you approve of my new name Mary. George dislikes double names and I could

not be Victoria, but it strikes me as curious to be rechristened at the age of 43.' This evoked one of her few known jokes. When a friend mentioned a certain notorious lady whose successive marriages had obliged her to change her name seven times, she replied: 'Well, I have had to change mine quite a lot: Princess May, Duchess of York, Duchess of Cornwall, Princess of Wales, Queen. But whereas mine have been by accident, hers have been by enterprise.'

'I regret the quieter, easier time we had,' Queen Mary wrote in 1910, 'everything will be more difficult now and more ceremonious.' That was true only of the public duties she shared with her husband. At the new King's desire, their private life in the royal palaces reverted from the age of Edward VII to that of Victoria. No longer was there bridge after dinner, much less the creaking of floorboards in the night; instead, a cup of tea, an hour with the last of the day's State papers for the King, some needlework for the Queen, then early to bed. A guest at Windsor said that it was like staying in a quiet vicarage. Max Beerbohm echoed the discontent of the fashionable world in a piece entitled *Ballade Tragique à Double Refrain*. Here are two stanzas from this imaginary exchange between a lord-in-waiting and a lady-in-waiting:

He: Last evening
I found him with a rural dean
Talking of District Visiting . . .
The King is duller than the Queen.

She: At any rate he doesn't sew;
You don't see him embellishing
Yard after yard of calico . . .
The Queen is duller than the King.

Both, however, were worthy of their inherited role. A guest at the Coronation in 1911 wrote to his wife: 'The Queen looked pale and strained. You felt she was a great lady, but *not* a Queen. She was almost shrinking as she walked up the aisle giving the impression that she would have liked to have made her way to her seat by some back entrance: the contrast on her return – crowned – was magnetic, as though she had undergone some marvellous transformation. Instead of the shy creature for whom one had felt pity, one saw her emerge from the ceremony with a bearing and dignity, and a quiet confidence, signifying that she really felt that she was Queen of this great Empire, and that she derived strength and legitimate pride from the knowledge of it.' In his own account of the Coronation, the King's tribute to his wife was brief but heartfelt. 'Darling May looked lovely, and it was indeed a comfort to me to have her by my side, as she has been ever to me during these last eighteen years.'

The legend has persisted of a henpecked Sovereign dominated by an imperious Consort. Wits spoke of King George the Fifth and Queen Mary the Four-Fifths. Not even physically did this jest reflect the truth. Although she appeared to be a tall, imposing woman who towered over her husband, that was an illusion. Her back was as stiff as a ramrod, and both hats and heels played a part in enhancing her stately deportment. She was in fact exactly the same size as the King: five feet, six inches.

In a wider sense, too, the King was the dominant partner in the marriage. For more than forty years, Queen Mary was the indispensable guardian of her husband's comfort and peace of mind, a perpetual shield against irritation and anxiety and ill health. To those ends she sacrificed some of her own personality, conforming to his every whim without resentment or even question. Neither in the upbringing of her children nor even in her choice of clothes was she permitted the discretion that any other wife would have taken for granted. Although self-imposed, her servitude was absolute.

It was revealed most obviously in the Queen's appearance. The King not only revered what had been fashionable in his early manhood, but expected his family and household to share the same conservatism of taste. The refusal of his eldest son to accept such restrictions strained an already uneasy relationship. Queen Mary, however, submitted to the King's almost oriental requirements with the meekness she brought to every aspect of their marriage. Her husband, she

never forgot, was also her Sovereign; and in response to his dictates she continued for the rest of her life to wear only such styles and colours as he decreed. 'The Queen had a wonderful success,' a courtier wrote satirically of the State visit to France in 1914. 'The Paris mob went mad about her, and it was rumoured that her out-of-date hats and early Victorian gowns would become next year's fashions.' A decade later she had still not abandoned her long, full skirts, her toques and her parasols. Occasionally she would make a timid excursion: a wide-brimmed hat in summer, perhaps, or a scarcely perceptible raising of a hem to show off her elegant ankles. But the King frowned upon the changes, and she relapsed into a style of timeless dignity. In India her jewels all but outshone those of the Native Princes; at a State ball she carried a massive treasure trove, borne as gracefully as her train of embroidered gold and silver thread eight feet long; at a Palace garden party, an awed guest compared her to the Jungfrau, 'white and sparkling in the sun.' Even on more mundane occasions, her apparel was not readily forgotten: a very large fur collar dyed purple, for instance, and a toque made entirely of artificial pansies.

Throughout the Great War of 1914–18, Queen Mary devoted her energies to charity and welfare work of many kinds. 'She would have made an excellent factory inspector,' the Labour Minister, Margaret Bondfield, later declared. In the royal household she rooted out extravagance with virtuous enthusiasm. Poussins and lamb were banished from the royal kitchens, to be replaced by fowls and mutton, though neither in profusion. No longer was each member of the family given a clean table napkin at every meal, but made use of that economical device the napkin ring. Then and for the rest of her life, the Queen's enemy was waste. She did not hesitate to descend on her eldest son's new apartment in St James's, examine the pattern he had chosen for his new curtains, substitute a cheaper yet equally serviceable material, and even wield a tape measure to prove that he had ordered six yards too much. Visiting Lady Curzon in the country, the Queen was distressed when her car ran over a lamb which had strayed on to the road. 'Still,' she told her hostess in a consoling yet practical way, 'you will be able to eat it.' And a visiting preacher who lunched at Sandringham was surprised to be given half a pear from the Queen's plate. As a guest in the country houses of others, however, her demands were less austere: freshly made barley water to be put in her bedroom every two hours, ice at night and not fewer than six clean towels every day. But she brought her own sheets and pillow cases.

The most responsible of all her duties was to safeguard the health and happiness of the King. After his accident in France, when thrown from his horse while inspecting troops, she insisted on accompanying him to the Western Front. 'This is the first lady to have a meal at my headquarters since War began!' Field Marshal Haig noted without enthusiasm. The Queen found it an exciting change from inspecting the rhubarb mould and rice pudding of workers' canteens. She even managed some sightseeing. Escorted by her eldest son, serving on the staff of an army corps, she walked the fields of Agincourt and Crécy. 'It was probably the first time that a Prince of Wales had visited the scene,' she wrote, 'since Edward the Black Prince was there at the time of the battle.'

In the post-war world, too, she was always at hand to ease the strain of those overseas State visits which the King detested. 'Very comfortable rooms,' he wrote of Brussels in 1922, 'but May lives at one end of the Palace and I at the other and the house is very large. It is not very convenient.' Queen Mary was no less wretched at being separated from her husband. But in the middle of the night she heard the sound of her bedroom door quietly opening. She switched on the light and there, peering round the screen, was what she described as 'his dear, sad little face.' He had found his way to her alone and in the dark.

It has sometimes been suggested that the Queen was on an altogether higher aesthetic plane than her husband. Her chosen fields of interest were royal iconography, particularly that of the descendants of King George III and

Coronation Luncheon at Guildhall, June 1911 by S. J. Solomon

Queen Charlotte; furniture; and the miniature, from the dolls' house to the trinkets of Fabergé. She was a dedicated researcher, annotator and labeller; but in all her life she never bought a really good or important picture, never patronized the most imaginative artists of her day. She would be less captivated by a Rembrandt or a Rubens than by a framed Hanoverian

princeling in bobtail wig and Garter ribbon.

The Queen brought both knowledge and the wiles of the predator to enlarging the Windsor collections. One is reflected in the descriptive labels, each in her own hand, attached to even the humblest of pieces; the other in those innumerable acquisitions which she bought or begged. Not all the anecdotes of her persistence are exaggerated. Visiting the homes of friends, acquaintances and strangers, sometimes self-invited, she would stand in front of a covetable object and pronounce in measured tones: 'I am caressing it with my eyes.' If that evoked no impulsive gesture of generosity, the Queen would resume her tour. But on taking her leave, she would pause on the doorstep and ask: 'May I go back and say goodbye to that dear little cabinet?' Should even that touching appeal fail to melt the granite heart of her host, her letter of thanks might include a request to buy the piece. Few resisted that final assault.

She could be formidable in other ways, too. The lady-in-waiting who presented her with a religious tract had it returned with the majestic rebuke: 'You are neither old enough nor good enough to give me this.' Then there was the young Duchess who, instructed to kiss the Queen's hand at a ball, left a perfect print of scarlet mouth on the back of the royal kid glove. 'She gave me one withering look that said all,' the culprit wrote, 'and I slunk away in disgrace.' And at Ascot one year she ordered a sporting peeress to be ejected from the Royal Enclosure for wearing a sailor's cap with the legend in gold lettering, 'HMS Good Ship Venus'. Even the landscape had to keep its distance. As the Queen arrived one day to inspect the new gardens at Windsor, a low-hanging branch of an oak grazed her toque. She gazed severely

Devonshire House Ball, 1897

at the offending limb but without comment.

The reign drew to a close, but not before the nation had celebrated its twenty-fifth anniversary. Together the King and Queen had come to symbolize both national pride and domestic virtue; together they shared the unsought acclamation of the Silver Jubilee. Within a year George V was dead. And as one King died, she paid homage to another. In a gesture both affectionate and historic, she took the hand of her eldest son and kissed it.

He proved unworthy of her homage. Queen Mary's first year of widowhood was clouded not only by grief and loneliness, but also by the determination of King Edward VIII to make Mrs Simpson his wife. 'If it was somebody else,' she sighed, 'but a divorced woman with two husbands!' Her pain and humiliation are epitomized in the letter she wrote to her wayward son after the Abdication: 'You will remember how miserable I was when you informed me of your intended marriage and abdication and how I implored you not to do so for our sake and for the sake of the country. You did not seem able to take in any point of view but your own. . . . I do not think you have ever realised the shock, which the attitude you took up caused your family and the whole Nation. It seemed inconceivable to those who had made such sacrifices during the war that you, as their King, refused a lesser sacrifice. . . . My feelings for you as your Mother remain the same, and our being parted and the cause of it, grieve me beyond words. After all, all my life I have put my Country before everything else, and I simply cannot change now.'

Queen Mary was nevertheless not too heartbroken to write another letter, asking him for the loan of his diamond star of the Order of the Garter to wear at his brother's Coronation in 1937. She made history by becoming the first Queen Dowager to attend such a ceremony. It was characteristic of her resilience. As long as her husband lived, she had centred her life entirely on his. Now she blossomed forth. She attended every court ceremony and celebration, went to the Derby, watched the tennis at Wimbledon, haunted art galleries and theatres, took her granddaughters on educational tours of Hampton Court and the Tower of London. In a single month she stayed in four country houses and at one of them *valsed* at a ball.

King George VI and Queen Elizabeth were kindness itself, inviting her to stay at Sandringham whenever she cared. Queen Mary wrote of one New Year celebration: 'We ladies put on funny hats for dinner which was amusing.' But she declined to spend the summer at Balmoral, which she had always hated: 'sitting on top of a wet mountain,' she called it. Instead she took possession of the Palace of Holyroodhouse, Edinburgh, motoring out each day to inspect the historic monuments and antique shops of Scotland. In September 1938 she travelled 1,687 miles by car. The following year, when her Daimler overturned after colliding with a lorry loaded with steel tubing, she walked down the rescuers' ladder as composed as if she had been descending the State staircase at Buckingham Palace.

She took a lively interest in politics, and was in the gallery of the House of Commons to hear Chamberlain announce that he was about to fly to Munich. It prompted a letter from the Kaiser for the first time since 1914, congratulating her on the Munich agreement, which both supposed would avert a second world war. He signed his letter, 'Your affectionate cousin, William.' Queen Mary, much moved by the restoration of a family link at a time of emotion, sent it to her son, King George VI, to be preserved in the Royal Archives. On balance she much preferred the Kaiser to Hitler, a vulgar fellow who, she observed after listening to a broadcast, spoke such abominable German.

Queen Mary spent the war years 1939–45 in the safety of Badminton, in Gloucestershire, as the guest of the Duke and Duchess of Beaufort (qq.v.). An unwilling exile from London, she did not care for the country, had never learned to ride and knew nothing of farming and hunting, the two staple occupations of her hosts. 'So *that's* what hay looks like,' she said one day to her niece. But clearing overgrown shrubberies so that young trees could be planted appealed to her sense of order and patriotism. Within the house she reclaimed some of her peacetime habits: putting on her jewels to dine each night, albeit off a sparse wartime menu, and laying out her Christmas presents according to the custom of Sandringham. There were visits to neighbouring country houses, fruitful rummages through the Badminton archives, needlework and reading, even a few visitors. The death of the Duke of Kent (q.v.) caused her much anguish, but her first thought was for the widowed Princess Marina, whom she set off to comfort in person.

Within two weeks of the end of the war with Germany she was back at Marlborough House, happily rearranging her furniture and treasures: not least a writing table bearing no fewer than ninety separate framed photographs, bibelots and other objects. She was delighted by the betrothal of her granddaughter Princess Elizabeth to Prince Philip of Greece. They were, she calculated, third cousins through Queen Victoria, second cousins once removed through King Christian IX of Denmark and fourth cousins once removed through King George III. Having inspected the wedding presents, she sent a request for any unwanted handkerchiefs with which to supply her charity bazaars. With the same sense of thrift she asked for flowers or chocolates left over from the dinner at the French Embassy given by President Auriol during his State visit to London; those were for herself. The birth of Prince Charles in 1948 evoked both generosity and a sense of history. She gave him a silver gilt cup and cover which George III had given to a godson in 1780: 'from my great grandfather to my great grandson 168 years later.'

Throughout the austerity of post-war Britain she refused any concession to her years. When Princess Elizabeth dined at Downing Street in 1947, she told one of the Labour Ministers, Hugh Gaitskell, that her grandmother's house was the coldest she knew, with hardly a fire anywhere. Gaitskell wrote: 'I asked if this was because she was spartan or because of the house, but she said, no – because of her national duty.' It was not her only personal contribution to solving Britain's economic problems: having toiled for several years on a needlework carpet, she sold it to Canada for £35,000.

In 1952 she mourned another of her sons, King George VI. Rising yet again above her own grief, she hastened to pay homage to her granddaughter and Sovereign. 'Her old grannie,' she said,' must be the first to kiss her hand.' Almost to the end Queen Mary drove out through the Park each day and not infrequently made a stop at some museum or gallery. On the eve of her eighty-fifth birthday she revisited her birthplace, Kensington Palace: not from nostalgia but to examine the Coronation robes worn by Queen Victoria. Queen Mary did not live to see the Coronation of Queen Elizabeth II. She died at Marlborough House on 24 March 1953. Not long before her death she said to a friend: 'I am beginning to lose my memory, but I mean to get it back.'

Masefield, John
(1878–1967)

Poet Laureate from 1930 until his death in 1967. He went to sea as a naval cadet at the age of thirteen, then worked in a carpet factory in

John Masefield

Yonkers, New York. His most celebrated work is *Reynard the Fox*, which reveals a deep knowledge and love of the English countryside. As Poet Laureate he wrote few commemorative pieces that bear either the weight of print or the test of time. But he was a modest man, and when sending his works for publication in *The Times* would enclose a stamped addressed envelope in case they failed to please.

Maud, Princess, Countess of Southesk
(1893–1945)

The younger daughter of the 1st Duke of Fife and his wife Princess Louise, the Princess Royal (qq.v), she was married in 1923 to Lord Carnegie, later 11th Earl of Southesk. On the night of the wedding, beacons were lit from Inverness to the Firth of Forth, a distance of more than a hundred miles, each visible to the next and all on land belonging to the families of either the bride or the bridegroom. Lord Carnegie served as aide-de-camp to Lord Chelmsford, the Viceroy of India, and managed his considerable Scottish estates.

Princess Maud with her two sisters, Princess Victoria (*left*) and Princess Louise (*right*)

The only child of the marriage is James Carnegie, born 1929, who on the death in 1959 of his mother's elder sister, Princess Arthur of Connaught (q.v.), succeeded her as 3rd Duke of Fife. Educated at Gordonstoun and the Royal Agricultural College, Circencester, he served in the ranks of the Scots Guards as a National Serviceman during the Malayan campaign of 1948–50.

Maud, Queen of Norway
(1869–1938)

The youngest daughter of King Edward VII and Queen Alexandra, she was married in 1896 to her cousin Prince Charles of Denmark. A prolonged legal squabble over the terms of their marriage contract cast its shadow for many years. Although prettier than her two sisters, Princess Louise and Princess Victoria (qq.v) she did not inherit the striking beauty of her mother. 'Princess Maud has dyed her hair canary yellow,' a lady-in-waiting wrote in 1899, 'which makes her look quite improper and more like a little milliner than ever.'

In 1905, after the dissolution of the unhappy union between Norway and Sweden, Prince Charles was elected to the throne of Norway as King Haakon VII. That any Sovereign should reign not by divine right but by the majority vote of a plebiscite outraged the more senior crowned heads of Europe. The Grand Duchess of Mecklenburg-Strelitz, Queen Mary's aunt, broke out into a rash of italics: 'A *revolutionary*

Coronation! such a *farce* ... makes me sick and I should say *you too!*' Her niece replied placidly: 'The whole thing seems curious, but we live in *very*, modern days.' The future King George V made the best of his sister's democratic ordeal by catching a twenty-eight-pound Norwegian salmon.

Queen Maud, shy, deaf and plagued by neuralgia, never adjusted to her new role. Her subjects thought her remote and disobliging; she thought them demanding and ungrateful. She consoled herself by laying out an English garden at Bygdö Kongsgaard. Each summer, too, she would spend at Appleton House, near Sandringham, where her brother made her feel quite at home with a deluge of royal banter. Noticing during a walk that she carried a separate handkerchief for her spaniel, he kept turning back to ask, 'Where are its galoshes?' and 'Don't forget its cough drops.'

Her only son succeeded his father as King Olav V in 1957. Born at Appleton and educated at Balliol College, Oxford, he won a Gold Medal for sailing at the Olympic Games of 1928. His bulky, genial figure stands out each year at the Remembrance Day service at the Cenotaph in Whitehall. He may also be seen doing his own Christmas shopping or lunching at Claridge's. As befits a monarch with the most modest of Civil Lists, he checks the bills item by item and counts his change.

Mensdorff, Count Albert
(1861–1945)

Cousin of King George V and Austrian ambassador in London, 1904–14. Albert Mensdorff-Pouilly-Dietrichstein, to give him his full name, spent much of his diplomatic career in London before being appointed ambassador in 1904 at the early age of forty-two. He was fortunate to retain the post for the next ten years. The Foreign Ministry in Vienna came to believe that he had so fallen in love with England as to be incapable of pursuing his country's interests. It

was a view shared by the British diplomatist Robert Vansittart (q.v.), who called the bachelor ambassador 'a flabby tabby, anglophil but impotent.'

Count Mensdorff owed his survival to a privileged position that outweighed any professional inadequacy. For he was a cousin of the British royal house twice over; his grandmother was a sister both of the Duchess of Kent, Queen Victoria's mother, and of Ernest I, Duke of Saxe-Coburg-Gotha, the Prince Consort's father. Mensdorff was thus on intimate terms with

Count Albert Mensdorff
by Spy

successive British Sovereigns and a constant guest in their houses. King George v even allowed him to wear the Windsor uniform, a blue evening coat with gold buttons and collar and cuffs of red: an honour usually confined to members of the royal family and a few favoured Prime Ministers. Mensdorff repaid his cousin's affection and trust by reporting, not to say betraying, every royal confidence to his masters in Vienna.

Mensdorff's connections and polished manners ensured him a place in British society. In August 1914, on the outbreak of hostilities with Germany, eight days elapsed before Britain declared war on Austria; the delay, someone joked, was to allow Mensdorff to complete his round of country-house visits. Even during that last strained week, with crowds demonstrating against Germany in the streets, the Austrian ambassador was asked to tea at Buckingham Palace; and an hour after Britain's belated declaration of war on Austria, he received a letter from the King hoping that he would soon be a welcome guest in London once more. It began, 'My dear Albert,' and ended, 'Ever your devoted friends and cousins, George and Mary.' The ambassador's departure for Vienna was scarcely that of an enemy. The Foreign Secretary, Sir Edward Grey, was in tears; a fashionable crowd saw him off at the station; there were shouts of, 'Three cheers for Count Mensdorff.'

In spite of that euphoric farewell, reports reached London during the war that he had spoken insultingly about England. It was therefore not until 1924 that he ventured to return. The King and Queen received their Austrian cousin cautiously. Mensdorff had tea at the Palace for the first time in ten years, but the reunion went unrecorded in the Court Circular. In 1925 he came to London again. 'A step forward,' he wrote in his diary, 'the Court Circular mentioned my presence at luncheon.' In 1926, no more than tea was offered. 'A certain carefulness,' he noted. 'I was not invited to Sandringham, where they are going next week.' At last, in 1927, Mensdorff was not only asked to Sandringham, where he had first stayed in 1890,

but also told that he could once more wear the Royal Victorian Order. Cousin Albert's rehabilitation was complete.

Middleton, Guy Willoughby, 11th Baron
(1887–1970)

Lord Lieutenant of the East Riding of Yorkshire and Knight of the Garter. His ancestors in the male line fought in all three classic battles of the Hundred Years War: Crécy, Poitiers and Agincourt. He himself, educated at Wellington College and Sandhurst, commanded battalions of Yorkshiremen in both world wars and was awarded the Military Cross.

He was a modest man. Replying to congratulations on being made a Knight of the Garter, he said: 'Yes, there was a bit of excitement here to begin with, but then my grandson caught his first salmon, so it was soon forgotten.'

A pillar of the Church of England, Middleton took trouble over the ecclesiastical patronage in his gift. When the Archbishop of York dined with him one night at Birdsall, he included a new curate among the guests. As the Archbishop was leaving, he said how much he had enjoyed meeting the curate and asked his host how he had discovered him. Lord Middleton replied: 'I advertised for him in *Horse and Hound*.'

Mildmay, Anthony, 2nd Baron
(1909–1950)

Gentleman rider and the Queen's first racing manager. Educated at Eton and Trinity College, Cambridge, he worked for three years in Baring Brothers, the merchant bank of which an uncle was senior partner. In 1933 he resigned to devote his life to steeplechasing. Although 6 feet 2 inches tall and long of limb, he was remarkably successful as an amateur rider. In the Grand National of 1936 he led from the start on his father's horse, Davy Jones, and would surely have won had not the buckle of his reins broken at the penultimate fence. As *The Times* wrote after his death: 'There never was a harder rider, a better loser or a more popular winner.'

His career as a jockey was interrupted by World War II, during which he served in the Welsh Guards with his old schoolfriend and racing trainer Peter Cazalet (q.v.). Mildmay was wounded and had another escape from death when a German bullet removed the earpiece of the radio earphones he was wearing in his tank. He was mentioned in despatches.

In 1949, the year after he had ridden Cromwell into third place in the Grand National, Mildmay was a guest at Windsor Castle for Royal Ascot. There he persuaded the Queen (now the Queen Mother) to buy a steeplechaser. She agreed that Mildmay should become her racing manager and look out for a suitable horse to be owned in partnership with her daughter, Princess Elizabeth. The result was the purchase of Monaveen, a bay gelding bred in Ireland. Trained by Cazalet, the horse soon won a race at Fontwell Park, carrying Princess Elizabeth's newly registered colours of scarlet, purple hooped sleeves and black cap: a variant of the Sovereign's racing colours. But within a few months Mildmay was dead, drowned while swimming off his estate on the coast of Devon. Later that year Monaveen broke a leg and had to be put down. The future Queen Elizabeth II's interest in horses turned to flat racing, leaving her mother to become the most enthusiastic and revered of all National Hunt patrons.

Milford Haven, Admiral of the Fleet Louis Mountbatten, 1st Marquess of (1854–1921)

Father of Earl Mountbatten of Burma and grandfather of Prince Philip, Duke of Edinburgh (qq.v.). He was born Prince Louis of Battenberg, eldest son of Prince Alexander of Hesse, who married morganatically Julie Hauke, daughter of a Polish politician. Prince

Alexander's wife was created Countess, later Princess of Battenberg, and gave the name to their children. In spite of the morganatic handicap, they were an ambitious family. A sister of Prince Alexander was married to the Tsar Alexander II of Russia; one brother of Louis briefly ruled Bulgaria; another married Queen Victoria's daughter, Princess Beatrice (q.v.).

As for Louis himself, he was allowed by his parents to become a naturalized British subject and to join the Royal Navy at the age of fourteen. There he served continuously for the next forty-six years, rising to Commander-in-Chief of the Atlantic Fleet in 1908 and First Sea Lord in 1912. He stood firm against Winston Churchill, who as civilian First Lord of the Admiralty was impatient with naval tradition and customs. When Churchill tactlessly persisted in trying to have a new warship named the *Oliver Cromwell* against the wishes of King George V, Prince Louis told him: 'All my experience at the Admiralty and close intercourse with three Sovereigns leads me to this: from all times the Sovereign's decision as to names for HM ships has been accepted as final by all First Lords.' That was the end of the matter.

In the last days of July 1914, when it fell to Prince Louis of Battenberg to mobilize the fleet for war, the operation was carried out with prompt efficiency. That, however, was not enough to protect a man of German name and accent from a vicious campaign of disparagement and insult. In October the Prime Minister noted: 'Our poor blue-eyed German will have to go.' On the following day Prince Louis resigned, 'driven to the painful conclusion that at this juncture my birth and parentage have the effect of impairing in some respects my usefulness at the Board of Admiralty.' Deeply wounded by the ingratitude of his adopted country, he disappeared into private life, consoled by the empty distinction of a Privy Counsellorship. Perhaps the most able naval officer of his generation, he spent the rest of the war compiling a three-volume history of medals.

In 1917, to appease the continuing public

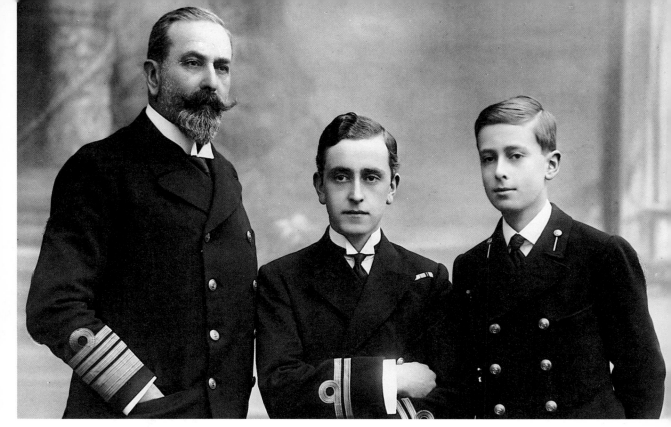

Louis, 1st Marquess of Milford Haven, with his two sons: George, Earl of Medina (later 2nd Marquess), and Lord Louis Mountbatten (later Earl Mountbatten of Burma)

hysteria against all things German, he was required to renounce his princely title and to anglicize his name. He emerged as Sir Louis Mountbatten, 1st Marquess of Milford Haven. On 4 August 1921, the anniversary of the outbreak of war seven years earlier, he was promoted to Admiral of the Fleet in belated recognition of his services to the Royal Navy. He died in the following month of a heart attack.

Victims of monstrous injustice are not always men of colourful character. Dreyfus, for instance, was never the life and soul of the officers' mess. So it was with Prince Louis of Battenberg. He was patriotic, honourable, industrious and efficient; but his intellectual cast of mind and reserved manner failed to win him a place in English society. His cousin and patron, Edward VII, was pained that Prince Louis should take a house in Pimlico. 'I thought only pianists lived there,' the King said. Like the Prince Consort before him, Prince Louis remained more than half a German: a good German, but still a German. 'These are the kind of administrative

blunders which are never made in Germany,' he wrote to the King's private secretary in 1907. Not even having got Lillie Langtry with child in the days of his youth was enough to convince old sea dogs that he could be trusted to command Nelson's navy.

Prince Louis married in 1884 his cousin Princess Victoria, the eldest daughter of the Grand Duke Louis IV of Hesse and Princess Alice, Queen Victoria's second daughter. They had four children. George, born in 1892, served in the Royal Navy, succeeded his father as the 2nd Marquess of Milford Haven and died of cancer in 1938. Louis, known in the family as Dickie, was born in 1900 and became Earl Mountbatten of Burma (q.v.). Alice, born in 1885, married Prince Andrew of Greece and was the mother of Prince Philip, Duke of Edinburgh. Louise, born in 1889, married King Gustav VI Adolf of Sweden.

In contrast to her husband, Victoria Marchioness of Milford Haven behaved with a fine disdain for convention. By the age of sixteen she had been taught to smoke by the Kaiser and relished the habit to the end of her life. She limped slightly at her wedding, having twisted her ankle leaping over a coal scuttle. Equally exuberant whether shooting pheasants or visiting museums, she painted, read philosophy, followed the latest developments in archeology. But like her daughter-in-law Edwina Mountbatten (q.v.) she could be tiresome, even aggressive, in flaunting socialist beliefs while clinging to the prejudices and privileges of birth, wealth and position. It was characteristic of that egalitarian princess to greet her husband's brand-new peerage in 1917 with a scornful reference to ennobled bankers and lawyers and brewers.

Lady Milford Haven survived her husband by nearly thirty years, dying at Kensington Palace at the age of eighty-seven. She thus lived to see her son become the last Viceroy of India, and a grandson married to Queen Elizabeth II.

Millar, Sir Oliver
(1923–   )

Surveyor of the Queen's Pictures since 1972. Educated at Rugby School and the Courtauld Institute of Art, he became Assistant Surveyor of the King's Pictures in 1947 and Deputy Surveyor in 1949. He succeeded Sir Anthony Blunt (q.v.) as Surveyor of the Queen's Pictures in 1972. Royal iconography has been his lifelong interest; even as a schoolboy, he filled his room with family trees and postcards of kings and queens. His catalogues of exhibitions and his longer published works are scholarly in substance, brisk and entertaining in style; nor has he ever allowed his place at court to colour his aesthetic judgment.

'It would be difficult,' Millar writes in *The Queen's Pictures*, published in 1977, 'to find a single important contemporary British or French picture acquired between the last years of Queen Victoria and the accession of King George VI.' He refers to Edward VII's 'inborn philistinism'; and regrets that Queen Mary's

Sir Oliver Millar

obsession with family likenesses prevented her from ever buying 'a really good or important picture.' One Scottish acquisition he singles out for particular scorn: 'Pettie's Bonnie Prince Charlie at Holyroodhouse, which might be chosen in an unguarded moment as a jacket for a novel by D.K.Broster, but would be more at home on a tin of Edinburgh rock in Princes Street.'

Elsewhere Millar writes that the Queen has given sittings for nearly one hundred portraits since 1937. He continues: 'Only a small number can be regarded as successful portraits or imaginative works of art. Recent paintings of domestic or equestrian scenes have demonstrated all too often weaknesses in construction, draughtsmanship, atmosphere and likeness. ... The photographer has, at least temporarily, vanquished the painter.'

Monckton of Brenchley, Walter, 1st Viscount (1891–1965)

Friend and adviser of King Edward VIII. He was born in Kent, the eldest son of a paper manufacturer. At Harrow he played cricket for the school against Eton in the celebrated 'Fowler's Match' of 1910; at Balliol College, Oxford, he took a Third Class in Classical Moderations followed by a Second Class in History. As President of the Oxford Union he came to know the Prince of Wales, a fellow undergraduate, although their friendship did not flourish until twenty years later.

In spite of an almost total blindness in one eye, Monckton served throughout the Great War in the Queen's Own West Kent Regiment and was awarded the Military Cross. He then embarked on a prosperous career at the Bar. He became a King's Counsel in 1930, Attorney-General to the Prince of Wales in 1932 and consitutional adviser to the Nizam of Hyderabad in 1933. It was during a visit to India in September 1936 that Edward VIII summoned him home to be his confidant throughout what came to be known as the Abdication crisis.

The essence of the problem was whether the King, as Supreme Governor of the Church of England, could marry a divorced woman yet keep his throne. He was in love with Wallis Simpson, already divorced from an earlier partner and now, at the King's prompting, seeking to be rid of her current husband. Monckton's role was at first no more than that of legal adviser. But in mid-November, following the sudden rift between Edward VIII and his Private Secretary, Alexander Hardinge (q.v.), Monckton agreed to be the link, even the mediator, between his Sovereign and his Prime Minister. The King later wrote:

'In the events that followed he played his part with a skill that impressed Mr Baldwin as much as it helped me. Despite the passions that were all too soon to envelop us, neither the Prime Minister nor I ever once had reason to complain of any misrepresentation or misunderstanding of our individual views. Undisturbed by the deafening hullabaloo in the Press, the intricate constitutional problems were handled calmly, expertly and always with dignity.'

On 20 October the King discussed with the Prime Minister for the first time what could no longer be regarded as a private matter; on 11 December he abdicated. Throughout those weeks Monckton shuttled between London and Fort Belvedere, the King's private residence near Windsor, about twenty miles from the capital. It was there that Edward VIII spent the last days of his reign in near seclusion, without a private secretary or equerry. On 3 December, Monckton was invited to make the Fort his temporary home; relieving the King's loneliness and listening to his interminable confidences by day and by night added to the burden.

The entrenched positions of the antagonists left scarcely any room for manoeuvre, much less compromise. For the past two years the King had been determined to make Mrs Simpson his wife. But Baldwin, whose bucolic torpor masked a shrewd political instinct, knew that a twice-divorced woman would be unacceptable as Queen. Either the King must renounce Mrs Simpson or he must give up the throne.

A third course was briefly considered: that the King be permitted to marry Mrs Simpson morganatically. This allowed a member of a royal house to contract a legal marriage with a woman of lesser birth who would not take her husband's rank and whose children would have no right of succession to the throne. Such a practice was not uncommon among European royal families. Queen Mary's grandfather, for instance, Duke Alexander of Württemberg, by choosing to marry a commoner, had excluded his children from the line of succession; they were consoled with the lesser family title of Teck. Lord Mountbatten, too, was descended from a morganatic branch of the royal family of Hesse. Monckton put little faith in a morganatic marriage between Edward VIII and Mrs

Walter Monckton (*left*) with the Duke and Duchess of Windsor and 'Fruity' Metcalfe

Simpson. He rightly surmised that the necessary legislation would be rejected by Parliament and prove equally unpalatable to the Dominions.

Monckton did, however, try to secure another measure on the King's behalf. The decree *nisi* which Mrs Simpson had secured against her husband in October would not become absolute until April 1937. There remained the danger that in the intervening months her close association with the King could lead to the intervention of other parties, whether moralizing or mischievous. It was for this reason that Monckton had urged the King to send her to the south of France and thus insulate them both from whispered innuendo. 'I was desperately afraid,' he afterwards wrote, 'that the King might give up his throne and yet be deprived of his chance to marry Mrs Simpson.' He therefore proposed that two Bills should immediately be introduced into Parliament; one giving effect to the King's Abdication, the other making the decree *nisi* of Mrs Simpson absolute forthwith. The Cabinet, however, rejected the plan. It disliked any notion of a bargain; and it asserted that the second Bill would affront the moral sense of the nation and provoke the very rumours it was designed to silence.

On 8 December, accompanied by Monckton, the King drove down to Fort Belvedere. There, for the last time, the Prime Minister pleaded with him to renounce Mrs Simpson and so retain his throne. He failed, and the elaborate machinery of Abdication was set in motion. Forty-eight hours later, after a last dinner at the Fort, Monckton listened to Edward VIII deliver his farewell broadcast. When it was over, the King stood up and putting his arm on Monckton's shoulder, said: 'Walter, it is a far better thing I go to.' After family farewells, Monckton accompanied him to Portsmouth and said goodbye to his friend and former Sovereign on board the destroyer that was to carry him into exile.

Throughout the crisis, Monckton had kept in close and sympathetic touch with Edward VIII's family. 'To give up all that for this,' was Queen Mary's sad comment to him as the tragedy drew to its close. He returned to London from Portsmouth at four o'clock on the morning of 12 December. Although physically exhausted and drained of emotion, he at once sat down in his club and wrote her a moving letter. 'Even his faults and follies,' he said of her son, 'are great.' Only then did he go to bed. The Duke of York, too, had maintained a friendly and trusting relationship with Monckton. As King George VI he at once showed his appreciation by making him a KCVO: the first knight of the new reign.

The months that followed that winter of discontent brought little relief to Monckton. While resuming his practice at the Bar, he continued to be involved in a succession of testing negotiations about the former King's title and finances. Some of the tasks laid on him by George VI were distasteful. One was to dissuade Edward from telephoning his brother with a stream of unsolicited advice on public affairs and private grievances. Another was to break the news to the newly created Duke of Windsor that his wife could not share his style of Royal Highness or the courtesies paid to it. Monckton would nevertheless incline punctiliously to the Duchess whenever they met. 'I find that my head bows very easily,' he said. Yet even on her wedding day he did not shirk the role of candid friend. 'I told her,' he later wrote, 'that most people in England disliked her very much because the Duke had married her and given up his throne, but that if she made him, and kept him, happy all his days, all that would change; but that if he were unhappy nothing would be too bad for her.'

His concern for the Duke's peace of mind also prompted him to urge the Prime Minister, Neville Chamberlain, and other members of the Cabinet to call on the Windsors at their home in Paris, and so relieve a growing sense of rejection. It was Monckton, too, who during the Duke's first visit to England since the Abdication tried to ease the strained relationship between the former King and his successor. Their meeting at Buckingham Palace was correct rather than cordial; it might have been glacial had he not excluded both the Queen and the Duchess of Windsor from the family reunion.

Throughout the war and after, Monckton remained the most steadfast of the Windsors' British friends, not least in refusing an offer of £100,000 to publish his account of the Abdication. He speeded them on their way to the Bahamas in 1940, stayed with them at Nassau in 1942 and entertained them during their post-war visits to London. Meanwhile he had his own career to pursue. On the outbreak of war he joined the newly created Ministry of Information, was sent on a mission to Russia then posted to Cairo as director of propaganda and information services. During the confrontation between the British Ambassador, Lord Killearn, and a fractious King Farouk, Monckton drafted an instrument of abdication which in the end was not needed. It drew from Clement Attlee the dry comment: 'He'd had practice.'

Monckton entered the House of Commons at a by-election in February 1951. When the Conservatives took office in October, Churchill pressed him to become Minister of Labour, 'since you have no political past.' 'I take it,' Monckton retorted, 'you do not expect me to have any political future.' He applied his conciliatory touch to a succession of industrial disputes. His critics complained that there seemed no limit to the price he would pay to avoid confrontation; but he did ensure a rare atmosphere of trust between a Conservative Government and the Trade Unions.

From December 1955 to October 1956 he was Minister of Defence in the Government of Sir Anthony Eden. Reluctant to endorse plans for the invasion of Egypt, he exchanged his department for the sinecure office of Paymaster General. He thus avoided some of the odium of the unsuccessful Suez adventure. In January 1957 he retired from active politics and was created a viscount. He had long coveted the post of Lord Chief Justice, the reversion to which had been promised him by both Churchill and Eden; but Lord Goddard would not stand down in favour of a man who had been through the divorce courts. Denied his judicial prize, Monckton found solace as chairman of the Midland Bank and the Marylebone Cricket Club. He interrupted these duties in 1959–60 to preside over the Advisory Commission on the Central African Federation.

Walter Monckton was attractive to women and enjoyed their favours with enthusiasm. He married in 1914 Mary Colyer-Ferguson, by whom he had a son and a daughter. The marriage was dissolved in 1947, when he married Bridget, wife of the 11th Earl of Carlisle and later Baroness Ruthven of Freeland in her own right. He died of arteriosclerosis on the eve of his seventy-fourth birthday and was succeeded in the family honours by his only son Gilbert, a major-general in the Army.

Moore, Captain Charles
(1880–1965)

Racing manager to King George VI and Queen Elizabeth II. He was the son of Arthur John Moore, of Mooresfort, County Tipperary, who sat in the House of Commons and was created a Papal Count in 1879. Charles fought in the Irish Guards during the Great War and was awarded the Military Cross. He built up a successful stud at Mooresfort and in 1937 was appointed to manage King George VI's stud at Hampton Court. The royal racing fortunes were then at a low ebb. Over the next quarter of a century both the King and his daughter, Queen Elizabeth II, won a succession of classic races. Moore worked well in harness with his fellow Irishman, the trainer Cecil Boyd-Rochfort (q.v.); but the knowledge and eye of the Queen herself in this field should not be underestimated.

Captain Moore married Lady Dorothie Feilding, a daughter of the 9th Earl of Denbigh, Lord-in-Waiting to Queen Victoria and King Edward VII, and Aide-de-Camp to King George V. One daughter of the marriage was the wife of Sir Godfrey Agnew (q.v.), Clerk of the Privy Council.

Like all breeders of horses, Moore favoured some lines of bloodstock at the expense of others. Unlike most, however, he would also take the pedigree of those owning the thoroughbreds into consideration. He retired in 1962, at the age of eighty-one, but continued to live at The Pavilion, Hampton Court. When the Queen and the Queen Mother called unexpectedly to see him one day, he was ill in bed, but came down to receive the royal visitors in his dressing-gown. This conversation then took place:

The Queen: 'How are you feeling?'
Moore: 'Well, Ma'am, I feel like a rabbit who has been bolted by a ferret.'
The Queen: 'I may have been called many things behind my back, but I have never been called a ferret to my face before!'

Charles Moore

He asked permission to refuse the knighthood offered to him by the Queen.

In 1965, although told by his doctors that he was too ill to travel, Moore returned to Ireland to die. He said: 'It is cheaper for me to go back to Mooresfort alive than dead. If I feel the journey by air is too much for me, I can always put my hat over my face and no one will notice till I arrive.'

Moore, Sir Philip
(1921–   )

Private Secretary to Queen Elizabeth II since 1977. The son of a member of the Indian Civil Service, he won a scholarship to Cheltenham College and an exhibition in Classics to Brasenose College, Oxford. Then the war intervened. he served in the RAF in Bomber Command, was shot down and spent three years as a prisoner of war. At Oxford he was given his Blues for hockey and rugby football (which in 1951 he played for England) and was in the Oxfordshire cricket XI.

Having won a place in the administrative class of the civil service, he became private secretary to the First Lord of the Admiralty, Lord Selkirk. When Selkirk was appointed United Kingdom High Commissioner for Singapore, he chose Moore to be his deputy. In 1965, the Minister of Defence, Denis Healey, selected him to become chief of public relations. The appointment annoyed the Institute of Professional Civil Servants, who protested that the post should have gone not to an administrative civil servant but to one trained in public relations. He did not remain long in Whitehall. Lord Cobbold (q.v.), as chairman of the Malaysia Commission of Inquiry, had been impressed by Moore's work in Singapore, particularly the cordial relations he had established with the Prime Minister of Singapore, Lee Kuan Yew. Cobbold had since become Lord Chamberlain of the Queen's Household, and now invited him to become an Assistant Secretary to the Queen. Moore took up his duties at the Palace in 1966, was promoted Deputy Private Secretary in 1972, and five years

Sir Philip Moore with Prince Edward, 1984

later succeeded Lord Charteris (q.v.) as Private Secretary.

Some think it was a mistake for Sir Philip Moore to abandon his career in the public service, where he would have been impressive in any senior post. In the role of the Queen's Private Secretary he has proved an able administrator, but slower and more cautious, less imaginative and amusing than his predecessors. He is married, has two daughters, is rarely found dining out and belongs to no clubs except the MCC.

Morshead, Sir Owen
(1893–1977)

Librarian of Windsor Castle, 1926–58. Educated at Marlborough, the Royal Military Academy and Magdalene College, Cambridge, he served with distinction throughout the Great War. He won the DSO, the MC, the Italian Croce di Guerra and five mentions in despatches. Returning to Cambridge after the war, he was elected a Fellow of Magdalene College and appointed librarian of its Pepys collection.

In 1926, on the retirement of Sir John Fortescue, Morshead was offered the post of Librarian at Windsor Castle. King George V always looked with favour on those who had borne arms; he had also received good reports on Morshead from his own second son, the Duke of York, who had known him at Cambridge.

As Librarian, Morshead made the Royal Archives more readily available to scholars than had some of his predecessors. Selections from Windsor's incomparable collection of old master drawings went on public display and a complete catalogue of that treasure trove was set in train. Morshead's published works, however, were disappointingly few.

He and his American wife, a handsome couple, were welcome guests of successive Sovereigns. He liked to recall how George V, noticing his Librarian's sparing diet, shouted

down the table: 'Morshead is not having any cream. Don't be afraid of it. It's ours, you know.' Queen Mary valued his charm as well as the eye of a connoisseur which he brought to her purchases in salerooms and antique shops.

During World War II he commanded a battalion of the Home Guard. In 1945 he once more tasted adventure. King George VI sent him by air to Germany to ensure the safety of some family letters, particularly those written by Queen Victoria to her eldest daughter, the Empress Frederick, after the Margravine of Hesse's house had been occupied by American troops.

In retirement, Morshead devoted much care to arranging his papers. Although urbane, even mannered in conversation, he could flourish a mordant turn of phrase; and his unpublished diary may one day be read with surprise as well as pleasure.

Mountbatten of Burma,
Louis Mountbatten, 1st Earl
(1900–1979)

Viceroy of India, Chief of Defence Staff and uncle of Prince Philip, Duke of Edinburgh. He was born at Frogmore House, near Windsor, the younger son of Admiral Prince Louis of Battenberg, a naturalized British subject later created Marquess of Milford Haven (q.v.), and Princess Victoria of Hesse, a granddaughter of Queen Victoria. Until 1917 he was known as Prince Louis Francis of Battenberg, though called Dickie to distinguish him from his father. When in that year the Admiral was obliged to relinquish his princely style and to anglicize the family name, Dickie assumed the courtesy title of Lord Louis Mountbatten, which he bore until he was himself created a peer in 1946.

He spent a childhood and youth of profound contrasts. He was both a great-grandson and godson of Queen Victoria. His mother's sister was married to the Tsar Nicholas II, who was also his father's cousin. Thus one of the first of the many uniforms he wore throughout life was the cuirass and helmet of the Imperial Household Cavalry given him by the Russian Emperor for Christmas 1905. He cherished no less a series of endearing little letters 'from your loving Anastasia.' In 1913 he followed his father, by now First Sea Lord, into the Royal Navy; and after three years at Osborne and Dartmouth emerged as a midshipman.

The outbreak of war in 1914 evoked an anti-German hysteria that forced his father, the most honourable and patriotic of men, to retire into private life. 'What d'you think the latest rumour that has got in here from outside is?' the fifteen-year-old naval cadet wrote to his mother from Osborne. 'That Papa has turned out to be a German spy and has been discreetly marched off to the Tower, where he is guarded by Beefeaters. . . . I got rather a rotten time of it for about three days as little fools . . . insisted on calling me German Spy and kept on heckling me and trying to make things unpleasant for me.' In later life Mountbatten would deny that his relentless ambition sprang from a desire to avenge his father's fate. Yet at least he was inspired by the example of that ill-used man; and it was with acute satisfaction and pride that forty or so years later he too assumed the appointment of First Sea Lord.

Mountbatten's ascent seemed effortless. He was born with enough royal blood to catch the indulgent eye of authority yet too little to blunt the spur of ambition. He first saw action in HMS *Lion*, the flagship of Admiral Beatty's Battle Cruiser Fleet, then transferred with his hero to HMS *Queen Elizabeth*, the flagship of the Grand Fleet. The war ended, and he spent a year at Christ's College, Cambridge, the nursery of Milton and Darwin, before serving in HMS *Renown* throughout the Prince of Wales's tours to Australia, India and the Far East. It was in Delhi that he proposed to Edwina Ashley (q.v.), the daughter of Lord Mount Temple and grand-daughter of Sir Ernest Cassel. They were married in St Margaret's, Westminster, in July 1922. The King and Queen were present and the Prince of Wales undertook the role of best man.

Mountbatten is coached by Charlie Chaplin.

Mountbatten had acquired a wife with looks as striking as his own and rich enough to protect them both from the risks of independent or adventurous judgment. They spent a protracted honeymoon in the United States, were received by President Harding and made a film with Charlie Chaplin.

In London the Mountbattens lived in Brook House, Park Lane, which Edwina had inherited from her grandfather; in Malta they took a villa and a yacht far beyond the means of other young officers in the Mediterranean Fleet. It was not so much the panache of their entertainment which aroused resentment as their simultaneous flaunting of socialist beliefs. Twice Lord Louis was blackballed for membership of the Royal Yacht Squadron; a spectator of the elections described the ballot-box as resembling caviar.

That playboy façade was deceptive. He became a specialist in communications and invented several ingenious devices for use at sea. In 1932, promoted to commander, he received his first ship, the destroyer HMS *Daring*. By the outbreak of war in 1939 he was a captain, in command of the 5th Destroyer Flotilla. It fell to him to bring back the Duke and Duchess of Windsor from France in HMS *Kelly*: the same unlucky ship which was torpedoed by a German E-boat in 1940, recommissioned, then sunk off Crete a year later. Mountbatten, decorated with the Distinguished Service Order, acquired a reputation as a dashing but accident-prone, even incautious leader. Perhaps it was what that dismal phase of the war demanded. King George VI, on being told that his cousin was to be given command of a certain aircraft-carrier, exclaimed: 'Well that's the end of the *Illustrious*!'

Instead he was chosen by Churchill to invigorate Combined Operations, with the rank of vice-admiral. The failure of the raid on Dieppe and the heavy casualties inflicted on Canadian troops renewed the enmity of Lord Beaverbrook and his newspapers. Mountbatten was unrepentant. He said: 'The raid has been described by people who do not understand what it achieved as a catastrophe. The losses were disturbing, but Dieppe taught the planners lessons that had to be learnt.' Like Admiral Fisher, he believed that the best scale for an experiment was twelve inches to the foot. Promoted yet again, Mountbatten ended the war as Supreme Allied Commander, South-East Asia. There he acquired the title of 'Supremo,' as much an accolade as an abbreviation, and bore it without embarrassment. Although his diplomatic touch charmed the Americans and the Chinese, but not the Dutch, the swollen size and

doubtful efficiency of his staff caused friction with other British commanders. Having seen the war against the Japanese to its end, he was created Viscount Mountbatten of Burma.

In February 1947, the Labour Government of Clement Attlee appointed him to succeed Lord Wavell as Viceroy of India, charged with completing the transfer of power by June 1948. If the hastily conceived and perhaps premature mission of the last Viceroy unwittingly provoked bloodshed and suffering, it at least left no legacy of hatred towards the British Raj, and may have averted a worse catastrophe. Mountbatten had hoped that after Independence he would become Governor-General of both India and Pakistan. But the persuasive charm which captivated Pandit Nehru failed to move the more mercurial Mr Jinnah, who let it be known that so demonstrative a friend of India would never be welcomed by her Moslem neighbour.

While in Delhi, the last Viceroy was created Earl Mountbatten of Burma. In lieu of a son, his elder daughter Patricia, married to the 7th Lord Brabourne, a film producer, was designated heir to his peerages by special remainder. His younger daughter Pamela is the wife of David Hicks, a decorator and designer.

The Viceroyalty of India was but an interlude in the career of an ambitious sailor. Having reverted to the rank of substantive rear-admiral, he successively commanded the 1st Cruiser Squadron in the Mediterranean; served as Fourth Sea Lord at the Admiralty; was promoted Commander-in-Chief, Mediterranean; and in 1955, not without opposition, he sat in his father's place as First Sea Lord. The rank of Admiral of the Fleet followed. In 1959 he became Chief of the Defence Staff and chairman of the Chiefs of Staff Committee. Throughout his years in Whitehall he initiated bold changes, not least the virtual integration of the Navy, the Army and the Air Force and the absorption of the three Service Ministries into a single Department. Even as a reformer, he retained a romantic attachment to the past. After a reception at the new Ministry of Defence, the wife of the Secretary of State said how much her arm ached after shaking hands with eight hundred guests. 'That is nothing,' he replied. 'My great-aunt, the Empress of Russia, used to have a blister on the back of her hand each Easter where the peasants had kissed it.'

When the present writer asked Mountbatten what he proposed to do after his retirement in 1965, he replied: 'I'm going to try not to die.' For the next fourteen years he succeeded. He inspired and raised money for United World Colleges, a chain of schools which he believed would contribute to a lasting peace. It was characteristic of his ebullience that, having refused to attend a State banquet at Buckingham Palace in honour of his old enemy the Emperor Hirohito of Japan, he called on him privately next day: not to apologize but to seek his financial support for the project.

He planned the opening to the public of Broadlands, the house he had inherited on his

Lord Mountbatten and Prince Charles

wife's death in 1960, with all the precision of a combined operation. He became the perpetual and ever willing counsellor not only of the royal family but of any who sought his help; and having solved the problem to his own satisfaction, he would not relent until his advice had been carried out to the letter. He also made films of his life and talked freely about the past with a picturesque recall that did not always bear historical scrutiny. In August 1979, while sailing with his family in a small boat off the west coast of Ireland, Mountbatten was murdered by an IRA bomb. He was eulogized as a Renaissance man and buried like a medieval emperor.

It is idle to speculate whether Mountbatten cared more for his royal blood or for his professional career. Like most of us, he wanted the best of both worlds; unlike most of us, he got it. By the unsentimental standards of genealogy, Mountbatten was royal but not very royal. His mother was a grandchild of Queen Victoria; he was thus three generations removed from the Sovereign. That, as it happens, is the precise relationship of Mr James Lascelles, the pop musician, to King George V. Yet it is exceptionally rare for him or others of comparable lineage to appear in the Court Circular or on the balcony of Buckingham Palace. Mountbatten had a secure place in both. He owed it partly to another royal connection; he was the uncle of Queen Elizabeth II's husband, his sister having married Prince Andrew of Greece and given birth to Prince Philip, later Duke of Edinburgh.

Mountbatten cultivated these relationships. During the defence cuts which followed the Great War he was saved from premature retirement by King George V himself as a gesture of reparation to Prince Louis of Battenberg. He made himself the confidant of the Prince of Wales, who took him round the world and acted as best man at his wedding. After the Abdication he unobtrusively transferred his personal friendship as well as his official allegiance to King George VI. He became the ever-welcome guest of the Queen and Prince Philip, the ever-favourite great-uncle of Prince Charles.

Yet it was not cupboard love which bound him to the House of Windsor. There was a touch of romanticism about the man of action which drew him to the most romantic of all institutions: the monarchy. He pored over its history, corresponded prodigiously, put his memories and his archives at the disposal of fellow students. It is tempting to compare him with Jane Austen's Sir Walter Elliot, who read no book other than the *Baronetage*: 'There he found occupation for an idle hour and consolation in a distressed one.' But it is not an exact parallel. Mountbatten had no need of such a volume; he knew it by heart. The present writer once heard him greet Princess Alexandra (q.v.) with the words: 'And how is my second cousin once removed?' Even during the turmoil of his months in India he compiled *Relationship Tables*, a volume ingeniously tracing his kinship with the dynasties of Europe. It was printed at the Viceroy's Press, Delhi, and bound in an appropriate purple. Five years later he produced an addendum, printed by the Press of the Commander-in-Chief, Mediterranean.

The laconic Mr Attlee said of him: 'Rather a Ruritanian figure, don't you think?' For Mountbatten, the Queen's uniform was not so much a working rig as a symbol of loyalty and devotion. He wore it as often as he could and on occasions when other senior officers in peacetime preferred plain clothes. A military colleague once complained: 'It is such a bore when Dickie telephones to say "full-dress uniform" and I have to retrieve my sword from the nursery.' On being appointed Colonel of The Life Guards, an unprecedented honour for a sailor, he bought a complete wardrobe of new uniforms; within a few days of entering his eightieth year he insisted on riding in the Queen's Birthday Parade, plumed, booted and cuirassed. Mountbatten also took an obsessive interest in medals and decorations, of which he himself had earned whole galaxies, including the Garter and the Order of Merit. There was one adornment to his uniforms of which he was even prouder: the three little gold ciphers denoting that he had served King Edward VIII, King George VI and Queen Elizabeth II as Personal Aide-de-Camp. His father had held the same appointment to the previous three Sovereigns.

For all his qualities of courage and leadership, of imagination and vigour, he did not escape disparagement, albeit in clubs rather than in pubs. His detractors accused him of impregnable self-assurance, of a relish for public acclaim, of treating subordinates brusquely, of political views that ill-accorded with his background and way of life. His memory is strong enough to bear such comment, and it must be left to history to distinguish between realism and ruthlessness, duty and ambition. Perhaps his only failure was to seek and win the prizes of life untrammelled by diffidence; to scorn that amateurishness which is the passport to every Establishment heart.

Mountbatten of Burma, Edwina Ashley, Countess
(1901–1960)

Wife of Earl Mountbatten of Burma (q.v.). She was the elder daughter of Colonel Wilfred Ashley, later Lord Mount Temple, a grandson of the philanthropist Earl of Shaftesbury; and Maud, only child of Sir Ernest Cassel, the German-born Jewish financier and intimate friend of King Edward VII, after whom Edwina was named.

Colonel Ashley and his family lived at Broadlands, in Hampshire, the house and landscape renovated by Capability Brown that had once been the home of Lord Palmerston. Maud died when Edwina was nine. After Wilfred Ashley's remarriage three years later, she became increasingly close to her Cassel grandfather. At Sir Ernest's death in 1921 she was left a fortune of £2 million, worth between £30 and £40 million in the currency of 1985, together with Brook House, a vast marble mausoleum in Park Lane, London. The death of Edwina's father later brought her both Broadlands and Palmerstons' Irish property: Classiebawn, a mock-Gothic castle and estate of 10,000 acres on the coast of County Sligo. Endowed with beauty and brains and great possessions, she was married in 1922 to Lord Louis Mountbatten, the most handsome and dashing young naval officer of his generation. It promised to be a match of fairy-tale perfection.

That is not quite how it turned out. The vitality and charm of the Mountbattens were shadowed by paradox. Royal condescension did not exclude reckless liaisons; or the insensitive flaunting of wealth a smoked-salmon brand of socialism. 'Chips' Channon (q.v.) was among those who doubted their sincerity. 'Politically,' he wrote of Edwina, 'she talked tripe, and pretended to be against all monarchy, she who is cousin to every monarch on earth. According to her they must all be abolished. How easy it seems for a semi-royal millionairess, who has exhausted all the pleasures of money and position, to turn almost Communist.'

Against these whimsical attitudes must be set Edwina Mountbatten's selfless concern for the relief of suffering. General Lord Ismay, Mountbatten's chief of staff in India and a man little given to flattery, wrote of the Viceroy's wife: 'She was utterly dedicated, completely indefatigable and uniquely experienced. Undaunted by fatigue, danger, disease or stench, or the most gruesome scenes, her errands of mercy took her to hospitals and refugee camps all day and every day, and a good deal of the night. She had the missionary zeal of a Florence Nightingale, and the determined courage of a Joan of Arc.'

Such sustained valour did not protect her from malicious whispers. Much has been said of her friendship with Pandit Nehru. It is an episode, however, that belongs more to the sociology of the British middle class than to the biography of Edwina Mountbatten. For what shocked her contemporaries at home was not so much the supposed intimacy of the relationship as the colour of the Indian Prime Minister's skin.

In January 1960 she flew to India to begin yet another ferocious tour of the Far East on behalf of the St John Ambulance Brigade, the Red Cross and the Save the Children Fund. After a

Edwina Mountbatten, 1925

few days with Nehru and his family in Delhi she left for Malaya, Singapore, Brunei and North Borneo. It was in the last of these that she suffered a fatal heart attack. Her body was brought back to England and by her own wish buried at sea off Portsmouth. The British destroyer bearing her remains was escorted by an Indian warship from which Pandit Nehru's personal wreath was cast into the waves.

Nicolson, Sir Harold
(1886–1968)

Diplomatist, man of letters and biographer of King George v. He was the younger son of Sir Arthur Nicolson, 11th Baronet, a shrewd ambassador in Madrid and St Petersburg who retired as Permanent Head of the Foreign Office and was created Lord Carnock. Born in the British Legation, Tehran, Harold was educated at Wellington College, which he loathed, and Balliol College, Oxford, for which he displayed a lifelong affection. In 1909 he followed his father into the Foreign Office. 'Harold,' declared his contemporary Robert Vansittart (q.v.), 'must learn to be formidable.' This the good-natured Nicolson never achieved. But by 1919 he was a valued official of the British delegation to the Peace Conference in Paris, on intimate terms with such statesmen as Lloyd George, Balfour and Curzon. There followed diplomatic posts in Tehran and Berlin that would probably have led to the highest of all. But in 1929 he resigned from the Service. His wife Vita Sackville-West, novelist and poet, detested the social life inseparable from senior missions; and Nicolson himself was increasingly attracted by the lure of letters and politics.

Even while *en poste* he had published perceptive and urbane works on Tennyson, Byron and Swinburne. He had also brought out *Some People*, a mercurial volume of essays that spared neither himself nor his diplomatic colleagues. Sir Percy Loraine, an ambassador of immense dignity and self-satisfaction, found himself pilloried

in its pages under the pseudonym Lord Bognor; he called it 'a cad's book.' The Foreign Secretary, Sir Austen Chamberlain, was about to deliver an official reprimand to its author; then he heard that the King had been shouting with laughter over it, and Nicolson went unrebuked. After his release in 1929 from official constriction, he wrote a satirical novel about the Foreign Office called *Public Faces*; several serious works on diplomatic negotiation; and two much-praised biographies, one on Lord Curzon, whose private secretary he had been, and another on his own father, Lord Carnock. He also became an accomplished and fluent journalist and broadcaster.

Nicolson achieved some of his political ambitions, too. After an unhappy flirtation with Sir Oswald Mosley's New Party, which had not yet degenerated into the British Union of Fascists, he was elected to the House of Commons in 1935 as a member of Ramsay MacDonald's National Labour Party, Conservative in all but name. He courageously opposed Neville Chamberlain's appeasement of the dictators and briefly held office in Churchill's wartime Coalition Government as Parliamentary Secretary to the Ministry of Information. After the war he was denied the peerage he had expected and retreated from the political scene.

In 1948, Sir Alan Lascelles (q.v.), Private Secretary to George VI, asked him to write the official biography of the King's father, George v, who had died in 1936. Among those who had recommended him for the task was G.M. Trevelyan, the most celebrated of British historians. Nicolson hesitated. His closest link with the royal family had been a wary friendship with King Edward VIII and Mrs Simpson (qq.v.), into whose circle he had been introduced by Lady Cunard and Lady Colefax (qq.v.). Throughout the year of the Abdication, however, he had come to disapprove of the match. It distressed him that 'that silly little man should destroy a great monarchy by giggling into a flirtation with a third-rate American.' (Although Nicolson included both Americans and Jews among his intimates, he rarely spoke of either breed without denigration; indeed, he affected to dislike all foreigners except the French and the Greeks.) In March 1937, having dined at Buckingham Palace at one of the first parties of the new reign, he wrote of the Queen, afterwards Queen Elizabeth the Queen Mother: 'Nothing could exceed the charm or dignity which she displays, and I cannot help feeling what a mess poor Mrs Simpson would have made of such an occasion. It demonstrates to us more than anything else how wholly impossible that marriage would have been.'

Even if by 1948 his association with the Duke and Duchess of Windsor had been wholly forgiven, he nevertheless doubted his fitness to write the life of George v. Mildly infected by his wife with the Bloomsbury virus, he despised both of the old King's favourite pastimes, shooting and stamp collecting. One he regarded as barbarous, the other, as he had written in an article for *The Spectator* only two years before, 'totally unworthy of man's unconquerable mind.' Fortunately a book on the personal life of the King had been written with sympathy by John Gore and published in 1941; Nicolson would be able to concentrate on the development of the monarchy during the reign.

That did not remove all Nicolson's misgivings. He was disturbed that he might not be allowed to write truthfully about his subject. Lascelles specifically warned him that anything discreditable about the Sovereign which he discovered would have to be omitted: he would be depicting as much a myth as a man. Still undecided, Nicolson consulted his two sons. The elder, Benedict (q.v.), until recently Deputy Surveyor of the King's Pictures, was against it; his father, he said, would become the Sir Gerald Kelly (q.v.) of literature. But the younger son, Nigel, himself a man of letters, was more encouraging. What finally tipped the balance was Queen Mary's belief that he would be the best person to write her husband's life. On 9 June 1948, Nicolson told Lascelles that he would accept the task.

It took him just three years to complete. The physical labour alone was considerable, not least

Harold Nicolson and his wife, Vita Sackville-West

in the hundred stone steps he climbed each day to reach the Royal Archives in the Round Tower of Windsor Castle. Sometimes, too, his spirits wilted at coveys of slaughtered partridges, albums of Cape Triangulars and George V's aesthetic indifference. The Duke of Windsor told Nicolson that he would never understand his father until he had seen York Cottage, Sandringham, where King George and Queen Mary brought up their large family. Nicolson duly wrote a supercilious description of 'a glum little villa, encompassed by thickets of laurel and rhododendron,' its furnishings 'indistinguishable from those of any Surbiton or Upper Norwood home.'

In spite of the threat of censorship mentioned by Sir Alan Lascelles, neither King George VI nor Queen Mary required him to remove more than a sentence or two from his text. Here and there, however, the author had smoothed over awkwardnesses from which George V would not have emerged quite so creditably: the King's vindictiveness against Admiral Lord Fisher, for instance, or his pressure on Lloyd George's Government in 1917 to withdraw an offer of asylum to the deposed Tsar Nicholas II lest his arrival in England should provoke republican demonstrations against the British monarchy.

Soon after the publication of *King George V* in August 1952, Queen Mary summoned Nicolson to Marlborough House, asking him to bring his own copy of the book with him. In it she wrote: 'This is a noble work about my dear husband.' Elsewhere the biography was received with equal acclaim; and although other writers have since published books about King George V, Nicolson's majestic *tour de force* has yet to be superseded either as a State portrait or an indispensable chapter of constitutional history.

The success of *King George V* brought him fame, money and a title; yet he found a little worm nestling in each of those golden apples. He disliked to be called a royal biographer, for that, he thought, implied a sacrifice of independence to courtliness. He enjoyed spending, largely on his friends, the huge sums that rolled in from his publisher, but failed to provide for taxation; when at length he received a demand from the Inland Revenue for £6,000 – perhaps ten times that figure in modern currency – it made his life miserable for years to come. Finally he was summoned to Buckingham Palace, where King George V's granddaughter made him a Knight Commander of the Royal Victorian Order: an award that recognized both the skill of the author and the rank of his subject. Nicolson, however, had earlier hoped to be made a Lord and thought that a knighthood, even one bestowed personally by the Sovereign, was rather middle class. Although he would not insult the Queen by refusing it, he wrote in his diary that he would have preferred 'a dozen bottles of champagne or a travelling clock.'

All in all, what many thought his most enduring literary triumph brought him scant pleasure. But he did enjoy telling the story of how, as he was waiting for a train one day, he met a Frenchman of his acquaintance who asked where he was going. Nicolson replied that he was on his way to Windsor Castle to seek material '*pour une biographie de Georges Cinq.*' The friend expressed surprise that there should be documents at Windsor about such a character – '*Quelle étrange personne, avec cette passion presque nymphomane pour les hommes.*' He thought Nicolson had said Georges Sand.

Nicolson, Benedict
(1914–1978)

Deputy Surveyor of the King's Pictures, 1939–47. The elder son of Sir Harold Nicolson (q.v.) and Vita Sackville-West, he was educated at Eton and Balliol College, Oxford. He studied art history at I Tatti, Florence, with Bernard Berenson, who said of him: 'There is something very important at the bottom of that well.' Sir Kenneth Clark (q.v.) was equally impressed. He found Nicolson a place at the National Gallery; and as Surveyor of the King's Pictures appointed him his deputy.

Ben Nicolson had scarcely begun his duties at the Palace when the outbreak of war drew him into the Army. He served in the ranks of an anti-aircraft battery at Chatham commanded by Victor Cazalet, MP, and composed largely of intellectuals and aesthetes. Commissioned into the Intelligence Corps, he became an authority on the interpretation of aerial photographs. As Captain Nicolson was able at this time to buy a Picasso and to lend his father £500, he presumably did not live on his military pay.

Shortly before the end of the war in 1945 he resumed his post of Deputy Surveyor of the King's Pictures under the new surveyor, Anthony Blunt (q.v.) One of his duties was to put the archives of the department in order. But he did not relish life at court, least of all the parlour games played after dinner at Windsor. One night, he recalled, a staid company of guests that included Anthony Eden, Stafford Cripps and General Lord Ismay were persuaded to arm themselves with brass pokers and shovels from the fireplace, form themselves into a squad and march past the King and Queen in slow time down the length of the drawing-room.

Nicolson resigned his appointment in 1947 on becoming editor of the *Burlington Magazine*. There he remained for thirty years, proud to see it flourish as one of the most respected journals of art history in the world. His own scholarship was rewarded by a CBE in 1971 and a Fellowship of the British Academy in 1977.

Norfolk, Henry Fitzalan-Howard, 15th Duke of
(1847–1917)

Earl Marshal of England. Succeeding his father at the age of twelve, he was sent to the Oratory School at Edgbaston, where he came under the personal supervision of Cardinal Newman. He studied abroad until embarking on his duties as leader of the Roman Catholic laity of England and their principal link with the Vatican. He devoted the greater part of his income to building churches and schools and to supporting charitable causes. Among the most solid of his monuments are the restored Arundel Castle and the cathedral church of St John, Norwich.

In 1895 the Duke accepted the office of Postmaster General in Lord Salisbury's Government, but resigned in 1900 to serve as a yeomanry captain in the South African War at the age of fifty-two. He was also the first Mayor of Westminster, Mayor of Sheffield and Chancellor of Sheffield University. As hereditary Earl Marshal of England, Norfolk was responsible for organizing the funerals of Queen Victoria and Edward VII, and the Coronations of Edward VII and George V. His industry and command of detail were not matched by the College of Arms, on whom he depended to carry out his instructions. No occasion was quite free from confusion and at the funeral of Edward VII the entire ceremonial had to be rewritten at the last moment by more skilled hands. The new King blamed his Earl Marshal. 'I love the Duke,' he said, 'he is a charming, honourable, straightforward little gentleman, no better in the world. But as a man of business he is absolutely impossible. Is it not hard on me?'

One lady-in-waiting described him as looking 'like the most insignificant of mechanics.' Certainly he had no sense of self-importance, and his middle years were clouded by much sorrow. His first wife, Flora Abney-Hastings, elder daughter of the first Baron Donington, died after ten years of marriage; and their only child, Philip, Earl of Arundel, was born blind and mentally retarded. Year after year his parents took the boy to Lourdes, praying for a miracle. Then came the day when they met a procession of pilgrims chanting the Magnificat: 'He hath filled the hungry with good things, but the rich He hath sent empty away.' The Duchess wept. '*We* shall get nothing,' she said.

Philip died in 1902. Two years later his father found happiness in a second marriage, to Gwendolen, Baroness Herries, by whom he had several children. The only son, Bernard, succeeded him in 1917 as 16th Duke of Norfolk.

Norfolk, Bernard Fitzalan-Howard, 16th Duke of
(1908–1975)

Earl Marshal of England. The only surviving son of the 15th Duke of Norfolk (q.v.), he succeeded to the family honours while still at the Oratory School, Edgbaston. He failed, however, to pass what in those days was an undemanding entrance examination to Christ Church, Oxford, particularly when the candidate was a duke. He was therefore commissioned into the 4th Royal Sussex Regiment, from which he transferred into the Royal Horse Guards; in later life he became chairman of the Territorial Army Council.

One of his first gestures of emancipation on coming of age in 1929 was to buy a racehorse. Racing remained a paramount interest, although his blue and scarlet colours were never carried to victory in a Classic. His enthusiasm was shared by his wife, Miss Lavinia Strutt, the only daughter of the 3rd Baron Belper, whom he married in 1937 and by whom he had four daughters. The Duke was a steward of the Jockey Club and in 1945–72 the Queen's Representative at Ascot. He was also chairman of the Sussex County Cricket Club, president of the Marylebone Cricket Club (MCC) and in 1962–3 manager of the MCC team which toured Australia. Batting once on his home ground of Arundel, the Duke stopped a ball with his pad and there was a loud appeal to the umpire, who happened to be his own butler. 'His Grace is not in,' that urbane functionary declared.

As hereditary Earl Marshal of England he bore responsibility for such State occasions as the funerals and Coronations of Sovereigns, the funeral of Sir Winston Churchill and the Investiture of the Prince of Wales. Early military training and the transaction of estate business gave him an assured authority that was rarely resented when tempered by his brisk commentary and dry humour. 'If the bishops don't

learn to walk in step,' the leader of the English Roman Catholic laity told the Anglican episcopate at a Coronation rehearsal, 'we shall be here all night.' When asked by an Eton boy whether it was true that the peers carried sandwiches in their coronets, the Duke replied: 'Probably. They are capable of anything.' His answer was equally droll when he was asked what would happen if it rained at the open-air Investiture of the Prince of Wales in Caernarvon. He said: 'We will get wet.' The only slip he is known to have made was in proposing to exclude television cameras from Westminster Abbey at the Coronation of Elizabeth II, lest they exposed the Queen to additional strain. In this he was supported by the Prime Minister, the Cabinet and the Archbishop of Canterbury. The Queen personally overruled them all and many millions throughout the world were thus able to share in the ancient ceremonial.

The Duke also reproached himself that the funeral procession of Sir Winston Churchill arrived at St Paul's Cathedral two minutes late. As during the preliminary planning in Churchill's lifetime it had taken three weeks to decide in what order the three Chiefs of Staff of the Armed Forces should march, the lapse may be forgiven.

Persistent economic pressure on the landowning classes, scarcely less rigorous under a Conservative Government than under Labour, obliged the Duke to sell some of his London property, including Norfolk House, St James's Square, land in Lincolnshire and much of the Sussex town of Littlehampton. This was regretted, for he was a conscientious and kindly landlord. During World War II he served as Parliamentary Under-Secretary for Agriculture in the Coalition Government of Winston Churchill, forming a cordial partnership with the Labour Minister, Tom Williams. He also played a prominent role in Sussex affairs and was Lord Lieutenant of the county.

Henry Channon, a guest of the Norfolks at Arundel in December 1936, wrote in his diary: 'We have the best rooms, but oh! how cold they are, and there is a gale blowing like at sea.' After

Coronation rehearsal, 1953: The Queen with the Duke of Norfolk

the war, the discomfort and expense of the castle prompted the Duke and his family to move to a dower house which they built on the Arundel estate. He liked plain living, and when taken to lunch at the Savoy Grill professed amazement at seeing 'these fellows eat enormous things with red wine.'

The Duke did all that was required of him as a Catholic: a word he pronounced, in the oldfashioned style, as 'Cartholic'. But his conservative temperament could not accept the restless changes in liturgy set in train by the Second Vatican Council, and he personally conveyed his misgivings to Pope Paul VI.

Norfolk, Miles Fitzalan-Howard, 17th Duke of (1915–)

Earl Marshal of England, He is the eldest son of the 3rd Baron Howard of Glossop (a greatgrandson of the 13th Duke of Norfolk) and the 11th Baroness Beaumont in her own right. His parents gave all their eight children names beginning with the letter M: Miles, Michael, Martin, Mark, Mariegold, Miriam, Miranda and Mirabel. Having succeeded to his father's title in 1971 and to his mother's in 1972, Miles succeeded his kinsman Bernard, 16th Duke of Norfolk (q.v.) in 1975.

Educated at the Roman Catholic public school, Ampleforth, and at Christ Church, Oxford, he was commissioned into the Grenadier Guards. During the war he won the Military Cross in Italy. He retired in 1967 as Director of Service Intelligence at the Ministry of Defence, with the rank of major-general. The Duke has since worked as a director of Robert Fleming, the merchant bankers; his friends like to remind him that on the day he went into the City, the pound was devalued.

As hereditary Earl Marshal, the Duke has so far been called upon to organize no ceremony more demanding than the annual State Opening of Parliament. In 1983, however, he arranged a reunion of several hundred Howards to celebrate the 500th anniversary of the dukedom of Norfolk. It included a service at the Tower of London, where several of his forebears have perished on the block. In the same year he was made a Knight of the Garter, thus following in the footsteps of most previous dukes and also, on his mother's side of the family, of Sir Miles Stapleton, a founder Knight of the Order in 1348.

The Duke disclaims any formal role as leader of the Roman Catholic laity in England. His views on religious topics are nevertheless heard with attention, and in 1984 he pleaded in brisk military language for some relaxation in Rome's attitude to birth control. He also declared his belief that Anglican orders were valid and that Catholic priests who adhered to the Campaign for Nuclear Disarmament were 'round the bend' in suggesting that the West could give up nuclear weapons while allowing the Soviet Union to keep them. 'When I talked about some of the Church's doctrine as bloody nonsense,' he said during the controversy, 'that was only an army way of saying I disagreed.' In 1982 he welcomed the Pope to England both as a Roman Catholic and a dedicated supporter of the ecumenical movement.

In 1949 the Duke married a distant cousin, Anne Constable Maxwell, an accomplished landscape painter and a tireless fund-raiser for charity. They have two sons and three daughters. The elder son, Edward, Earl of Arundel, sells industrial gas in Shoreditch. One daughter is married to the actor Patrick Ryecart, another to television interviewer David Frost, the son of a Methodist minister. The Norfolks have several houses, in all of which they live modestly: a tiny mews house in London; a small country house near Henley-on-Thames; a flat in Arundel Castle, now a family museum open to the public; and Carlton Towers, in Yorkshire, a huge Victorian pile by Pugin that belonged to the family of the Duke's mother, the Stapletons. Ebullient and approachable, Miles Norfolk tempers the pride and dignity of his inheritance with a lively humour and the kindest of hearts.

Ogilvy, Hon. Angus
(1928–   )

Husband of Princess Alexandra (q.v.). The younger brother of the 13th Earl of Airlie and grandson of Mabell Countess of Airlie (qq.v.), he is the second of the three sons of the 12th Earl, Lord Chamberlain to Queen Elizabeth the Queen Mother. He was educated at Eton and Trinity College, Oxford, then spent two years in the Scots Guards as a National Serviceman.

His betrothal to Princess Alexandra in November 1962 took their circle by surprise. He was thirty-four, she twenty-five; they had been close friends and confidants for so long that their marriage had seemed an increasingly remote prospect. The wedding took place in Westminster Abbey on 24 April 1963, preceded by a spectacular party given by the Queen at Windsor Castle and organized by her inspired impresario, Lord Plunket (q.v.). Forthright and independent, Ogilvy declined a peerage; and rather than ask the Queen for a grace-and-favour house, he bought the lease – on a mortgage – of Thatched House Lodge, Richmond Park, a spacious property previously occupied by Group Captain Sir Louis Greig, former equerry and tennis partner to King George VI. Not until many years later were the couple given the use of a small apartment in St James's Palace, so that they could change for an evening engagement without driving out to Richmond Park and back.

Both Ogilvy's brothers have made successful careers in the City: David, now Earl of Airlie, as a merchant banker, and James as a stockbroker. On leaving the Army, Angus joined the group of companies formed by Harley Drayton, with widespread interests in banking and finance, television and newspapers, shipping and railways. One business in which Drayton had a substantial shareholding was an ailing Rhodesian company called Lonrho. In 1961 he despatched his bright young man, Ogilvy, to Salisbury

Angus Ogilvy with his fiancée, Princess Alexandra, and his parents, the Earl and Countess of Airlie, 1963

in search of someone to breathe fire into Lonrho. Ogilvy discovered 'Tiny' Rowland, former railwayman and farmer, who agreed to take on the task. Within fifteen years, Lonrho's annual profits rose from £150,000 to almost £100 million, and have continued to multiply.

Ogilvy's own seat on the board of Lonrho, however, was to cast a temporary shadow over his career. In 1976 a Board of Trade investigation into the company declared that he had been 'negligent' in fulfilling his duties. In a detailed refutation, Ogilvy noted fifty-eight errors of fact in the report and many wrong assumptions. Since the document was protected by legal privilege, he could not challenge the inspectors' strictures in a court of law, as he would have wished. He therefore declared that 'the only honourable thing to do' was to resign all his directorships. Two companies, to their credit, Rank Organization and MEPC, refused to accept his resignation. He has since joined the board of Sotheby's, the auction house. Angus Ogilvy's punctilious reaction to the episode was much respected in the City and beyond. At most, his judgment as a director of Lonrho may have been at fault; his probity remained intact. Even those who regretted his association with so mercurial a company as Lonrho realized his need of an ample income: not to spend on himself but to enable his wife to bear a full programme of royal engagements on what was then an in-adequate Civil List.

Angus Ogilvy devotes much hard work to charitable causes, including youth clubs, help for the aged and research into cancer and rheumatism. In spite of a painful ailment of the spine, he is, as Johnson said of Boswell, a very clubbable man: energetic, nervous, musical, drily humorous and a tremendous talker.

Paget, Lady Victor
(1892–1975)

She was Bridget, younger daughter of the first and last Baron Colebrooke, a Permanent Lord in Waiting to King George V and Master of the Robes to King Edward VIII. Her marriage to Lord Victor Paget, a brother of the 6th Marquess of Anglesey, was dissolved in 1932. Lady Victor was at one time a close friend of King Edward VIII when Prince of Wales. She used to say: 'How vulgar of those American women to call him David. Either one calls him Sir or one calls him Darling.'

Penn, Sir Arthur
(1886–1960)

Private Secretary and subsequently Treasurer to the Queen, later Queen Elizabeth the Queen Mother. Educated at Eton and Trinity College, Cambridge, he fought throughout the Great War in the Grenadier Guards, was wounded, mentioned in despatches and awarded the Military Cross and the French Croix de Guerre. Like so many young men of his generation, he was more than a little in love with Lady Elizabeth Bowes-Lyon, whom he later served with devotion. He never married. Courtly yet humorous, he was a knowledgeable student of music and painting, and excelled at innumerable pastimes: shooting, fishing, tennis, golf, gardening, carpentry, even bricklaying. He combined his royal duties with the chairmanship of King and Shaxson, the City firm of billbrokers, and left a fortune of nearly £400,000.

Philip, Prince, Duke of Edinburgh
(1921–   )

Husband of Queen Elizabeth II. He was born at Mon Repos, a royal palace in Corfu, on 10 June 1921, the only son of Prince Andrew of Greece, a brother of King Constantine I, by his wife Princess Alice of Battenberg, daughter of the 1st Marquess of Milford Haven and sister of Earl Mountbatten of Burma (qq.v.). Prince Philip's birth placed him sixth in line of succession to the Greek throne: a precarious heritage. In the autumn of 1922, Prince Andrew, who had commanded an Army Corps in the disastrous campaign against Turkey, was arrested by the revolutionary Government that had seized power in Athens. Six other scapegoats, the Commander-in-Chief and five senior ex-Ministers, were put on trial and shot. That would have been Prince Andrew's fate, too, had

Coronation rehearsal, 1953: Sir Arthur Penn

the British Government not secured his release through the efforts of an unofficial envoy.

In later years Lord Mountbatten claimed that the mission had been inspired by King George v and buttressed by the despatch of the cruiser HMS *Calypso* to the Piraeus. The truth was less colourful. George v approved of the plan but did not initiate it; and the revolutionary Government allowed Prince Andrew to leave Greece only on condition there was no overt threat by the British naval presence. HMS *Calypso*, far from steaming into Phaleron Bay with decks cleared for action, was used only to transport Prince Andrew and his family to safety. His son Philip, then aged eighteen months, was said to have been carried on board the British cruiser in an orange box. The humiliating treatment of Prince Andrew by his compatriots left a scar on his son's memory; and although in recent years Prince Philip has shown much kindness to his exiled Greek cousin, King Constantine ii, he has never displayed affection for his native land.

As Philip's parents drifted apart, he was dumped on his grandmother, the Dowager Marchioness of Milford Haven, at Kensington Palace. It became the nearest thing he had to a London home throughout a restless but not unhappy childhood. There is a mistaken belief that he was brought up by his uncle, Lord Mountbatten. It was in fact Mountbatten's elder brother, the 2nd Marquess of Milford Haven, who acted as his guardian and saw to his education. The boy lived fitfully with his mother in Paris until old enough to go to Cheam, the preparatory school in Surrey. Then came an interlude in Germany. He stayed with one of his four sisters, the wife of the Margrave of Baden, at Salem, near Lake Constance. It was here that Kurt Hahn (q.v.) had helped the Margrave's father to establish a school run on enlightened principles. When Hahn, a Jew, was driven out of German by Nazi oppression in 1933, he refounded the school at Gordonstoun, in Scotland. In the following year, Prince Philip became a pupil.

The Prince's competence at both work and games was leavened by high spirits. 'Often

naughty, never nasty,' Hahn wrote of him. He became captain of cricket and hockey, a trustworthy seaman, guardian (or head prefect) of the school. In the outdoor training and self-reliance which Gordonstoun taught lay the seeds of the Duke of Edinburgh's Award Scheme. Hahn was no sycophant, and his final report on the boy was reassuringly objective: 'Prince Philip is a born leader, but will need the exacting demands of a great service to do justice to himself. His best is outstanding – his second best is not good enough.'

In 1939 he passed into the Royal Naval College, Dartmouth, as a special entry cadet, taking sixteenth place out of thirty-four. The outstanding naval careers of a grandfather and two uncles inspired him to succeed; but it was without family influence that he won the King's Dirk as the best cadet of his year. He served throughout the war in the Mediterranean, the Far East and elsewhere. At the Battle of Matapan in 1941 he was in charge of searchlights in HMS *Valiant*. 'Thanks to his alertness and appreciation of the situation,' his Captain wrote, 'we were able to sink in five minutes two eight-inch-gun Italian cruisers.' It brought him a mention in despatches. Prince Philip also witnessed the final surrender of Japan in September 1945, on board the American battleship *Missouri* in Tokyo Bay.

The Prince first met his future wife when she visited Dartmouth with the King and Queen a few weeks before the war. She was then thirteen, he five years older. With the fair good looks of a Viking and a young man's self-confident charm, he won her heart at sight. They corresponded and sometimes he was asked to Windsor. As early as January 1941, the well-informed 'Chips' Channon, mp, met him at a cocktail party in Athens and wrote in his diary: 'He is to be our Prince Consort and that is why he is serving in our Navy.' The Greek royal family looked forward to the match. Princess Elizabeth's parents, however, were more cautious. 'We both think she is too young for that now,' the King wrote to Queen Mary in March 1944, 'as she has never met any young men of her own age.' He went on: 'I like Philip. He is intelligent, has a good sense of humour and thinks about things in the right way.'

Time seemed to be the only obstacle. In the same year the King told Mountbatten that he would like Philip to acquire British nationality so that he could help the royal family with their public duties; since the death of the Duke of Kent in 1942, there remained only himself and the Duke of Gloucester. Prince Philip had already determined to become a British subject, if for no other reason than to qualify for a permanent commission in the Royal Navy. Nor did King George of the Hellenes, as the head of his family, raise any objection. But the instability of Greek politics required the Prince to postpone his application. The future of the monarchy lay in the balance, and his change of nationality could be interpreted either as a provocative gesture of British support for the institution or as an equally unwelcome pointer to its impending collapse. Then there was the problem of the name by which he would be known. That of the Royal House of Greece and Denmark, Schleswig-Holstein-Sonderburg-Glucksburg, clearly would not do. Eventually it was decided that he should take the anglicized version of his mother's name of Battenburg. In March 1947 the London Gazette at last announced the metamorphosis of HRH Prince Philip of Greece and Denmark into Lieutenant Philip Mountbatten, Royal Navy.

The whole elaborate process, it emerged twenty-five years later, had been unnecessary. In 1972 the British courts upheld the submission of Prince Ernest Augustus of Hanover that all descendants of the Electress Sophia, the mother of King George I, were by an Act of 1705 *ipso facto* British subjects. Prince Philip, who can claim such descent through both his parents, has thus been a British subject from birth.

Even after his naturalization, he and Princess Elizabeth had to wait another four months before the King would consent to his daughter's betrothal and another three before it was solemnized in Westminster Abbey on 20 November. Lieutenant Mountbatten had in the meantime undergone further changes, in both religion

and status. In October 1947 he formally relinquished membership of the Greek Orthodox Church and was received into the Church of England by the Archbishop of Canterbury, Geoffrey Fisher (q.v.). And on the day before the wedding he was made a Royal Highness, a Knight of the Garter, Baron Greenwich, Earl of Merioneth and Duke of Edinburgh. 'It is a great deal,' the King said, 'to give a man all at once.' There was more to come. Although the Duke of Edinburgh continued to be known informally as Prince Philip, he had renounced his princely title of Greece without acquiring that of the United Kingdom; he was thus a Royal Highness but not a Prince. This anomaly was rectified in 1957, when on the advice of the Prime Minister, the Queen granted him the style and title of a Prince of the United Kingdom. He was made a Knight of the Thistle in 1952, Grand Master of the Order of the British Empire in 1953 and a member of the Order of Merit in 1968; but he does not hold, and is thought to have declined, the Grand Cross of the Royal Victorian Order, the Queen's reward for personal service.

In spite of King George VI's intention that his son-in-law should relieve him of his own burden of royal duties, few demands were made on Prince Philip. He was able for the next few years to combine marriage to the heir to the throne with his career as a naval officer. He worked in the operations division of the Admiralty; joined a staff course at the Royal Naval College, Greenwich; was posted to the Mediterranean Fleet as first lieutenant of the destroyer *Chequers*; promoted lieutenant-commander in command of the frigate *Magpie*. His uncle had meanwhile returned from India to command the 1st Cruiser Squadron, and the two couples shared the pleasures of life ashore in Malta. The Prince and Princess might have hoped to continue thus for perhaps another decade. George VI was not yet fifty-two when his daughter married, and statistically at least could be expected to reign for another twenty years. George V had died at seventy, Edward VII at sixty-eight; Queen Victoria at eighty-one, William IV at seventy-one, his father George III at eighty-one.

It was not to be. In July 1951, the King's ill health required Prince Philip to return home on indefinite leave from the Navy. He accompanied Princess Elizabeth on a tour of Canada and the United States in October, and at the end of January flew off again with his wife for East Africa, Australia and New Zealand. In Kenya, on 6 February 1952, they received news of the King's sudden death at Sandringham, and at once flew home. Grief was not their only emotion. For the new Queen it was a call to duty, premature but not altogether unexpected. For Prince Philip it seemed to signal the end of personal freedom. 'He looked as if you had dropped half the world on him,' a secretary noted. Where once he had taken the day-to-day decisions of married life, he now found his initiative courteously stifled by the Household.

The Queen heaped her husband with honours and promoted him to the highest rank in all three Services; but he was made aware of his inferior status in several unfortunate ways. Under the mistaken belief that only a Queen Consort may occupy a throne by the side of the Sovereign at the State Opening of Parliament, the Prince was until 1967 relegated to a mere chair. Queen Mary went further. She confided to a friend her opinion that the Sovereign should drive alone to and from the Abbey on Coronation Day, with her husband in a separate coach.

Although this was never seriously considered, Queen Mary had earlier been responsible for another indignity. Hearing of Lord Mountbatten's boast that the Queen's family name was now no longer Windsor but Mountbatten, she hastened to warn the Prime Minister of this apparent presumption. Churchill at once summoned the Cabinet, which formally advised the Queen to put the matter beyond doubt. This statement was accordingly issued in April 1952:

'The Queen today declared in Council her Will and Pleasure that She and Her Children shall be styled and known as the House and Family of Windsor, and that Her descendants other than female descendants who marry and their descendants shall bear the name of Windsor.'

Lord Mountbatten had in fact been correct in his claim, for he was referring only to the family name, which by English usage is that of the father. He was an experienced enough genealogist to know that the name of the Royal House remained Windsor. The Queen, by her enforced declaration of April 1952, not only reaffirmed the continuation of the House of Windsor but also deprived her descendants of the right to bear their true family name of Mountbatten. In 1960, however, after 'further consideration,' she issued a second declaration replacing the family name of Windsor by that of Mountbatten-Windsor. While removing the slur of the past eight years from Prince Philip, it otherwise served no practical purpose. The new name was to be borne only by those descendants of the Queen 'who will enjoy neither the style, title or attributes of Royal Highness, nor the titular dignity of Prince, and for whom a surname will be necessary.' Thus it will not operate until the Queen has great-grandchildren in the male line: at least until the turn of the century.

It may be mentioned in passing that the terms of the 1960 declaration were broken in 1973, when Princess Anne was married to Captain Mark Phillips. Although she was and remains both a Royal Highness and a Princess, the marriage register referred to her as 'Anne Elizabeth Alice Louise Mountbatten-Windsor.' This use of the surname in the second rather than the third generation was, Buckingham Palace stated, at the Queen's express wish and without her seeking the advice of her Ministers. It did not establish a precedent. When Prince Charles married Lady Diana Spencer in 1981, his entry in the register bore no surname.

Another pinprick inflicted on Prince Philip during the early years of the reign would scarcely be worth relating except to illustrate his magnanimity. The Sovereign is Colonel-in-Chief of all five regiments of Footguards. Each regiment also has a Colonel, sometimes but not always a member of the royal family, whose relationship with its officers and men is closer and more domestic. The Queen herself had as Princess Elizabeth been Colonel of the Grenadier

Guards from 1942 until her accession, when she became Colonel-in-Chief. In 1952, as one of the first acts of the new reign, she proposed to confer the cherished appointment of Colonel on her husband. She had reckoned without the insolence of certain senior officers of the regiment. They made it plain that while they could not refuse to accept the Prince as their new Colonel, they would not welcome him. Rather than challenge such prejudice, the Queen appointed a retired general to the vacant post.

As for Prince Philip, in the following year he became Colonel of the Welsh Guards on the retirement of the octogenarian Earl of Gowrie, VC. He was well received by a regiment proud of its friendliness and civility. 'What is unique about us?' he said one night when dining with the officers. 'I will tell you. It is the only regiment in which the Colonel is legally married to the Colonel-in-Chief.' The union was not broken until 1975, when the Prince of Wales was thought to have a higher claim on his father's appointment. The Queen, reluctant to sever her husband's long connection with the Household Troops, suggested once more that he should become Colonel of the Grenadier Guards. A less generous-minded man than Prince Philip, recalling the snub he had received from the regiment in 1952, might have refused out of hand. As it was, he accepted, and has established an agreeable relationship with a later generation of Grenadier officers.

That appointment is but one of a hundred and more diverse interests that the Prince has acquired over the years. It is tempting to compare his vigour and versatility with that of the Prince Consort, who could as soon compose a Te Deum as design a model pigsty. But the exercise would be profitless. Albert was a political animal; Philip is not. The influence of the Prince Consort lay in his assumption of the duties of Private Secretary to the Sovereign. He interviewed and wrote to her Ministers, criticized their submissions, drafted the Queen's official letters and memoranda. His role was not unconstitutional. The Prince Consort, as Gladstone put it, was a power behind the Queen, not a power behind the Throne. He helped his wife to make up her mind on all the complexities of home and foreign affairs; but the conclusions, once adopted, were hers and hers alone. She was as much entitled to draw on her husband's knowledge and opinions as on a book or newspaper.

Unlike Queen Victoria, who did not appoint a permanent Private Secretary until after her husband's death, the modern Sovereign has a small but able secretariat that undertakes all Prince Albert's political functions. There is thus no need for her to call on her husband for guidance; nor is it likely that he would wish to embroil himself in the sensitive day-to-day issues of government. But by undertaking a relentless programme of public engagements at home and abroad, he has made himself no less well informed than was Prince Albert in his day. That experience is always at the Queen's disposal.

The relationship between Prince Philip and his uncle Lord Mountbatten has been consistently exaggerated; it was one of affection and admiration but not dependence. Yet they share characteristics more often found in the thrusting professional classes than in the royal cousinage of Europe: an intelligence that does not welcome contradiction, an impatience that excludes urbanity, a warmth of heart masked by competitiveness. For all their love of polo and shooting and sailing, their knowledge of farming and wildlife, neither has been cast in the traditional mould of the country gentleman. These qualities have jarred on more lethargic contemporaries and exposed uncle and nephew to good-humoured mockery. 'He is what in our family passes for an intellectual,' a member of the royal circle once said of Prince Philip.

It is a taunt of which he need not be ashamed. He has mastered an impressive range of subjects: education, health, science, conservation, industrial relations, sport. He knows whose brains are worth picking and how to distil those loans into well-shaped and fluently delivered speeches. He does not lack self-confidence. 'I am not a graduate of any university,' he told a conference of rectors and vice-chancellors. 'I am not a humanist or a scientist, and oddly enough I don't regret it. I owe my allegiance to another of the world's few really great fraternities, the fraternity of the sea. At sea you will find all the conflicts that man has had to contend with now and in the past: the fear of the unknown, the power which is greater than man and his machines, the necessity to reconcile human frailties to scientific gadgets.'

Specialist audiences do not welcome intrusion by the inspired amateur on their preserves. After Prince Philip had visited a Cambridge college as Chancellor of the University, a senior academic observed: 'He was wonderful with the kitchen staff, quite good with the undergraduates, lamentable with the dons.' Nor do industrialists care to be told to 'pull their fingers out' or trade unionists to shake off their antidiluvian ways: at least not by a Prince hot foot from two months at Balmoral. Perhaps he finds this discouraging. 'People,' he sighs, 'would rather be bored than offended.'

Prince Philip has long tried to wean the country from this bland taste by practising what he calls dontopedalogy: the science of opening your mouth and putting your foot in it.

His sharp, bantering humour can unintentionally wound. The Queen's shoemaker did not think it funny to be told that her feet were always aching. Nor did the Brazilian admiral who was asked if he had won his dazzling display of medals on the artificial lake of his country's capital, Brasilia. 'Yes, Sir,' the victim replied, 'not by marriage.' Sometimes the Prince's words are misrepresented. He was not lacking in sympathy for the unemployed when he envied their leisure. And possibly he was not on oath in his greeting to General Stroessner, the long-serving dictator of Paraguay: 'It's a pleasant change to be in a country that isn't ruled by its people.'

The Press is a favourite target, perhaps because the Prince was now and again included in the vendetta waged by Lord Beaverbrook against the Mountbattens. At least Prince Philip has been able to dispel the legend that the royal family cannot hit back. 'The *Daily Express*,' he said, 'is a bloody awful newspaper. It is full of

lies, scandal and imagination.' There was also some good clean fun when he visited Gibraltar and threw nuts indiscriminately at the apes and the journalists. But he was wrongly accused of having turned a garden spray on the Press at the Chelsea Flower Show; it was one of his sycophants.

Occasional saloon-bar jokes about modern art have brought Prince Philip the undeserved label of philistine. It is an absurd caricature of a man who has made discerning additions to the royal collections; personally designed a charming new fountain for the private gardens of Windsor Castle; and shown a talent for painting landscapes that would adorn any summer exhibition at Burlington House. ('You paint like royalty,' Lord Beaverbrook assured Arnold Bennett, but the artist was not flattered.)

Prince Philip adopts a broad canvas, too, for both the spoken and the written word. It is a bold and well-read man who delivers the Rede Lecture at Cambridge on the theme of *Philosophy, Politics, Administration*. His search for truth emerges in *A Windsor Correspondence*, an exchange of letters with the Dean of Windsor, Michael Mann (q.v.) on Christianity and evolution. It reveals what might already have been suspected: his attachment more to the ethics of Christianity than to its doctrine. It is all part of his determination to get to the root of things, whether photographing birds or driving a four-in-hand; the economics of shooting pheasants at Sandringham and growing mushrooms at Windsor; the education of his children and the art of cooking sausages on television.

For almost forty years, this able, stimulating, provocative man has complemented and fortified the work of the Queen without ever attempting to eclipse her in the public mind. Suggestions that he be given some distinctive title are not new. 'It is a strange omission in our constitution,' Queen Victoria wrote in 1856, 'that while the wife of the King has the highest rank and dignity in the realm after her husband assigned to her by law, the husband of a Queen regnant is entirely ignored by law.' In the earliest days of her reign, Queen Victoria urged her first

Prime Minister to give Prince Albert the title of King Consort. Melbourne was horrified. 'Let's hear no more of it, Ma'am,' he advised, 'for if you once get the English people into the way of making Kings, you will get them into the way of unmaking them.' So eventually she compromised on the title of Prince Consort. It would add as little to Philip as it did to Albert; for no man deserves recognition more nor needs it less.

Phillips, Captain Mark
(1948–   )

Husband of Princess Anne (q.v.). He is the only son of Major P. W. G. Phillips, MC, late 1st King's Dragoon Guards, by his wife Anne Patricia Tiarks, daughter of a brigadier in her husband's regiment. He is thus descended from the Rev. Johann Tiarks, a pastor of the Reformed Lutheran Church, who emigrated from Germany in 1820 and became chaplain to the Duchess of Kent, Queen Victoria's mother. Captain Phillips is also a kinsman of the celebrated Miss Adeline Horsey de Horsey, who married the 7th Earl of Cardigan, leader of the Charge of the Light Brigade, and outlived her irascible husband by almost half a century.

Mark Phillips was educated at Marlborough and Sandhurst and in 1969 commissioned into the 1st The Queen's Dragoon Guards (as his father's and grandfather's regiment had now become after amalgamation). On 14 November 1973 in Westminster Abbey he married Princess Anne. In the following year the Queen appointed him one of her personal Aides-de-Camp and a Commander of the Royal Victorian Order. He retired from the Army in 1978 to become a student at the Royal Agricultural College, Cirencester, and to farm at Gatcombe Park, Gloucestershire: formerly the property of the Conservative statesman Lord Butler and a century earlier the home of the economist David Ricardo.

Phillips shares with Princess Anne a love of country life and horses. He is an Olympic gold medallist and was four times winner of the Badminton Three-Day Event. In spite of his equestrian brilliance, it is said that some members of his wife's family do not find him as clever as they; but the intellectual gulf has probably been exaggerated. To all such rumours and to Princess Anne's strong personality he responds with good humour. 'Well,' he said on the birth of his son Peter in 1977, 'at least I've done something right.' He won another rosette in 1981 with the birth of his daughter Zara.

Plunket, Patrick, 7th Baron
(1923–1975)

Deputy Master of the Household to Queen Elizabeth II. He came of a colourful line. The 1st Baron was for ten years Lord Chancellor of Ireland, during which, it was said in the English House of Commons, he annually amassed for himself and his family offices worth £28,000, or £700,000 in the currency of 1985. The 2nd Baron was a Bishop; the 3rd a Queen's Counsel; the 4th an Archbishop; the 5th Governor-General of New Zealand; the 6th, with his wife, was killed in air crash, leaving his eldest son Patrick orphaned at fourteen.

Educated at Eton and Magdalene College, Cambridge, Plunket served in the Irish Guards during the war and was wounded. He was successively equerry to George VI and to the present Queen who in 1954 appointed him Deputy Master of the Household. Handsome and debonair, he was one of those bachelors of easy manners and taste who are always in demand at court. His flair for entertainment was exceptional. King Edward VII used to say: 'I do not know much about *Arrt*, but I think I know something about *Arrangement*.' Patrick Plunket knew about both. He liked the challenge of a splendid occasion and met it with imagination and panache. There would be vast pyramids of white flowers: delphiniums and eremurus and peonies; or a whole syringa tree in bloom, rising from a great malachite pot. And along the tables would be ranged treasure troves of silver unused since the reign of George IV. Sometimes he would create a palace, sometimes a country house: never an hotel.

Plunket contributed much ingenuity to the conversion of the private chapel at Buckingham Palace, badly damaged during wartime air-raids, into a public picture gallery. The Queen's Gallery, opened in 1962, has since displayed the richness and variety of the royal collections.

His knowledge was also in demand as a trustee of both the Wallace Collection and the National

Patrick Plunket

Prince Philip at the Royal Windsor Horse Show, 1984

Mark Phillips at Badminton, 1978

Art-Collections Fund. As a private collector, he acquired many a bargain. Among them was an oil sketch by Rubens, *The Death of Hippolytus*, picked up cheaply in the saleroom because there were doubts about its authenticity which Plunket did not share. When the experts at length confirmed his judgment, its value soared. It was later accepted by the Government in lieu of death duties on Plunket's estate, and assigned to the Fitzwilliam Museum, Cambridge.

Plunket died at the age of fifty-one after a long and distressing illness. Another of his pictures, *A Coast Scene in Normandy* by Bonington, was given to the Queen by his family in memory of her servant and friend. The Queen in turn chose and gave the site for a memorial to him in the Valley Gardens, Windsor Great Park: a little wooden temple containing a seat that overlooks Virginia Water. Plunket's friends raised a fund to build the pavilion and also to endow scholarships in the art of preserving ancient buildings.

Ponsonby, Sir Frederick, later 1st Baron Sysonby
(1867–1935)

Keeper of the Privy Purse to King George V. The second son of Sir Henry Ponsonby, Queen Victoria's Private Secretary, Fritz (as his family and friends called him) was educated at Eton and commissioned into the Duke of Cornwall's Light Infantry, from which regiment he transferred to the Grenadier Guards. As aide-de-camp to Lord Elgin when Viceroy of India he was selected in 1895 to become equerry and assistant private secretary to the Queen, remaining at court for the last forty years of his life. He did, however, extricate himself to serve in the South African War in 1901–02, and again in the Great War when at the age of forty-seven he rejoined the Grenadiers as a junior officer, fought on the Western Front and was mentioned in despatches.

Ponsonby was loyal and industrious, a master of medals and decorations, and in time an unrivalled authority on what his mother called 'all the little miseries of etiquette.' Yet he was too outspoken to be the perfect courtier, and his long career was punctuated by differences with three successive Sovereigns. He offended Queen Victoria by disparaging the social pretensions of her Indian Secretary and favourite, the Munshi Abdul Karim; for a year she barely spoke to him and never once asked him to dine. His independence of mind and unsought advice made Edward VII (whom he served as assistant private secretary) bellow with rage. And of his years with George V, he wrote: 'The King hated all insincerity and flattery, but after a time he got so accustomed to people agreeing with him that he resented the candid friend business. At one time he took a dislike to me as he thought I invariably disagreed with any views he happened to express, but after a time regarded me as an unavoidable critic.'

That ungracious confession scarcely took account of the King's self-doubts and lack of confidence, particularly during the early part of the reign. He had one candid courtier in Sir Charles Cust (q.v.); two could be depressing. The King nevertheless promoted Ponsonby to be Keeper of the Privy Purse and Treasurer, loaded him with stars and ribbons and in 1935 made him a peer, albeit with reluctance. (The Prime Minister, Ramsay MacDonald, had proposed the King's Private Secretary, Sir Clive Wigram, for a peerage. The King thought Ponsonby less deserving, but with characteristic kindness did not want to wound his feelings by ennobling one old servant and not another.)

Fritz Ponsonby was tall and thin, as elegant on the grouse moor as at a court ball. He expected the same sartorial perfection in others, and would condemn to social extinction any man who wore suede shoes or too shiny a set of buttons on his tail coat. Both writing and painting found a place in his busy life. To the annoyance of the King and the ex-Kaiser he published in 1927 an unauthorized edition of the letters of the Kaiser's mother, the Empress Frederick, Queen Victoria's eldest daughter. He also liked to try his hand at copying old masters from the royal collection. The King jocularly maintained that Fritz used to keep the originals after replacing them by his copies.

Had Ponsonby been so enterprising, it might at least have relieved his perennial shortage of money. In youth he gambled, once losing £500, twenty times that sum in the currency of today, during a single night's play at baccarat; and having married and produced a family on the slender stipend of an equerry, he was never free from financial worry. This he tried to alleviate in

a number of ingenious ways. Among his unfruitful schemes were writing film scripts and raising the treasure of King John from the Wash.

Pope-Hennessy, James
(1916–1974)

Biographer of Queen Mary. The younger son of Major-General L.H.R. Pope-Hennessy and Dame Una Pope-Hennessy, the biographer of

James Pope-Hennessy

Dickens, he was also the brother of Sir John Pope-Hennessy, director of the British Museum. Educated at Downside School and Balliol College, Oxford, he served briefly and resentfully as private secretary to the Governor of Trinidad and Tobago, then from 1940 to 1944 in the War Office.

He established his reputation as a biographer with a two-volume life of Monckton Milnes, Lord Houghton, the Victorian man of letters, social reformer and friend of Swinburne. The life of his own grandfather, Sir John Pope-Hennessy, the colonial governor, also brought him much praise. It was from Lady Pope-Hennessy that James inherited a measure of Malayan blood and oriental good looks: high cheekbones, straight black hair, dark hooded eyes and a pallid complexion.

The most acclaimed of Pope-Hennessy's seventeen books was *Queen Mary*, published in 1959. It remains the masterpiece of royal biographies: lively yet respectful, impeccable scholarship dowered with Proustian insight, as much a smiling intimate portrait as an evocation of a vanished age. He also wrote some literary sketches, much enjoyed by his friends but published only after his death, of those whom he had interviewed while writing *Queen Mary*. They not only reflect his sharpness of eye and ear but also offer some enticing footnotes to history. It astonished some readers of his portrait of the Duke of Windsor to learn that the Duke, having contributed £4,000 of the £8,000 required to put up a monument to King George v at Windsor, was not invited to the ceremony of dedication; and that in 1951, when writing *A King's Story*, the Duke was refused permission by Winston Churchill to quote from letters Churchill had sent him during the Abdication crisis, in case they should mar his chances of winning the impending general election.

Pope-Hennessy also wrote with characteristic irreverence: 'It is *courtiers* who make Royalty frightened and frightening: taken neat ... they are perfectly all right. This does not mean that they are as others, but you can get on to plain terms with the species, like an ornithologist

making friends with some rare wild duck.'

Good-humoured irony was only one of Pope-Hennessy's many gifts. He was scintillating in conversation, affectionate and generous in friendship, free from any prejudice of class or colour. Yet he was also burdened by misfortune of his own making. He squandered an ample income on disastrous sexual liaisons and other extravagances. In 1974, at the age of fifty-eight, he died at the hands of some disreputable acquaintances who, having heard him boast of the huge sums promised for his as yet unwritten life of Noel Coward (q.v.), were naïve enough to suppose that he kept the money in his house and brutal enough to murder him for it. It was a tragic end which shocked yet did not altogether surprise his friends.

Probyn, General Sir Dighton
(1833–1924)

As a cavalry officer during the Indian Mutiny of 1857 he won the Victoria Cross; but few ever set eyes on the decoration, which lay concealed behind a patriarchal beard that flowed down to his navel. He joined the household of the future Edward vii in 1872, serving first the King and later the widowed Queen Alexandra for almost half a century. As Comptroller and Treasurer he did not find it easy to inspire thrift in either the Sovereign or his Consort. King Edward dissolved his own early debts by making almost half a million pounds from his stud of racehorses; but not even Probyn's quixotic refusal to accept a salary from Queen Alexandra could balance the accounts of his improvident but adored 'Blessed Lady'. He was still struggling to manage her uneasy finances when he died at the age of ninety-one.

Sharp-tongued and choleric, with a detestation of Irish Home Rule, Indian Nationalism and Jews, Probyn was sometimes subdued by apoplectic fits. Queen Mary once witnessed such a collapse, and the difficulty of bystanders in

General Sir Dighton Probyn, V.C.

opening the tight collar of his uniform; thereafter she always carried a sharp penknife in her reticule.

Ramsay, Lady Patricia
(1886–1974)

She was born Princess Patricia of Connaught, the younger daughter of the Duke of Connaught (q.v.), Queen Victoria's third son, and his wife Princess Louise of Prussia. The Duchess of Connaught, the child of an unhappy marriage that had ended in separation, proved a domineering partner and an unsympathetic mother. She insisted that Princess Patricia, or Patsy as she was called in the family, should wear her sister's cast-off clothing: a custom often followed in even the most aristocratic of Victorian households. What went beyond the

Lady Patricia Ramsay and her infant son

bounds of acceptable thrift was the Duchess's refusal to provide her daughter with well-fitting shoes. To the end of her days, the Princess suffered from painfully deformed feet.

Nor, until she was thirty-three, could Princess Patricia marry the man of her choice: the Hon. Alexander Ramsay, a younger son of the 13th Earl of Dalhousie and a serving naval officer. For more than a decade she was deterred from accepting his repeated proposals by a lack of self-confidence that her mother did nothing to discourage as well as the custom that princesses should not marry commoners. It is true that in 1871 her aunt Princess Louise, Queen Victoria's fourth daughter, had married the Marquess of Lorne (qq.v.); and that in 1889 another Princess Louise, the eldest daughter of the Prince and Princess of Wales, had married the Earl of Fife (qq.v.). Unlike Captain Ramsay, however, both those suitors were heirs to great estates; Lorne succeeded his father as 9th Duke of Argyll and Fife was created a Duke. The death of the Duchess of Connaught in 1917 removed the most implacable opponent of her daughter's love match; and in 1919 the more relaxed, postwar attitude of King George v allowed him to smile on Princess Patsy's desire.

Two days before her wedding in Westminster Abbey, she asked to relinquish her royal style and title, and was henceforth known as Lady Patricia Ramsay. For the next fifty-five years she led an almost entirely private life. The public knew of her only as an accomplished artist in oils, water colours, pen-and-ink and gouache, who exhibited her work with reluctance. Her early paintings were of flowers, marine life and tropical vegetation. Later she turned to abstracts, experimenting boldly with bright colours and strong contrasts that owed something to Gauguin and Van Gogh. Her cousin Princess Marie Louise called them 'modern, very modern,' which she did not intend to be a compliment.

Alexander Ramsay, who was knighted in 1937 and retired with the rank of admiral in 1942, died in 1972. Lady Patricia outlived him by two years.

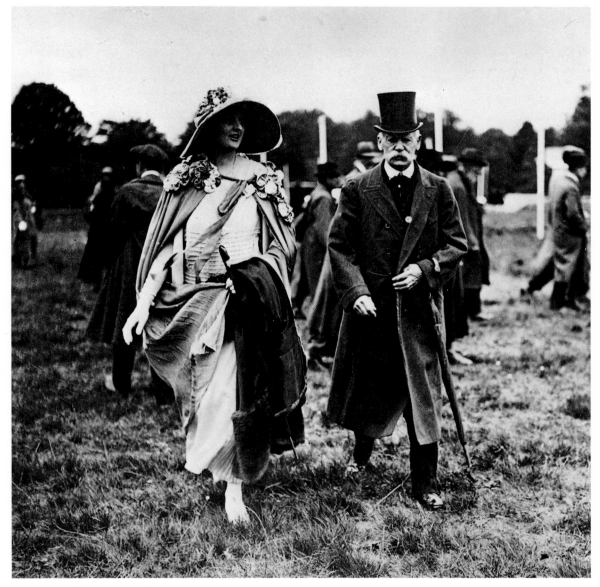

The Duke of Richmond and his guest. Royal Ascot, 1923

Richmond, Charles Henry, 7th Duke of
(1845–1928)

Host to King George v and Queen Mary each summer for Goodwood races, in Sussex. The royal party were entertained to a succession of elaborate meals, the menus for which were submitted to Buckingham Palace for approval each April. Nearly forty specially hired servants crowded into the house a mile from the racecourse, as well as an orchestra. The Duke's grandson once attached a pedometer to the butler, Mr Marshall, for a single day in race-week; it registered nineteen and a half miles. The Duke celebrated the departure of his royal guests by dining off plain beef and carrots.

The tradition of hospitality was continued by his son, the 8th Duke, and his grandson, the 9th and present Duke, skilled alike as a painter and motor-racing driver. Whenever the Sovereign won a race, the trophy was placed on the table at dinner that night, surrounded by home-grown magnolias. One year the electricity supply failed just before the Queen arrived. The Duke sent to nearby Chichester for 200 candles and borrowed a pair of generators from an RAF station. The sound of revelry by night, a family tradition, thus went uninterrupted.

State business, however, sometimes intruded. Five plaques in the drawing-room of Goodwood House record that successive Sovereigns have presided over meetings of the Privy Council in race-week; Edward VII in 1908; George V in 1924 and Elizabeth II in 1953, 1955 and 1957.

Rigby, Sir Hugh
(1870–1944)

Surgeon to successive Sovereigns. In 1917 he successfully operated on Prince Albert, later King George VI, to short-circuit a gastric ulcer that for the past two years had eluded diagnosis by other medical authorities and caused the poor young prince untold pain and discomfort. Rigby was assisted in his task by Sir Frederick Treves, who in 1902 had so deftly removed Edward VII's appendix that the patient was able to sit up on the following morning and smoke a cigar.

In December 1928, before either sulphonamides or antibiotics were available for the treatment of toxic infections, Rigby's surgical skill was again in demand at Buckingham Palace. As George V almost succumbed to a general septicaemia of the blood, Rigby removed one of the King's ribs so that the seat of the infection, an abscess behind the diaphragm, could be drained. Although the operation brought the patient instant relief, and indeed saved his life, fragments of the bone remaining at the site of the incision prevented the wound from healing for several months. Rather than cause public alarm, the King nevertheless agreed to attend a Thanksgiving Service at Westminster Abbey in July 1929. But he was furious with his doctors and surgeons. 'Fancy a Thanksgiving

Sir Hugh Rigby, 1920

Service,' he told them, 'with an open wound in your back!' He was obliged to endure yet another visit to the operating theatre, and later could be heard complaining to a Cabinet Minister: 'They called it a minor operation, Mr Lansbury, and they opened me from *here* to *here*.'

Roussin, René

Chef de cuisine to King George VI. He carried the majestic style of the Edwardian Age up to the very brink of World War II. Here is but one stage in the preparation of his *cailles à la royale*, served at Windsor on 14 June 1938 to the Ascot

Week guests of the King and Queen: 'The heads of the quails are at this stage rejoined to the breasts, being held in place by concealed wooden toothpicks. It is usual to make eyes for the heads by putting a minute round of truffle in the centre of a little circle of white of egg.'

Yet Roussin was not a proud man, and would as contentedly cook kippers for the King, albeit in his distinctive way. The fish were successively boned, forced through a wire sieve, gently cooked with béchamel sauce, blended with fresh cream and a liberal pinch of cayenne pepper, spread on toast, put in the oven, garnished with parsley and served very hot on a folded table napkin.

Runcie, The Most Rev. Robert
(1921–)

Archbishop of Canterbury since 1980. The grandson of a Scottish draper and son of the chief electrical engineer at the Tate & Lyle sugar refinery in Liverpool, he grew up in modest circumstances. His father had to retire through failing eyesight, and by 1939 was quite blind. This imposed both financial and emotional strains on the family. Among Robert's lighter duties were taking his father to football matches and describing the play; he was also required to

Archbishop Runcie and the Princess of Wales, 1982

read aloud the latest racing news. From Merchant Taylors' School, Crosby, he won scholarships to Brasenose College, Oxford, where he spent four terms before being called up for the Army.

Service in the Senior Training Corps at Oxford entitled him to express a choice of regiment. Proud of his Scots blood, he suggested the King's Own Scottish Borderers. He was instead invited to consider the Scots Guards, who had suffered severe casualties in North Africa and were in search of reinforcements. In reply to his worried inquiry about the need for a private income, Runcie was told that in wartime even officers of the Brigade of Guards could live on their pay. So he took the King's shilling, went through gruelling courses at Pirbright and Sandhurst, and emerged as an ensign, or second-lieutenant, in the 3rd (Tank) Battalion of the Scots Guards. Many of his brother officers came from landed families; all had been to public schools, mostly Eton. At first he felt, and perhaps was made to feel, an intruder. But his exceptional good humour and strength of character rapidly won him friendships that endure to this day.

Almost all those with whom he served were later to play a role in national life. They included William (later Viscount) Whitelaw, the Home Secretary; Sir Charles (later Lord Maclean, q.v.), Chief Scout and Lord Chamberlain; Lord Cathcart, major-general and a deputy-Speaker of the House of Lords; Lord Michael Fitzalan-Howard, major-general and Marshal of the Diplomatic Corps; Lord Bruce (later Earl of Elgin), president of the Boys' Brigade and Lord High Commissioner to the General Assembly of the Church of Scotland; Peter Balfour, chairman of Scottish and Newcastle Breweries; and Sir Hector Laing, chairman of United Biscuits. The chaplain of the battalion, the Rev. George Reid, became a chaplain to the Queen and Moderator of the General Assembly of the Church of Scotland.

A week before the invasion of German-occupied France in June 1944, Runcie entered Canterbury Cathedral for the first time to attend a service of dedication. But the Scots Guards did not cross the Channel until mid-July. They then fought their way through closely wooded country unsuitable for armoured warfare and suffered heavy casualties. Runcie was fortunate to survive the entire campaign without a scratch. He won the Military Cross for leading his tanks into an exposed position under fire to destroy enemy guns that were holding up the advance. In the last days of the war he made history as a tank commander by capturing a German submarine that lay off the Baltic coast.

Returning to Oxford in 1946, he read Greats: a searching test of classics, philosophy and history that makes it the most arduous of university disciplines. His industry and concentration, all the more impressive after five years as a soldier, brought him a coveted First Class. But he was no hermit. He played cricket and hockey and was elected president of the Brasenose junior common room. To balance an earlier allegiance to Labour politics, Runcie joined the Conservative association; his frivolity, however, incurred the disapproval of a former president called Miss Roberts, who as Margaret Thatcher would one day uphold Tory orthodoxy on a larger stage.

Shrinking, as his contemporaries supposed, from the rough and tumble of public life, he determined to take Holy Orders. He studied theology at Westcott House, Cambridge, was ordained in 1950 and spent the next two years as a curate on Tyneside. Much as he enjoyed his pastoral duties, he felt drawn to the academic world, which welcomed so promising a recruit. From 1952 until his consecration as Bishop of St Albans in 1969 he was successively chaplain and vice-principal of Westcott House, dean and assistant tutor of Trinity Hall, Cambridge, and principal of Cuddesdon College, Oxford.

In 1957 he married Rosalind Turner, daughter of J. W. Cecil Turner, reader in law at Trinity Hall. They spent their honeymoon in Nice, where Robert acted as *locum tenens* to the Anglican chaplain: an undemanding post except for the decrepitude of his flock which obliged him to conduct three funerals during the first week. In 1960 the comfort and stimulation of

Cambridge gave way to nine austere years at Cuddesdon. They cannot have been easy for a young wife with two small children. Tradition imposed a monastic regime on staff and students alike, whether married or celibate. All meals except lunch on Saturdays had to be eaten in college; women were scarcely ever allowed on the premises; wives and fiancées of ordinands had to live at least two miles away. Not even the enlightened Runcies could make more than a token dent in the heartless system they inherited. 'Lindy' Runcie would sometimes declare: 'Too much religion makes me go pop.' One solace to her fitful loneliness was the love of music she had inherited from her grandfather, a tenor with the Carl Rosa opera company. Both enjoyed the cruises run by Swan Tours during which Robert lectured on classical sites in the eastern Mediterranean; one reform which he refused to make at Cuddesdon was the relaxation of compulsory Greek.

It came as no surprise either to the Church of England or to Runcie himself when in 1969 the Prime Minister, Harold Wilson, submitted his name to the Queen as Bishop of St Albans. His duties took him far beyond the diocese. He presided over a national reorganization of theological colleges and accepted the chairmanship of both the commission for reunion with the Orthodox Churches and the committee which advises the BBC and its rivals on religious broadcasting. Such was the confidence Runcie inspired that after only five years at St Albans he was asked to succeed Donald Coggan, the new Archbishop of Canterbury, as Archbishop of York – admittedly after two other candidates had refused. He decided that he could not yet abandon his diocese. In 1979, however, there came a more pressing request: that on Coggan's retirement he should become Archbishop of Canterbury and Primate of All England. Mrs Runcie, who enjoyed giving piano lessons and writing a music column for the *Hertfordshire Advertiser*, had no doubt what her husband's answer should be. 'The only way I ever want to leave St Albans,' she declared defiantly, 'is feet first in a coffin.'

He too hesitated, and at No. 10 Downing Street discussed the appointment with the Prime Minister. Mrs Thatcher asked him for his decision as soon as possible. By the time he had made up his mind, she was in Lusaka for the conference of Commonwealth Prime Ministers. In the middle of one session there was an interruption as a despatch box of the utmost urgency arrived for Mrs Thatcher. Her secretary unlocked it and handed her a single strip of paper. Under the gaze of a hundred anxious eyes, she read: 'Runcie accepts.' In such bizarre circumstances he agreed to become the 102nd Archbishop of Canterbury. He is also the first to have been chosen not by the Prime Minister but by the Crown Appointments Commission: a body of clergy and laymen which presents two names to the Prime Minister, who in turn selects one of them for submission to the Sovereign. But there is no reason to believe that Mrs Thatcher would have made a different choice if acting alone. Any prelate who kept pigs for a hobby, it was surmised, must surely be a Stanley Baldwin at heart. The Government paid him the compliment of postponing Budget Day by twenty-four hours so that the Cabinet and other Members of Parliament could attend his enthronement in Canterbury Cathedral.

As a churchman, Runcie displays conservative beliefs, at least when measured against the endemic radicalism of almost the entire bench of bishops. He is cautious about permitting remarriage in church after divorce and welcoming homosexuals into the priesthood. He also opposes the ordination of women, not on theological grounds but because it would obstruct reunion with the Orthodox Churches. Runcie made another ecumenical gesture by receiving Pope John Paul II at Canterbury. Indeed, there is nowadays scarcely any great Anglican occasion to which representatives of other faiths are not bidden.

Politically, the Archbishop has sometimes followed in the wake of his predecessor, William Temple, by embroiling himself in economic problems for which there are no specifically Christian solutions: the coal strike of 1984, for

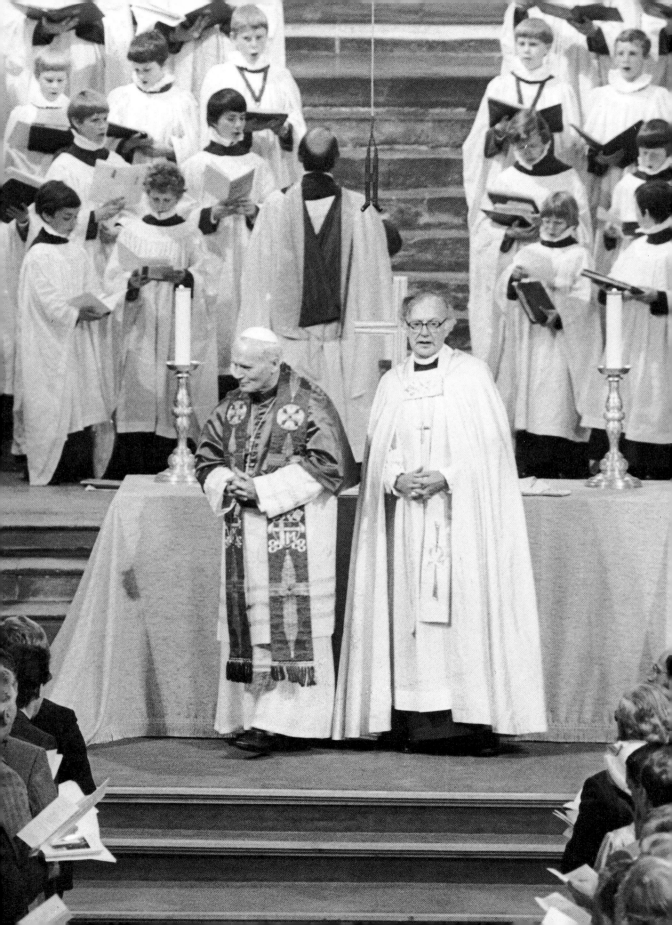

instance. The most controversial of all his sermons was that preached at St Paul's Cathedral after the Falklands campaign of 1982. Instead of exulting over a fallen enemy, as some expected, he told a congregation that included Mrs Thatcher and her Cabinet: 'War is a sign of human failure and everything we say and do in this service must be in that context.' The Archbishop continued: 'In our prayers we shall quite rightly remember those who are bereaved in our own country and the relatives of the young Argentinian soldiers who were killed. Common sorrow could do something to reunite those who were engaged in this struggle. A shared anguish can be a bridge of reconciliation.' It was the voice not only of a Christian but also of the first Archbishop of Canterbury ever to have borne arms for his King and country.

In May 1985, his sermon in Westminster Abbey on the fortieth anniversary of Victory in Europe won a wider acceptance. He described how, during the Allied Liberation of Holland, he had seen a parish priest encourage his flock to empty their houses of furniture and throw it into the river to form a causeway for the tanks of the Scots Guards. 'I was moved and humbled by their sacrifice,' the Archbishop said.

'What an unctuous bugger,' Runcie once heard his father exclaim during a broadcast by Archbishop Lang. That is not a failing of the present Archbishop. In private life he is the kindest and most generous-minded of men, with an irreverent sense of humour. He likes, for instance, to recall the notice he saw on the frontier between Israel and Jordan: 'Double crossing is allowed only to diplomats and to certain bishops.' His sermons are simple and sincere, yet worthy of any national occasion. 'Here is the stuff of which fairy tales are made,' were his opening words at the wedding of the Prince of Wales. And at the service for the eightieth birthday of the Queen Mother, he quoted from an earlier Queen Elizabeth: 'Though God has raised me high, yet this I count the glory of my crown, that I have reigned with your loves.' Runcie had caught both the mood of the hour and the spirit of the dynasty.

Archbishop Runcie with Pope John Paul II. Canterbury Cathedral, 1982

Salisbury, Frank O.
(1874–1962)

Painter of royal portraits and public occasions. The son of a plumber and glazier, he was born in Hertfordshire, educated mostly at home and apprenticed to a manufacturer of stained glass at St Albans.

He continued to paint grandiose compositions on historical themes long after the genre had ceased to appeal to public taste. A characteristic example, completed in 1910, hangs in the East Corridor of the House of Commons: *Henry VIII and Catherine of Aragon before the Papal Legate at Blackfriars*. Later examples, equally rich in colour and complex in design, include *The Burial of the Unknown Warrior* (1920) and *The Heart of the Empire* (1935), recording the Service of Thanksgiving for King George V's Silver Jubilee. He was unfortunate, however, in depicting the wedding in 1922 of Princess Mary to Viscount Lascelles (qq.v.). Cramped for space on his canvas, he deliberately omitted one of the bridesmaids. His choice of victim could hardly have been less inspired. It was Lady Elizabeth Bowes-Lyon, who in the following year became Duchess of York and in 1936 Queen.

Although Salisbury's portraits were said to owe something to the photographer's art, he was called upon to paint many members of the royal family, five Presidents of the United States, five British Prime Ministers and three Archbishops of Canterbury. He exhibited at the Royal Academy for the first time in 1899 and was disappointed never to be elected a member. King George VI made him a Commander of the Royal Victorian Order and he was similarly honoured by the King of Italy.

Salisbury cultivated an opulent style. He built himself a sham-Jacobean house in Hampstead which he called Sarum Chase; drove his own Rolls-Royce; and dressed, as Sir Kenneth Clark wrote, 'like a Harley Street gout specialist, with purple stock and cameo tie-pin.'

Salisbury, Robert Gascoyne-Cecil, 5th Marquess of
(1893–1972)

Statesman and friend of the royal family. He was the eldest son of the 4th Marquess, grandson of the 3rd Marquess, Queen Victoria's last Prime Minister, and a descendant of William Cecil, Lord Burghley, Queen Elizabeth I's Lord High Treasurer.

Brought up at Hatfield, the most political house in England, he was given leave as an Eton schoolboy to watch the House of Lords throw out Lloyd George's Budget of 1909. From Christ Church, Oxford, he joined the Grenadier Guards in 1914, but appendicitis at first caused his rejection for active service. He overcame the caution of the medical board by promising he would drink a glass of milk at 11 o'clock each morning in the trenches. Lord Cranborne (as he was known until succeeding to his father's marquessate in 1947) fought with his battalion and was awarded the French Croix de Guerre before being invalided home. After the war he worked in the City as a billbroker, then sought election to the House of Commons. From 1929 until 1941, when he was called up to the House of Lords in his father's lifetime, he sat for South Dorset, where the family have substantial estates.

'The Cecils,' Winston Churchill used to say, 'are always ill or resigning.' The first of Cranborne's two quixotic resignations took place in 1938 when, as Parliamentary Under-Secretary at the Foreign Office, he followed his Secretary of State, Anthony Eden, into the wilderness in protest at Neville Chamberlain's supine attitude towards the dictators. Churchill, however, recalled both men to join his Coalition Government in 1940. Cranborne occupied a succession of Cabinet offices and was Leader of the House of Lords from 1942. He is believed to have refused the Viceroyalty of India owing to indifferent health, but served in the post-war

Governments of Churchill and Eden. In January 1957, on Eden's resignation after the Suez venture, he was asked to advise the Queen in her choice of a new Prime Minister. Salisbury (as he had become in 1947) conducted a personal poll of leading Conservatives to discover whether they favoured 'Rab' Butler or Harold Macmillan. 'Well,' he inquired, with his much-imitated difficulty in pronouncing the letter 'r,' 'is it to be Wab or Hawold?'

Having helped to secure the premiership for Macmillan, to whom he was related by marriage, he remained in the reconstructed Cabinet for only two months before resigning. This time he disapproved of the decision to negotiate with Archbishop Makarios, the Cypriot leader, over the future of the island. Until then it had been widely thought that Salisbury was indispensable to any Conservative Government; but in a political climate already affected by Macmillan's wind of change, his departure created scarcely a ripple. He remained active, however, in defence of the white settler's dwindling role in Africa, particularly in Rhodesia. A man of exceptional courtesy in private life, he was nevertheless a hard-hitting politician who in 1961 offended his own party by publicly describing the Colonial Secretary, Iain Macleod, as 'too clever by half'; and by comparing his methods to those habitually displayed at the bridge table. Salisbury could take as well as give hard knocks. When during a debate in the Lords on Rhodesia he omitted to make the customary declaration of his financial interests there, another peer explained sarcastically: 'Of course whereas we have interests, the Cecils have responsibilities.' And in reply to Salisbury's plea on behalf of Britain's 'kith and kin' in Rhodesia, President Kaunda of Zambia observed: 'I don't suppose many of them get past the gates of Hatfield House without paying half a crown.'

'Bobbety' Salisbury loved his family home and made it more beautiful than at any time since its completion in 1612 by the 1st Earl. Like all Cecils, he took an aggressive interest in Anglican liturgy and would brook no interference from cleric or layman in the order of

The Marquess of Salisbury by Orpen

worship of his private chapel. The Bishop of St Albans once suggested that this quatrain be omitted from the hymn 'All things Bright and Beautiful':

The rich man in his castle,
The poor man at his gate,
God made them, high or lowly,
And order'd their estate.

Salisbury refused. He believed in an established society and the virtues of hereditary rule. But that did not preclude either an unselfish nature or a modest, even frugal private life. After hearing a fully choral morning service in the chapel at Hatfield, he might catch a Green Line bus to Westminster; and a junior official, waiting for him by appointment in the House of Lords, would hear the Lord President of the Council running down the passage so that his visitor should not be kept waiting. Sometimes, however, he seemed to lack the common touch. He was in his seventies before he visited Brighton for the first time, to speak at a Conservative conference. 'Yes,' he said of that popular resort, 'it is just as one imagined it would be.'

A lifelong friend of the royal family, Salisbury was one of seven new Knights of the Garter created by King George VI after the Order had become the Sovereign's personal prerogative in 1946. It was Queen Elizabeth the Queen Mother, whom he had known since the days of their youth in Hertfordshire, who gave him portraits of his ancestors to hang at Hatfield: one of the great Lord Burghley, another of Robert, 1st Earl of Salisbury. Year after year in successive reigns, he and his wife, a daughter of Lord Richard Cavendish, would be asked to Balmoral. There he would be serenaded on his birthday with verses composed by Arthur Penn (q.v.); and in spite of the spectacles which perched on his nose, he acquitted himself well in the grouse butts. But he was no match for the Queen Mother when they played that most cunning of card games, racing demon, after dinner. 'Oh, ma'am,' he sighed, 'I am suwwounded by howwible, howwible Queens.'

He died in his seventy-ninth year after much silent suffering and is buried at Hatfield.

Sargent, Sir Malcolm
(1895–1967)

Orchestral conductor. The son of a coal merchant and amateur musician, he was educated at Stamford School and articled to Haydn Keeton, the organist of Peterborough Cathedral. In 1914 Sargent became organist of Melton Mowbray parish church, an appointment interrupted by war service in the 27th Durham Light Infantry. He received generous help from local patrons that enabled him to become a pupil of Benno Moiseiwitsch. At twenty-four he was the youngest Doctor of Music in the country. Sir Henry Wood invited him to conduct his composition, 'Impressions on a Windy Day' in the 1921 season of the Promenade Concerts, the beginning of an association that was to bring him immense popular acclaim. The most versatile and reliable of conductors, he was no less at ease with the choral masterpieces of Bach, Handel and Elgar than with Gilbert and Sullivan operettas or the Diaghilev Ballet. Modern British composers owed him an especial debt.

In spite of these triumphs, Malcolm Sargent endured much misfortune. A tubercular infection laid him low from 1932 to 1934; and his domestic life was later shattered by a marriage that ended in divorce and the death of a much-loved daughter from polio. He sought solace in a frenetic social round and a restless programme of travel; always he was a generous host, a genial guest and the pride of his tailor. But at heart he was a lonely man, easily scarred by professional disparagement.

Sargent's delight in royal occasions sometimes exposed him to drollery. It was alleged that at a Buckingham Palace party, while talking to one acquaintance, he was joined by another from overseas, whom he hastened to introduce:

'This is my friend the King of Norway.'
'Denmark,' said the visitor.

He was, however, much encouraged when in 1937 the Queen brought Princess Elizabeth and Princess Margaret Rose to hear him conduct one of his Robert Mayer concerts for children. No less pleasing was his conversation with King George VI after a rousing performance of *Rule Britannia*:

'You will in future always include that in the programme when I am present.'
'But, Your Majesty, how can I include *Rule Britannia* if I am about to conduct a sacred work like the *St Matthew Passion*?'
'No problem at all. I shall not be there.'

Last night of the Proms

Sassoon, Sir Philip, 3rd Baronet
(1888–1939)

Politician, connoisseur and friend of the royal family. He was born in Paris, the only son of Sir Edward Sassoon and his wife Aline, daughter of Baron Gustave de Rothschild. Sometimes called the Rothschilds of the East, the Sassoons had reputedly been driven out of Spain in the fifteenth century, settled in Mesopotamia, founded a great merchant house in Bombay and so moved to England. Here, within scarcely more than a generation, they had acquired two baronetcies and the friendship of the future King Edward VII.

Philip Sassoon was educated at Eton and Christ Church, Oxford, where he took a Second Class in History. Having at the age of nineteen the right to elect for either British or French nationality, he chose British. But for the rest of his life he retained a slight sibilant accent which, with his sleek dark looks, made him seem never quite an Englishman.

On the death of his father in 1912 he inherited a title, a fortune and the parliamentary constituency of Hythe, in Kent, which he represented at Westminster until his death twenty-seven years later. During the Great War, as a junior captain in the yeomanry, he became private secretary to Sir Douglas Haig, the Commander-in-Chief on the Western Front, who valued his talent for political liaison and conciliation. When in 1917 the Field Marshal wished to show his gratitude by making Sassoon a Companion of the Order of St Michael and St George, the War Office explained that no officer below the rank of major could receive so high a decoration. Haig promoted him.

Sassoon's Ministerial career was less meteoric. Appointed Parliamentary Under-Secretary for Air in 1924, he held the same post until 1929 and again from 1931 to 1937, when he became First Commissioner of Works. The appointment enabled him to bring a trained eye and the tastes of an aesthete to the care of royal palaces and public buildings. He entertained with oriental splendour at his own three houses: in Park Lane, London; at Trent Park, New Barnet; and at Port Lympne, near Hythe, where more than one conference of Allied statesmen took place under his roof.

Lord Hugh Cecil, MP, used to say that of all his acquaintances, Sassoon alone combined immense wealth with an amiable temperament. But others who enjoyed his ready hospitality repaid him with sly disparagement and anti-Semitic jokes. Winston Churchill, who painted a well-known picture of the Blue Room at Trent, said: 'When you are travelling to an unknown destination, it is wise to attach a restaurant car to the train.' And Lord D'Abernon, renowned alike for his ambassadorial skills and the chiaroscuro of his financial dealings, boasted of having poured all the bath salts into his bath in order to be revenged on his host for the Crucifixion.

Sir Philip Sassoon loved the entire royal family. An exotic butterfly, he would flit from palace to palace bearing expensive presents. 'He had,' wrote Henry Channon (q.v.), 'a prolonged and hazardous friendship with the Prince of Wales whom he worshipped, though their intermittent quarrels were famous. He was also intimate with the King, Queen and Queen Mary – royalties haunted his house always, and he was loyal to them as he was to no-one else. Politicians he dropped as soon as they fell from power.'

In April 1939, although suffering from a severe attack of influenza, Sassoon insisted on accepting an invitation to Windsor. It cost him his life. A streptococcal infection set in and he died, unmarried, on 3 June. He was fifty. His sister, Sybil, Marchioness of Cholmondeley, inherited the best of his pictures; they hang at Houghton, her house in Norfolk, where on her ninetieth birthday in 1983 the Queen and the entire royal family assembled to congratulate her. To a cousin, Mrs David Gubbay, Sassoon left a tax-free annuity of £11,000 a year. To produce this, it was stated in the courts, would require a capital sum of £10,425,000.

Snowdon, Antony Armstrong-Jones, 1st Earl of
(1930–   )

Former husband of Princess Margaret (q.v.). He was born in London on 7 March 1930, the only son of Ronald Armstrong-Jones, by his wife Anne Messel, later Countess of Rosse.

Both sides of his pedigree reveal inherited talent. His paternal grandfather, Sir Robert Armstrong Jones, of Plas Dinas, Caernarvon, was a leading authority on the treatment of mental illness. Sir Robert's son, Ronald Armstrong-Jones, a barrister, was educated at Eton, served in the Army in both world wars, became a Queen's Counsel in 1954 and hyphenated his name. In 1925 he married Anne, only daughter of Leonard Messel, by whom he had two children: Antony, created Earl of Snowdon, and Susan Anne, who married the 6th Viscount de Vesci. His marriage was dissolved in 1934. He subsequently married Carol Coombe, an Australian actress; and after that marriage had ended in divorce, he married thirdly Jenifer Unite, an air hostess. Anne Armstrong-Jones, Lord Snowdon's mother, subsequently married Michael, 6th Earl of Rosse.

Snowdon's maternal grandfather, Leonard Messel, came of a German-Jewish family who made a fortune in the City of London and settled in Sussex. Leonard was educated at Eton and Oxford, married the only daughter of Linley Sambourne, the *Punch* artist, and was the father of Oliver Messel, the designer, and of Anne, the mother of Lord Snowdon. His home, Nymans, went up in flames in 1947, destroying his fine collection of herbals; but its famous gardens are open to the public and his collection of fans is to be found in the Fitzwilliam Museum, Cambridge.

Tony, as he is called by family and friends, was four years old when his parents divorced. He spent much of his childhood on his stepfather's estates at Birr, in Ireland, and Womersley Park,

in Yorkshire. From Sandroyd, a preparatory school in Surrey, he went to Eton: a polite, unobtrusive boy who, as in later life, preferred the engineering workshop to the library. At Jesus College, Cambrige, he read Natural Sciences, then switched to Architecture but failed to complete the course. He did, however, cox the winning Cambridge Eight against Oxford in 1950: a remarkable achievement for a victim of poliomyelitis. (A decade or so later, when he and Princess Margaret entertained the current Cambridge crew at Kensington Palace, they took the precaution of putting away all their more fragile objects for the evening. The oarsmen turned out to be quiet, beautifully mannered and addicted to nothing stronger than orange juice.)

Armstrong-Jones began his career as a professional photographer apprenticed to Henry Nahum, better known as Baron. He first set up on his own in a room in Albany so small that his sitters had to squat on the floor to be photographed. Then he constructed a more spacious studio in a disused ironmonger's shop in Pimlico. His business flourished and he was invited to photograph most members of the royal family. He was something of a perfectionist; at a conference of the Institute of Directors, he asked one member to put out his cigar as the blue smoke would spoil his pictures. In 1958 he published a book of photographs entitled *London*. That was the year he first met Princess Margaret. After a clandestine courtship they were married in Westminster Abbey in May 1960.

Soon after his betrothal, the Queen decided that he should receive an Earldom so that the children of the marriage could bear a higher rank and style than that of commoner. As his family had long lived in Caernarvon that name would have been a natural choice. But there was already an eighteenth-century Earldom of Carnarvon (the heir to which is Lord Porchester, the Queen's racing manager). So Armstrong-Jones tentatively chose to become Earl of Arvon, the borough in which lay his ancestral home, Plas Dinas. Then the whole matter of the peerage was shelved for more than a year, until shortly before the birth of his first child. In the meantime, the former Prime Minister, Sir Anthony Eden, had been created Earl of Avon. To avoid confusion, Armstrong-Jones thereupon chose Snowdon as his title. The new Earl's godfather, Sir Michael Duff, Lord Lieutenant of Caernarvonshire, was annoyed; he owned the mountain. Although something of an embarrassment to the young photographer, the unearned Earldom served its purpose. It enabled the son of Princess Margaret and Lord Snowdon, born in November 1961 and called David, to bear the courtesy title of Viscount Linley, after his great-great-grandfather, Linley Sambourne; and their daughter, born in May 1964, to be styled Lady Sarah Armstrong-Jones.

Snowdon resented the attempts of some popular newspapers to depict him as a male Cinderella who had emerged from obscurity to wed the Queen's sister. When, during the first two years of marriage, he and Princess Margaret occupied a small grace-and-favour house in Kensington Palace, he would point out that he had been brought up in far more luxury at Birr Castle or Womersley Park; that for the first time since Eton he was living in a bed-sitter; that he did not live off his wife but had made a substantial nest-egg as a photographer; and that the *Daily Express* had always treated him with respect as a rich dilettante who condescended to let the newspaper publish some of his photographs.

To demonstrate his independence, he joined the staff of the *Sunday Times* in 1962 as a salaried artistic adviser and photographer. Rival newspapers engaged in a battle for readership objected to the appointment; the *Observer*, for instance, wrote scathingly that the Queen's brother-in-law had been put into circulation. Although the grumbles soon died away, his professional assignments were not without piquancy. On one occasion he accompanied a well-known journalist who went by appointment to interview a public man. When they arrived at his country house, the grandee graciously welcomed the journalist. 'I hope you will

stay to lunch,' he said. 'Your photographer can have a sandwich at the pub in the village.' Snowdon, who had meanwhile been preparing his cameras, now emerged from the car. He later said: 'I should have thought more of our host had he stuck to the original arrangement. But I'm afraid he then asked me to lunch, too.'

Snowdon designed a new aviary for the London Zoo and over the years has devoted much care and ingenuity to the problems of the old and the disabled. He was also handy about the house. When he and Princess Margaret moved into a larger wing of Kensington Palace, he veneered the doors and designed much of its modern furniture and fittings.

In 1969 he was given a wider stage for his talents when as Constable of Caernarvon Castle (an appointment he had received in 1963), he worked in uneasy harness with the Earl Marshal, the 16th Duke of Norfolk (q.v.) and the College of Arms in planning the Investiture of the Prince of Wales. It was an imaginative blend of pseudo-ancient custom and modern contrivance produced on a cheese-paring budget. As in 1911, when Lloyd George inspired a similar spectacle in Caernarvon Castle for the Investiture of Edward, Prince of Wales, it had a political motive: to pacify and flatter those Welsh people who felt themselves ignored by an English-orientated central Government. The ceremony on 1 July 1969 was in fact preceded by fifteen terrorist explosions. Snowdon rejected the elaborate schemes of heraldic decoration proposed by the College of Arms; nor were there red carpets, striped awnings, special seats for important guests or even shelter in the event of rain. To throw the occasion open to the television cameras, the arena contained little more than a huge Perspex canopy weighing more than a ton and bearing the Prince of Wales's feathered insignia. He did not always have his way. The Prince, for instance, instead of wearing a plain gold band on his head, was given a fussy modern version of a traditional coronet. Nor was the uniform which the Constable designed for himself much admired: a green tail coat that buttoned to the neck, matching trousers but no

Lord Snowdon with *left to right*: Viscount Linley, Prince Andrew, Lady Sarah Armstrong-Jones, and Princess Margaret

hat. For his contribution to the pageant, he was made a Knight Grand Cross of the Royal Victorian Order.

By now Princess Margaret and her husband had been married for nine years and seemed to have reached a sensible understanding about their respective working hours. She performed her royal engagements; he immersed himself in a busy career as photographer, designer and film maker. It soon became apparent, however, that this division of public interests was reflected in their private lives. There were times when neither troubled to hide these marital tensions; and since many of their friends were chosen from outside the discreet ranks of court and county, rumours of infidelity and insult gained currency. In 1976 it was announced that they

had agreed to live apart, but that there were no plans for divorce proceedings. Two years later they were divorced.

It was more of a tragedy for Princess Margaret than for her husband. When in 1955 she was obliged to renounce her love for Group Captain Townsend, she had publicly acknowledged the Church's ban on remarriage after divorce; in doing so she had effectively condemned herself to prolonged loneliness once her marriage to Snowdon was at an end. He, by contrast, never having committed himself to that doctrine, was free to remarry. In the same year as his divorce he did so. His bride was Lucy Lindsay-Hogg, the daughter of a textile designer and former wife of a film director, who had acted as Snowdon's production assistant. There is a daughter of the marriage. The family lives quietly in Kensington, little more than half a mile from the home of Princess Margaret.

Spencer, Edward John, 8th Earl
(1924–   )

Father of Diana, Princess of Wales. The Spencer fortunes were founded on sheep. Sir Robert Spencer, created a peer in 1603, was reputed to own 19,000 of them and to be as rich as any man in the kingdom. That did not protect him from being put in his place when in the House of Lords he taunted the Earl of Arundel with the treason of his father and grandfather, both of whom had died on the scaffold. Arundel retorted that his ancestors had indeed suffered for serving their King and country – at a time when Lord Spencer's ancestors were keeping sheep. For this pleasantry Arundel was committed to the Tower.

The family estates at Althorp, in Northamptonshire, were further enriched in the eighteenth century by a splendid bequest from Sarah, Duchess of Marlborough, to her favourite grandson, John Spencer, whose son was in 1765 created Earl Spencer and Viscount Althorp. Thus began the present line. The 2nd Earl collected a library of 40,000 volumes, including fifty-eight Caxtons. (A century later, his grandson the 5th Earl, a victim of the agricultural depression, sold it for £250,000 – perhaps £7 million in the currency of 1985; it is now known as the Rylands Library, part of Manchester University.) He has another claim to fame. As First Lord of the Admiralty during the Napoleonic Wars he promoted Nelson out of turn, then despatched him to the Mediterranean to win the Battle of Aboukir Bay. His son the 3rd Earl made an even deeper mark on history before succeeding to the family honours. As Viscount Althorp, MP, he was Chancellor of the Exchequer and the Leader of the House of Commons who ensured the passing of the Great Reform Bill of 1832. A dedicated farmer, he also helped to found the Royal Agricultural College, Cirencester, where the present Earl was a pupil in the next century.

On the death of the childless 3rd Earl, the title passed to his brother Frederick, a sailor and collector of china who was successively Lord Chamberlain and Lord Steward at the court of Queen Victoria. Statesmanship emerged once more with his son the 5th Earl, who was twice Lord Lieutenant of Ireland; when Mr Gladstone retired in 1894, he wished Spencer to succeed him as Prime Minister, but the Queen preferred Lord Rosebery. His half-brother the 6th Earl was renowned for what a parliamentary commentator called 'his incomparable shirt-front, his irreproachable cuffs and his miraculous collar.' As Lord Chamberlain to King Edward VII, he proved an oppressive stage censor; thus at the first London performance of Richard Strauss's *Salome* he required Madame Ackté, in the title role, to apostrophize an empty platter rather than display the severed head of John the Baptist. In the Great War, he raised a private army of Brownies for patriotic purposes. Spencer's wife, a sister of Maurice Baring, was an accomplished violinist who would serenade her children to sleep on a Stradivarius.

Albert John, known as Jack, succeeded his father as 7th Earl in 1922. He brought knowledge and taste to the task of preserving, arranging and adding to the Althorp collections; but the portrait of himself he commissioned Augustus John to paint is no more successful a likeness than that of Queen Elizabeth the Queen Mother by the same artist. Spencer had few social graces. Devoted to his possessions, he expected visitors to display a discernment scarcely inferior to his own; those who failed the test did not readily forget the experience. He was more at ease with museum curators than with fellow landowners, although he undertook many local duties and was for fifteen years Lord Lieutenant of Northamptonshire. He was generous in opening his muniment room to scholars; not even the most eminent, however, could afford to relax. He once came on Winston Churchill, at work in the Althorp archives on his life of the 1st Duke of Marlborough, smoking a cigar. 'I ripped it right out of his mouth,' Spencer related, 'and stamped it out on the floor.' Another visitor was packed off in disgrace for having sat on a chair covered with the host's own needlework.

For many years the 7th Earl Spencer ran two old-established dining clubs: the Society of Dilettanti, for aesthetes and museum men, and the Roxburghe, for bibliophiles. At the first of these he announced one evening that as the Society had accumulated a comfortable cash balance, he proposed giving part of it to the National Art-Collections Fund. The late Duke of Wellington protested that some of it ought to be used to improve the Society's dinners. 'Must we,' he asked with patrician disdain, 'have boarding-house dishes like sardines on toast?' Spencer's reply was deceptively mild. 'I have never been in a boarding-house,' he said, 'but we often have sardines at Althorp.' He died in 1975 and was succeeded by his only son, the 8th Earl and father of the Princess of Wales.

Edward John, known in the family as Johnnie, was born in 1924 and educated at Eton and the Royal Military College, Sandhurst. As Viscount Althorp he served in the war with the Royal Scots Greys and in 1950 was appointed an equerry to George VI. The present Queen confirmed him in the post but he resigned in 1954 to farm in Norfolk. He married in the same year Frances Roche, younger daughter of the 4th Baron Fermoy and his wife Ruth (q.v.). There are four surviving children of the marriage. The only son and heir, Charles, has since 1975 borne the courtesy title of Viscount Althorp. Of the three daughters, the eldest, Sarah, is married to Neil McCorquodale, a distant kinsman of Raine, Countess Spencer (see below); the second, Jane, to Robert Fellowes, an Assistant Private Secretary to the Queen since 1977, whose father, Sir William Fellowes, was for nearly thirty years the much-revered Agent at Sandringham; and the youngest, Diana, to the Prince of Wales. The children were brought up at Park House, on the Sandringham estate, where Frances herself had been born. When her marriage to Spencer

foundered in 1969 she married Peter Shand Kydd and now lives near Oban in Argyllshire.

The present Earl betrays not a trace of that acerbic self-absorption which made his father so insensitive a parent. It is from his mother, Lady Cynthia Hamilton, a daughter of the 3rd Duke of Abercorn, that he inherits a warm heart and generous nature: qualities which have ensured him the love and loyalty of his children through times of marital stress. On the death of his father in 1975 he inherited Althorp; and in the following year he married Raine (q.v.), formerly Countess of Dartmouth.

For nearly thirty years Spencer was a member of the Northamptonshire County Council. He has also taken on other public duties, including the chairmanship of the National Association of Boys' Clubs. Although not as possessive of his treasures as was his father, he is quietly knowledgeable and delights in displaying the glories of Gainsborough and Reynolds by candlelight. A skilled photographer, he filmed the scenes outside Buckingham Palace on the day his daughter was betrothed to the Prince of Wales.

Spencer, Raine, Countess
(1929–   )

Wife of the 8th Earl Spencer and stepmother of Diana, Princess of Wales. She was born in 1929, the daughter of Alexander George McCorquodale and his wife Barbara Cartland (q.v.). In 1948 she married Gerald, 9th Earl of Dartmouth, by whom she had three sons and two daughters. The marriage was dissolved in 1976. She then married, as his second wife, the 8th Earl Spencer (q.v.).

She had earlier given many years of energetic public service. The scourge of obstructive officials, she was a member of the Westminster City Council, of the London County Council and of the Greater London Council. She has done much for the preservation of ancient buildings and the encouragement of tourism, and is on the advisory council of the Victoria and

Albert Museum. Her most recent publication is a book on British spas, a handsome volume with photographs by her husband; royalties from its sale have been given to spa towns, to restore wrought iron and other architectural features.

She furthers her enterprises with panache and persuasion. Under her direction, Althorp, the Spencer seat in Northamptonshire, has been drastically restored, albeit at the cost of selling certain family treasures. The cleaning of the pictures and furniture has revealed many forgotten delights; and if the redecoration of some of the rooms appears unnaturally bright, it will return to its faded grandeur within a century or two. Lady Spencer has also established several thriving businesses to help maintain the fabric of the house: hiring of its crimson dining-room for private entertainment and a shop resembling Aladdin's cave in the old stables.

Her relentless powers of organization and her skill in the arts of publicity have not endeared her to the more costive of her Northamptonshire neighbours, and she has been discouraged from taking much part in the public life of the county. A metropolitan at heart, she is more at ease in a London drawing-room of *literati* than tramping through fields of kale in the shooting season. Dazzlingly turned out on any occasion, Raine Spencer once gently chided a fellow guest for not wearing more of her famous family jewels. 'Ah,' her diffident friend replied, 'but you see I am only a country countess.'

Not the least of her virtues has been as the guardian of her husband's health. A few years ago he caught pneumonia after an operation and did not respond to the established treatment. As he lay at death's door, his wife remembered that one of her friends, Bill Cavendish-Bentinck, later Duke of Portland, was the chairman of Bayer UK. So she asked him whether the pharmaceutical division of his company could provide an alternative remedy. By chance there was a new compound awaiting clinical trials. It was rushed to the hospital; and where so many others had failed, this succeeded. Shortly afterwards the Spencers bought a house at Bognor, where King George v had convalesced in 1929.

Lord and Lady Spencer, 1983

Stamfordham, Arthur Bigge, 1st Baron (1849–1931)

Private Secretary to King George v. The son of a Northumberland parson, he was educated at Rossall School and the Royal Military Academy, where he was a fellow cadet with the Duke of Connaught (q.v.). As a young officer in the Royal Artillery, he formed a close friendship with the Prince Imperial, son of the deposed Emperor Napoleon iii, who while serving in the British Army had been posted to Bigge's battery. Although in hospital with fever when the Prince was ambushed and killed during the Zulu War of 1879, Bigge was later chosen to escort the Empress Eugenie to the scene of the tragedy. That in turn brought him to the notice of Queen Victoria, who in 1880 appointed him to be her Assistant Private Secretary. On the death of Sir Henry Ponsonby in 1895, Bigge succeeded him as Private Secretary.

During his first year at court, Bigge discovered that the Queen's Scottish retainer, John Brown, could be no less formidable than the Sovereign herself. Having been promised a day's fishing at Balmoral, he was dismayed when Brown appeared in his room with a stern countenance: 'Ye'll not be going fishing,' Bigge was told. 'Her Majesty thinks it's about time ye did some work.' And work he did, until his death in harness half a century later. The old Queen insisted that all business with her Private Secretaries, and even with her Ministers in Attendance, should be conducted in writing; nor would she allow a typewriter to intrude on her correspondence. To relieve the strain on her failing eyesight, Bigge changed his hand to a fine flowing script and used ink as thick and black as pitch.

Sir Arthur, as he became in 1895, also learned that those who serve Sovereigns must be as attentive to small matters as to large. At the prompting of the Queen, he spent eighteen months persuading a reluctant War Office to grant a favoured bandmaster the honorary rank of second-lieutenant; Bigge's campaign, coinciding with the South African War, was ultimately as successful but no less gruelling.

On the Queen's death in 1901, he might reasonably have expected to become Private Secretary to the new King. Edward VII, however, wished to retain Sir Francis Knollys, who had been with him for the past thirty years. Bigge was instead offered the post of Private Secretary to the King's only surviving son, the future George V, who as heir to the throne needed an experienced counsellor. In a strictly hierarchical sense his appointment was a demotion. That, however, was of no importance to a man of his modesty. As it turned out, he remained with his new master until his own death in 1931, serving him successively as Duke of Cornwall, Prince of Wales and King. Although Bigge's judgment was occasionally headstrong, his contribution to the strength and stability of the monarchy during those thirty years can scarcely be exaggerated.

Slight of build and unassuming in manner, he was a perennial pillar of strength during the future King's apprenticeship. Prince George recognized the debt he owed to Bigge. 'What would have happened to me,' he wrote in 1907, 'if you had not been there to prepare and help me with my speeches. I can hardly write a letter of any importance without your assistance.' On the death of Edward VII three years later, the burden redoubled. Throughout some of the most turbulent events in British history, Bigge was always at hand to guide an inexperienced monarch through the quicksands of political crisis. Yet in the very first months of the new reign, even that paragon of private secretaries displayed a want of judgment that could have been disastrous.

It happened in November 1910 when the Liberal Government of H.H. Asquith proposed to curb the powers of an hereditary and overwhelmingly Conservative majority in the House of Lords by introducing a Parliament Bill. Fearing that the Lords would thwart the plan by rejecting the Bill time after time, the Prime Minister demanded a secret undertaking from the King: that in the event of a renewed Government victory after the next general election, the King would create enough new Liberal peers – several hundred of them if need be – to swamp Conservative opposition in the House of Lords and so ensure the passage of the Parliament Bill.

The King was affronted, and with justice. Asquith, it seemed, was not prepared to trust him to do his duty when the need arose, but was asking for a promise to act in ill-defined circumstances. Two alternative courses now faced George V. He could either swallow his anger and give Asquith the undertaking demanded: a promise which the Prime Minister could then make known and wield as a political weapon whenever it suited him. Or he could refuse, insisting that it was the duty of a constitutional monarch to *act* on his Prime Minister's advice but not to *make promises*.

Bigge urged the King to follow the second course, whatever the consequences: and these could indeed have been perilous. For Asquith and his colleagues would instantly have been provoked to resign, thereby forcing the King to find a new Prime Minister. The only other candidate was A.J. Balfour, leader of the Conservative opposition; but as his party held a minority of seats in the Commons, he might well have declined to form a new Government. The King would then have been obliged to recall Asquith and, with damaged reputation, surrender on such terms as the Liberal leader demanded. Even if Balfour had agreed to form a Government, his lack of a majority in the Commons would have led him to ask the King for a dissolution of Parliament. The general election which must then have followed would have been fought on two issues: whether an hereditary House of Lords should be permitted to destroy the legislative programme of a democratically elected House of Commons, and whether the King had behaved correctly. The Liberals would have claimed that he was in unholy alliance with the peers against the people; the Conservatives that he was defending the constitution against a revolutionary intrigue.

Whatever the outcome of the poll, the King would have been the loser. A Liberal victory would have delivered him once more into Asquith's hands, chastened and defenceless; a Conservative victory would in retrospect have justified his resistance to Asquith, but at a cost of alienating, perhaps permanently, Liberal respect and goodwill.

Such were the hazards to which Bigge would have exposed the King in pursuing what he called 'a bold, fearless and open line of action.' It is fortunate that he was not the King's only confidant. On the death of Edward VII six

months earlier, Francis (by now Lord) Knollys had been invited to remain in office as joint Private Secretary to George V; and whereas Bigge counselled defiance to Asquith's demand, Knolly's pursued a more conciliatory path. 'I feel certain,' he told the King, 'that you can safely and constitutionally accept what the Cabinet propose and I venture to urge you strongly to do so.' The King, having pleaded in vain with the Prime Minister to change his mind and withdraw his request for a promise, reluctantly took Knollys' advice. As it turned out, he was never required to make a mass creation of Liberal

Lord Stamfordham with George V in the garden of Buckingham Palace during the Great War

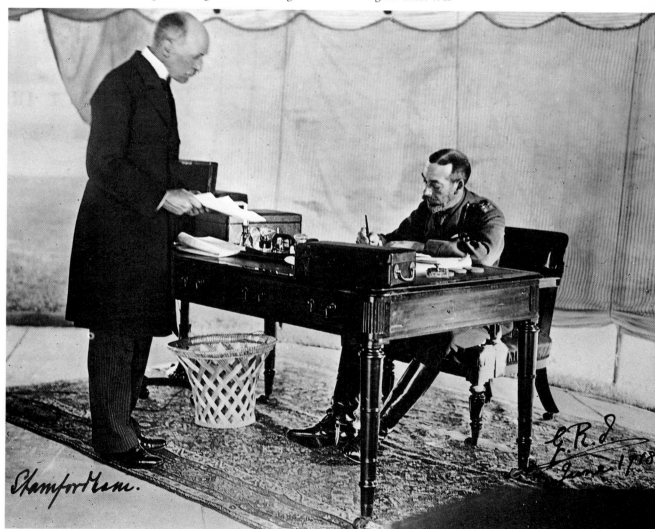

peers; rather than provoke such a drastic measure, the House of Lords agreed to the Parliament Bill, albeit by a narrow majority. And although the King was left with a sense of grievance against the Prime Minister, the two men worked well enough together until Asquith's fall in 1916.

The King's resentment did not extend to Bigge; he had merely thought it more prudent to follow the course advocated by Knollys. In the Coronation Honours of 1911, Knollys was advanced from Baron to Viscount and Bigge was created Baron Stamfordham, the name of the Northumbrian village of which his father had been vicar. The two Private Secretaries meanwhile continued uneasily in double harness. Each cherished his master's interests; but Knollys was at heart a Liberal, Stamfordham a Conservative. Knollys believed that the throne could best be preserved by submission to Ministerial advice; Stamfordham (as we shall now call him) feared that each successive erosion of the royal prerogative heralded the destruction of both the monarchy and a stable society.

Throughout the remaining years of the Liberal Government, Asquith and his colleagues regarded Knollys as a friend at court, Stamfordham as an enemy. 'I received from him yesterday,' the Prime Minister complained to Knollys in 1912, 'a letter which both in tone and substance is quite unexampled in my communications with the Crown.' And when Knollys retired in 1913, leaving Stamfordham as the sole Private Secretary to the King, the Cabinet discussed the change. 'Everyone lamented the loss of Knollys,' one Minister noted, 'and the influence of Stamfordham, whose wings the P.M. earnestly desired should be clipped.' Such was the impression which the most correct, cautious and politically impartial courtier of the 1920s left on the previous decade.

With the outbreak of war in 1914, resentment between Buckingham Palace and Downing Street was submerged in the need for national unity. On ceasing to be Prime Minister in December 1916, Asquith wrote to Stamfordham: 'The times have not been easy, and of late

more than difficult, but our task has been lightened by complete mutual confidence and ever-growing friendship.' The burden which Stamfordham bore throughout the war was daunting. No aspect of home or foreign policy, of military strategy or parliamentary business, escaped his notice or his pen. As the watchdog of the King's prerogatives, he let nothing go by default, however trivial. On the eve of the Battle of Loos, he solemnly rebuked the Prime Minister for failing to consult the Sovereign about a new Dean of Ripon.

There was renewed friction with Asquith's successor, Lloyd George, over his neglect of the King's wishes, particularly in the matter of military appointments. During one celebrated conflict, the Prime Minister told Stamfordham that the King was encouraging mutiny by taking up the cause of senior officers whom the Government had decided to dismiss. Lloyd George's antipathy spread to the staff at No. 10 Downing Street, who would keep the King's Private Secretary waiting on a wooden chair in the hall and fail to rise to their feet when he entered their office.

Stamfordham was not unduly disturbed by such discourtesy. 'We are all servants here,' he used to tell his fellow courtiers, 'although some are more important than others.' His own most memorable service to the monarchy has passed into history. In 1917, when there were persistent though unfounded whispers about George V's patriotism, the King decided that those members of his family who bore German titles such as Teck or Schleswig-Holstein or Battenberg should abandon them in favour of British surnames. But what was his own family name? Perhaps Guelph, perhaps Wettin: none could be certain. What then should replace it? Tudor-Stewart, Plantagenet, York, England, Lancaster and Fitzroy were all considered but for one reason or another rejected. It was then, amid unanimous approval, that Stamfordham suggested Windsor. 'Do you realize,' the former Prime Minister, Lord Rosebery, told him, 'that you have christened a dynasty?' In Britain, the proclamation of the House of Windsor revived patriotic fervour. Germany was less respectful. The Kaiser said he would be delighted to attend a performance of that well-known opera, '*The Merry Wives of Saxe-Coburg-Gotha.*'

Wise, industrious and peppery, Stamfordham worked on throughout the uneasy peace of the 1920s. Whichever political party held office, he was never too busy with affairs of State to notice and, in the King's name, rebuke a lapse of duty or a breach of custom. Such surveillance extended even to Ministers' clothes. Lord Birkenhead, the Lord Chancellor, was furious at receiving a letter of pained reproach for having arrived at Downing Street wearing a country suit instead of a frock coat and top hat. 'I don't like the King's brown bowler hat,' he was said to have observed, 'but I am not always writing to him about it.' When a Labour Government first took office under Ramsay MacDonald in 1924, Stamfordham showed himself to be a more flexible and considerate mentor. He hoped that those Ministers who could not afford the expense of a new suit of court dress might have recourse to 'Messrs. Moss Bros., which is I believe a well-known and dependable firm.'

Stamfordham married in 1881 Constance Neville, daughter of a parson in Somerset, by whom he had a son, killed in action in 1915, and two daughters. Having christened a dynasty of monarchs, he founded another of royal servants. His grandson, Michael Adeane (q.v.) became Private Secretary to Queen Elizabeth II, and Michael's son, Edward Adeane, Private Secretary to Charles, Prince of Wales.

Stuart of Findhorn, James, 1st Viscount
(1897–1971)

Equerry to King George VI and Secretary of State for Scotland. The third son of the 17th Earl of Moray, descended from an illegitimate son of King James V of Scotland, he went to school at Eton; but he liked to say that his education did not begin until 1940, when he joined Winston Churchill's wartime Government. He served throughout the Great War in the Royal Scots and was awarded the Military Cross and bar. Stuart then spent eighteen months as equerry to the Duke of York, later King George VI.

He brought a cheerful insouciance to his duties. Once when the Duke wanted to watch cricket, his equerry took him to a deserted Lord's; the match was being held at the Oval. He had similar difficulty in finding Lambeth Palace, where the Duke was late in arriving for the Archbishop of Canterbury's dinner party.

Stuart later claimed in his memoirs to have introduced the Duke of York to his future bride,

James Stuart

Lady Elizabeth Bowes-Lyon (q.v.), at a dance in the Ritz Hotel in 1921. In fact they first met at a children's party in 1905, and later at the house of Lord Farquhar (q.v.) in Grosvenor Square.

In 1922, unwilling to continue living on an equerry's salary of £450, out of which he had to pay a valet, Stuart went off to seek his fortune in the oilfields of Oklahoma. But he was back in 1923 to enter the House of Commons as a Conservative and to marry Lady Rachel Cavendish, a daughter of the 9th Duke of Devonshire and sister of Lady Dorothy Macmillan. He was Government Chief Whip 1941–5, and Secretary of State for Scotland 1951–7, when he was made a peer.

Stuart remained on cordial terms with the royal family. Having been accidentally peppered with shot by his neighbour on the grouse moor, he once arrived at Balmoral with his face covered in sticking plaster. In reply to the Queen's anxious inquiry, he told her how he had first driven to the local hospital for an injection of penicillin, then to the nearest hotel for a 'small refreshment', which in Scotland means a double whisky.

'But, James,' the Queen said, 'you should surely not have had that after the penicillin?'

'You know, Ma'am, that's exactly what the barmaid said.'

Susan
(1944–1959)

Matriarch of the royal family's corgis, she lay concealed at the Queen's feet when as Princess Elizabeth she left Buckingham Palace in an open carriage to begin her honeymoon with Prince Philip.

And Susan begat Honey, who begat Bee, who begat Heather, who begat Foxy, who begat Brush, who begat Geordie, who begat Smoky, who begat Spark, who begat Diamond.

Going back nine generations in the Queen's family tree brings us to King George I, who was born in 1660.

Teck, Prince Francis of
(1870–1910)

Second son of the Duke and Duchess of Teck and a younger brother of Queen Mary. The black sheep of the family, he was removed from Wellington College for assaulting the headmaster. And although he fought with gallantry in the British Army, winning the Distinguished Service Order, he was rarely free from debt.

The most catastrophic of these financial crises occurred in 1895, when he was stationed in Dublin with his regiment. Owing the bookmakers £1,000, the penniless Prince determined to extricate himself by putting £10,000 on a supposedly unbeatable horse to win £1,000. The horse took a negligent view of its responsibilities, allowing itself to be beaten into second place. Thus Francis was left owing £11,000, perhaps twenty times that amount in the currency of today. To avoid a public scandal, his brother-in-law, the future King George V, and other members of the family settled his huge losses.

It was not the last of his outrages. After the death of his mother in 1897 he bestowed her emeralds on his ageing mistress. Prince Francis died at the age of forty from the effects of a minor operation. At his funeral, Queen Mary wept publicly for the only time in her life. She also took care to recover the family emeralds.

Townsend, Group Captain Peter
(1914–   )

Equerry and Deputy Master of the Household to King George VI and equerry to Queen Elizabeth II. The son of an Indian Army officer serving in the Burmese administration, he was born near Mandalay but educated in England. From his public school, Haileybury, he went to the RAF College, Cranwell, where the instructors reported 'his reluctance to attempt anything which might make him noticeable.' There was irony too in the commission he received from King George V: 'To our trusty and well-beloved ... greeting.'

As a fighter pilot he shot down in February 1940 the first German bomber to fall on English soil since the Great War. He emerged from twenty months of combat by day and night with the Distinguished Service Order and the Distinguished Flying Cross and Bar; but also with the shattered nerves of a brave man overcoming perpetual fear. 'The fight had gone out of me,' he wrote, 'I had flown myself to a standstill.' He found comfort in his marriage to Rosemary Pawle, the daughter of an army brigadier, who bore her husband two sons. Townsend was meanwhile given a succession of staff and training posts, none of which he enjoyed. Then came the crucial moment of his career. He was summoned to the office of the Chief of Air Staff in Whitehall and told: 'If you don't find the idea particularly revolting, I propose to recommend you for the job of equerry to His Majesty. The appointment will be for three months.' In his memoirs, *Time and Chance*, the Group Captain records that his wife, on hearing the news, threw her arms round him and exclaimed, 'rather indecently', he thought: 'We're made.' His comment was unchivalrous, hers the stuff of tragedy.

Townsend took up his duties at Buckingham Palace at the beginning of March 1944. They were not onerous: little more than welcoming the King's visitors and showing them into his presence. Most of his fellow courtiers had been selected not, as he had, on past achievement but through some family or other personal connection with the royal household. But Townsend, exceptionally handsome and with a nervous charm reflecting that of the King, soon felt at ease in that largely aristocratic world. His appointment of three months was extended indefinitely. It thus fell to him during the post-war Labour Government to receive his own cousin, Hugh Gaitskell, Minister of Fuel and Power and later Chancellor of the Exchequer.

'The fact that Hugh was a socialist,' Townsend wrote, 'caused me, secretly, I am ashamed to say, some embarrassment. . . . There was not a single socialist – at least above stairs – in Buckingham Palace.'

It seemed to some observers that the King's affection for Townsend was almost that of a father for his son. The equerry certainly displayed something of Queen Elizabeth's magical touch in soothing that troubled spirit, particularly during the strain and exhaustion of the royal tour of South Africa in 1947. That year he became a Commander of the Royal Victorian Order for personal services to the Sovereign. Other Heads of State recognized his worth. The King of Denmark made him a Knight of Dannebrog, conducting the informal ceremony in his shirtsleeves; President Auriol of France, with even less regard for protocol, sent him the insignia of an Officer of the Legion of Honour in a brown envelope by post. George VI also put Adelaide Cottage, in Windsor Park, at the disposal of the Townsends. Once the tea house of Queen Adelaide, the consort of William IV, it proved a delightful retreat in summer, but cold and damp in winter.

In 1950, Townsend was promoted to be Deputy Master of the Household. Although this consolidated his role of attentive favourite, it was at the expense of his family happiness. Those of both sexes who wed courtiers are obliged to endure frequent and sometimes prolonged separation. Most resign themselves to it; a few do not. Increasingly lonely at Adelaide Cottage, Rosemary Townsend sought a life of her own. In December 1952 she was divorced by her husband, and two months later married John de Laszlo, son of the portrait painter whose work adorns so many royal residences. In those days a sharp distinction was made at court between the so-called innocent and guilty parties in a divorce. Townsend was adjudged innocent and thus not required to relinquish his household appointment.

He had meanwhile fallen in love with someone sixteen years younger than himself: no bar in itself to remarriage, except that she was the

The Duke of Teck, 1870

King's daughter. He wrote of Princess Margaret: 'She was a girl of unusual, intense beauty, confined as it was in her short, slender figure and centred about large purple-blue eyes, generous, sensitive lips and a complexion as smooth as a peach. She was capable, in her face and in her whole being, of an astonishing power of expression. It could change in an instant from saintly, almost melancholic, composure to hilarious, uncontrollable joy. She was, by nature, generous, volatile. She was a *comédienne* at heart, playing the piano with ease and verve, singing in her rich, supple voice the latest hits, imitating the famous stars. She was coquettish, sophisticated. But what ultimately made Princess Margaret so attractive and lovable was that behind the dazzling façade, the apparent self-assurance, you could find, if you looked for it, a rare softness and sincerity.'

Townsend's appointment at the Palace lapsed with the death of the King in 1952. He was instead made Comptroller to the widowed Queen Mother, who with her younger daughter now moved to Clarence House. In that more intimate circle, he and Princess Margaret grew ever closer. By the spring of 1953 they were ready to tell the Queen of their attachment and to seek her blessing to their proposed marriage. Startled but sympathetic, the Queen reacted like any head of a family confronted by an unexpected match. She asked her sister to wait a year. Simultaneously, Townsend broke the news to the Queen's Private Secretary, Sir Alan Lascelles (q.v.), who was equally startled but not at all sympathetic. He told the would-be suitor: 'You must be either mad or bad.'

Lascelles was doubtless shocked by the presumption of any courtier, and a commoner to boot, who sought the hand of the Queen's sister. But his sense of outrage was not so much personal as constitutional. The Royal Marriages Act of 1772 required all members of the royal family to seek the Sovereign's consent before contracting a marriage; and Lascelles well knew that as Supreme Governor of the Church of England, the Queen could not flout its doctrines by permitting her sister to marry a divorced

man. On reaching the age of twenty-five, it is true, Princess Margaret would be free to marry the man of her choice without the Queen's consent; but even then she would have to plead with Parliament if she were to retain her royal privileges.

As soon as Townsend had unburdened himself to Lascelles, the Private Secretary consulted the Prime Minister. Churchill agreed that to avert any risk of an open scandal, Townsend must leave the country. The Queen disagreed. Sympathetic to her sister's predicament if not to the doctrine of remarriage after divorce, she thought Townsend's proposed banishment unnecessarily severe. It would be enough, the Queen said, if he were to leave Clarence House and return to Buckingham Palace as one of her own equerries.

No mention of the attachment had yet reached the British Press. On Coronation Day, however, as Princess Margaret was waiting to leave the Abbey, she was seen to brush a speck of fluff from Townsend's uniform amid much shared laughter. This innocent though possessive gesture at once caught the interest of foreign journalists; British newspapers, more restrained, waited another eleven days before abandoning themselves to romantic speculation. This time the Prime Minister insisted that Townsend, still a serving officer, must leave the country. He was offered a choice of posts as Air Attaché at British diplomatic missions overseas: Brussels, Johannesburg or Singapore. Resentful at being bundled out of England, he chose the first, so that at least he would not be too far separated from his schoolboy sons.

For the next two years Townsend carried out his duties as Air Attaché, enjoyed the social life of Brussels, became a dedicated and popular amateur jockey. Meanwhile he and Princess Margaret corresponded regularly and at a brief reunion in London in July 1954 renewed their pledges of love. On 21 August 1955, her twenty-fifth birthday, Princess Margaret was released from some of the restrictions of the Royal Marriages Act; no longer would she need to seek the Queen's permission to marry Group Captain

Townsend. Such freedom, however, was illusory: she would still have to give one year's notice of her marriage to the Privy Council and to renounce her royal status and Civil List. It was not until 13 October that Princess Margaret and Peter Townsend met once more at Clarence House. For thirteen days, in the glare of publicity, they discussed their future. At last, on 24 October, for reasons both spiritual and material, they decided not to marry. The news was given to the world five days later. The disappointed suitor then returned to Brussels. (For a fuller account of this episode, see *Margaret, Princess*.)

Townsend was still well-regarded in the RAF and at forty-two not without the prospect of high command. But he felt too rooted in the past to resume his Service career: a survivor, as it were, of the age of windjammers. he continued as Air Attaché for a year, then followed the traditional path of those disappointed in love: not quite big-game hunting in Africa, but a solitary journey round the world by car. This enterprise, covering 60,000 miles and lasting eighteen months, was financed by the *Daily Mail*; he stipulated, however, that its promotion and publicity should make no mention of either the royal family or of his own personal affairs.

In March 1958 he called on Princess Margaret for the first time since their enforced separation two and half years before. His choice of Clarence House for the reunion exposed them both to renewed speculation; and there were some who suspected him of seeking the limelight, even of wishing to eclipse the Queen's State visit to Holland that very week. Although it would not have been difficult for the two old friends to have met again in a more secluded place, he has never attempted to see Princess Margaret since. 'Public curiosity killed our long and faithful attachment,' he wrote. That may be one reason. Another is that in the following year he married a pretty Belgian girl half his age, Marie-Luce

Group Captain Peter Townsend. Also in the group are, *left to right*, the Duke of Gloucester, the Princess Royal, Princess Margaret, the Queen and the Duke of Beaufort, 1955.

Jamagne, whom he had met at a horse-show in Brussels. She has borne him a son and two daughters.

Townsend tried his hand at several ventures – as film maker, wine shipper and publicist – before settling down with his family in France as an industrious and successful writer. His books include *Duel of Eagles*, an account of war in the air between the RAF and the Luftwaffe; *The Postman of Nagasaki*, on the effects of dropping the second atomic bomb on Japan in 1945; and *Time and Chance*, an emotional autobiography.

Vansittart, Sir Robert, 1st Baron
(1881–1957)

Sir Robert Vansittart

Diplomatist. Educated at Eton, Vansittart joined the Diplomatic Service in 1903 and in 1930 was appointed Permanent Under-Secretary at the Foreign Office. Eight years later he was removed by the Prime Minister, Neville Chamberlain, and given the newly created but ineffectual post of Diplomatic Adviser to the Government. He would perhaps have had more success in his opposition to Chamberlain's policy of appeasing Hitler and Mussolini had he used a terser, less epigrammatic style in his official papers. 'I have read your memorandum,' King George V once told him, 'not all of it, of course.' Vansittart noted what he called this 'encouragement to brevity,' but did not mend his ways.

Victoria, Princess
(1868–1935)

The second daughter of King Edward VII and Queen Alexandra. One sister was married to the Duke of Fife (q.v.), the other to the future King of Norway; but Victoria remained a lifelong though unwilling spinster. Her mother was largely responsible for this unhappiness. The Danish-born Queen frowned on any alliance with a German prince; and there were few other suitors available for a British princess. Lord Rosebery had once been thought a possible husband after the death of his first wife, Hannah Rothschild, but the match did not prosper. The future Prime Minister was after all twenty years older than Princess Victoria, of a neurotic temperament and bored by court ceremonial.

Robbed of her prize, she became a little indiscreet in her attachments. At Windsor in 1908, she and the diplomatist Lord Granville danced the whole evening after dinner, the servants having rolled up the carpet. 'I thought it not quite approved of,' a guest noted. One friend remained faithful to mother and daughter alike. Old Admiral Fisher wrote in 1912: 'Princess Victoria, who used to be scraggy, lanky and anaemic, has developed into an opulent figure with a rosy plump face! She looked very

handsome and I told her so, and her tall figure makes her most imposing now.' But the Princess found few opportunities to exercise her new-found charms. With the death of King Edward VII, his widow had retired to Sandringham, insisting that her unmarried daughter should accompany her as a perpetual companion and lady-in-waiting. And so the lonely years slipped away. In 1922 King George gave his sister a small bolt-hole in Kensington Palace which she was occasionally able to use. But it was not until Queen Alexandra's death in 1925 that Princess Victoria, by now approaching sixty, could escape from the ghosts of Sandringham to set up her own establishment. For the last decade of her life she lived at Coppins, in Iver, Buckinghamshire, an ugly but comfortable villa which she bequeathed to her nephew, Prince George, Duke of Kent.

Even as a girl, Princess Victoria had been noted for her sharp tongue, particularly when she turned it against her new sister-in-law, Princess May of Teck, later to be Queen Mary. 'Now do try to talk to May at dinner,' she would beg a guest with false solicitude, 'though one knows she is deadly dull.' Contemptuous of Princess May's morganatic blood and jealous of her superior education and talents, Princess Victoria grew ever more splenetic. In the spring of 1925, the King invited her to take a much-needed holiday from her vigil at Sandringham and to accompany him and the Queen on a Mediterranean cruise in the royal yacht. It proved an unhappy family reunion. The Queen's love of natural beauty and historic sites served to inflame the philistinism of her sister-in-law, who not only subjected her to a torment of mockery, but also invited the King to join in the cruel sport. 'I am glad to be back,' the Queen wrote on returning from what was to have been the treat of her life.

Princess Victoria was also reputed to make mischief in the family during her daily telephone chat with the King. At least it produced one of his favourite stories: the occasion when her telephone bell rang at the usual hour, and she took up the receiver and said, 'Hallo you old fool.' The voice of the operator broke in: 'Beg pardon, Your Royal Highness, His Majesty is not yet on the line.'

Her death in December 1935 so distressed the King that for the only time in his life he could not face his public duties and cancelled the State Opening of Parliament. 'No one ever had a sister like her,' he wrote in his diary. Within two months he too was dead.

Victoria Eugénie (Ena), Princess
later Queen of Spain
(1887–1969)

Born at Balmoral, she was the only daughter of Princess Beatrice, Queen Victoria's youngest child, and Prince Henry of Battenberg, who became a naturalized British subject, served in the Army and died of fever during the Ashanti campaign of 1896. Except on formal occasions she was called Ena, the Gaelic name chosen by Queen Victoria to mark her granddaughter's Scottish birth. Some maintain that the infant princess should have been baptized Eua, but that the Minister who performed the ceremony misread the Queen's handwriting.

In 1905 the young King Alfonso XIII of Spain came to England in search of a bride. Rejected by Princess Patricia of Connaught, he won the hand of her cousin, Princess Ena, who was required to renounce her faith as a Protestant and to be received into the Roman Catholic Church. Her conversion aroused bigotry in Britain, not least in the royal family, and doubts about her sincerity in Spain. The stiff Spanish court also wondered whether one of the supposedly up-start Battenbergs was worthy of a Bourbon.

Worse was to come. There are no formal photographs of Princess Ena wearing the dress in which she was married on 31 May 1906. It was drenched in the blood of footmen and horses, blown to pieces by an anarchist's bomb as the wedding procession returned to the royal palace in Madrid. Tragedy continued to haunt the marriage. King Alfonso yearned for a succession

Queen Ena of Spain

of healthy male heirs to strengthen his precarious line against dynastic intrigue and republicanism. But of their four sons, two suffered from haemophilia and a third from a post-operative malady that affected both hearing and speech. Don Juan, father of King Juan Carlos of Spain (1938–   ), alone grew to robust manhood.

King Alfonso believed, or perhaps affected to believe, that his mother-in-law had deceived him by concealing a family spectre. For it is now recognized that Queen Victoria was a carrier of haemophilia, or the bleeding disease; transmitted through three of her daughters, it ravaged the dynasties of Germany, Russia and

Spain. The King, cheated of his hopes, brought his marriage to an end in all but name. At the best of times an impatient and inconsiderate lover, he now embarked on bouts of philandering that caused Queen Ena distress and humiliation. It was even whispered that Alfonso preferred to make love to his mistresses on black satin sheets because they showed up the exceptional whiteness of his skin.

Although no such scandal touched the reputation of Queen Ena, she did not escape criticism. Like her aunt the Empress Frederick, she refused to conform to the customs and rigid protocol of her adopted country. Her loud laugh was said to resemble 'something from the stable'; she smoked openly; and her opera glasses were constructed to black out rather than magnify the more disgusting evolutions of a bull-fight.

In 1931 the Republican revolution drove the Spanish royal family into exile. Adversity, far from healing the rift between the King and Queen, drove them to a formal separation. Alfonso died in Rome in 1941, his wife in Lausanne twenty-seven years later. To the end of her long life Queen Ena retained her beauty, her imperiousness, nearly all her jewellery and a catholicity of friendship that included Marlene Dietrich and Noel Coward.

Wagner, Sir Anthony
(1908–   )

Garter King of Arms 1961–78. He descends from Melchior Wagner, the son of a hatter to the court of Coburg, who emigrated to England, was naturalized in 1709, married the daughter of a Huguenot refugee and became hatter to George I and George II.

Anthony, the son and grandson of schoolmasters, was a King's Scholar at Eton, where he fagged for Eric Blair, better known as the novelist George Orwell. An exacting genealogist even as a schoolboy, Wagner came to the conclusion that the rightful King of England was not George V but Rupert of Bavaria; and when obliged as Captain of the School to say a Latin grace that included the name of the King, he substituted Rupert for George. The Provost of Eton, Montague Rhodes James, realizing that this was the conviction of a scholar rather than a youthful impertinence, dealt gently with him. He merely required Wagner to refer to 'the King', without declaring which one he had in mind.

By 1931 Wagner had so far overcome his scruples as to accept the office of Portcullis Pursuivant in the College of Arms. It is this body, founded in 1484, which by royal authority regulates the grant of heraldic arms in England and carries out certain ceremonial duties. Wagner was promoted to Richmond Herald in 1943 while simultaneously serving in the ministry of Town and Country Planning. In 1961 he became Garter King of Arms, the executive head of the College under the titular control of the Earl Marshal of England (see *Norfolk, 15th, 16th and 17th Dukes of*).

He was required in 1973 to resist a Bill for the reform of the College of Arms introduced into the House of Lords by Lord Teviot, a young Conservative peer and former bus conductor with an interest in genealogy. The measure was defeated by forty-nine votes to twenty-eight. On reaching the age of seventy, Wagner did not follow recent custom by retiring but stepped down a rung to become Clarenceux King of Arms, responsible for the grant of arms south of the River Trent.

An erudite genealogist, Wagner has published family trees linking Queen Elizabeth I with Shakespeare; Queen Elizabeth II with King David of Israel; and Dr Johnson with his disdainful patron, Lord Chesterfield. He is less at ease when called upon to determine matters of etiquette, but recalls with mournful satisfaction his settlement of a dispute between two Labour peers as to their relative precedence in a procession.

Wales, Charles, Prince of
see *Charles, Prince*

Wales, Diana, Princess of
see *Diana, Princess of Wales*

Weir, Sir John
(1879–1971)

Physician to many members of the royal family, some of whom he converted to an acceptance of homeopathic remedies. This occasionally caused friction between Weir and more orthodox medical advisers; but he was a genial, anecdotal man, whose reassuring bedside manner, old-fashioned whiskers and Scots accent disarmed criticism. He put as much faith in diet and exercise as in medicine bottle and pill box. The young Prince of Wales, driving himself to exhaustion in the 1920s, was rationed to four cigarettes a day and two small slices of cold beef for lunch; his younger brother, the future King George VI, was told to play more golf. Weir attended Queen Elizabeth II at the birth of her children and remained one of her physicians until almost his ninetieth year. Having been advanced through every grade of the Royal Victorian Order from Commander to Knight Grand Cross, he received the exceptional honour of the Royal Victorian Chain in 1949.

Wheeler-Bennett, Sir John
(1902–1975)

Official biographer of King George VI and Historical Adviser to the Royal Archives. The son of a prosperous businessman who refused a peerage from Lloyd George, he was brought up in affluence. But at the age of thirteen he became a wartime casualty when a German plane dropped a bomb on his school at Westgate-on-Sea. The shock left him with a stammer that persisted until Lionel Logue (q.v.), the speech therapist, effected a cure fifteen years later. From Westgate he went on to Malvern College, but ill

health prevented him from going up to Oxford. Instead he travelled abroad. The greater part of his time between the wars he spent in Germany, observing her people and her problems with relentless curiosity. Thus equipped, Wheeler-Bennett wrote a succession of volumes on which his reputation rests. He was conscious, perhaps too conscious, of having received no academic training in the history of diplomacy; but what he lacked in the scrutiny of State papers he gained in his personal knowledge of public men and their motives. He was early to recognize the evil of the Nazis and to warn all who would listen of their menacing ambitions.

During the war Wheeler-Bennett helped to establish the British Information Services in New York and worked in political intelligence. Afterwards he was made British editor-in-chief of the captured archives of the German Foreign Office and taught at Oxford. With his new American wife he lived outside the university, in the patrician comfort of Garsington Manor, where a generation earlier Lady Ottoline

Sir John Wheeler-Bennett

Morrell had entertained her Bloomsbury friends.

In 1953, on the recommendation of Harold Nicolson (q.v.), he was appointed to write the official life of King George VI, who had died in the previous year. He undertook the task with a thoroughness relieved by romanticism. Five years later he produced a volume of almost 900 pages: as much a political history of the reign as a biography of the monarch. Some readers deplored how little its sombre style reflected the sparkle of the author's conversation. But as his friend and publisher, Harold Macmillan, observed: 'There is a gulf properly fixed between the frivolity of the spoken word and the decorum of the printed text.' Wheeler-Bennett was made a KCVO and appointed the first incumbent of a new post, Historical Adviser to the Royal Archives. In 1974 he was advanced to GCVO. These marks of his Sovereign's favour pleased him immensely.

Jack Wheeler-Bennett looked the part of the gentleman scholar. His bearing was military, his manners elaborately courteous. He eschewed the corduroy trousers and leather elbow-patches of needier dons; no pen ever protruded from his pocket. Hat, stick and gloves were his accoutrements; eyeglass and carnation completed the Edwardian ensemble. Yet as Harold Macmillan noted, his features were strangely un-English, almost those of a German princeling. Some who knew of his pre-war intimacy with the Kaiser would whisper that he was in fact his near-kinsman. This Wheeler-Bennett denied with vehemence. 'My dear mother,' he would say, 'never even met a Hohenzollern in her life.'

Whitby, Sir Lionel
(1895–1956)

As a young pathologist he was invited to join the team of medical men who successfully fought to save the life of George V in the winter of 1928–9. Their task would have been much easier had the sulphonamide drugs been available to fight the King's streptococcal infection of the chest. But it

was not until the next decade that Whitby's own research into diseases of the blood led him to establish sulphapyridene, originally called M and B 693 (after the firm of May and Baker, in whose laboratories it was synthesized).

In the Great War, Whitby was wounded and lost a leg; in World War II, he was in charge of blood-transfusion services. He later became Master of Downing College, Cambridge, and Vice-Chancellor of the University.

Wigram, Sir Clive
later 1st Baron
(1873–1960)

Private Secretary to King George V. The son of an official in the Madras Civil Service, he was born in India and educated at Winchester College. There he became a legendary cricketer and won the public schools rackets championship. From the Royal Military Academy he was commissioned into the Royal Artillery, later exchanging into the 18th Bengal Lancers. Between tours of duty as aide-de-camp to two successive Viceroys, Elgin and Curzon, he fought on the North-West Frontier and with Kitchener's Horse in South Africa. Wigram served as assistant to the chief of staff during the first Indian tour of the future George V in 1905–06 and was soon afterwards appointed an equerry. On the King's accession in 1910 he became Assistant Private Secretary, retaining the office until he succeeded Lord Stamfordham (q.v.) as Private Secretary in 1931.

Although approaching forty, Wigram embarked on his new responsibilities with humility. Finding his lack of foreign languages a handicap, he gave up his lunch hour in favour of French lessons. His command of English was always robust but idiosyncratic. Years of glory on the cricket field had taught him to pepper both conversation and correspondence with sporting metaphors. He wrote after a general election: 'I have just come back from Downing Street and found the Prime Minister in great fettle. His side have batted well in this Test Match and there is no doubt that the Skipper declared his innings closed at the right moment.' And when noting a succession of visits of foreign ambassadors to Windsor, Wigram concluded: 'On hearing them, I thank God more and more that I am an Englishman.'

His fellow Assistant Private Secretary, Frederick Ponsonby (q.v.), was pained by such bravado. 'His horizon is limited,' he wrote, 'and he does not seem to be able to take a broad-minded view of the many perplexing questions that come here. He has the true British contempt for all foreigners which is now rather out of date, and his political views are those of the ordinary officer at Aldershot.' But the King thought himself 'indeed lucky in having found a man like him.' And even the critical Stamfordham wrote to Wigram's mother: 'His natural power of looking ahead, his accurate mind and common sense, his charming and patient temper, his untiring energy and industry have enabled him to achieve successfully what would have baffled not one man but several.'

Wigram also acquired the courtier's art of attaching equal weight to the trivial and the momentous. On the eve of the Battle of Passchendaele he could be found ruminating on whether women munition workers about to be inspected by the Queen should or should not remove their gloves before shaking hands. With the coming of peace he was called upon to decide the colour of the crown that should adorn a governor-general's writing paper.

He was nevertheless a reformer, who realized that one necessary way of disarming republicanism was to present the public with a full and accurate picture of the monarchy at work. He wanted 'a well-paid Press representative, with an office at Buckingham Palace, and sufficient sums for propaganda purposes should be forthcoming.' Such an appointment was in fact first made in 1918, but its usefulness depended on the tact and understanding with which a Press Secretary

Sir Clive Wigram

met the ever-growing demands of newspapers. Until well into the reign of Elizabeth II, relations between the Palace and the Press remained lamentable (see *Colville, Commander Sir Richard*).

Through lack of foresight, Wigram believed, several imaginative gestures had gone unnoticed. He thought it tragic that the King's wartime gift of £100,000 to the Treasury had not been allocated to a scheme for the working classes; and he was disappointed at the tepid response to a proposal that convalescent soldiers and their families could use the gardens of Buckingham Palace. He pleaded for well-publicized royal visits to industrial areas and closer links with the trade unions. More cynically, he suggested that teachers and the clergy should be invited to the Palace in greater strength: 'Preachers propagate better than most people the gospel of devotion to the throne.' But he feared the obstructiveness of 'the Palace Troglodytes, who shudder when any changes are proposed and consider any modification of the present Court functions as lowering to the dignity and status of the Sovereign.' It is a measure of their resistance to change that Wigram thought himself almost a revolutionary when he confessed to Archbishop Lang: 'I go as far as saying that trains and feathers at Court should be abolished.' Sure enough, it needed a second world war to sweep away those frivolous adornments.

On the death of Lord Stamfordham in March 1931, the King had no hesitation in choosing Wigram as his successor. Others were less enthusiastic, and he remains unjustly underrated. Sir John (later Lord) Reith, of the BBC, echoed a widely held view when he said of Wigram: 'He is always very genial, but it seems to take a good deal to make him understand things.' Wigram, it is true, was never the intellectual equal of Stamfordham, but their contrasting styles seemed to widen the gap. Stamfordham, slight of build and self-effacing, was attuned to the council chamber; Wigram, large and ebullient, to the playing field or the grouse moor. One was punctilious, even peppery; the other affable and of a ready humour. Stamfordham's letters were

cast in a formal language that lent itself more to rebuke than to encouragement; Wigram's pen jogged merrily along through thickets of sporting allusion. Yet in the economic and political crisis which occupied the latter months of 1931 – he called it 'my first Test Match' – not even Stamfordham could have displayed a firmer touch.

Wigram, who received a peerage in the Silver Jubilee honours of 1935, served the King to the end. It was to him that George V, within hours of his death, put the memorable question: 'How is the Empire?' He remained with Edward VIII for the first six months of the new reign, then withdrew into semi-retirement as Lieutenant-Governor of Windsor Castle. Here, in its moat garden, he revealed exceptional qualities of hand and eye. He produced the nearest ever to a black dahlia and is immortalized in the horticultural world by a primula from Nepal called *P. Wigramiana*.

In 1912 Wigram married Nora, daughter of Sir Neville Chamberlain, Inspector-General of the Royal Irish Constabulary. Their younger son Francis was killed in action with the Grenadier Guards in 1943: yet another victim of the cruel fate which has spared few Court families during the present century.

Windsor, Wallis Warfield, Duchess of (1896–   )

Formerly Mrs Ernest Simpson, formerly Mrs Earl Winfield Spencer; wife of the Duke of Windsor, formerly King Edward VIII (q.v.). Myths continue to cling to her ancestry, birth and upbringing: that she came of humble stock, was born several years before her third husband and was the daughter of a lodging-house keeper. She was in fact born in the summer resort of Blue Ridge Summit, Pennsylvania, on 19 June 1896, almost exactly two years after King Edward VIII. Her father, Teakle Wallis Warfield, was a Warfield of Baltimore, Maryland, and her mother, Alice Montague, a Montague of Virginia: two long-established and respected families. The child was baptized Bessiewallis, later abbreviated to Wallis. Her father, whose health did not allow him to work, died five months after the birth of his daughter, leaving Mrs Warfield impoverished. She and her daughter moved to a cheap hotel, from which they were rescued by one of the Montague family, Aunt Bessie Merryman. Wallis received a good education, made friends and in 1916 married Earl Winfield Spencer, an officer in the air arm of the United States Navy. Neurotically jealous and an alcoholic, he proved an unsatisfactory husband. There were separations and reunions until, in 1927, much to the dismay of her family, his wife divorced him. In the following year she remarried.

Ernest Simpson was the son of an American mother and an English father, the head of a firm of shipbrokers with interests on both sides of the Atlantic. Eight months younger than Wallis, he was born in New York and cut short his studies at Harvard in 1918 to sail for England, serve in the Coldstream Guards and become a naturalized British subject. His wife later said of him: 'Reserved in manner, yet with a gift of quiet wit, always well dressed, a good dancer, fond of the theatre, and obviously well read, he impressed me as an unusually well-balanced man.' For the first time in her life she was able to display her inspired gifts for household management and hospitality. She bought fine furniture, silver and glass for their flat in Bryanston Square, near Hyde Park, and entertained with flawless yet unobtrusive skill.

No touch was overlooked. 'In planning a dinner,' she wrote, 'I wanted each item, whether it was trout, partridge or grouse, to be of the same size. I had noticed that this small detail, besides making for symmetry, has the merit of reducing a hostess's area of possible embarrassment. With everything the same size there is no chance of the platter arriving at the far end of the table bearing only a token; and, conversely, there is no necessity for the hostess to make conversation while the guest-of-honour probes

an irregular assortment for a modest helping.' Even when a few friends dropped in for cocktails, Cecil Beaton noticed, there were eight different kinds of hot hors-d'œuvres and green grapes stuffed with cream cheese. Forty years later, as her third husband was dying in Paris, two English doctors who had flown over to examine him were not allowed to see the patient until they had eaten their way through one of her ambrosial luncheons.

In either 1930 or 1931 she met the Prince of Wales for the first time. Already more than a little captivated by the American way of life, he was amused by what a friend called her 'voracious vivacity'. Neither then nor later did she look like a woman who would cost a king his throne. She was trim and *soignée*, yet without either the ageless beauty or the ambitious eye of a Cleopatra. Certainly she was not the American adventuress of legend who lured a golden-haired boy from the paths of duty and devotion. Edward, Prince of Wales, approaching his thirty-eighth year and embroiled with a succession of married mistresses, needed no luring. Increasingly bored by the constraints of monarchy, he found solace in her friendship, then in her love. He flaunted his infatuation to the world. By 1935, still married to her husband, Mrs Simpson was the chatelaine of Fort Belvedere and the Prince's constant companion abroad, sometimes chaperoned by Mrs Merryman, sometimes not.

As early as 1934, the Prince later confessed to Walter Monckton (q.v.), he had determined to marry Mrs Simpson; or, to put it less romantically, he was plotting to make another man's wife his own. Nobody suspected the role which the Prince intended for her. 'She is,' Henry Channon (q.v.) wrote in his diary for January 1935, 'a nice, quiet, well-bred mouse of a woman with large startled eyes and a huge mole.' Yet already she had begun to enjoy the influence if not the power of a royal favourite. That month, when the telephone was out of order, she personally rang up the Postmaster General. Three months later, Channon noted: 'She has already the air of a personage who walks into a room as though

Mrs Simpson by Cecil Beaton

she almost expected to be curtsied to.' The Prince positively delighted in her possessiveness, as when she made him cut down his smoking, smarten his appearance, pay more attention to his State papers. Both could have profited from a lesson or two in constitutional history before his accession in January 1936 as King, Defender of the Faith and Supreme Governor of the Church of England. Edward VIII might then have recognized that not even the most popular of monarchs could make a woman with two living husbands his wife, much less his Queen, and Mrs Simpson that she could never be more than either the mistress of the King or the wife of the ex-King.

Blind to these political realities, the lovers conspired to remove by divorce the only obstacle that seemed to stand in their way: a complaisant Ernest Simpson. After prolonged discussion with lawyers, Mrs Simpson's action charging her husband with adultery was set down for hearing in October. Even that near-formality was endangered by the recklessness with which the King had compromised her throughout the first nine months of his reign. She was seen without her husband not only in the privacy of Fort Belvedere but on semi-State occasions at St James's Palace; on a summer cruise in the yacht *Nahlin* and at Balmoral on their return. The King was besotted. Lady Diana Cooper (q.v.) a guest in the *Nahlin*, saw him go down on his hands and knees to pull Mrs Simpson's dress from under the feet of her chair. His chivalry went unrewarded. 'Well,' she said, 'that's the *maust* extraordinary performance I've ever seen.'

As the date of the divorce action approached, the King's love for Wallis Simpson ceased to be a matter only of the heart. The Prime Minister, Stanley Baldwin, reminded him that the Sovereign dare not condone remarriage after divorce. The King replied that if he could not make Mrs Simpson his wife, then he would abdicate. Other solutions were suggested, such as a morganatic marriage, but rejected by the British and dominion Governments (see *Monckton of Brenchley, Viscount*). On 3 December, Mrs Simpson left for the south of France, 'to remove myself from the King's life,' as she told a friend. It was followed four days later by a statement to the Press:

'Mrs Simpson, throughout the last few weeks, has invariably wished to avoid any action or proposal which would hurt or damage His Majesty or the Throne. Today her attitude is unchanged, and she is willing, if such action would solve the problem, to withdraw from a situation that has been rendered both unhappy and untenable.'

However sincerely meant, this offer to renounce the King changed nothing; the King would not renounce Mrs Simpson. Within twenty-four hours she was also exposed to undeserved humiliation. Her solicitor, Theodore Goddard, flew out to Cannes at the Prime Minister's request to see whether she would withdraw her divorce action against Ernest Simpson, the decree not yet having been made absolute. The mission proved fruitless; the King instructed her by telephone to let the divorce proceed so that he could marry her as soon as the law allowed. It happened that Goddard, who suffered from a heart ailment and was unused to flying, took with him his physician. The Press, discovering that this practitioner had once been attached to a London maternity hospital, assumed that Mrs Simpson was pregnant; and the rumour gained currency. Even then she was not free from misadventure. Five months later, as she prepared for her wedding, there appeared on the Order Paper of the House of Commons a genuine and innocently drafted measure entitled Edinburgh Royal Maternity and Simpson Memorial Hospital Order Confirmation Bill.

Meanwhile her ordeal continued. The King, having rejected Baldwin's last appeal to renounce Mrs Simpson, signed his Instrument of Abdication and prepared to leave England. Before addressing Parliament that afternoon, the Prime Minister chivalrously asked the King whether there were any particular points the King would like him to emphasize. The King told him that there were two. The first was a personal declaration of loyalty to his brother, the new King. The second was a request for Baldwin to tell the nation that 'the other person most intimately concerned had consistently tried to the last to dissuade the King from the decision which he had taken.' Baldwin read out the first note, but either ignored or forgot the second.

The Prime Minister rightly claimed that in refusing to contemplate a Queen with three living husbands he had overwhelming support both at home and from the Dominions. What added to the resentment against Mrs Simpson was an equally emphatic belief: that Edward VIII had been ensnared by an *American*: the representative of a culture then considered brash if not positively barbaric. Half a century later, such prejudice seems unthinkable. In 1936 it permeated every level of society. Harold Nicolson (q.v.), who took a liberal view of the Christian marriage vows, wrote in his diary: 'Mrs Simpson is a perfectly harmless type of American, but the whole setting is slightly second-rate.' During Edward VIII's brief reign, the transatlantic spell cast by Mrs Simpson revealed itself in such small ways as the introduction of three-decker toasted sandwiches at Balmoral and the King's reference to 'the Ammurican Government' when he opened Parliament. Nor was it as a subaltern in the Grenadier Guards that he learned to wear suede shoes with an otherwise immaculate khaki uniform. One of the saddest vignettes of his life was Fort Belvedere on the evening of 10 December 1936, his last complete day as Sovereign. He had only four guests to dine with him: all brought into his life by his future wife. It was a sign of things to come. Throughout the long years of exile in France, Manhattan was never far away: the brisk wisecracks, the rattle of ice, the *Wall Street Journal*.

On 3 June 1937, at a French château lent by a naturalized American of Nazi sympathies, Wallis Simpson was married to the newly created Duke of Windsor; thereafter her story merges with his. No member of the royal family attended the wedding of the woman who might have been Queen; nor, like other brides, was she permitted to assume the rank and style of Royal Highness borne by her husband. King George VI and his Ministers had seen to that. She was, and remains, a duchess; but the nearest she came to a royal progress was when touring Hitler's Germany with the Duke in 1937 and as the wife of the Governor of the Bahamas from 1940 to 1945. Sometimes she called it Elba, at other times St Helena.

At the end of the war the Duke refused to live in an England which still denied his own status to his wife. Instead, he and Wallis embarked on a restless routine that took in the more agreeable resorts of Europe and the New World but remained rooted in Paris. 'My duty as I saw it,' the Duchess wrote, 'was to evoke for him the nearest equivalent to a kingly life that I could produce without a kingdom.' It was not until 1953 that she found the ideal setting: a small château and park in the Bois de Boulogne, near Neuilly. Once the residence of General de Gaulle, it was let to them by the City of Paris at a token rent. That satisfied the Duchess's craving for cosmopolitan society. Almost simultaneously the Duke found a small country property, le Moulin de la Tuilerie, where he could re-create the pleasures of gardening at Fort Belvedere.

In both houses, his wealth and her taste combined to produce an artistry of entertainment that had scarcely any rival. Rooms of great beauty glowed with candlelight; furniture, carpets, objects, silver, flowers, food and wine were all of the best; cohorts of servants were as well drilled as guardsmen but less obtrusive. Such was the stage: but what of the leading lady? The Duchess has retained almost to the end an elegance that owes something to artifice, more to the fashion houses of Paris, most to dazzling jewellery of simple design on which the Duke spent a sizeable part of his fortune. She has of course attracted disparaging whispers over the years, some envious, others malicious. Yet the marriage that King George VI and his Ministers thought so insecure in 1937 endured until her husband's death thirty-five years later.

It was then, for the first and last time, that Wallis, Duchess of Windsor, was received almost as a Queen. Flown from Paris to London in a royal aircraft and lodged in Buckingham Palace, she stood by the side of Elizabeth II in St George's Chapel, Windsor, at the Duke's sombre yet splendid funeral. Among those royal mourners she looked less out of place than might have been imagined. A year later she returned for a few hours to place flowers on her husband's grave. Then failing health condemned her to a twilight world where she remains to this day.

Wedding day: the Duke and Duchess of Windsor

ACKNOWLEDGMENTS

The author would like to express his gratitude to Caroline Zubaida, of Weidenfeld & Nicolson, for the exceptional care, competence, and cheerful encouragement she has brought to the production of this book.

ILLUSTRATION ACKNOWLEDGMENTS

The author and publishers wish to thank the following institutions, agencies and photographers by whose kind permission the illustrations are reproduced on the pages indicated.

The pictures on pages 53, 187 (Copyright © reserved), 204, 267, 281 are reproduced by Gracious Permission of Her Majesty The Queen; Godfrey Argent 15, 279; Bassano 209; BBC Hulton Picture Library 6, 63, 65, 68, 69, 101, 103, 105, 138, 145, 148, 151, 153, 175, 192, 194, 204 (*left*), 222, 247, 257, 275 (*right*), 277; Cecil Beaton photographs, courtesy of Sotheby's London 41, 47, 56, 224–5, 240, 243, 284, 287; Reproduced with permission of the Bodley Head 217; Camera Press, London, 35, 38, 150, 210 photo by Richard Slade; Courtauld Institute of Art by permission of the Marquess of Salisbury, Hatfield House, 255; Courtesy Lord Halifax, KL Photographers 183; Barry Swaebe 143; E. T. Archive 30, 31 collection of Lord Edward Pelham Clinton; Fleet Fotos 184–5;

John Frost Newspaper Library 77; Tim Graham Picture Library 23, 25, 26, 45, 67, 83, 91, 95, 104, 133, 137, 160, 161, 163, 172, 215 (*right*), 241, 249, 261, 264; Grenfell family papers 66; Guildhall Art Gallery, City of London 200–1; The Illustrated London News Picture Library 34, 146, 248; Imperial War Museum 8, 18; Kobal Collection 57; Leeds City Council 71; Lords Gallery London 117; Mansell Collection 22, 38 (*right*), 147, 176–7, 246; Mary Evans Picture Library 28, 55, 152, 180, 272; Museum of London 113; National Portrait Gallery 84, 140 (*left*), 205, 206, 269; Desmond O'Neill 182; The Pilgrim Press Ltd 178–9; David Poole P.R.P. reproduced by Gracious Permission of Her Majesty The Queen, 46, 168; Popperfoto 21, 39, 140 (*right*); The Photo Source 24 photo by Chris Ware 27, 29, 32, 36, 50, 61, 64, 107, 131, 136, 142, 155, 157, 164–5, 168, 170, 202, 215 (*left*), 231, 233, 252, 274–5; Rex Features 219; Scottish National Portrait Gallery 17.

Picture Research: Anne-Marie Ehrlich